NATURAL RESOURCES
IN CANADA

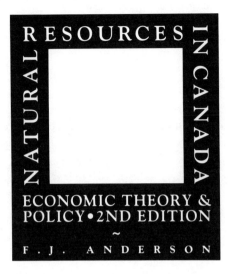

NATURAL RESOURCES IN CANADA

ECONOMIC THEORY & POLICY • 2ND EDITION

~

F . J .   A N D E R S O N

Nelson Canada

Canadian Cataloguing in Publication Data

Anderson, F.J.
  Natural Resources in Canada

2nd ed.
Includes bibliographical references and index.
ISBN 0-17-603509-5

1. Natural resources—Economic aspects—Canada.
2. Natural resources—Government policy—Canada.
I. Title

HC113.5.A53 1991   333.7'0971   C91-093154-2

Publisher   Ric Kitowski
Acquisitions Editor   Dave Ward
Manager, Editorial Services   Jean Lancee
Editor   Jane Hammond
Art Director   Lorraine Tuson
Cover Design   John Robb
Text Design   Janet Riopelle
Cover Photograph   Gary Cralle/The Image Bank Canada

Printed and bound in Canada
1   2   3   4   5   6   7   WC   94   93   92   91

OTABIND   The pages in this book open easily and lie flat, a result of the Otabind bookbinding
process. Otabind combines advanced adhesive technology and a free-floating
cover to achieve books that last longer and are bound to stay open.

This book was printed on 50 lb ECP Recycled paper, which is acid-free and approved under
Environment Canada's "Environmental Choice Program". It contains a minimum of 50%
"post commercial" recycled fibre, of which a minimum 5% is recycled "post consumer" fibre.

▮ CONTENTS

Preface   ix

■ PREFACE

The prominence of natural resources issues in Canadian contributions to economic theory and policy is the motivating force for a textbook designed to introduce students to natural resources economics in a Canadian context. The first edition of *Natural Resources in Canada* seemed to play a useful role in this respect. But time marches on and the natural resources field is a changing one. Many new contributions and perspectives appeared in the 1980s and continued to be relevant at the beginning of this new decade; these include a stronger interest in the environment, a topic deliberately excluded from the previous edition. The present edition attempts to bring in new work and has a completely new chapter on the environment. Case studies in the previous edition have been dropped, partly to accommodate new material and partly because they had become dated.

The content that I have selected reflects what I hope is a reasonable blend of economic theory applied to natural resources and environmental problems for the 1990s. As with the previous edition, this book is intended for students with a background in intermediate microeconomic theory. The book can be used in different ways. If the focus is to be on extractive resources, for example, then the new environmental material in chapter 3 can be skipped. If, on the other hand, the instructor wants to concentrate on the unifying themes in the utilization of extractive and environmental resources without getting into taxation and rent capture issues, then chapter 5 can be omitted.

The optional material on optimal control theory in the appendices has been altered and expanded in this edition. The basic optimal control framework is set out in the appendix to chapter 2 with extensions to environmental issues and fisheries management in chapters 3 and 7.

My thanks to Bob Cairns at McGill University and to Tom Harris at Lakehead University, both of whom provided detailed comments on the previous edition. Many of their efforts still show up in the present version. Other colleagues at Lakehead provided critical assistance in the revised chapters of this edition: Crandall Benson (chapter 6), Norm Bonsor (chapter 3), and George Kondor (chapter 2). I am very grateful for their help and I hasten to exonerate them from blame for any shortcomings in the final results. My natural resources students have laboured through the first edition and drawn my attention to problems of analysis and exposition which I have tried to remedy here. Dave Ward at Nelson Canada, who first suggested that a revised edition would be worthwhile, and Production Editor Jane Hammond have offered much-needed support throughout the project.

Freda Brown's typing and organizational skills were invaluable in manuscript preparation of both editions, and I am very much indebted to her for her friendly, careful, and patient work. My thanks also go to the staff

x

of the reference department of the library at Lakehead: their professional help was instrumental in assembling materials and locating government documents.

Finally, my wife, Lynda, and my children, Elizabeth and Karl, were all sources of encouragement in different ways. I am always grateful to them as I think they know.

Thunder Bay, Ontario

CHAPTER ONE

NATURAL RESOURCES
AND THE CANADIAN
ECONOMY

▌ INTRODUCTION AND OVERVIEW

Canada's role as a world producer of natural resource commodities is probably the most distinctive feature of its economy. The development of the Canadian economy has been written as a sequence of natural resource ventures from fish, fur, and square timber in the colonial period through wheat, pulp and paper, lumber, and minerals in the twentieth century. This so-called *staples theory* of growth was the distinctive contribution of an earlier generation of Canadian economists and interest in the role of natural resources and the management of resources is a continuing theme in Canadian economics.

As expected, natural resources extraction sectors are significant contributors to Canadian real income in today's economy. Table 1.1 shows the breakdown of Canada's Gross Domestic Product at Factor Cost (GDP) into

1

TABLE 1.1   Real Gross Domestic Product at Factor Cost* 1988

SECTOR	REAL GDP	PERCENT
Canada Total	395.8	100.0
Agriculture	10.2	2.5
Fishing and Trapping	.8	.2
Logging and Forestry	2.9	.7
Mining	23.7	6.0
Manufacturing	78.0	19.7
Construction	28.2	7.1
Transport/Storage	18.2	4.6
Communications	12.0	3.0
Other Utilities	11.5	2.9
Trade and Services**	146.7	37.0
Other	64.3	16.3

*In billions of constant 1981 dollars. GDP at factor cost = GNP at market prices – investment income received from non-residents + investment income paid to non-residents – indirect taxes net of subsidies – residual error of estimate.
**Includes wholesale and retail trade; finance, insurance, and real estate; community, business, and personal services.

Source: Statistics Canada: *Gross Domestic Product by Industry* (February 1989) (15–001).

its sectoral components. The GDP is a measure of the value of goods and services produced within Canada's geographical boundaries after deducting inputs of intermediate goods and indirect taxes (net of subsidies) paid to governments. Thus GDP equals income received by factors of production (including foreign-owned capital). The relationship between GDP and GNP at market prices is indicated in the note to Table 1.1.

Consider the mining sector in Table 1.1. Mining GDP is measured as $23.7 billion or 6 percent of the Canadian total. Mining GDP measures incomes received by factors of production co-operating in the production of minerals and ore concentrates. These incomes include wages, returns to capital, and rents to the resource. Mining taxes are included in the mining sector's GDP, since they are classified as income taxes even though they are now viewed as rents to the provincial Crown as the owner of the resources. Part of the return to mineral resources is not actually included in the sectoral measurement of mining GDP since royalties levied on well-head prices of oil and gas are classified as investment income received by provincial governments. These returns are included in total GDP even though they are not included in the GDP of the mining sector. In addition, some other mining revenues received by governments (e.g., payments for oil and gas leases) are classified as indirect taxes and therefore excluded from GDP by definition. Similar problems in the use of GDP estimates

TABLE 1.2   Leading Exports by Commodity Category* 1988

RESOURCE CATEGORIES

Newsprint Paper	6.6
Woodpulp	6.3
Lumber	5.5
Crude Petroleum	4.0
Natural Gas	3.0
Fish and Fish Products	2.7
Precious Metals and Alloys	2.6

NON-RESOURCE CATEGORIES

Passenger Autos and Chassis	16.7
Motor Vehicle Parts	10.8
Trucks and other Vehicles	7.9
Wheat	4.6
Industrial Machinery	4.1
Aircraft, Engines, Parts	3.0
TV, Telecommunications Equipment	3.0
Office Machines and Equipment	2.9
Total Commodity Exports	137.1

*In billions of current dollars.

Source: Statistics Canada: *Summary of Canadian International Trade* (65–001).

appear in forestry as well. Income earned in the production of hydroelectric power is included in transportation, communication, and utilities in Table 1.1. A conservative estimate based on hydro's share in overall electricity generation would place it at 1.5–2.0 percent of total GDP. Significant hydro rents are passed forward to final users in the form of low prices relative to other forms of energy. The size of hydro rents is discussed further in chapter 5. With these shortcomings in mind, Table 1.1 provides some indication of the relative importance of extractive sectors in Canadian economic activity.

The key role of natural resources industries in Canada's exports is indicated by Table 1.2. Though Canada has diversified its economy into manufactures and services, natural resource commodities are still the driving force in international trade. Among the country's leading ten export categories, natural gas, newsprint, woodpulp, lumber, petroleum and coal products, and crude petroleum are prominent contributors to Canada's export earnings.

The extractive sectors vary considerably in their regional significance. Mining, forestry, and fishing make up a much larger share of provincial GDP in Newfoundland, Saskatchewan, Alberta, British Columbia, and the northern territories than in the central regions and the Maritimes. Newfoundland's strong dependence on extractive incomes is primarily due to mining, forestry, and fishing. Mining is also crucial to the Saskatchewan and Alberta economies. In Alberta's case, oil and gas account for the largest percentage of provincial GDP earned in extractive activities. Saskatchewan relies both on oil and gas production and on potash (an essential component of fertilizers). British Columbia's extractive sectors emphasize forestry, oil and gas, and metal mining (mainly copper). The Yukon and Northwest Territories are also heavily dependent on mining with zinc as the most important mineral. Hydroelectric power is of enormous importance to Quebec. Because of its dominance in oil and gas production, Alberta is responsible for over 50 percent of income earned in Canadian mining. Ontario accounts for the largest share of incomes earned in metallic mining.

Canada's extractive activities provide raw materials for the primary manufacturing sectors of the economy. Forestry supplies logs to the lumber and pulp and paper industries, mineral ores and concentrates move into international markets as well as to domestic primary metal industries, crude oil from the Prairies moves to refineries on the west coast and as far east as Montreal. Hydroelectricity is a crucial industrial input in pulp and paper and primary metal manufacture. The coastal fisheries supply fish processing plants in British Columbia and the Atlantic Provinces. About 30 percent of total manufacturing is primary manufacturing though not all of Canadian primary manufacturing relies on Canadian resources. For example, Canadian smelters and metal refineries handle quantities of imported ores and mineral concentrates, and oil refineries in the Atlantic region are still strongly dependent on imported crude oil. At the same time, significant amounts of Canadian resources do not enter Canadian primary manufacturing processes: unprocessed metallic minerals are exported along with hydroelectric power and decreasing quantities of crude oil.

Just as the significance of the extractive sectors varies from region to region, so does the significance of resource-processing industries. The Atlantic Provinces and British Columbia have manufacturing sectors that are dominated by resource processing. In the Atlantic region, pulp and paper mills and fish processing plants are dominant manufacturing activities that rely on local resources. In British Columbia, sawmilling and pulp and paper make up almost half of value-added in manufacturing. Even in Quebec and Ontario, 20–30 percent of incomes earned in manufacturing rest on primary activities. The pulp and paper industry is of particular importance in central Canada and especially in Quebec. The primary metal industries, dominated by iron and steel mills, make up over 8 percent of value-added in Ontario manufacturing.

Overall, mining is clearly the dominant resource sector, followed by hydroelectric power and forestry. In terms of value-added, pulp and paper is Canada's largest manufacturing industry, followed by sawmilling and the manufacture of motor vehicle parts. Iron and steel is the fourth largest industry; smelting-refining and petroleum refining are Canada's seventh and eighth largest manufacturing industries respectively.

The pronounced differences in the importance of individual resources to particular regions shape both economic and political interests in Canada and have often led to sharp conflicts between provincial and federal government policies in the resources field. Control over oil and gas revenues and production was an important issue in federal-provincial relations in the 1970s. Saskatchewan policy makers were in disagreement with the federal government (and with U.S. authorities) over potash taxation and pricing policies in the 1960s and 1970s. Resource revenue controversies have spilled over into metallic mining industries as provincial governments have attempted to capture greater shares of mining revenues through new taxation mechanisms.

The important role of the natural resources sectors as suppliers of inputs to primary manufacturing, earners of revenue in export markets, and the mainstays of specific regional economies automatically leads to the question of how Canada might survive without resources. Would the disappearance of a major resources sector cause a significant decline in Canadian incomes (GDP) in the long run? How does the long-run impact of "resource disappearance" compare with short-run effects of reduced outputs in our extractive sectors? Should Canadians take steps to modify our "hewers of wood and drawers of water" image by encouraging further processing of natural resources prior to export?

The implications of changes in the sizes of Canada's extractive sectors and the possibilities of further processing of natural resources are recurrent themes in Canadian economics. The earlier work of Innis, Lower, and MacIntosh taught Canadians to think in terms of an overlapping succession of export opportunities based on extractive resources.[1] This *staples theory* of economic growth, in which fish, timber, wheat, and minerals earn the incomes in foreign markets that permit the development of domestic activity, has had a strong appeal for economic historians and economic theorists alike, even though the approach has been challenged more recently. In an important theoretical contribution, Chambers and Gordon (1966) advanced the argument that the absence of a major Canadian resource—in their example, the wheatlands of the Prairies—would have had only a modest impact on the country's economic growth during the pre–World War II period. The Chambers-Gordon argument sparked controversy. Staples theorists were anxious to refute their findings and, in the ensuing discussion, estimates of the contribution of the Prairie wheat boom to per capita incomes in the early part of the twentieth century were revised and revised again, both by Chambers and Gordon and by others.

The framework used by Chambers and Gordon (CG) is hypothetical and long run in nature. Labour and capital are allowed to migrate from the hypothetically absent natural resources sector to other industries in this

FIGURE 1.1

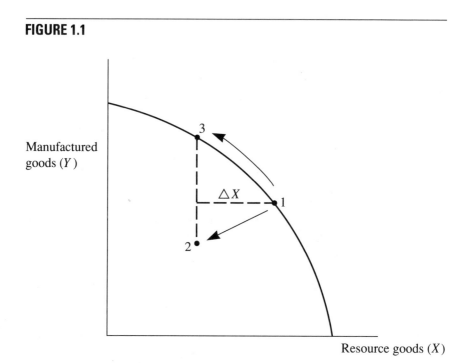

kind of analysis. The economy takes maximum advantage of its substitution capabilities, altering its allocation of labour and capital toward manufacturing production to compensate for the disappearance of a natural resource. Boadway and Treddenick (1977) have developed a similar long-run model to measure the economic importance of Canada's mining industries. As discussed below, these long-run approaches produce quite different economic implications for the Canadian economy than the short-run results of a decline in extractive activity. Short-run results of a "resource disappearance" would be more drastic, as representatives of the extractive industries and primary manufacturing industries often point out.

In the short run, productive activities are basically *complementary* rather than *substitutable* as they are in the long run, a message implicit in Keynesian multiplier analysis. The hypothetical elimination of, say, the Canadian logging industry would reduce incomes earned in logging and forest products manufacture to virtually zero. Incomes would also decline in domestic industries supplying the logging and forest products sector. The decline in incomes leads to a drop in domestic consumption, which spreads the decline in activity to other sectors. The result is a drop in income equal to some multiple of the initial reduction. Figure 1.1 uses a hypothetical production possibilities frontier (PPF) to contrast long- and short-run approaches to the importance of natural resources. Beginning at a full-employment position (point 1), a decline in natural resources activities carries the economy to a position inside the PPF in the short run, reflecting the complementary (multiplier) response of overall activity to a decline in natural resources production (point 2). In the long run, labour and capital previously used in the resource sector can shift over to the production of non-resource goods. Instead of moving to a point inside the PPF, the structure of the economy is altered toward the production of more non-resource goods and less resource goods (point 3).

The next three sections of this chapter examine the short- and long-run impacts of declines in resources sector activity—"resource disappearances"—in greater detail. The final section examines the related "further processing argument": under what circumstances should Canada adopt a policy of restricting the export of raw materials or of encouraging additional processing of raw materials? The "resource disappearance" issue and the "further processing" issue are closely connected since, in the one case, we are inquiring into the impact of *removing* specific natural resources activities from the economic system while, in the other, we are inquiring into the effect of *adding* specific resources-using industries to the economy.

■ RESOURCE INDUSTRIES AND SHORT-RUN SHOCKS

A Basic Input-Output Model

In the short run, a decline in economic activity in one part of the economy leads to a decline in purchases of goods and services from other parts of the economy. As factor incomes decline, consumption falls off. The initial drop in economic activity spreads throughout the system and produces a multiplicative effect on total income. Input-output analysis provides a way of quantifying the operation of complex multiplier processes. Input-output models can be divided into two types: *open* models and *closed* models. In the open versions, household expenditures on consumption goods are exogenous while, in closed versions, household expenditures are made to depend on household income through the consumption function so that households become part of the endogenous operation of the economy. In what follows, we shall consider closed models.

A very simple closed input-output model involving a natural resource industry, a manufacturing industry, and a household sector can be written out as follows:

Resources $\qquad$ $X - a_{11} X - a_{12} Y - b_1 H = x$ $\qquad$ (1)

Manufactures $\qquad\qquad\qquad Y - a_{21} X - a_{22} Y - b_2 H = y \qquad\qquad$ (2)

Households $\qquad\qquad\qquad H - a_{31} X - a_{32} Y = 0 \qquad\qquad$ (3)

Expressed in dollar terms, each of the coefficients (a_{11}, a_{12}...b_1, b_2) indicates the number of dollars of a particular input required per dollar of a particular output. These are the *input-output coefficients*. Thus, a_{11} shows the number of dollars worth of input X (resources) required per dollar of output of X (resources), a_{21} shows the number of dollars worth of input Y (manufactures) required per dollar of output X (resources), and so on. The coefficients b_1 and b_2 are the household expenditure coefficients, showing the number of dollars worth of X and Y purchased per dollar of household income. Equation (1) shows that taking the total value of resource output X and subtracting the amount of resources needed to produce resources ($a_{11}X$), the amount of resources needed to produce manufactures ($a_{12}Y$), and the amount of resources needed to satisfy household demand (b_1H, where H stands for household income), gives the resources "left over" to satisfy other demands (x). These other demands, which are exogenous to the structure of the model, are called *final demands* and consist of investment expenditures on resources, government purchases of resources, and exports of resources (net of imports). A similar interpretation applies to the manufacturing sector in equation (2). In equation (3), we begin with household income (H) and subtract income earned from producing resources ($a_{31}X$) and manufactures ($a_{32}Y$). The result is zero, indicating that income payments from the resources and manufacturing sectors are assumed to be the *only* sources of household income.

Examining multiplier impacts in input-output models usually involves introducing changes in exogenous final demands (x and y) into the model and calculating the resulting effects of such changes on total household income H. As we shall see below, this is not quite the same thing as examining the effect of a "resource disappearance" but it is a very important concept in its own right.

Equations (1), (2), and (3) involve three unknown variables (X, Y, H), the values of which have to be solved in terms of the known input-output coefficients (a_{11}, a_{12}...b_1, b_2) and the assumed final demand levels (x and y). One can proceed to the solution of the system by simply substituting one equation into another or by more sophisticated methods.[2] The resulting solution for household income is

$$H = \{[a_{21}a_{32} + a_{31}(1 - a_{22})]x + [a_{12}a_{31} + a_{32}(1 - a_{11})]y\}D^{-1} \qquad (4)$$

where $D = (1 - a_{11})(1 - a_{22}) - b_1 a_{21} a_{32} - b_2 a_{12} a_{31} - b_1 a_{31}(1 - a_{22}) - b_2 a_{32}(1 - a_{11}) - a_{12} a_{21}$. If there is an increase in final demand for the resource ($\Delta x > 0$) while the final demand for manufactures remains constant ($\Delta y = 0$), the effect on household income or GDP is then simply

$$\Delta H = \{[a_{21}a_{32} + a_{31}(1 - a_{22})]\Delta x\}D^{-1}$$

and the final demand multiplier is

$$\Delta H/\Delta x = [a_{21}a_{32} + a_{31}(1 - a_{22})]D^{-1} > 0 \qquad (5)$$

The final demand multiplier is the ratio of the increase in household income or GDP to the initial increase in the final demand for the resource after all interactions in the closed input-output system have worked themselves out. In typical Keynesian style, equation (5) quantifies the short-run reaction of income to exogenous shocks in the final demand for resources. Changes in final demand are not the same thing as "resource disappearances" however. How should a resource disappearance due, say, to depletion, be handled?

Depletion implies an exogenous reduction in the *total* value of resource output X in equilibrium rather than an exogenous change in final demand x. If X changes exogenously, then x can be treated as endogenous: a fall in the economy's total output of resources will lead to an automatic decline in exports or an increase in imports of resources. Since x appears only in equation (1), we can start the resource disappearance model by just omitting equation (1) and concentrating on equations (2) and (3). Writing them out again, we have

Manufactures $\qquad\qquad Y - a_{21} X - a_{22} Y - b_2 H = y \qquad (6)$

Households $\qquad\qquad H - a_{31} X - a_{32} Y = 0 \qquad (7)$

Suppose resource production X changes by an amount ΔX. Final demand for manufactures remains fixed so that $\Delta y = 0$. Taking first differences of equations (6) and (7) with $\Delta y = 0$,

$$\Delta Y - a_{21}\,\Delta X - a_{22}\,\Delta Y - b_2\,\Delta H = 0 \qquad (8)$$

$$\Delta H - a_{31}\,\Delta X - a_{32}\,\Delta Y = 0 \qquad (9)$$

Eliminating ΔY from equations (8) and (9) and isolating the ratio $\Delta H/\Delta X$,

$$\Delta H/\Delta X = [a_{21}a_{32} + a_{31}(1 - a_{22})][1 - a_{22} - b_2a_{32}]^{-1} \qquad (10)$$

Equation (10) shows the response of total household income to a change in gross production X in the resources sector. We can call it the resource disappearance multiplier to distinguish it from the final demand multiplier in equation (5). If we know ΔX, we can solve for ΔH from equation (10). Knowing ΔX and ΔH, we can solve for ΔY from either equation (8) or (9). The decline in gross production in the resources sector lowers the demand for manufactures as inputs into resources and lowers household incomes earned in resources production. The fall in household income causes a further decline in the demand for manufactures, and a further decline in income until the system stabilizes. (In Figure 1.1, the fall in X leads the system from point 1 to point 2 where both X and Y are lower than at point 1.) Notice that once ΔX, ΔY, and ΔH are known, the endogenous change Δx could be found from equation (1) if desired, i.e., $\Delta x = \Delta X - a_{11} \Delta X - a_{12} \Delta Y - b_1 \Delta H$. Notice also that, by definition,

$$\Delta H / \Delta X = (\Delta H / \Delta x)(\Delta x / \Delta X) \tag{11}$$

Since the change in gross production exceeds the change in final demand for resources, $\Delta x / \Delta X < 1$. This means that $\Delta H / \Delta x > \Delta H / \Delta X$. The final demand multiplier is larger than the resource disappearance multiplier. We should also note, however, that the resource disappearance multiplier only takes into account the magnified impact of reduced output of resources on incomes earned in resource extraction and the demand for other goods by the extractive sector and by households. We are assuming that sectors that use resources as inputs can replace these inputs out of final demand (x) on world markets. If this replacement is not possible, there will be further "forward linked" effects on domestic resource-processing sectors and a much larger fall in domestic household income.

Multiplier Estimates for Resources

In a survey of multiplier studies undertaken by Nickel, Gillies, Henley, and Saunders (1978) for Canadian mining, a range of final demand multipliers were reported. These multipliers fall in the range of 1.4 to 2.0.[3] Calculated multiplier values tend to be smaller for smaller geographical areas owing to larger leakages from the chain of income creation in the form of imports of intermediate inputs and final consumption goods. If the Canadian mining industry suddenly disappeared with the smelting and refining sectors shifting over to foreign sources of ores and concentrates, what might happen to Canadian GDP in the short run? Taking the multiplier approach quite literally, the direct effect in 1988 would have been an immediate loss of $24 billion in GDP as shown in Table 1.1. This loss would then be multiplied to produce the final effect on GDP as industries supplying the mining sector contract and force contraction on other industries and on household spending. Using a resource disappearance multiplier of 2, the loss would be nearly $50 billion or 12 percent of GDP. If the smelting and refining sectors were unable to replace their Canadian supplies of ores and concentrates with other supplies, the contraction would be even larger. The regional impact of a cessation of mining activity would be truly devastating for certain provinces. The mining industry (principally oil and gas) makes up about 20 to 25 percent of Alberta's GDP, for example. Elimination of the petroleum sector in this region could reduce incomes by 30 to 40 percent.

Clearly the *potential* for multiplicative declines in GDP as a result of adverse final demand shocks or depletion of resources in an economy like

Canada's is substantial. In fact, however, the likelihood of sudden reductions of large magnitude in extractive activity because of depletion depends very much on the size of the region or country in question. For large and diversified geographical areas—a large province or Canada as a whole—wholesale resource disappearance is both *a priori* improbable and historically unprecedented. But for smaller regions and towns, the dangers are very real indeed. For nonrenewable resources, continuing production depends upon the replacement of old deposits with new discoveries. For a small area, the probability that the new deposits (if discovered) will be conveniently located to absorb factors of production previously engaged in extracting the old depleted deposits is quite low. Even for renewable resources such as forests, depletion is quite possible in the absence of deliberate regeneration (chapter 6). A 1977 study of single-industry towns in Canada undertaken by the Department of Regional Economic Expansion showed that 25 percent of Canada's population outside census metropolitan areas lives in single-industry communities of which 40 percent are dependent on logging and forest products and 10 percent are dependent on metal mines and mineral processing.[4] The closing of mines at Uranium City in Saskatchewan, Schefferville in Quebec, and Lynn Lake in Manitoba, for example, completely destroyed the economic bases of these communities. For Canada as a whole, "resource disappearances" in the form of sudden closures of extraction or processing facilities owing to depletion are ordinarily offset by new resource developments in other regions.

At the national level, then, final demand shocks will be more important than "resource disappearance" shocks. Resource depletion affects particular resources at particular times and in particular regions, but final demand shocks due to worldwide booms or recessions can affect a wide range of activities across the country at the same time. Canada has a highly open economy with a ratio of merchandise exports to GDP of over 25 percent. Whatever products the country and its individual regions specialize in, Canadians can expect to experience sizable exogenous final demand shocks simply because of the high degree of openness of our economy and its regions. Does our strong specialization in natural resources exports (Table 1.2) expose us to unusually large risks associated with fluctuating world demands?

A study that attempted to answer this question was carried out by Gray (1975). In his comparisons of resource-based sectors and secondary manufacturing sectors, Gray found that resource industries did exhibit higher variances of employment and output than manufacturing industries over the 1961 to 1973 period but that there was no statistically significant difference in these variances when forestry was removed from the resources industries sample. Gray also concluded that the observed differences in employment and output variances were also large among industries *within* the manufacturing sector and that many manufacturing industries were a good deal *less* stable than some resource extraction and processing industries. Since these comparisons include any instability in resources sectors that might be associated with depletion and discovery, resource industries came off quite well in the comparison. Forestry, though, does seem to be an unstable industry that is highly sensitive to international fluctuations in demand. Demand shocks can be a very serious problem in specific regions as well. The impact of the 1981–82 downturn on British Columbia, the Sudbury region, and northern Quebec and Labrador was particularly severe owing to the strong dependence of these areas on exports of lumber, nickel, and iron ore respectively.

Problems with Multiplier Estimates

Multiplier analysis and multiplier estimates confirm that depletion or adverse demand shocks have the potential to reduce GDP significantly in the short run. Given the usefulness of the multiplier approach for the analysis of short-run responses to expenditure changes and localized changes in resource stocks, how accurate are estimates of multipliers likely to be? Do they have their own shortcomings? The following quotation sums up many of the criticisms that are often made of the assumptions on which multiplier analysis rests:

> Despite their apparent respectability in government and within. . .industry, multiplier and impact studies make far too many simplistic assumptions to warrant the implications drawn for them. They assume a perfectly elastic supply of all factors of production and neglect the role of the price mechanism entirely. They assume fixed investment and other final demands including exports, neglect all financial considerations, neglect the exchange rate and capital flows, and assume fixed input-output coefficients.[5]

If production factors are not available to meet an expansion of demand for an industry's product, the operation of the multiplier chain will be altered. The scarce factor's price may increase and the industry will fail to expand its inputs from other sectors. If relative prices change, households and industries will alter the quantities supplied and demanded of inputs and outputs, introducing variations into estimated values of multiplier coefficients. If firms respond to changing sales by altering their investment plans, a new source of induced expenditure change additional to household consumption would have to be added to the model to capture the full economic impact. During an expansion, interest rates tend to rise, altering expenditure plans. When economic activity rises, imports will increase and this tends to create a balance of payments deficit. If, as a result, the value of the Canadian dollar declines, exports will be stimulated so that industries' final demands rise, again modifying the income-generation sequence. In addition, any change in the exchange rate alters the relative costs of domestic and foreign commodities used as industrial inputs so that the input-output coefficients showing requirements from domestic industries may alter.

The catalogue of shortcomings of multiplier analysis leads to a great deal of skepticism about the precision to be attached to numerical multiplier values. The multiplier *concept* certainly retains its relevance as a description of short-run complementarity among industries in response to exogenous shocks, but actual measurement of multiplier values is very sensitive to specific assumptions.

▮ ECONOMIC EFFICIENCY AND WELFARE IN THE LONG RUN

Assessing the importance of natural resource stocks to the Canadian economy in the long run requires that we develop a suitable framework to describe, in simple terms at least, how an economy allocates its factors of production among competing uses to produce a long-run mix of resource goods along with other goods and services. We should note that the decision to specialize in the production of certain goods does not act to constrain domestic consumption, provided domestic consumers can exchange goods and services with other countries on world markets. The fact that an economy like Japan is unable to produce many resource goods is not necessarily problematic provided it can specialize in the production of other types of goods (automobiles, electronics, fabricated steel) and export them to obtain its needed natural resource goods as imports. By the same token, a Canada devoid of many of *its* natural resources industries might be able to adapt in a similar manner in the long run.

Unlike the short-run complementarity/multiplier approach, long-run models of economic structure assume that labour and capital are mobile among industries so that one sector of the Canadian economy can be expanded with fixed total supplies of factors of production by taking factors out of other sectors. In the case of capital, factor mobility extends beyond Canada's borders. The model developed in this section makes the assumption of constant returns to scale: each industry has a production function relating its output to its inputs such that doubling all inputs doubles output. Implicitly, each factor of production exhibits diminishing marginal productivity. Factors of production are fully employed so that expansion of the output of one industry requires a reduction in the output of at least one other industry. Taking two industries for illustration, a production possibility frontier (PPF) links society's maximum production from either industry to the output level of the other industry (Figure 1.1). The *opportunity cost* of an increase in the output of extractive resources (X) is the required reduction in the output of manufactures (Y) in this two-industry case.

The bowed-out (concave to the origin) nature of the PPF requires the

FIGURE 1.2

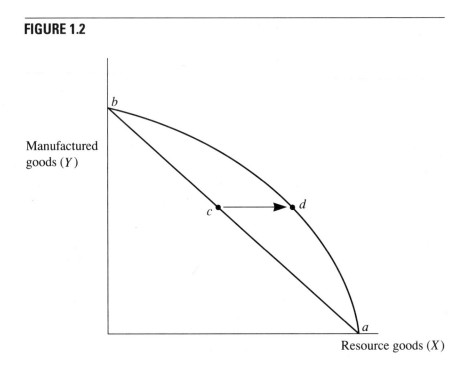

assumption of two (or more) factors of production which are used in
different proportions in the two industries. Assume the factors of production to be capital and labour. Referring to Figure 1.2 and beginning at point
a where all of society's endowments of labour and capital produce
extractive outputs, consider a movement along the straight line from *a* to *b*
by transferring bundles of capital-labour (in the same ratio as their total
supplies) from the extractive sector to the manufacturing sector. The
straight line reflects the constant returns to scale assumption operating in
both industries. Along this straight line, both industries show a common
ratio of labour to capital in production equal to the ratio of total factor
supplies (endowments) in the economy. Moving on a straight line path
between *a* and *b* is not usually the most efficient way to proceed, however.
Consider point *c*. At *c*, both industries use the same labour-capital ratio,
that is, they have the same *factor-intensity*. It is probable—indeed likely—
that manufacturing output can be maintained at *c* while extractive
resources output can be expanded by altering relative factor intensities. If
labour and capital are denoted by L and K and resources and manufacturing outputs are denoted by X and Y, the following equations show what
happens to outputs as levels of factor use change in each industry:

$$\Delta X = MPP_L^x \, \Delta L_x + MPP_K^x \, \Delta K_x \qquad (13)$$

$$\Delta Y = MPP_L^y \, \Delta L_y + MPP_K^y \, \Delta K_y \qquad (14)$$

The symbol MPP_L^x is the marginal productivity of labour in industry X (resource goods). Similar interpretations apply to MPP_K^x, MPP_L^y, and MPP_K^y. Marginal productivity is the ratio of the change in output (say ΔX) to the change in a factor input (say ΔL) with the other input held constant. When both input levels change, equations (13) and (14) show the resulting output changes. Referring back to point c, hold manufacturing output constant ($\Delta Y = 0$). Now, begin altering the relative factor supplies allocated to each industry. Suppose extractive resources output is an inherently capital-intensive activity relative to manufacturing. Moving horizontally from point c will involve $\Delta K_x > 0$ and $\Delta L_x < 0$ (increasing capital-intensity in resources output). Since capital is being removed from manufacturing and labour is being added (to keep $\Delta Y = 0$ in equation (14)), $\Delta K_x = -\Delta K_y > 0$ and $\Delta L_x = -\Delta L_y < 0$ since factors of production added to one of the industries must be removed from the other. Eventually, point d will be reached at which further shifts in relative factor intensities cannot increase extractive resources output so $\Delta X = 0$.

At this point equations (13) and (14) become

$$MPP_L^x \, \Delta L_x + MPP_K^x \, \Delta K_x = 0 \qquad (15)$$

$$MPP_L^y \, \Delta L_y + MPP_K^y \, \Delta K_y = 0 \qquad (16)$$

Equation (16) equals zero because we have been assuming all along that manufacturing output is to be held constant. Equation (15) equals zero because we have arrived at the point at which increasing the capital-intensity of the extractive resources sector relative to manufacturing can offer no increase in the output of extractive resources. Equations (15) and (16) can be rearranged to read

$$MPP_L^x / MPP_K^x = -\Delta K_x / \Delta L_x \qquad (15A)$$

$$MPP_L^y / MPP_K^y = -\Delta K_y / \Delta L_y \qquad (16A)$$

Remembering that full-employment of labour and capital implies $\Delta K_x = -\Delta K_y$ and $\Delta L_x = -\Delta L_y$, (15A) and (16A) can be consolidated into a single efficiency condition:

$$\textit{Efficiency Condition 1}: \ MPP_L^x / MPP_K^x = MPP_L^y / MPP_K^y \qquad (17)$$

This efficiency condition must apply at every point like d along the production possibility frontier. It states that the marginal rate of technical substitution between labour and capital must be the same in both industries in order to maximize the output of X given an arbitrarily fixed output of Y.

Satisfaction of equation (17) also helps to explain why the PPF is concave to the origin: provided efficient factor intensities are *different* for the two sectors, points like d will lie further from the origin than points like c on the straight line joining a and b. So the PPF begins at a and ends at b but lies outside straight-line acb at points intermediate to a and b. In a sense, efficiency condition 1 simply requires that factors of production are allocated to industries so as to squeeze the most output out of the economy. It does not say what combination of output on the PPF will, or should, be chosen.

Under conditions of perfect competition, equality between the ratios of the marginal productivities of factors of production in the two industries—efficiency condition 1—is automatically satisfied. Consider profit-maximizing firms in industry X (resources goods). They will want to hire labour until the marginal revenue product of labour equals the wage rate for labour. The same will be true for capital and for firms in industry Y. Denoting the prices of resource goods and manufactures as P_x and P_y, the wage rate as w, and the price of capital (its rental rate) as R, the profit-maximizing factor-hiring conditions in the resource goods sector are

$$MPP_L^x P_x = w \qquad (18)$$

$$MPP_K^x P_x = R \qquad (19)$$

In the manufacturing sector Y, the optimal hiring conditions are

$$MPP_L^y P_y = w \qquad (20)$$

$$MPP_K^y P_y = R \qquad (21)$$

Consolidating equations (18) through (21) by dividing (18) by (19) and (20) by (21),

$$MPP_L^x / MPP_K^x = w/R = MPP_L^y / MPP_K^y \qquad (22)$$

Firms in both industries maximize profits by equating the ratio of marginal factor products to the factor price ratio. In doing so, they collectively end up satisfying efficiency condition 1 which defines the location of the economy's PPF.[6]

Once the economy is located on its PPF, the slope of the PPF measures the marginal cost of one commodity in terms of the other. This can be established by noting that the transfer of labour from industry X to industry Y causes a loss of output $\Delta X = MPP_L^x \Delta L_x$ and a gain $\Delta Y = MPP_L^y (-\Delta L_x)$ where $\Delta L_x < 0$. So the slope of the PPF is $\Delta Y/\Delta X = -MPP_L^y / MPP_L^x$. The marginal cost of X, denoted as MC_x, is $MC_x = w/MPP_L^x$ [i.e., $(\Delta \text{Cost}/\Delta L_x)/(\Delta X/\Delta L_x)$]. Similarly, the marginal cost of Y is $MC_y = w/MPP_L^y$. Thus,

FIGURE 1.3

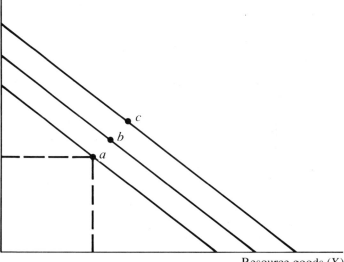

Manufactured goods (Y)

Resource goods (X)

$$\Delta Y/\Delta X = (-w/MPP_L^x)/(w/MPP_L^y) = -MC_x/MC_y \qquad (23)$$

If, as we want to assume in examining long-run models, the country can engage in international trade, it is important to compare the terms-of-trade (the international ratio of export to import prices) with the domestic cost ratio (MC_x/MC_y) which measures the slope of the PPF. Just like individuals, entire economies are constrained in their consumption combinations by a budget constraint. Figure 1.3 illustrates a system of such constraints. Suppose the economy is able to produce some combination of manufactures and resource goods given by point a in Figure 1.3. Further suppose that the world prices of resource goods and manufactures are beyond the control of the country under discussion and are fixed at P_x^*, and P_y^*, respectively. In this case, the combinations of goods available to the residents of the country are shown by the straight line with slope $-P_x^*/P_y^*$ passing through a.[7] If the country can produce combinations b or c in Figure 1.3, the possible consumption combinations available to its residents expand to include the areas inside the budget constraints of slope $-P_x^*/P_y^*$ passing through b or c. Maximizing the available combinations of manufactures and resource commodities involves moving to the *highest* budget constraint consistent with the economy's productive potential.

FIGURE 1.4

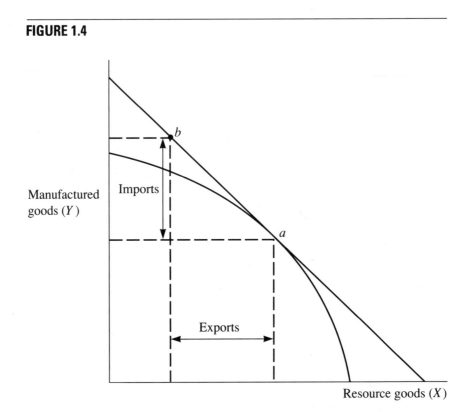

Figure 1.4 combines the previous two diagrams to illustrate the maximum consumption combinations available to the economy assuming full employment of its factors of production (labour and capital). In addition to efficiency condition 1 defining the location of the PPF, the slope of the PPF must equal the world price ratio. Any budget constraint outside the one shown in Figure 1.4 cannot be achieved because of the limitation on the economy's productive potential set by its PPF.

At point a, a second efficiency condition is satisfied: equality between the domestic marginal cost ratio (MC_x/MC_y) and the world price ratio:

$$\textit{Efficiency Condition 2}: \ MC_x/MC_y = P_x^*/P_y^* \qquad (24)$$

Given the opportunities presented to exchange at the world price ratio (P_x^*/P_y^*), the country's consumers may decide to consume at point b. With the economy producing at point a, exports of resource commodities in the amount indicated by Figure 1.4 are used to purchase the indicated volume of manufacturing imports. Notice once again that efficiency condition 2 will be satisfied automatically under perfect competition since firms in each industry will be maximizing profit as described by equations (18) through (21). Thus, under perfect competition, $MC_x = P_x^*$ and $MC_y = P_y^*$.

To complete the present discussion of efficiency conditions, note that point b will represent an optimum from each consumer's point of view provided consumers are maximizing their utilities subject to their individual incomes and the prices P_x^* and P_y^*. Suppose individual i's total expenditure on X and Y is given by M^i. Satisfaction of his/her budget constraint means that

$$M^i = P_x^* \, X^i + P_y^* \, Y^i \tag{25}$$

where X^i and Y^i refer to the consumer's feasible consumption levels for goods X and Y. Suppose the consumer's utility function is $U^i = U(X^i, Y^i)$. Using the difference notation again with a fixed level of expenditure M^i so that $\Delta M^i = 0$,

$$0 = P_x^* \Delta X^i + P_y^* \Delta Y^i \tag{26}$$

$$\Delta U^i = MU_x^i \Delta X^i + MU_y^i \Delta Y^i \tag{27}$$

where MU_x^i and MU_y^i stand for the marginal utilities of the two goods to individual i. To maximize utility, each individual must adjust his purchases so that any rearrangement $(\Delta X^i, \Delta Y^i)$ that satisfies (26) cannot increase utility, i.e., in the utility-maximizing consumption pattern for X^i, Y^i, $\Delta U^i = 0$. Solving equations (26) and (27) with $\Delta U^i = 0$ produces the third efficiency condition:

Efficiency Condition 3: $MU_x^i / MU_y^i = P_x^* / P_y^*$ (28)

The final efficiency condition is the usual budget-line–indifference-curve tangency result for utility-maximizing consumers. We assume that the consumption choice at point b in Figure 1.4 meets efficiency condition 3.

Notice that satisfaction of efficiency conditions 1 and 2 simply amounts to maximizing the economy's national income at international prices by moving to the highest possible level of national income $(P_x^* X + P_y^* Y)$ subject to the feasibility constraint set by the PPF. Satisfaction of efficiency condition 3 allows consumers to rearrange their expenditures relative to point a through exports and imports to give themselves the highest possible utility level at point b.

The following section utilizes the long-run model of efficient production and consumption to examine how such an economy adapts to changes in its natural resources endowments. Two such models are discussed: the Boadway-Treddenick (1977) model of a current mining-sector "resource disappearance" and the Chambers-Gordon (1966) model of the contribution of Prairie agriculture to the Canadian economy in the pre–World War I period. Each model approaches the long-run adaptation problem in slightly different ways.

■ THE LONG-RUN VALUE OF NATURAL RESOURCE STOCKS

The Boadway-Treddenick Model

Boadway-Treddenick (BT) examined the long-run implications of the hypothetical removal of Canada's metallic mining industries from the economy. The BT model has fifty-six industrial categories. Each sector utilizes labour and capital and inputs from other sectors in accordance with the 1966 Canadian input-output table. To simplify the interpretation of their results, all the non-mining sectors are here treated as a single collection of industries; "manufacturing" for short. Using Figure 1.5, output in the mining sector is measured on the X-axis and the aggregate output of other industries ("manufactures") appears on the Y-axis. The mining sector uses a higher capital-labour ratio than the manufacturing sector. The PPF linking mining sector and manufacturing sector outputs is shown in Figure 1.5. At the existing world prices of minerals and manufactures, the economy is in long-run equilibrium at point a. Mineral resources are sufficiently abundant that mining output at point a is unconstrained by the availability of minerals so that the return to minerals (economic rent) is zero. All income in the economy, therefore, accrues to capital and labour. All the efficiency conditions of the previous section are assumed to be satisfied at the production point a and the consumption point b. Note that the economy is exporting mining output and importing manufactures at b.

Now suppose that all the mineral resources that support mining activity are removed from the Canadian economy—a long-run resource disappearance. The resulting effects of removing the mining sector are shown in Figure 1.5. When the mining sector is removed, the economy's production point shifts to point c from point a. Since it is no longer possible to produce mining output, the economy shifts all of its capital and labour factors into the production of manufactures. Provided the economy is still able to trade at the *same* world prices as before, its new income line is parallel to the old and is the straight line cd. The inward shift of the income constraint is caused by the relatively capital-intensive nature of mining. The economy has lost an opportunity to utilize its capital endowments in a relatively capital-intensive sector by exporting the difference between production and consumption in this sector. A valuable international trade opportunity has vanished and the cost is shown by the magnitude of the inward shift of the income line.

BT add to this effect a second possible effect. Since the economy no longer produces mining output, its international trade orientation is reversed. Instead of exporting minerals and importing manufactures, it now imports minerals and exports manufactures. The supply of minerals in the world economy has decreased and the supply of manufactures in the

FIGURE 1.5

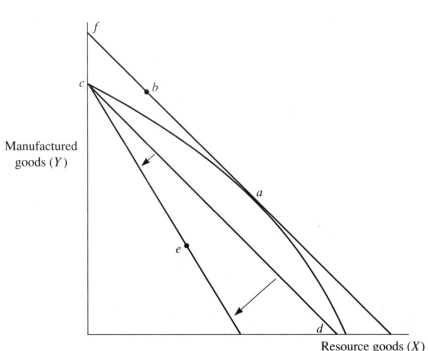

world economy has increased. The new exports of manufactures lower world prices of manufactures so P_y (the world price of manufactures) falls. The loss of Canadian mineral supplies raises the world price of minerals so P_x (the world price of mining commodities) rises. Since the slope of Canada's income line is $-P_x/P_y$, there is a terms-of-trade effect. Canada's final income constraint emanating from point c is *steeper* than cd (as indicated by the directional arrows in Figure 1.5), reflecting the rise in P_x/P_y. Canada's final consumption point is shown as point e.

Though the BT model contains some additional complications owing to their more realistic disaggregated treatment of the manufacturing sector in Figure 1.5, the two effects described are the fundamental causes of economic losses when mining is removed. The manufacturing sector must increase its capital intensity to absorb the large quantities of capital released by the demise of mining (the factor price ratio w/R is higher at point c than at point a in Figure 1.5). We could refer to this loss as a *factor proportions effect*. The loss of mining output and the expansion of manufactures adds an additional loss by altering world prices and we might refer to this as a *terms-of-trade effect*.

If the capital intensity of the mining sector had been equal to the capital intensity of the manufacturing sector and if world prices remained unaffected by the elimination of mining, the BT model would not show any economic losses. If both sectors had the same capital intensity, then the PPF would have been a straight line (see the discussion in the previous section) and production at *b* would only occur if the income line and the PPF were superimposed (the same line). Elimination of mining would move the economy to point *f* and Canadian consumers could simply trade back to *b* at the original world prices.

Using approximate measures of the factor proportions effect and the terms-of-trade effect, BT measured the losses involved in the shift of the consumption combination from point *b* to point *e* in Figure 1.5. They concluded that the welfare loss to Canadians from a complete cessation of metallic mining output would be small. This is particularly true when capital is mobile between Canada and other countries. In the capital mobility case, the factor proportions effect is minimal because the removal of Canadian mining industries does not force capital into manufacturing, rather the excess capital released by the disappearing mining sector can be absorbed at a constant rate of return in other countries.[8] In essence, the PPF is nearly linear so that point *c* almost coincides with point *f* in Figure 1.5. Nor did the authors find a large terms-of-trade effect. Removing Canadian metallic minerals output from world markets and adding additional Canadian manufactures to world output had little effect on the world prices of these goods.

The Chambers-Gordon Model

The Chambers-Gordon (CG) model is similar in many respects to the BT model.[9] The international capital mobility assumption is introduced by CG at the outset. With capital internationally mobile at a fixed rate of return, the two factors of production in fixed supply in the Canadian economy are labour and natural resources in the CG model. In contrast to the BT model, the CG model assumes that natural resources are valuable as scarce productive inputs and receive incomes in the form of economic rent. When natural resources disappear, economic rents also disappear. Natural resources are specific to their respective extractive industries. Canada is a price taker in all international markets so that world prices of manufactures and natural resource commodities do not change when Canadian supplies of these commodities change. Thus, there are no terms-of-trade effects in the CG model.

With natural resources and labour as the only immobile factors of production, the bowed-out PPF simply represents the effect of diminishing returns to labour in resources production. Each unit of labour removed from the manufacturing sector subtracts a constant amount of manufactured output. As the extra units of labour are added to the resources sector, the marginal product of labour in resource goods declines since labour is being added to fixed inputs of natural resources. Figure 1.6 illustrates this. Again, the economy is maximizing national income at world prices at point a where the income line with slope $-P_x/P_y$ is tangent to the PPF. The slope of the PPF is $\Delta Y/\Delta X$ and measures the marginal cost of obtaining extra resource goods in terms of manufactures.

Panels A and B of Figure 1.6 show the optimal allocation of the economy's resources between manufactures and resources production in two equivalent ways. Panel A shows the PPF tangency interpretation while panel B gives the same information as the intersection of the marginal cost of resource goods ($MC = -\Delta Y/\Delta X$) with the fixed world price of resource goods in terms of manufactures (P_x/P_y). Point a represents the same efficient output mix decision in both panels. In panel B, the shaded area over the marginal cost curve and under the price line measures *economic rent* accruing to the natural resource. On each unit of resources output produced, the economic rent on that unit is the difference between price and its marginal cost. Adding up over all resource units produced from zero to a produces the shaded rent area. Since the two panels are equivalent and panel B graphs the slopes of the curves in panel A, the rent *area* in panel B corresponds to the *distance bc* in panel A.

Now subtract the resource industry from the economy. Since the economy can no longer produce resource goods, it allocates all its labour (and any required mobile capital) entirely to manufacturing and goes to point c in panel A. National income (measured in manufactures) falls by bc in panel A (equal to the shaded area in panel B). This loss corresponds to removal of economic rent. The CG model, therefore, argues that the loss to the Canadian economy from a natural resource disappearance just equals the economic rent that would have been earned on the resource had it been present. This could be referred to as the *rent effect*.

Synthesis of Models

The BT and CG models are essentially complementary. The BT model ignores the rent effect entirely by simply assuming that resources are very abundant prior to their complete disappearance. In contrast, the CG model places all its emphasis on losses of rent that occur with a natural resource disappearance. The CG model assumes away the very losses that are at the heart of the BT model: the factor proportions effect and the terms-of-trade effect. In a two-factor (labour-capital) model, the assumption of internationally mobile capital leaves only a single immobile factor (labour) in each country, turning the PPF into a straight line. The mobile capital assumption thus removes the factor proportions effect. As noted above, BT found very little in the way of a factor proportions effect with strong capital

FIGURE 1.6

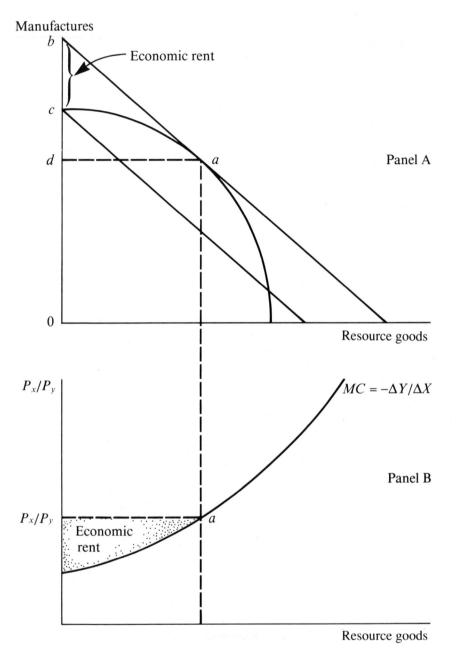

mobility. The terms-of-trade effect is also absent if the economy is a price taker on world markets. In this case, changes in its structure do not alter the prices it faces on its exports and imports.

Synthesis of the BT and CG models is straightforward. Referring back to Figure 1.5, the movement from point a to point c (removal of the extraction sector) can cause income losses *both* because of a loss of rent (CG) and because of the loss of an opportunity to absorb immobile capital (BT). Both the rent effect and the factor proportions effect are incorporated in the bowed-out shape of the PPF. Point e then takes into consideration both of these effects *plus* the terms-of-trade effect.

Adding losses of economic rent to the BT estimates of long-run losses owing to the removal of mining seems not to make very much difference to their conclusions. A very rough way of estimating economic rent would be to use provincial revenues raised from mining taxes which are, in many cases, attempts to capture mineral resource values for the owners, usually the provincial Crown. In 1980–81, for example, provincial mining revenues amounted to about $650 million compared to Canada's 1980 GDP of $270 billion. On this very crude estimate, elimination of mining rents would have reduced 1980 GDP by less than 0.25 percent. So, one might conclude that BT's decision to ignore losses of economic rent is a sensible one. But when rents are examined for other natural resources sectors, the magnitudes can be very different. Consider oil and gas. In the same year (1980–81) the Economic Council of Canada estimated oil and gas revenues, including Crown royalties, freehold royalties, lease sales, and miscellaneous revenues of $6 billion. This was a period in which oil and gas prices were being held below world levels. Had oil and gas prices been allowed to move up to world price levels and the resulting revenue increases passed back to resource revenues, the latter would have increased from $6 billion to $24 billion which was nearly 9 percent of 1980 Canadian GDP. In this case it is clear that rent loss from the disappearance of petroleum deposits would have been significant. According to the same set of Economic Council estimates, rents on hydroelectric resources (especially in Quebec) and forest resources (especially in B.C.) are also of some importance, particularly at the regional level. So, depending on the sector and the circumstances, rent effects can be large or small.[10]

Turning to the terms-of-trade issue, it now seems agreed that the major shortcoming of the CG model is its neglect of possible price changes. Lewis (1975) stresses that the removal of a resources sector requires the manufacturing sector to switch over from an import-competing role to an export role. The existence of transportation costs and other trade barriers among countries will almost certainly mean that such a shift will require a fall in the price of manufactures. To this observation should be added the fact that Canada is an important supplier of certain resource commodities on world markets: 20 to 25 percent of world nickel production (excluding the U.S.S.R.), 20 to 25 percent of zinc production outside the U.S.S.R., 35 percent of potash production, 50 percent of asbestos production, and 35 percent of world newsprint production, to mention some significant ones. Elimination of Canadian output in any of these categories would probably raise world prices.

The absence of a factor proportions effect in the CG model has not inspired much criticism. Despite its formal appearance in the BT discussion, most observers seem content with the assumption that long-run international capital mobility prevents different capital intensities in extraction and manufacturing from having an impact on relative factor prices (w/R) when one sector expands at the expense of the other. Gains from the availability of Canadian natural resources do not, therefore, accrue from the presence of resource extraction as a way of utilizing Canadian capital endowments provided capital-owners can choose among alternative international locations. This is of particular relevance when it is recalled that a substantial fraction of the capital stock in extractive industries is owned outside Canada and would presumably return to its countries of origin in the absence of Canadian resources extraction opportunities.

A general criticism levied against the CG model, and applicable to BT as well, involves the question of the impact of resources on the *size* of the Canadian economy and the impact of economic size on unit costs of production in domestic manufacturing (e.g., Caves 1971). One might argue that the presence of resources industries leads to linkages that increase the sizes of other sectors and generate economies of scale. Since the present models assume constant returns, this argument cannot be effectively handled without changing the analytical framework. If scale effects *are* present, it would be necessary to add them to the other three effects on per capita income discussed above.

■ THE RESOURCE-PROCESSING OPTION

Some General Arguments

The desire by Canadians to engage in further processing of natural resources before export through, for example, provincial quotas on log exports, encouragement of petrochemical facilities in Alberta, and smelting-refining of metallic ores in Canada have the reverse impact to that created by removing certain sectors from the economy. Efficiency condition 2 (in the next to last section) proposes marginal cost pricing as the correct product mix condition. All units of a commodity for which marginal cost (the slope of the PPF) is less than price (the slope of the income line) can be efficiently produced in the sense that adding these units to the economy's activities raises its national income at world prices (refer to Figures 1.3 and 1.4 and the accompanying discussion). Conversely, if activities are added for which marginal costs are greater than prices, national income falls. Under competitive conditions, activities that increase national income will automatically appear, while those that lower national income will not. There is, therefore, a *prima facie* argument to the effect that the absence of processing activities from the economy under competitive conditions signals that such activities would make a negative contribution to national income and should not be undertaken on efficiency grounds.

The efficiency argument is not necessarily a clincher of course. Most statements of preference for more resource processing in Canada allude to a wider range of issues. In the words of one observer,

> ...the political preference in Canada may be to encourage more processing and manufacturing because this would provide benefits in the form of pride in Canadian abilities and entrepreneurship if more final products were made at home and in the form of greater control over the final use of the country's resources. By contrast, the economist's assessment of the benefits would be based on the much narrower judgement of whether the wealth of the country would be enhanced if Canada had the opportunity to add more value to its resources before they were exported.[11]

In addition to the sense of pride and resource control, the advantages of job creation implied by encouraging further processing is usually stressed in the further processing argument. The jobs-creation argument for further processing has a short-run look about it since, in the long run, jobs created in processing come about by moving along the PPF and eliminating jobs elsewhere. Still, the Canadian economy only rarely operates on its PPF. When we are inside the PPF, should we not welcome processing jobs?

Aggregate demand stimulation is an argument that can apply to the encouragement of a whole range of economic activities during a recession and not just to further processing activities. We can increase investment in plant and equipment, exploration for new resources, consumption, or government activities using monetary and fiscal policies. Why pick resource processing if its long-run effect is to shift factors of production out of activities that can make a larger contribution to national income? The stimulation of resource processing is a long-run structural policy, not a short-run stabilization measure. The federal government is not clear on the distinction between short- and long-run issues in resource processing:

> Further processing of mineral resources has been a continuing objective of Canadian public policy, because it provides employment, increases value added, promotes regional development, and increases tax revenues.[12]

This statement ignores the basic economic question of alternatives: why is further processing to be preferred to other economic activities that could accomplish the same list of goals: providing jobs, helping disadvantaged regions, and generating income and tax revenues. One returns to the original question: can the real income constraint be pushed outward, to the potential benefit of all Canadians, by substituting resource processing activities for other activities, or is the reverse likely to be the case?

As indicated by the efficiency discussion above, economists are typically conservative on this question. Suppose the revenues to be derived from an expansion of resource processing could cover all the opportunity costs of labour and capital involved along with the costs of intermediate inputs so that a net surplus emerges. Why, in such a case, have private profit-maximizing investors overlooked such an opportunity? The simplest answer is that private investors, like everyone else, are not infallible. Perhaps specific resource-processing activities that could increase national income in the long run *have* been overlooked by the private sector. But if this is the case, the question to be asked is still the same one that ought to have been asked by astute private investors: would the value-added in a particular processing project exceed the costs of factors of production allocated to the project from alternative uses? The answer requires resort to the facts of particular projects and industries.

Two basic approaches to encouraging processing are characteristic of Canadian policy. One approach is to place quotas on the export of unprocessed resources; the second is to subsidize processing itself. The former strategy has been pursued in the forestry sector. Both the federal and provincial governments restrict exports of unmanufactured timber (logs, pulp chips, and certain other mill residuals) with a view toward promoting domestic manufacturing in the form of sawmilling and pulp and paper production. The same approach has been used with fisheries to direct unprocessed fish caught by Canadian fishermen to domestic fish-processing plants. Unprocessed fish export restrictions have come under attack under our international trade obligations, however, and it is becoming more difficult to use this method of guaranteeing employment in the processing sector. Subsidization of processing is the typical approach in the minerals sector and usually takes the form of processing tax breaks in provincial mining tax legislation.

Analysing Log Export Restrictions

British Columbia's log export controls offers an interesting example of the negative impact of this kind of policy on net incomes generated in natural resources activities. If B.C. sawmillers could pay as much for B.C. logs as Japanese importers, then log prices in B.C. would not be affected by quotas. That this is not so has been argued by Pearse in his Report of the Royal Commission on Forest Resources. Pearse pointed out that logs exported to Japan from the U.S. Pacific Northwest in the early 1970s were often sold at prices *double* those received for logs sold on the Vancouver Log Market.[13] The following effects have been identified:

FIGURE 1.7

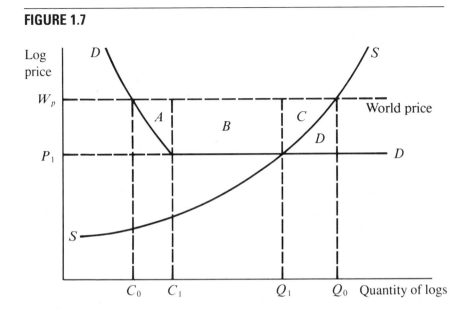

1. The reduced price of B.C. logs tends to reduce the economic rents that accrue to timber resources in the province.
2. Reduced log prices discourage logging activity since some marginal timber will no longer be worth utilizing as log prices fall below harvesting costs. Part of the timber resource becomes uneconomic.
3. Reduced log prices lower the cost of lumber production in B.C. Under competitive conditions, domestic lumber prices will decline as a result, leading to expanded domestic demand for B.C. lumber.
4. B.C. sawmillers are able to compete in Asian lumber markets as a result of the reduced domestic log prices they pay, so lumber exports and production are larger than in the absence of the log export quota. This is the intended effect of the log export quota.

The above points suggest that the further processing objective implicit in log export quotas is achieved at the expense of economic rent to the B.C. forest resource and at the expense of distortion in the amount of logging production and domestic lumber consumption. These points are illustrated in Figure 1.7. *DD* is the demand curve for logs by domestic sawmillers. The downward sloping section of *DD* shows the domestic demand for logs derived from domestic lumber consumption. At a sufficiently low price for logs, *DD* becomes perfectly elastic because sawmillers can export logs *in the form of lumber* at the fixed log price P_1. *SS* shows the supply curve of logs from the harvesting sector. When export controls are absent, the world price of logs (W_p) sets the domestic price. Total production is Q_0, domestic log consumption for domestic lumber manufacture is C_0, and log exports are $C_0 Q_0$. When log exports are prohibited, the world log price ceases to apply to the domestic market, and the domestic log price drops to the level at which domestic sawmills can sell lumber into the export market (P_1). Notice that the difference $W_p - P_1$ is the cost advantage of foreign over domestic sawmills translated into a price differential on domestic logs.

Domestic log production now drops to Q_1 from Q_0, reflecting the lower price received for logs. Domestic log consumption rises from C_0 to C_1. Exports of logs, now in the form of lumber, fall from $C_0 Q_0$ to $C_1 Q_1$. Figure 1.7 labels three types of losses to the domestic economy. Area *A* is a loss owing to distortion of domestic consumption. The demand curve over the range $C_0 C_1$ shows the maximum prices that consumers are willing to pay for logs in that quantity interval. When these prices are subtracted from the world prices that *could* have been obtained in the absence of the quota, area *A* is the resulting loss.[14] Area *B* shows the loss of timber rent on the export volume $C_1 Q_1$. Had this volume been exported as logs rather than lumber the price would have been higher by $W_p - P_1$ and rent would have been higher by the area ($W_p - P_1$) times $C_1 Q_1$. Area *C* shows the loss brought about by discouraging domestic log production from Q_0 to Q_1. The supply curve between Q_1 and Q_0 shows the marginal costs of producing logs over this interval. When these marginal costs are subtracted from the world price of logs (W_p), the resulting producers' surplus is area *C* which is lost when output shrinks from Q_0 to Q_1. Thus, in total, prohibition of log exports leads to economic losses adding up to areas $A + B + C$.

The loss caused by the artificial encouragement of domestic consumption (area *A*) is sometimes referred to as the *consumption loss*. The loss caused by discouraging domestic production (area *C*) is called the *production loss*. These losses come about because consumption and production decisions in the domestic economy are distorted by the resource processing policy. The consumption loss comes about from the failure to satisfy efficiency condition 3 in the next to last section. The production loss comes about from failure to satisfy efficiency condition 2. Even if these distortions were absent, the decision to switch from exporting logs to exporting lumber reduces returns to the domestic economy by the difference between the value of logs to the more efficient foreign sawmilling sector and their value to domestic sawmills (area *B*).

Another way of encouraging processing is to subsidize resource inputs to the domestic processing sector, perhaps by offering tax rebates to domestic processors. Figure 1.7 can be used to illustrate the effects of this kind of policy as well. Suppose the subsidy per unit of the resource processed is set exactly equal to $W_p - P_1$ in Figure 1.7. This subsidy is the *minimum* amount required to permit domestic processors (sawmills, in this case) to compete on world markets. The domestic processors pay the world price for logs (W_p) but their cost per log is reduced to P_1 as a result of the subsidy. Since W_p is being paid for logs, the total log supply is Q_0. Since sawmillers are paying P_1, competition among sawmills in the domestic sector expands domestic log consumption from C_0 to C_1 as before, leading to loss area A again. With log output set at Q_0, exports are C_1Q_0. Instead of receiving the world price for unprocessed logs (W_p), the economy receives only P_1 equal to the world price net of the subsidy required to sell logs in the form of lumber in export markets. The economic loss on processed log exports is, therefore, $(W_p - P_1)$ multiplied by the export volume C_1Q_0, which is equal to areas $B + C + D$ in Figure 1.7. The *minimum* total loss from eliminating unprocessed log exports through a processing subsidy per log is shown by areas $A + B + C + D$ and is larger by area D than the loss resulting from prohibition of unprocessed exports. The reason for the difference is that export prohibition discourages output of the unprocessed resource, and the resulting reduction in exports relative to the subsidy option reduces the social losses involved. With the log export prohibition policy, the cost of the program falls initially on the harvesting sector as log prices decline. The harvesting sector reduces output from Q_0 to Q_1 in response. The latter response is missing from the subsidization case in which the taxpayers absorb the cost of the policy directly. The subsidization policy, though more costly, also implies a higher level of employment and activity in the harvesting sector than the export quota approach. Indeed, while the log export quota adds processing jobs, it reduces employment in the logging sector.

The foregoing discussion of processing incentives suggests that, except in cases where income-expanding opportunities have been overlooked by the private sector, encouragement of processing will generally involve losses to the economy as a whole. Measured at constant world prices, the economy's long-run level of national income is reduced by substituting inefficient resource-processing activities for other activities. The magnitude of the losses depends on the exact method used to stimulate processing.

■ CONCLUSIONS AND THE NEXT STOP

The focus in the present chapter has been on the contribution that natural resources extraction activities make to the Canadian economy in the short and long run. Multiplier analysis shows that painful short-run consequences follow from adverse demand shocks in resources extraction sectors and from resource disappearances. Even though multipliers are hard to quantify with precision and multiplier analysis suffers from theoretical shortcomings, the approach serves to highlight important expenditure complementarities among different sectors in the Keynesian short-period.

In the long run, when factors of production can be reallocated from one sector to another, reductions in the level of extractive activity produce different and less serious effects on real income. The BT and CG models have been used to describe the nature of the contribution that extractive activities make to real income in the long run. If the Canadian economy operates in a world of mobile capital in the long run and world commodity prices cannot be much affected by Canadian outputs, the message of the CG model is that returns to the resources themselves, in the form of economic rents, act as a good measure of the real income gains that Canadians receive from natural resources extraction. In some cases, where world prices are sensitive to Canadian outputs (i.e., Canada is not a price taker on world markets), the calculation of gains and losses have to be modified by terms-of-trade effects.

Decisions to alter the long-run structure of the economy in favour of additional resource processing can also be approached using the efficiency framework developed here. On the issue of encouraging further process-ing, economists, unlike most government policy makers, remain skeptical. Unless the private sector's ability to mobilize factors of production in response to profit opportunities is laid open to question, resource-process-ing incentives are likely to cause economic losses. Factors of production are withdrawn from activities in which their incomes exceed the incomes to be earned in domestic processing and domestic consumption decisions are distorted.

Throughout the long-run efficiency discussion in this chapter, we have assumed that an expansion of natural resources extraction activities in the Canadian economy can be measured by the amount of "manufactures" that must be given up along the production possibilities frontier (PPF). The slope of the PPF measures the opportunity cost of additional natural resources products. This approach has permitted us to draw on well-established models of long-run economic efficiency. Using the marginal cost of resources production along the PPF is not, however, the full story on the opportunity cost of resources production. It is certainly true that an expansion of resources extraction is costly in terms of other goods that could have been produced during the current period. But it is also true that using natural resource stocks to produce *current* outputs of natural resource goods can mean that these resource stocks are not available to produce natural resource goods for the *future*. Obtaining the maximum social returns from natural resources over time requires that the connection between current extraction decisions and the costs of future extraction be built into analytical models of resource use. Chapter 2 explores the economics of choice extended to this time dimension by examining efficient extraction sequences for nonrenewable resources.

■ NOTES

1. Excerpts and references to the staples literature can be found in W.T. Easterbrook and M.H. Watkins, eds., *Approaches to Canadian Economic History* (Toronto: McClelland & Stewart, 1971). R.E. Caves and R.H. Holton, *The Canadian Economy: Prospect and Retrospect* (Cambridge, Mass.: Harvard University Press, 1959) is a classic illustration of the staples-driven approach to domestic income determination. See also R. Pomfret, *The Economic Development of Canada* (Toronto: Methuen, 1981).

2. The system can be solved using Cramer's Rule or by matrix inversion methods suitable to computer programming. See, for example, A.C. Chiang, *Fundamental Methods of Mathematical Economics* (New York: McGraw-Hill, 1984), Chap. 5.

3. The multipliers calculated here are referred to as Type-A multipliers in the input-output literature. They are the ratio of the final increase in household income to the initial change in expenditure. Type-B multipliers are the ratio of the final change in household income to the initial change in household income. Type-B multipliers are larger than Type-A multipliers because not all of the initial expenditure change is received as an initial increase in household income. Some reported multipliers are Type-B. Further discussion can be found in W. Miernyk, *The Elements of Input-Output Analysis* (New York: Random House, 1965).

4. See Department of Regional Economic Expansion (DREE), *Single-Industry Communities* (Ottawa: DREE, 1977).

5. R. Boadway, quoted in P. Nickel, et al., *Economic Impacts and Linkages of the Canadian Mining Industry* (Kingston: Queen's University Centre for Resource Studies, 1978).

6. Equation (22) can also be obtained by assuming cost minimization by firms in both industries. The ratio of the marginal products of the two factors is the slope of the firm's isoquant (the marginal rate of technical substitution) which is equated to the slope of the firm's isocost (w/R) in the cost-minimization problem.

7. Beginning at a, the country's consumers can exchange (export) units of resource goods in amount ΔX earning export revenue $P_x\Delta X$ and import units of manufactures ΔY equal to $P_x\Delta X/P_y$. Thus, the slope of the income line (budget constraint) is $\Delta Y/\Delta X = -P_x/P_y$ as stated.

8. If there are many industries in the manufacturing sector, the factor proportions effect will be zero provided the sector removed (mining) has a capital-labour ratio that lies within the range of the capital labour ratios of the various industries in the manufacturing sector. As discussed in the text, the factor proportions effect also disappears if capital is perfectly mobile internationally.

9. The specific problem dealt with in CG is not the same as the one dealt with in BT though. In the CG model, prairie wheatlands and the wheat economy are hypothetically removed against the background of the early twentieth century Canadian economy, while BT deal with the hypothetical disappearance of Canada's metallic minerals sector in the 1960s and 1970s.

10. The Economic Council of Canada's rent estimates for the early 1980s are discussed further in chapter 5.

11. L. Silver, *The Pursuit of Further Processing of Canada's Natural Resources* (Montreal: C.D. Howe Research Institute, 1975), p. 10.

12. Energy, Mines, and Resources, *Mineral Policy: A Discussion Paper* (Ottawa: 1981), p. 105.

13. P.H. Pearse, *Timber Rights and Forest Policy in British Columbia*, 2 vols. (Victoria: Royal Commission on Forest Resources, 1976), Vol. 1, p. 308.

14. Loss measure A assumes that there are negligible income effects operating on the domestic demand curve for logs.

■ FURTHER READING

Useful treatments of the regional significance of natural resources industries in Canada with spatial perspectives can be found in

Anderson, F. *Regional Economic Analysis: A Canadian Perspective.* Toronto: H.B.J. Holt, 1988.

McCann, L.D., ed. *Heartland and Hinterland.* Toronto: Prentice-Hall, 1987.

A straightforward presentation of the kind of input-output and impact-multiplier analysis used in this chapter is

Miernyk, W.H. *The Elements of Input-Output Analysis.* New York: Random House, 1965.

The Boadway-Treddenick and Chambers-Gordon models of the impact of natural resources disappearances on economic welfare are contained in

Boadway, R., and J. Treddenick. *The Impact of the Mining Industries on the Canadian Economy.* Kingston: Queen's University Centre for Resource Studies, 1977.

Chambers, E., and D. Gordon. "Primary Products and Economic Growth: An Empirical Measurement." *Journal of Political Economy* 74 (1966): 315–32.

Resource processing arguments are examined in

Silver, L. *The Pursuit of Further Processing of Canada's Natural Resources.* Montreal: C.D. Howe Research Institute, 1975.

CHAPTER TWO

MODELS OF NONRENEWABLE RESOURCE USE

∎ INTRODUCTION

This chapter and chapter 4 deal with theoretical and empirical issues of natural resources scarcity. The economic models of resources scarcity in the following sections deal with nonrenewable resources. Renewable resources models utilize many of the principles developed for nonrenewable models and are developed in detail in subsequent chapters on forestry and fishing.

Among theoretical models in the natural resources field, the theory of the optimal exhaustion of minerals is probably the best known. The theory of optimal exhaustion is directly traceable to a pathbreaking article by Hotelling (1931) in which many later developments were foreshadowed.[1]

Hotelling's treatment was the starting point for a revival of interest in the theory of nonrenewable resources in the 1960s and 1970s.

A key feature of simple models of resource exhaustion is the presence of a fixed stock of the resource under examination. Consumption of a unit of the nonrenewable resource at one moment in time precludes its use at other moments. This means that using a resource unit at one moment in time carries an opportunity cost, sometimes referred to as a "user cost" in the form of the benefits forgone by using the resource later on. Another way of putting the problem is to say that holding units of the resource instead of consuming them permits benefits to appear at later points in time. When the problem is put this way, natural resource conservation becomes part of *capital theory* in which present costs are incurred to acquire future benefits.

Since Hotelling's model is the basis for subsequent work in the theory of natural resources utilization, it is this model that is examined in the first section of the present chapter. Subsequent sections add further (modern) complications to the Hotelling structure and inquire into the role of markets in achieving the kinds of resource allocation patterns required by the theories. The present chapter has two major themes. The first theme involves contrasts between the exhaustion of resources and the depletion of resources. Most nonrenewable resources models look forward to ultimate exhaustion of mineral stocks in the Hotelling tradition, but newer treatments allow for the possibility that depletion of minerals may be taking place without assuming that actual exhaustion is in the offing.[2] The second theme involves our expectations of what the price system can reasonably be expected to accomplish by way of conserving nonrenewable resources for the future and the policy options available to alter the timing of nonrenewable resource extraction.

▌ THE HOTELLING MODEL

The Two-period Case

The simplest initial approach to Hotelling's model is to adopt a two-period time horizon. Society is endowed with a known stock of resources (say 200 units). These resources are homogeneous in the sense that the unit cost of converting them from their natural state to finished products is constant at, say, $10 per unit of final product (refined minerals).[3] Society's demand curve for the final product at time t is $\pi_1(q_1)$, where π_1 is the price of the final product and q_1 is final product output at time t. At time $t + \Delta t$ the demand curve is $\pi_2(q_2)$.

Figure 2.1 illustrates society's position if it allocates its available resource stock equally between the two periods: 100 units in t and 100 units in $t + \Delta t$. The demand curves in both periods are assumed identical.

FIGURE 2.1

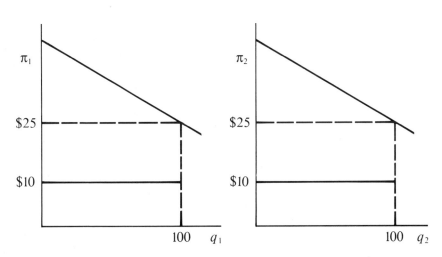

At the output level of 100 units, consumers are willing to pay $25 for the last unit. The unit cost of producing the final product is $10. The difference between product price and unit cost is $15. Given the existing plan of allocating 100 units to each period, mining firms can afford to offer resource owners $15 per unit for their resource units. If competition among mining firms is perfect resource owners will indeed receive $15 as a rental payment on each unit of resources extracted. Total (scarcity) rent in each period is $1500. If society's resource endowment disappeared, but it could acquire perfectly substitutable final products at $25 per unit to replace the missing resources, its loss would be $1500 per period: the Chambers-Gordon type of measurement discussed in chapter 1.

The result illustrated in Figure 2.1 is optimal only if society applies a zero discount rate to future benefits. Suppose, on the contrary, that capital assets yield 10 percent per period in this economy (after depreciation). Since 90.9¢ invested at t will grow to $1.00 at time $t + \Delta t$ elsewhere in the economy, society should insist on the same 10 percent rate of return on resource stocks as it could obtain by holding capital assets in, say, manufacturing. In Figure 2.1 society actually receives a zero rate of return: resource owners who hold units from period t to period $t + \Delta t$ find that those units are worth the same at $t + \Delta t$ as they are at t ($15 per unit). Using a 10 percent rate of discount over the interval Δt, the resource owner receives a present-valued return of $15/(1 + 0.1) = $13.64 on resource units marketed at $t + \Delta t$ compared to $15 on units sold at time t. A unit transferred from period $t + \Delta t$ to period t improves wealth by $1.36 (= $15 − $13.64).

FIGURE 2.2

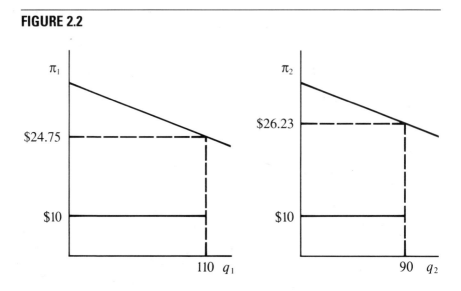

Figure 2.2 shows the equilibrium position that results when enough units of the resource have been transferred from consumption at $t + \Delta t$ to t to equalize the present value of resource units in both periods. Consumption in period t has risen from 100 to 110 units, while consumption in period $t + \Delta t$ has dropped from 100 to 90 units. Resource owners receive $26.23 − $10 = $16.23 for each unit of resources sold at $t + \Delta t$ and $24.75 − $10 = $14.75 for each unit of resources sold at t. Society cannot increase its wealth by shifting units from one period to the other. This is so because the present value of a unit of resources sold at $t + \Delta t$, $16.23/(1 + 0.1)$, equals the value at t, $14.75. The present value of wealth has indeed been increased by adopting the allocation in Figure 2.2 rather than that in Figure 2.1. In Figure 2.1, total wealth is ($15)(100) + ($15)(100)/(1 + 0.1) = $2864. In Figure 2.2, total wealth is (14.75) (200) = $2950.

The difference between the product price (π) in either of the periods and marginal production cost (C) is the *net price*. The net price can also be referred to as the *in situ* value of the resource, the royalty, the scarcity rent per unit of the resource, or the resource's marginal user cost. In period t the net price is $24.75 − $10 = $14.75. In period $t + \Delta t$ the net price is $26.23 − $10 = $16.23. Since, in equilibrium, the present value of the net price at $t + \Delta t$ equals the net price at t, the situation in Figure 2.2 can be stated algebraically as

$$\pi(t) - C(t) = [\pi(t + \Delta t) - C(t + \Delta t)]/(1 + r\Delta t) \qquad (1)$$

where, in the present example, $\pi(t) = \$24.75$, $\pi(t + \Delta t) = \$26.23$, $C(t) = C(t + \Delta t) = \$10$, $r = .1$, and $\Delta t = 1$.[4] If the net price is denoted as $p = (\pi - C)$, equation (1) can be written as

$$p(t) = p(t + \Delta t)/(1 + r\Delta t) \tag{2}$$

If equations (1) and (2) are not satisfied, society can increase its wealth (the present value of its income stream) by shifting resource use between periods. Rearranging (2),

$$\{[p(t + \Delta t) - p(t)]/\Delta t\}/p(t) = r \tag{3}$$

Equation (3) states that, in equilibrium, the rate of growth of the net price between the two periods must equal the rate of discount (r). If continuous compounding is adopted by allowing Δt to shrink toward zero then (3) can also be written in continuous (calculus) notation as

$$(dp/dt)/p = r \tag{4}$$

where dp/dt is the limit of $[p(t + \Delta t) - p(t)]/\Delta t$ as Δt approaches zero. Equality between the rate of growth of the net price and the rate of discount is a fundamental condition of intertemporal nonrenewable resources allocation in the Hotelling model. Condition (4) must be satisfied in the context of the constraint on the total availability of the resource: output at time t (110) plus output at $t + \Delta t$ (90) has to add up to the total available stock (200).

Extension to Many Periods

Intuitive extension of the Hotelling results to many time periods is straightforward. Condition (4) must now apply in comparing any two adjacent moments in time, otherwise it would be possible for society to increase wealth by reallocating resources production from one period to another just as in the two-period model. Total resources output taken over all periods must add up to the stock of resources available.

Models of the Hotelling type are *exhaustion* models precisely because a known total stock of the nonrenewable resource is allocated to resource production over a finite number of periods at the end of which production ceases and the stock is exhausted. Implicit in this is the requirement that, at the moment of exhaustion, the price of the product (π) has risen to the point at which the quantity demanded of the product is zero, referred to as the *choke price*. In Figures 2.1 and 2.2, the choke price occurs when the product demand curve meets the vertical axis. This requirement is *not* met in our two-period model because of the assumption that only two periods are to be used for production. When the number of periods is endogenous, however, product price (π) must reach the choke price (π_{max}) at the moment of exhaustion. Suppose the choke price is reached with units of the resource stock left over. If this happens, the leftover units of stock cannot be sold and are worthless. This indicates that extraction rates should have been higher all along the extraction path. Suppose, on the other hand, that the choke price is reached with total extraction over all time periods greater than the initial stock. Obviously this result is not feasible. The optimal extraction program, therefore, requires that the choke price π_{max} be reached at the same time that the last unit of the available stock is used up.

Returning for a moment to the two-period case in equation (1), the net price as a *user cost* can be illustrated. Recalling that the net price (p) equals product price (π) minus marginal production cost (C), (1) can be written as

$$\pi(t) = C(t) + p(t + \Delta t)/(1 + r\Delta t) \qquad (1A)$$

At time t, product price equals marginal cost where marginal cost is defined as marginal production cost (C) *plus* marginal user cost equal to the discounted value of the natural resource at time $t + \Delta t$. The user cost is, therefore, the opportunity cost of using the natural resource unit in the present instead of saving it for future use.[5]

The appearance of a positive net price for nonrenewable resources in the Hotelling model reflects the fixed stock assumption. If resources were to exist in unlimited quantities, net prices would be zero in the Hotelling framework. The price of the product (π) would, as in other competitive market structures, approach marginal production cost (C). Marginal production cost consists of the marginal cost of finding the resources plus the marginal cost of mining and milling.[6] With an unlimited stock of homogeneous resources available, there is no special reason to predict real cost increases either at the exploration phase or the production phase. This type of model has been called a "frontier model" (Howe 1979) or a "cornucopian model" (Brooks 1973).

The Hotelling model, in the simple form so far discussed, predicts increasing prices for resources and for resource products. Net prices are expected to rise at a rate approximating the rate of interest: 10 percent (per annum) in the example used here. Product prices rise because net prices rise. In the two-period model of Figures 2.1 and 2.2, the 10 percent increase in the net price from period t to $t + \Delta t$ produces a 6 percent increase in the price of the product from $24.75 to $26.23.

The rising net price in the Hotelling model comes about because society is assumed to require the same rate of return (10 percent) on assets held as resources as they could obtain by selling resource units and investing in, say, manufacturing capital. As one writer has put it,

> The only way that a resource deposit in the ground and left in the ground can produce a current return for its owner is by appreciating in value. Asset markets can be in equilibrium only when all assets in a given risk class earn the same rate of return, partly as current dividend and partly as capital gain. The common rate of return is the interest rate for that risk class. Since resource deposits have the peculiar property that they yield no dividend so

long as they stay in the ground, in equilibrium the value of a resource deposit must be growing at a rate equal to the rate of interest.[7]

Appreciation of the net price is what gives resources a positive rate of return in the Hotelling model so that units will be saved (conserved) for future periods.

The optimality condition implied by the Hotelling rule is sensitive to the rate of interest used to discount future net prices. Society is arranging things so that the value of resources at the margin (the net price) has to rise at 10 percent per annum. This means that the marginal benefit $(\pi - C)$ of an extra unit of resources at $t + \Delta t$ is, after discounting at 10 percent, equal to the marginal benefit $(\pi - C)$ of an extra unit of the resource now (at t). But what rate of discount should be used? In the preceding examples, the discount rate chosen is the rate of return on capital assets in other sectors of the economy. Some writers have argued that a *collective* approach to saving decisions would increase saving and bring down the rate of interest below this level. This argument suggests that observed rates of interest are higher than the rate that would prevail with collective saving patterns.[8] Others argue that individuals are simply too short-sighted in their saving decisions, particularly when saving goes into capital for the benefit of future generations of people. If these arguments are true, perhaps the rate of interest should be lower under ideal circumstances. But the rate of return would be lower not just on resource deposits but on capital assets in general. Unless a *comprehensive* reduction in rates of return is contemplated for society as a whole, resource deposits should meet *existing* rates of return on other capital assets. Lowering the rate of return on resource deposits through a slower rate of increase of net prices in the Hotelling model is thus made contingent on generally lower rates of return throughout the economic system. In the absence of a general reduction in rates of return, resource deposits ought to be required to earn the same rates of return as other assets; that is, capital held in the form of resources should meet the opportunity cost of that capital as measured by rates of return in other sectors.

Throughout the preceding discussion terms like "net price" have been used to describe the marginal value of resource units to society. The Hotelling rule, for example, equates the present value of net price in all periods and, in the process, equates the present marginal value of resource units at all points in the extraction horizon. The expression "net price" suggests that the Hotelling solution to optimal resource use can be achieved by a system of markets. It turns out that some very strong assumptions are needed to conclude that a market system will actually be capable of duplicating socially optimal resource use over time. In particular, one has to assume that markets for units of the resource are both *complete* and *competitive*. The completeness assumption means that forward markets must exist for resource units bought and sold at future dates.

The competitive assumption is shorthand for perfect competition in which markets for all dates are populated by large numbers of well-informed buyers and sellers engaged in private wealth-maximization. A detailed discussion of these market assumptions is reserved for the final section of this chapter. Before dealing with the market question, some modifications of the basic Hotelling model will be considered. In the basic model, units of the resource stock are assumed to be homogeneous. In his own work, Hotelling recognized that the quality of remaining resources was likely to deteriorate, raising marginal production cost (C), as extraction proceeded. The integration of this idea into models of nonrenewable resources use and the resulting modification of equation (4) was left to subsequent researchers, however.

Removal of the fixed resource stock assumption and the introduction of rising marginal production cost as extraction proceeds produces a somewhat different kind of nonrenewable resources model. The differences are particularly noticeable when technological progress is allowed to operate on production costs. The following section modifies the Hotelling model to bring these changed assumptions into the analysis.

■ GENERALIZING THE HOTELLING MODEL

Adapting the basic Hotelling model to incorporate declining resource quality as extraction proceeds leads to a generalized version of the exhaustion model. Figure 2.3 contrasts the resource supply assumptions of the Hotelling model with the modifications introduced in this section. Panel A (the Hotelling version) shows that marginal production cost (C) remains constant right up to a point of resource exhaustion where cumulative production adds up to the fixed resource stock constraint. Panel B (the modified Hotelling model) assumes that marginal production cost is a gradually increasing function of cumulative output. If a resource stock constraint exists at all, it appears as a final vertical section of the rising cost curve in panel B (dashed line).

The increase in marginal production cost as cumulative production takes place reflects two factors. First, exploration may become less productive as the most likely mineral-bearing areas are examined initially and less likely prospects are deferred for subsequent exploratory work. Second, and more important, new discoveries may involve a movement to lower grade mineral ores as the best deposits are used up first. Table 2.1 shows the decline of copper ore grades for major producing countries including Canada over the period from 1960 to 1976. The percentage of metallic copper contained in copper-producing ores declined during this period to about half its initial value for the world as a whole and to about 35 percent of its initial value for Canada. Natural resources use generally proceeds from the higher quality to the lower quality resources. This

FIGURE 2.3

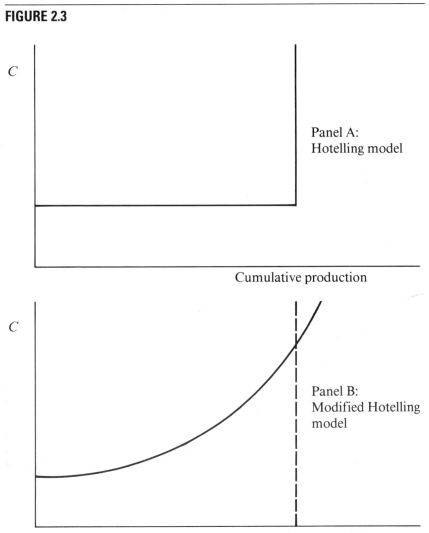

C

Panel A:
Hotelling model

Cumulative production

C

Panel B:
Modified Hotelling
model

Cumulative production

sequencing is sensible: with positive discount rates, cost increases should
be postponed as long as possible. It should be noted though that new
discoveries will often involve higher grades than existing orebodies: the
case of the rich Hemlo gold discoveries on the north shore of Lake Superior
in the early 1980s is an example.

The modified Hotelling model sets out optimum conditions for the use
of a nonrenewable resource that is subject to rising production costs as

TABLE 2.1   Evolution of copper ore grades in Canada, other major producing countries and the world

	1960	1968	1976
		(percent)	
Canada	1.70	0.90	0.62
United States	0.80	0.77	0.71
Chile	1.97	1.29	1.07
Peru	0.91	0.98	0.93
Zaire	4.00	4.00	4.05
Zambia	3.71	3.40	3.02
Philippines	—	0.54	0.50
Mexico	—	0.60	0.67
Papua New Guinea	—	0.47	0.61
World	2.03	1.20	0.96

Source: Energy, Mines and Resources, *Mineral Policy: A Discussion Paper* (Ottawa: Supply and Services, 1981).

extraction proceeds. These optimum conditions are usually derived using the mathematics of optimal control. In what follows, a more intuitive approach is used (readers interested in a proof of the optimum conditions using control theory are referred to the appendix to this chapter).

Consider two periods, t and $t + \Delta t$ in the sequential use of a nonrenewable resource subject to rising marginal production cost with cumulative production. A decision is to be made at time t either to hold or extract a marginal unit of the resource stock. If the unit is extracted at time t then the return to society consists of its net price $p(t)$. If the unit is held over until time $t + \Delta t$ and sold at that time, the present value of the net price received by society is $p(t + \Delta t)/(1 + r\Delta t)$ where, as before, r is the continuous discount rate. Since the unit cost of extraction depends on the size of the remaining stock, the decision to hold an extra unit of the stock over the period Δt and extract it at time $t + \Delta t$ lowers the cost of extraction during the interval Δt. Suppose the change in unit cost caused by an increase in the stock size is $\Delta C/\Delta X < 0$. Denoting the instantaneous rate of extraction as q, total extraction is $q\Delta t$ and the change in overall extraction cost brought about by holding the extra unit of stock is $(\Delta C/\Delta X)q\Delta t < 0$. If the unit is extracted immediately in period t, society will receive the net price $p(t)$ but will sacrifice the chance to hold extraction cost down over the period Δt and will also sacrifice the present value of the unit if it were extracted at $t + \Delta t$. So the *net* benefit from immediate extraction is $p(t) + (\Delta C/\Delta X)q\Delta t - p(t + \Delta t)/(1 + r\Delta t)$. Additional units should be added to the stock at t (depletion deferred to $t + \Delta t$) until the net benefit of such additions equals zero, i.e. until

$$p(t) + (\Delta C/\Delta X)q\Delta t - p(t + \Delta t)/(1 + r\Delta t) = 0 \qquad (5)$$

Multiplying through by $(1 + r\Delta t)$, equation (5) becomes

$$p(t)(1 + r\Delta t) + (\Delta C/\Delta X)q\Delta t(1 + r\Delta t) - p(t + \Delta t) = 0 \qquad (6)$$

Rearranging (6),

$$rp(t)\Delta t = p(t + \Delta t) - p(t) - (\Delta C/\Delta X)q\Delta t(1 + r\Delta t) \qquad (7)$$

Dividing both sides of (7) through by Δt,

$$rp(t) = [p(t + \Delta t) - p(t)]/\Delta t - (\Delta C/\Delta X)q(1 + r\Delta t) \qquad (8)$$

We now permit the time interval (Δt) and therefore the size of the stock change (ΔX) to shrink toward zero. Now the rate of change of the net price $[p(t + \Delta t) - p(t)]/\Delta t$ becomes dp/dt, the stock effect on unit cost $\Delta C/\Delta X$ becomes dC/dX, denoted by C_x, and $r\Delta t$ approaches zero. Equation (8) becomes

$$rp = dp/dt - C_x q \qquad (9)$$

which is the result derived using optimal control (dynamic optimization) in the appendix to this chapter. This condition must be satisfied at every point in the evolution of production of the nonrenewable resource.

Equation (9) equates the holding cost of an additional unit of the resource stock (rp) to the marginal return on an extra unit of the stock. The marginal return is divided into two parts: a capital appreciation component (dp/dt) and a return consisting of postponement of the cost increase that would otherwise have occurred if the resource unit had been extracted $(-C_x q)$.[9]

The modified Hotelling model allows for two different kinds of exhaustion. The first type—*complete exhaustion*—occurs when there is a finite limit to the stock of available resources as shown by the dotted vertical line in panel B of Figure 2.3. In that case the net price terminates at a positive value just as it does in the simple constant-cost Hotelling version. The difference is that the net price grows at a rate equal to the rate of interest in the simple model (equation (4)) and at a rate *lower* than the rate of interest in the modified version (equation (9)). The second kind of exhaustion is *incomplete exhaustion*. In this case the dotted vertical line is absent in panel B of Figure 2.3. Larger and larger amounts of cumulative production involve ever higher levels of marginal production cost with no definite limit set on the resource base. Production ceases only when marginal production costs have risen so high that they threaten to exceed the maximum price (π_{max}) that consumers are willing to pay for the resource product (the choke price). When the choke price is reached $C = \pi_{max}$ and the final (terminal) net price is $p = \pi_{max} - C = 0$. Resources are exhausted in an economic sense. Even though additional units are available they are not worth extracting because consumers cannot be found

FIGURE 2.4

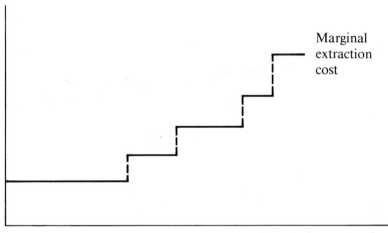

Marginal extraction cost

Cumulative production

to pay the high production costs involved in dealing with such low-grade deposits. Since the terminal net price is zero in an incomplete exhaustion model, a positive net price ($p > 0$) earlier in the development of the resource industry implies that not only is the rate of growth of net price less than the rate of interest, it is actually negative.

In some cases the simple Hotelling model is combined with differing grades. Each grade lasts for a finite period of time so that marginal production cost rises in a series of discrete steps (Figure 2.4). Within each grade the simple Hotelling result obtains, and the net price rises at a rate equal to the rate of interest. The transition from each grade to the next lower grade is abrupt and is accompanied by a sharp drop in the net price (Figure 2.5). Consider two successive grades. The net price for the higher grade is rising at the rate of interest so that owners of these deposits will be content to dispose of them at any point in the initial finite time interval during which the high-grade deposits last. Since the poorer grade deposits command a *lower* net price, the price increases during the first time interval are large enough to provide a yield on the poorer grade that exceeds the rate of interest. So the owners of the poorer grade are content to hold their deposits off the market until the higher grade deposits are used up. When exhaustion of the high-grade deposits occurs (point A in Figure 2.5) the net price p ($= \pi - C$) drops abruptly and then begins rising again at the rate of interest. The price of the product (π) must be the same at point A whether or not the product is produced from the higher or from the lower

FIGURE 2.5

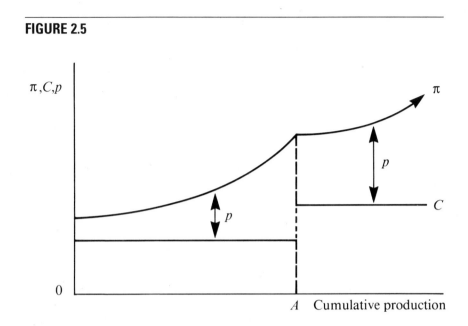

A   Cumulative production

grade resources. At point *A* the rate of increase of the product price (π) slows down because the net price (still growing at r) is now a smaller component of product price ($\pi = p + C$). As the model proceeds through a series of grades, the net price may rise or fall on average since it is rising *within* grades and falling at the points of transition *between* successive grades. As the number of grades is increased, the stepped cost structure in Figures 2.4 and 2.5 approaches a continuous curve like panel B of Figure 2.3. The quantity of mineral in each grade gets smaller and smaller so that, in the limit, cost rises continuously as production proceeds and the behaviour of net price is described by equation (9).

There is no reason to be dogmatic about the choice of continuous or step-wise cost increases because of depletion.[10] Where depletion tends to increase costs more or less steadily, the continuous version of the model has advantages, since the net price will always be subject to downward pressure as depletion forces the mineral industry to higher and higher cost sources all the time. If, on the other hand, resource utilization involves moving from higher to lower grades only occasionally with long periods in which production takes place from a single type of deposit, the step-wise model is more useful.

An interesting example of the application of the step-wise model to energy resources is contained in an optimal energy use model developed by Nordhaus (1979). In the Nordhaus model, the steps in Figures 2.4 and 2.5 involve worldwide transitions from conventional oil and gas production through coal, synthetic oil and gas, to nuclear power in four different energy-using sectors. Nordhaus visualizes the world as moving toward an essentially inexhaustible energy source in the form of breeder nuclear power while using up its exhaustible fossil fuel energy sources along the way. At the point at which exhaustible energy sources disappear, the net price of the last exhaustible source plus its production cost ($p + C$) gives an energy price (π) exactly equal to the cost of producing energy from the inexhaustible source. From then on the net price is zero ($\pi = C$) because resource exhaustion is no longer relevant. The world relies exclusively on nuclear energy from breeder reactors. Nordhaus calls this ultimate energy source the "backstop technology." At the moment when the backstop is reached, society's cumulative energy consumption must equal the total available stock of the exhaustible energy sources.

The development of the simple Hotelling model of optimal resource exhaustion in the preceding section and the modified Hotelling approach described in this section have been presented without reference to technological changes that may be operating to reduce marginal production costs (C) over time as new discovery and extraction techniques increase the productivity of labour and capital in resources sectors. The next section is devoted to this issue. All of the models in this section and the previous one predict exhaustion—complete or incomplete—over the planning horizon spanned by resource production. When technological change is added, the simple Hotelling model still predicts that society runs out of resources since a finite resource stock inevitably produces complete exhaustion. However, as the following section explains, the modified Hotelling model with rising production costs and no resource stock constraint responds differently to the introduction of cost-reducing technical change. In a range of cases, technological progress may be rapid enough to offset the rising costs brought about by depletion so that no definite limit can be assigned to the available stock of economic resources.

∎ THE IMPACT OF TECHNICAL CHANGE

The most straightforward method of incorporating technical change into exhaustion models is to assume that marginal production costs are influenced by time. In this case the marginal production cost function can be written as

$$C = C(X, t) \tag{10}$$

where X measures the remaining stock of the resource and t is the time variable that incorporates (exogenous) technological change. Examining the separate marginal effects of depletion and technological change,

$$dC/dt = \partial C/\partial X \cdot dX/dt + \partial C/\partial t = -C_x q + \partial C/\partial t \qquad (11)$$

The change in C taking place during a very short time interval is being broken down into two effects. The first effect—already described by equation (9)—measures the impact of depletion on cost during the short time interval dt. The current level of output reduces the remaining stock X so $dX/dt = -q$. As the remaining stock falls, unit production cost increases so $C_x < 0$. The second effect isolates the impact of technical change on marginal production cost and is given by $\partial C/\partial t$ in equation (11). Since $\partial C/\partial t$ is negative (time reduces marginal production cost as new techniques are utilized), the *overall* effect of time on production cost could be positive or negative. Depletion tends to raise C while technical advance tends to lower it. In the words of one observer,

> ...exploration, guided by geological concepts and skills, is a systematic process in the long term, tending to detect first those deposits that are largest, highest grade, closest to surface and closest to market. Consequently, the best deposits will, on average, be discovered, developed, and exhausted first. Lower quality or smaller deposits remain for the future. Thus, depletion causes the cost of mineral supply to rise over time. Fortunately, there is a second offsetting force which is also at work: advances in technology. Such advances may include revised geological concepts, more efficient and extensive exploration techniques as well as improved mining and mineral processing methods. Advances in technology act to reduce the cost of mineral supply. The resultant of these depletion and technological forces determines whether the economics of mineral exploration are in fact deteriorating or improving with time.[11]

The presence of technological change does not alter the resource owners' basic decision-making framework. Equation (4) is still valid for the simple Hotelling model, and equation (9) still describes the optimal path for the net price when production costs are subject to the pressure of depletion. Figure 2.6 illustrates the behaviour of the simple Hotelling model with technical progress. Marginal production cost (C) is declining as time passes ($\partial C/\partial t < 0$). Resource owners are still maximizing net wealth over time, so that the net price p is growing at the rate of interest. The product price (π) is illustrated as falling at first and then rising. Since product price is net price plus marginal production cost,

$$d\pi/dt = dp/dt + dC/dt \qquad (12)$$

From equation (4), dp/dt is positive and equals rp. With technical progress dC/dt is negative in the simple Hotelling model. In the early stages of exhaustion, the net price is low and falling marginal production cost dominates the behaviour of product price so that $d\pi/dt < 0$. Later on, when p is larger, the movement of the product price is dominated by the rising net price so that $d\pi/dt > 0$. The resulting U-shaped behaviour of π as exhaus-

FIGURE 2.6

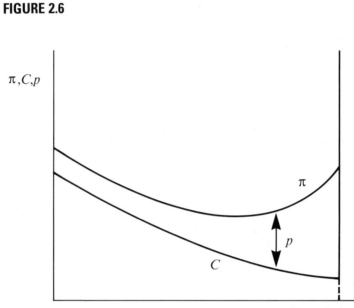

Cumulative production

tion proceeds is illustrated in Figure 2.6. Exhaustion is still inevitable here because of the fixed resource stock but product prices may experience an extended period of decline before turning up to choke off consumption as exhaustion approaches.

Turning to the *modified* Hotelling approach, equation (9) describes the optimal behaviour of net price over time. In order to interpret the impact of technological change, it is useful to write equations (9), (11), and (12) together:

$$rp = dp/dt - C_x q \tag{9}$$

$$dC/dt = -C_x q + \partial C/\partial t \tag{11}$$

$$d\pi/dt = dp/dt + dC/dt \tag{12}$$

As Slade (1982) has shown, this system can be reduced to a single equation showing the impact of technological change on product price movements ($d\pi/dt$). If equation (9) is substituted into equation (12), the following emerges:

$$d\pi/dt - dC/dt - C_x q = rp \tag{13}$$

Adding $\partial C/\partial t$ to both sides of (13),

$$d\pi/dt - dC/dt - C_x q + \partial C/\partial t = \partial C/\partial t + rp \qquad (14)$$

Since $dC/dt = -C_x q + \partial C/\partial t$ (equation (11)), the last three terms on the left-hand side of (14) cancel leaving

$$d\pi/dt = \partial C/\partial t + rp \qquad (15)$$

which states that optimal product price may be rising or falling depending upon the speed of technological progress. The interpretation of equation (15) depends upon whether the nonrenewable resource has a fixed stock or not.

Consider, first, models with a fixed resource stock. The simple Hotelling model is the basic case. With $\partial C/\partial t < 0$, the simple Hotelling model begins with falling product price provided p is small enough at the outset. But p is growing at the rate of interest so that, eventually, rp is large enough to overwhelm the forces of technological progress and $d\pi/dt$ becomes positive, choking off demand for the resource product at the point of resource exhaustion as described above (Figure 2.6). The requirement that demand be choked off as exhaustion is approached is common to all models in which a fixed stock appears. The net price increases to ensure that this result will occur.

When production cost rises with cumulative extraction ($C_x < 0$), and there is *no* fixed limit on the resource stock available, the results are different. If exhaustion did occur in this framework, it would have to be because marginal production cost has risen high enough to equal the choke price π_{max}. At this point the net price would equal zero, a situation of *incomplete exhaustion* as described earlier in this chapter. In equation (15) a zero net price with cost-reducing technological change ($\partial C/\partial t < 0$) would give rise to a falling product price ($d\pi/dt < 0$). If product prices were falling at the point of (incomplete) exhaustion, consumption of the product would start up again. A contradiction appears: if resources are no longer being depleted but technical progress is proceeding, new economic resources appear on the scene, counter to the assumption that exhaustion has occurred.

The conclusion is clear: incomplete exhaustion *cannot* occur if production costs are subject to downward pressure from technological advance. Baumol (1986) has drawn attention to this feature of nonrenewable resource models with technological progress. What is happening here is that new techniques are continuously converting noneconomic stocks of resources into economic stocks by lowering their unit extraction costs (C) below the choke price (π_{max}). Of course, technological progress may be quite slow so that continued production over the very long run must be small to prevent the rising costs of depletion from overwhelming the beneficial effects of technical progress. One possibility is that technical progress can offset the cost consequences of depletion for long periods (if not indefinitely) in such a way that the price of resource products (relative to other goods and services) remains approximately stationary (see chapter 4). If such constancy of real prices were to occur in an optimal use model of the type described by equations (9), (11), and (12), then equation (15) would become

$$d\pi/dt = \partial C/\partial t + rp = 0 \qquad (16)$$

so that the net price equals $(-\partial C/\partial t)/r$. If, to continue the example, technological progress is occurring at a regular relative rate so that real unit costs are declining in the minerals sector at, say 2 percent per annum, then $(\partial C/\partial t)/C = -.02$. If the discount rate is, say, 10 percent (in real terms), then equation (16) can be written as

$$p/C = -[(\partial C/\partial t)/C]/r = .02/.10 = .20 \qquad (17)$$

placing the net price at 20 percent of unit cost (C) or 16.7 percent of product price (π). This is, of course, a highly simplified representation of a steady-state process in which the contest between depletion and technological progress is fairly equal. It is only one possibility among many, but it does illustrate that including technological change in the modified Hotelling model means that resource exhaustion is only one possibility. Indeed, exhaustion is only inevitable if a fixed resource stock assumption is built into the nonrenewable resources model.

■ CAN FREE MARKETS DO IT?

Forward Markets and Expectations

The basic Hotelling model and the modified versions that allow for cost increases due to depletion and cost reductions due to technical progress describe optimal approaches to nonrenewable resource use. These optimal models lie at a considerable distance from the operation of actual market mechanisms. In standard economic terminology there is considerable room for *market failure*, that is, inability on the part of the market mechanism to reproduce the results described by the models. In order to illustrate the problems confronting a market approach to nonrenewable resource extraction, we will consider a simple example of the basic Hotelling model.

The total stock of a homogeneous nonrenewable resource is assumed to be 324 units. Each unit can be extracted at a cost $C = \$10$. During each period, the product demand function is $q = 110 - \pi$. The assumed rate of discount is 10 percent. Table 2.2 illustrates the optimal extraction and pricing path for the problem. The net price (p) in column 2 follows the Hotelling rule, rising at 10 percent per period from \$42.41 in period 1 to the terminal net price of \$100.00 in period 10. The product price path in column 3 is obtained by adding the constant \$10 extraction cost to the net

TABLE 2.2   An optimal extraction example

(1)	(2)	(3)	(4)	(5)
t	p	π	q	X
1	42.41	52.41	57.59	324.08
2	46.65	56.65	53.35	266.49
3	51.32	61.32	48.68	213.14
4	56.45	66.45	43.55	164.46
5	62.10	72.10	37.90	120.91
6	68.30	78.30	31.70	83.01
7	75.13	85.13	24.87	51.31
8	82.65	92.65	17.35	26.44
9	90.91	100.91	9.09	9.09
10	100.00	110.00	0.00	0.00

Note: See text for assumptions.

price path. Each period's output in column 4 is obtained from the demand function ($\pi + q = 110$). Column 5 shows the remaining stock (X) obtained by subtracting the previous period's output from the previous period's stock. At the terminal point (period 10), the current extraction rate is zero and the remaining stock is zero.

The results in Table 2.2 can be obtained by a *central planner*. The planner solves the problem using the asset equilibrium condition given by the Hotelling rule in equation (3) together with the terminal condition requiring $X = 0$ when $q = 0$. If a *market* mechanism is to be used instead of the planning mechanism, some very strict assumptions are needed. First, the units of the resource must be owned by a set of competitive agents. Each agent can supply any number of the resource units he or she owns at any point in time by incurring the extraction cost of $10 at the chosen time of disposal. To make rational supply decisions, each owner must be aware in period 1 of prices that will be obtained at *all* points in time. With these prices known, owners can decide when to dispose of their resource holdings.

To obtain knowledge of all prices at the beginning of the process requires a *spot* market to establish the period 1 net price and a set of *forward* markets to establish net prices for periods $t \geqslant 2$. Each market reaches equilibrium when the quantity of resource units supplied in that period equals the quantity demanded. When equilibrium is reached in all periods, the quantity to be supplied in each future period becomes a forward delivery contract at the equilibrium price. For example, from Table 2.2, equilibrium implies that the futures price is $p = \$68.30$ for period 6. Resource owners contract to deliver 31.70 units of the resource to purchasers in period 6 at this price with the contract entered into in period 1. Since resources are perfect substitutes on the supply side provided the present value of the net price is the same in all periods, the Hotelling rule emerges. Since all markets must also clear in equilibrium and total supply in all periods equals the available stock (324 units), the terminal condition ($X = 0$; $q = 0$) is a consequence of market-clearing behaviour.

The assumption that competitive forward markets exist in period 1 for all future periods means that markets are *complete*. If the forward markets are missing from the model then there is no decentralized pricing mechanism to establish optimal extraction results. If forward markets are missing, resource owners can only decide on how many units to supply in period 1 based on their *expectations* of net prices in future periods.

Once expectations are admitted into the analysis, it becomes unlikely that present decisions can be thought of as rational in the light of unknown future events. In the most extreme case,

> ...the only information available to producers is the history of the industry, the current situation, and the individual's hopes, fears, and expectations about the future price of resources....current production plans depend in large measure on unfounded expectations about the future where waves of propaganda, optimism, or pessimism can overwhelm "rational" entrepreneurs....[12]

In the absence of central planning or forward markets, there is nothing to ensure that expected net prices correspond to the optimal net prices in column 2 of Table 2.2. When markets are incomplete, *market failure* occurs as a matter of definition. Without forward markets, sellers of resource units have no method of co-ordinating their actions. Even if each seller could form an accurate expectation of future demands for resources as a *whole*, no individual seller knows what other sellers are planning to do in response to demand and what prices will therefore emerge. Each seller is free to assume, for example, that other sellers are saving resource supplies for the future so that future net prices will be low. The appropriate wealth-maximizing response is to sell now. With everyone selling now, the future is not provided for. It might be argued that low current net prices will act as a signal that scarcity and higher net prices will prevail in the future. This type of expectation could work to promote conservation for the future. But it could also be that a decline in current net prices leads to an expectation of further declines in the future which promotes disposal of stocks in the present.

How Large is the Resource Stock?

The issue of expectations and forward markets is not the only problem faced by the Hotelling model. Though Hotelling himself was not perfectly clear on the matter, the available stock of resources (324 units in the present example) refers to *undiscovered* resources and not just to reserves of minerals. Society need not be concerned about using up the last unit of reserves of a mineral since consumption of reserves is being accompanied by reserve additions brought about by new discoveries. What is important is the ultimate stock of resources from which new discoveries are made to replace current production. Since available resource stocks have yet to be established as reserves through the exploration process, it is natural to find controversy concerning the actual magnitude of such resources. The assumption that the resource stock *is* known to the extent necessary to permit forward delivery contracts over an extended time horizon (say twenty-five years and beyond) is not realistic. In fact, it is not optimal to spend money to establish (discover and prove up) resource stocks that will not be used for many years or decades. There is little evidence that reserves are held for future use beyond the projected requirements of particular mining facilities:

> ...ore "reserves" of a country are, essentially, merely the sum of the working inventories of unmined ore of all existing and prospective mines....It would be premature and uneconomic for a company to develop reserves at a mine—a costly process—beyond the needs of a rational mining plan...[13]

The modified Hotelling model presents added difficulties. In this version, it is not only necessary to know all the stocks available, it is also necessary to predict the behaviour of extraction cost (C) for these stocks as resource depletion unfolds in the future. Resource owners have to know the exploration, development, extraction, and processing costs associated with transforming resource prospects under their own control to marketable products.

The basic structure of the optimal extraction model can be preserved only if exploration and development cost per unit of resources is reasonably certain for each prospect. This may be the case if each owner controls a large enough area of mineral rights to take advantage of the "law of large numbers" such that a particular exploration/development budget leads to a reasonably certain number of resource units. Referring to the copper industry, Herfindahl put this problem in the following way:

> ...if the areas in which copper deposits may be found are large and there is sufficient knowledge of the general characteristics of these areas to permit reasonably good prediction of the success of the exploration efforts of the industry as a whole, then the finding and production of copper will be taking place in a relatively stable environment.[14]

When the geographical area of ownership of prospects is small, however, the owner is unlikely to have any clear idea of what exploration activity will turn up, if anything. Ownership of the results of exploration activity could involve large resource stocks or none at all.

Property Rights and Market Structure

To summarize so far, optimal extraction requires a complete and competitive set of forward markets and the ultimate stock of resources and their extraction costs must be known to the owners of resource prospects. In addition, it is essential that resource prospects *are* actually under secure ownership (tenure). Suppose resource prospects are well-defined in terms of the magnitudes of resource stocks and their extraction costs. If Individual A "owns" a resource prospect and decides to incur exploration and development costs later in the extraction sequence, then the resources must still be there when he or she subsequently decides to prove them up and produce them. If the prospects are not under secure ownership so that other producers can help themselves to the unproven stocks, then there is no incentive for Individual A to delay in proving up the stocks. This *common property* or *open access* problem is prominent in environmental economics and in the exploitation of fish stocks and is discussed in greater detail in chapters 3 and 7.

A further problem on the supply side involves the information-generating aspects of exploration expenditures. Exploration results may convey valuable information to producers other than the producer undertaking the expenditure so that *external benefits* are conferred on other searchers for resource deposits:

> The information externality arises when the spatial orientation of deposits is such that the discovery of one deposit conveys valuable information to those searching nearby. Such information externalities can, if not exploited by those making the initial discovery, lead to insufficient expenditure by the resource sector (private cost exceeds the social cost for new discoveries).[15]

In essence, if Individual A locates resources under mineralogical conditions that are similar to those characterizing Individual B's prospects, then Individual B is receiving an (unpriced) external benefit in the form of valuable information. Since Individual A is not compensated for the information, her or his incentive to explore and reveal such information is impaired. This effect acts in the opposite direction to the open-access effect: the information externality slows down the rate of depletion, while the failure to treat mineral prospects as private property speeds up the rate of depletion.

It seems entirely likely that the absence of forward markets for resources stretching decades into the future is not just a cause of uncertainty but is also a result of uncertainty. If resource owners could form fairly accurate expectations of the true costs of producing additional units of resource products from prospects under their secure control, this could be an important step forward in rational nonrenewable resource planning. In this type of environment, owners of prospects *might* be willing to enter into forward contracts for future delivery of resources. If, at the same time, the users of resource products could anticipate their own future demand functions, they *might* also be willing to enter forward-purchasing contracts. The fact that long-term forward markets have not developed, therefore, may imply that uncertainties are too large on either or both sides of the supply/demand process. On the supply side, resource owners may feel that mineral prospects are too uncertain to justify anything approaching firm forward delivery commitments. On the demand side, resource users may also feel that uncertainty about their own future costs and market prospects militates against definite forward-purchasing plans for the resources they use as inputs.

Even if resource owners and users were willing to enter into forward contracts based on solid information about the future, two additional issues can be raised. The first, mentioned earlier in this chapter, concerns the discount rate (r) used in comparing net prices and cost changes over time. Private and social decisions will not coincide unless private and social discount rates coincide. As discussed above, however, this type of market failure (if present) is of a very general kind requiring economy-wide corrective action rather than specific action in resources sectors.

A second problem concerns the competitive structure of resources markets. The use of a system of forward markets to allocate nonrenewable resources over time will only be efficient if there are large numbers of buyers and sellers—perfect competition. Suppose, by contrast, that resource ownership in a particular minerals industry is under monopolistic control. For a competitive owner, the value of a unit of the resources is the net price. Wealth is maximized by equating the present values of the net price over time leading to the Hotelling rule in equation (4). For a monopolistic owner, however, the value of a unit of the resource is its marginal profit equal to ($MR - C$) where MR is marginal revenue in the product market. The monopolistic owner maximizes wealth by equating the present values of ($MR - C$) over time. The resulting pattern of resource use over time is generally *different* from the pattern that would be selected by competitive resource owners. Indeed, very special assumptions are needed to reach the opposite conclusion. These assumptions are that marginal production cost (C) is zero and the elasticity of demand for the product is constant irrespective of output.[16] If marginal production cost is zero, equation (4) becomes $(d\pi/dt)/\pi) = r$. For a monopolist, it is true that $MR = \pi(1 - 1/\epsilon)$ where ϵ is the elasticity of demand for the monopolist's product. If ϵ is constant, then $dMR = d\pi(1 - 1/\epsilon)$ and $dMR/dt = d\pi/dt \cdot (1 - 1/\epsilon)$. As a result, if equation (4) is satisfied so that $(d\pi/dt)/\pi = r$ then it is automatically true that $(dMR/dt)/MR = r$. The output plan selected by the competitive market structure in which the net price ($p = \pi$) is growing at each moment at the rate of interest *also* ensures that the marginal profit

(MR) is growing at the rate of interest as a monopolistic owner requires. If, more realistically, marginal production cost is positive and elasticity (ϵ) varies as output varies, satisfaction of equation (4) will *not* produce the same growth rate for a monopolist's marginal profit ($MR - C$). So the monopolist would pick a different output pattern over time to make ($MR - C$) grow at the rate r. Most observers feel that the monopolist will satisfy this requirement by restricting present output and expanding future output; production is delayed and conservation promoted.

■ CONCLUDING OBSERVATIONS

The results of the previous section can be summarized. Partly due to uncertainty surrounding future mineral supplies and demands, long-term forward markets for resources do not exist. Owners of resource prospects do not adopt long-range planning in their wealth maximization objectives. As a result, delaying the process of exploration/extraction to produce the positive net prices for the lowest quality resources currently utilized does not take place. Uncertainty and the absence of forward markets makes it difficult to know just how much delay is optimal, though it is clear that a zero net price (no delay) is too low when depletion is taking place. Resource prospects should command positive net prices (rents). Failure to delay production to produce positive net prices is equivalent to non-ownership of the resource prospects themselves: no one finds it worthwhile to hold such prospects since others may initiate exploration on them at any time. As Gaffney has pointed out,

> ...the absence of tenure virtually guarantees abuse, for no one can profit from his own forbearance. That is familiarly true of our streets and parks, for example. It is even more true of exhaustible resources, whose optimal use over time requires forbearance. [17]

Market processes may diverge from optimal use even if enough information combined with secure ownership is present. If private and social discount rates differ, transition to a lower rate of return on all social assets would slow down resource depletion. By this standard, current rates of depletion are too rapid. In contrast to the above biases toward excessive use, markets may also incorporate some weaker biases toward conservation. Information externalities may slow down exploration processes while, at the same time, impairing the efficiency of the search process. If monopolistic elements are present, these will also affect depletion rates and usually in the direction of greater conservation.

Finally, if net prices approach zero under existing institutional and market arrangements, policy action could be used to generate positive net prices for nonrenewable resource stocks. A tax on each unit of resources added to the known stock could be used to drive a wedge between the product price (π) and marginal production cost (C) leading to a positive net price ($\pi - C > 0$). Such a corrective tax policy will be discussed further in chapter 5 where it will be referred to as a *depletion tax*. It is unlikely that enough information exists to permit a depletion tax system to duplicate the exact requirements of optimal use, but it could be a step in the right direction.

■ APPENDIX: INTRODUCTION TO DYNAMIC OPTIMIZATION

A Framework for Dynamic Optimization

The purpose of this section is to introduce optimal rules for natural resource utilization beginning from simple maximization principles. To make our results useful not only for the nonrenewable resource problems of this chapter but also for later problems involving pollution (chapter 3) and renewable fisheries resources (chapter 7), the resource utilization problem developed here takes a fairly general form. The list of further readings offers alternative and complementary treatments of dynamic optimization.

The basis of dynamic optimization lies in the Lagrange method. The Lagrange method is first illustrated for a simple problem. Suppose we are dealing with the two-period Hotelling model of the present chapter. There is a fixed endowment of the homogeneous natural resource denoted by X_0 and it is desired to maximize discounted net benefits over two periods subject to the constraint that the outputs of the two periods add up to X_0. The problem can be stated as follows:

Maximize $V = \rho[B(q_1) - C \cdot q_1] + B(q_0) - C \cdot q_0$ (A1)

Subject to $X_{t+1} - X_t = -q_t$ ($t = 0,1$)   (A2)

where V is the present value of net benefits, q_0, q_1 are the outputs in the two periods, and $B - C \cdot q$ stands for net benefit. Net benefit is total benefit B minus total cost (equal to constant unit extraction cost C multiplied by output q). The discount rate is r so that $\rho [= 1/(1 + r)]$ is the discount factor applied to net benefits in period 1. The constraints are written in a dynamic form, indicating that the stock in period $t + 1$ (X_{t+1}) equals the stock in period t (X_t) minus the flow withdrawal from the stock at t (q_t). Since $t = 0,1$, there are two constraints here: $X_2 - X_1 = -q_1$ and $X_1 - X_0 = -q_0$. Since $X_2 = 0$ as a terminal condition in the two-period problem, these two constraints actually boil down to the single constraint: $q_0 + q_1 = X_0$. We have left the constraints in their more general form (A2), however, because it is easier to generalize to many periods using this form for the constraints.

A simple way of thinking about the benefit function B is to assume

FIGURE 2A.1

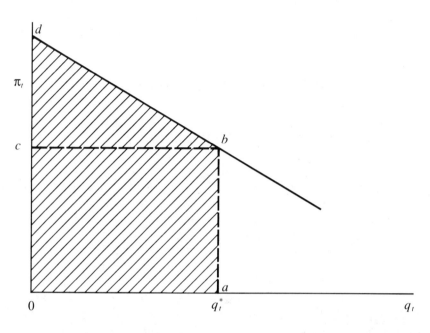

that it is the area under the aggregate demand curve for the resource product. Referring to Figure 2A.1, B consists of the total amount consumers pay for all units of the resource product ($0abc$) plus the consumers' surplus (dbc). A small change in output of the resource product leads to a marginal benefit—dB/dq—which is measured by the price of the product, denoted by π.

The Lagrange optimization method uses (A1) and (A2) to construct the Lagrangian expression

$$L = V + \rho^2\lambda_2(X_1 - q_1 - X_2) + \rho\lambda_1(X_0 - q_0 - X_1) \qquad \text{(A3)}$$

where the constraint in implicit form is multiplied by a Lagrange multiplier for each period.[18] The Lagrange multiplier has been expressed as a present value. For example, since the stock in period 2 is constrained by values of q_1 and X_1, the Lagrange multiplier for X_2 is discounted to period 0 by multiplying it by ρ^2 (and similarly for stock X_1). Notice that X_0 is fixed and X_2 is fixed (at zero) in (A3). Maximizing V subject to the constraint is equivalent to maximizing L without constraint. The necessary conditions for maximizing L are obtained by setting the partial derivatives of L with respect to the stock and flow variables (X, q) as well as the Lagrange multipliers equal to zero:

$$\partial L/\partial q_0 = \partial V/\partial q_0 - \rho\lambda_1 = [\pi_0(q_0) - C] - \rho\lambda_1 = 0 \qquad (A4)$$

$$\partial L/\partial q_1 = \partial V/\partial q_1 - \rho^2\lambda_2 = \rho[\pi_1(q_1) - C] - \rho^2\lambda_2 = 0 \qquad (A5)$$

$$\partial L/\partial X_1 = \rho^2\lambda_2 - \rho\lambda_1 = 0 \qquad (A6)$$

$$\partial L/\partial(\rho^2\lambda_2) = X_1 - q_1 - X_2 = 0 \qquad (A7)$$

$$\partial L/\partial(\rho\lambda_1) = X_0 - q_0 - X_1 = 0 \qquad (A8)$$

Substituting (A6) into (A4) and (A5) produces the standard Hotelling rule:

$$\pi_0 - C = \rho(\pi_1 - C) \qquad (A9)$$

Notice that the net price in period 1 ($p_1 = \pi_1 - C$) is defined as $\rho\lambda_2$ which incorporates the one-period lagged effect of decisions in period 1 on the next period's stock. A similar interpretation applies to $p_0 = \pi_0 - C$.

Since equations (A4) through (A8) are only necessary conditions for the problem in (A1) and (A2), it must also be ascertained that second-order conditions for a maximum of L are strictly satisfied. The second-order conditions will be strictly satisfied provided the objective function V is strictly quasi-concave and the feasible set defined by the constraints is convex. In the present case V is strictly quasi-concave provided that $d^2B(q)/dq^2 < 0$, i.e. the demand functions are downward-sloping. In all subsequent problems we will assume that these second-order conditions are met.[19]

The foregoing Lagrange optimization method can be generalized quite easily to problems involving many periods. We can also include stocks of resources as well as flows in the benefit and cost functions as well as more complex types of resource stock behaviour over time. Consider the following problem:

Maximize $\qquad V = \sum_0^\infty \rho^t[B(q_t,X_t) - C(X_t) \cdot q_t] \qquad (A10)$

Subject to $\qquad X_{t+1} - X_t = f(X_t) - q_t \qquad (A11)$

Society wants to maximize the present value of net benefits over an infinite time horizon, subject to stock-flow constraints. Here, the benefit and cost functions include not only the flows of resource output (q_t), they also allow for *stock effects* operating on benefits and costs through the amount of the resource stock in existence at each point in time (X_t). In the modified Hotelling model, for example, suppose the total *economic* stock of the resource is X_0. This economic stock consists of all units of the resource for which unit extraction cost C is less than or equal to the "choke price" (π_{max}). If cumulative production up to time t is denoted by x_t, then the remaining stock is $X_t = X_0 - x_t$. If we assume that $dC(X_t)/dX_t = C_x < 0$, then we are assuming that unit cost rises with cumulative production as we move to higher and higher cost ores. Including the stock X_t in the benefit function could make sense in pollution models (discussed in chapter 3) where stocks of pollutants affect the flow of environmental benefits received by society.

Equation (A11) also generalizes the constraint to allow for the possibility that the stock grows or declines over time. With a renewable resource like fish, for example, the stock grows as a result of net reproduction and the growth of existing fish (chapter 7). In some cases, stocks of pollutants will decline over time due to the regenerative capacity of the environment (chapter 3). In these cases, the change in the stock $(X_{t+1} - X_t)$ is the net result of its natural growth or decline $[f(X_t)]$ and any current decisions to add to or subtract from the stock (q_t).

Just as in the two-period Hotelling model, equations (A10) and (A11) can be used to form the Lagrangian expression:

$$L = V + \sum_0^\infty \{\rho^{t+1}\lambda_{t+1}[X_t + f(X_t) - q_t - X_{t+1}]\} \qquad \text{(A12)}$$

Equation (A12) is analogous to (A3). Maximizing (A12) with respect to q_t and X_t,

$$\partial L/\partial q_t = \partial V/\partial q_t - \rho^{t+1}\lambda_{t+1} = \rho^t[\pi(q_t, Xt) - C(Xt)]$$
$$- \rho^{t+1}\lambda_{t+1} = 0 \quad \text{(A13)}$$

$$\partial L/\partial X_t = \partial V/\partial X_t + \rho^{t+1}\lambda_{t+1} \cdot (1 + f_x) - \rho^t\lambda_t = 0 \qquad \text{(A14)}$$

where f_x is the derivative of f re X_t. Equations (A13) and (A14) are analogous to equations (A5) and (A6). Notice that the final term in (A14) emerges from (A12) by recognizing that X_t appears in *two* of the constraints just as X_1 did in the two-period problem. Noting that $\partial V/\partial X_t = \rho^t(B_x - C_x \cdot q_t)$ where B_x and C_x are the partial derivatives of B and C with respect to X_t, (A13) and (A14) can be simplified to

$$p_t = \pi_t - C = \rho\lambda_{t+1} \qquad \text{(A15)}$$

$$\rho\lambda_{t+1} - \lambda_t + (B_x - C_x \cdot q_t) + \rho\lambda_{t+1}f_x = 0 \qquad \text{(A16)}$$

where, as usual, p_t denotes the net price.

Equation (A15) simply sets output in period t so that the marginal value of using an extra unit of the stock to produce current output $(\pi_t - C)$ equals the sacrifice in the value of next period's stock. Equation (A16) states that units should be added to the stock until all the present-valued marginal benefits of doing so equal zero. Adding a unit will improve present-valued benefits if: (1) the present value of the unit as part of next period's stock $(\rho\lambda_{t+1})$ exceeds its current value (λ_t) which is true if the capital appreciation on an additional unit of stock exceeds its holding cost; (2) the unit provides positive marginal benefits over the period in the form of improved willingness-to-pay by consumers (B_x) or unit cost reductions (C_x) on all units extracted in the current period (q_t); (3) the unit grows so that extra units of stock (f_x) are available in the next period. These extra units have a present value of $\rho \lambda_{t+1}$.

Equations (A15) and (A16) are discrete time conditions for dynamic optimization. If we want to express them in continuous time notation, this can be done by shrinking the time interval Δt and allowing the stock adjustment to take place continuously. Define r as an instantaneous rate of discount so that $\rho = 1/(1 + r\Delta t)$. Stock changes take place immediately so that benefit flows from stock changes must be multiplied by Δt to capture their full effect over the time interval Δt. With these requirements in mind, equation (A16) becomes

$$\lambda_{t+\Delta t}/(1 + r\Delta t) - \lambda_t + (B_x - C_x \cdot q_t)\Delta t + \lambda_{t+\Delta t}f_x\Delta t/(1 + r\Delta t) = 0$$

or, multiplying by $(1 + r\Delta t)/\Delta t$,

$$(\lambda_{t+\Delta t} - \lambda_t)/\Delta t - r\lambda_t + (B_x - C_x \cdot q_t)(1 + r\Delta t) + \lambda_{t+\Delta t}f_x = 0 \quad \text{(A17)}$$

As Δt is allowed to approach zero, $(1 + r\Delta t)$ approaches one and $\lambda_{t+\Delta t}$ approaches λ_t. This also implies that $p_t = \rho\lambda_{t+\Delta t} = \lambda_{t+\Delta t}/(1 + r\Delta t)$ approaches λ_t. Equation (A17) becomes

$$dp/dt - rp + (B_x - C_x q) + pf_x = 0$$

or

$$rp = dp/dt + (B_x - C_x q) + pf_x \quad \text{(A18)}$$

Equation (A18) states that the marginal holding cost of holding an extra unit of resources (rp) must equal the marginal benefits from holding the extra unit in terms of appreciation of its net price (dp/dt) plus any current increase in net benefits $(B_x - C_x q)$ caused by holding the extra unit of stock plus any growth in the extra unit of the stock, valued at the net price (pf_x).

The continous time problem is, in fact,

$$\textit{Maximize} \quad V = \int_{0}^{\infty} e^{-rt} \{B[X(t),q(t)] - C[X(t)] \cdot q(t)\}\, dt \quad \text{(A19)}$$

$$\textit{Subject to} \quad dX/dt = f[X(t)] - q(t) \quad \text{(A20)}$$

where the summation operator "Σ" in the discrete time version is replaced by the continuous summation (integration) operator "$\int$". The continuous time discounting factor ρ^t is e^{-rt}. Instead of using the Lagrangian approach, the necessary conditions for the continuous time problem can be obtained by setting up the *Hamiltonian function* defined by

$$H = \{B[X(t), q(t)] - C[X(t)] \cdot q(t)\}e^{-rt} + \mu(t)\{f[X(t)] - q(t)\} \quad (A21)$$

where $\mu(t)$ is the present value of the Lagrange multiplier, i.e., $\mu(t) = \lambda(t)e^{-rt}$. The necessary conditions for the maximization problem can be written as

$$\partial H/\partial q = 0; \quad d\mu/dt = -\partial H/\partial X; \quad dX/dt = \partial H/\partial \mu \quad (A22)$$

The first condition, known as the *maximum principle* in control theory simply maximizes the Hamiltonian with respect to the *control variable* (q) and is already familiar from the discrete version discussed above. The maximum principle has $\partial H/\partial q = (\pi - C)e^{-rt} - \lambda e^{-rt} = 0$ implying that λ is simply the current net price $p = \pi - C$. The second condition, known as the *costate* or *adjoint equation*, is also familiar from what has already been done. Since $\mu(t) = \lambda(t)e^{-rt}$, $d\mu/dt = d\lambda/dt \cdot e^{-rt} - r\lambda e^{-rt}$. The costate equation is, therefore,

$$d\mu/dt = d\lambda/dt \cdot e^{-rt} - r\lambda e^{-rt} = -\partial H/\partial X = (-B_x + C_x q - \lambda f_x)e^{-rt} \quad (A23)$$

Simplifying (A23) and substituting the net price p for λ reproduces equation (A18). Finally, the condition that $dX/dt = \partial H/\partial \mu$ in (A22) simply reproduces the constraint (A20). Thus the three necessary conditions on the Hamiltonian in (A22) are exactly equivalent to the necessary conditions derived earlier using the Lagrange technique.

As discussed in the main body of the chapter, the conditions in (A22) must be met subject to certain end-point requirements referred to as *transversality conditions* in control theory. In nonrenewable resource problems, the initial condition identifies the stock of the resource in existence at the beginning of the utilization horizon (X_0). At the end of the extraction sequence, at, say, T, the rate of extraction must be zero ($q_T = 0$) and the value of any remaining units of the resource must be non-positive, i.e. $\lambda(T)X(T) \leq 0$. Valuable units of the resource stock should not be left over when extraction comes to an end. In the simple Hotelling model, the terminal condition is satisfied by the complete exhaustion condition $X(T) = 0$. In the modified Hotelling model with extraction cost increasing as the stock is used up, any remaining units of the stock at T are uneconomic to extract such that $\lambda(T) = 0$.

Our nonrenewable resource problems are simplified cases of the general problem set out in discrete form in (A10) and (A11) and in continuous form in (A19) and (A20). Since nonrenewable resources do not grow or decline, $f(X) = 0$ and therefore $f_x = 0$. Since we are not assigning any benefits to the existing stock of nonrenewables, X does not enter the benefit function B. This means that $B_x = 0$. With these simplifications, the asset equilibrium condition in (A18) becomes

$$rp = dp/dt - C_x q \quad (A24)$$

which is equation (9) in the main body of the chapter. When the remaining stock has no effect on extraction cost so that $C_x = 0$, then equation (A24) simplifies further to the basic Hotelling rule in equation (4).

A Dynamic Programming Example

The usual solution method for dynamic optimization problems is by *backward recursion*. The procedure is to identify the terminal end-point condition and use the necessary conditions for the optimization problem to iterate the values of the state and control variables backwards until the initial conditions for the problem are met. We can use the simple Hotelling model as an illustration. The net price is $p = \pi(q) - C$ so that $dp/dt = (d\pi/dq)dq/dt = \pi_q dq/dt$ since unit extraction cost (C) is a constant. The adjoint equation is $rp = r[\pi(q) - C] = dp/dt$. By substitution, $r[\pi(q) - C] = \pi_q dq/dt$. Thus, the dynamics of the control and state variables for the simple Hotelling problem are

$$dq/dt = r[\pi(q) - C]/\pi_q \qquad (A25)$$

$$dX/dt = -q \qquad (A26)$$

Writing the dynamic equations in discrete time notation,

$$q_t - q_{t-1} = r[\pi(q_{t-1}) - C]/\pi_q \qquad (A27)$$

$$X_t - X_{t-1} = -q_{t-1} \qquad (A28)$$

Following the example in the chapter, assume that the available stock is $X_0 = 324$, the product demand function is $\pi = 110 - q$, $C = 10$, and the discount rate is $r = .10$. From the demand function, $\pi_q = -1$. The terminal requirement for period T is $X_T = 0$ and $q_T = 0$. Setting $q_T = 0$ allows us to solve for q_{T-1} from (A27). The value of q_{T-1} together with $X_T = 0$ gives X_{T-1} from (A28). Returning to (A27), we can now solve for q_{T-2} and then use (A28) again to solve for X_{T-2}. Working backwards in this way reproduces the results in Table 2.2. The backward recursion ends at $T - 9$ when $X_{T-9} = 324$.

Valuing Society's Resource Endowments

What does the preceding optimization analysis say about the value of the resource stock to society? Figure 2A.2 illustrates a single period in the sequence of resource extraction decisions represented by the optimal model. Since we are assuming (for simplicity) that unit extraction cost is dependent only on cumulative production but not on the current extraction rate, marginal cost is horizontal at level C in Figure 2A.2. Since the net price $(\pi - C)$ is positive, the presence of the resource allows society to earn

FIGURE 2A.2

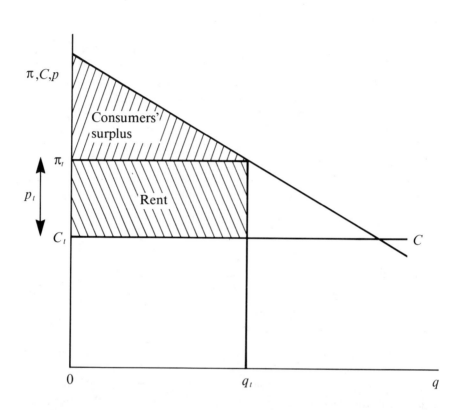

resource rent equal to the net price multiplied by the current extraction rate
(q). In addition, society gains the consumers' surplus equal to the triangu-
lar area shown. The gain to society over the extraction horizon is each
period's resource rent plus consumers' surplus summed and discounted
over the life of the resource. This gain is measured by the value of the
objective function V in equation (A10) or (A19).

The gain can be compared with the gains identified by Boadway and
Treddenick (1977) and by Chambers and Gordon (1966) as discussed in
the previous chapter. The consumers' surplus area is present because
changes in the extraction rate lead to changes in product prices. If product
prices are fixed—say by world markets—product price is independent of
the rate of extraction. The demand curve for the resource product is
perfectly elastic at the world price. In this case, changes in the rate of
domestic extraction produce a zero terms-of-trade effect and all gains are
measured by the present value of resource rents (Chambers and Gordon).

Note that the factor-proportions effect is also absent in Figure 2A.2 as a consequence of the assumption that marginal extraction cost (C) is fixed with respect to the current extraction rate.

▌NOTES

1. See S. Devarajan and A. Fisher, "Hotelling's 'Economics of Exhaustible Resources': Fifty Years Later," *Journal of Economic Literature* 19 (1981): 65–73.
2. See, for example, D. Levhari and N. Liviatan, "Notes on Hotelling's 'Economics of Exhaustible Resources'," *Canadian Journal of Economics* 10 (1977): 177–92; M.E. Slade, "Trends in Natural Resource Commodity Prices: An Analysis of the Time Domain," *Journal of Environmental Economics and Management* 9 (1982): 122–37. A vigorous attack on the exhaustion assumption appears in J. Simon, *The Ultimate Resource* (Princeton: Princeton University Press, 1981), Chaps. 1–3.
3. Unit cost is average and marginal extraction cost: individual mines are assumed to be identical and in long-run equilibrium. Also the number of units of the resources required per unit of final product is taken as fixed in this chapter. Variability of the resource input per unit of product output is discussed in chapter 4.
4. The discounting term in equation (1) has been written to facilitate a shift to continuous compounding later in this section. Over the interval Δt, continuous compounding raises the value of \$1 to $\$1 \cdot e^{r\Delta t}$. The term $e^{r\Delta t}$ is closely approximated by $1 + r\Delta t$ for "small" values of $r\Delta t$ using the McLaurin expansion $e^{r\Delta t} = 1 + r\Delta t + (r\Delta t)^2/2! + (r\Delta t)^3/3! \ldots$.
5. The original application of the concept of user cost to natural resource problems is A.D. Scott, "Notes on User Cost," *Economic Journal* 63 (1953): 368–84.
6. Since exploration and development spending precede actual mining costs, these "up-front" expenditures must be carried forward (compounded) at the ruling rate of interest (r) and added to mining costs to arrive at overall extraction cost (C).
7. R. Solow, "The Economics of Resources or the Resources of Economics," *American Economic Review* 64 (1974): 1–14.
8. S. Marglin, "The Social Rate of Discount and the Optimal Rate of Investment," *Quarterly Journal of Economics* 77 (1963): 95–111; A.K. Sen, "Isolation, Assurance, and the Social Rate of Discount," *Quarterly Journal of Economics* 81 (1967): 112–24.
9. The return $(-C_x q)/p$ is sometimes called the own rate of return. If the net price is constant, the own rate of return equals r in the modified Hotelling model. See R. Dorfman, P. Samuelson, and R. Solow, *Linear Programming and Economic Analysis* (New York: McGraw-Hill, 1958), pp. 309–25.
10. Both approaches were introduced into the resources literature simultaneously. Gordon introduced the continuous depletion approach characterized by equation (9); see R.L. Gordon, "A Reinterpretation of the Pure Theory of Exhaustion," *Journal of Political Economy* 75 (1967): 274–186. Herfindahl

brought in the discontinuous model illustrated in Figures 2.4 and 2.5; see O. Herfindahl, "Depletion and Economic Theory," in M. Gaffney, ed., *Extractive Resources and Taxation* (Madison: University of Wisconsin Press, 1967).

11. B. Mackenzie, "Looking for the Improbable Needle in a Haystack: The Economics of Base Metal Exploration in Canada," *CIM Bulletin* 74 (1981): 116.

12. P. Davidson, "Natural Resources," in A. Eichner, ed., *A Guide to Post Keynesian Economics* (White Plains, New York: Sharpe, 1978), pp. 155–56.

13. J. Zwartendyk, "Mineral Exploration in Canada: The Needs and the Prospects," *Foreign Investment Review* (Spring 1978): 17.

14. O. Herfindahl, *Copper Costs and Prices* 1870–1957 (Baltimore: Johns Hopkins, 1959), p. 232.

15. R. Anderson, "Resource Conservation and Pricing," *Resources Policy* 3 (1977): 78–86.

16. Constant elasticity of demand means that the demand curve is asymtotic to the vertical price axis. No matter how large price (π) becomes, quantity demanded remains positive. In this case resource exhaustion is also asymtotic: the total amount of the stock used approaches the fixed available stock as a limit.

17. M. Gaffney, ed., *Extractive Resources and Taxation* (Madison: University of Wisconsin Press, 1967), p. 112.

18. The Lagrange method is developed in A.C. Chiang, *Fundamental Methods of Mathematical Economics* (New York: McGraw-Hill, 1984), Chap. 12. See also, for example, J. Conrad and C. Clark, *Natural Resources Economics: Notes and Problems* (New York: Cambridge University Press, 1987), Chap. 1; M.J. Fryer and J.V. Greenman, *Optimisation Theory: Applications in OR and Economics* (London: Edward Arnold, 1987), Chap. 2.

19. On second-order conditions, see, for example, Chiang, *Fundamental Methods*, Chap. 2. A useful introduction to the convexity-concavity requirements is in H. Gravelle and R. Rees, *Microeconomics* (London: Longman, 1981), Chap. 2.

■ FURTHER READING

As the appendix implies, the development of optimal models of nonrenewable resource use over the past twenty years has relied heavily on mathematical techniques, specifically on the optimal control approach. The following articles and books (approximately in ascending order of difficulty) offer explanations of these techniques:

Conrad, J.M., and C.W. Clark. *Natural Resource Economics: Notes and Problems*. New York: Cambridge University Press, 1987, Chaps. 1 and 3.

Dixit, A.K. *Optimization in Economic Theory*. New York: Oxford University Press, 1976, Chap. 9.

Dorfman, R. "An Economic Interpretation of Optimal Control Theory." *American Economic Review* 59 (December 1969) (note errata in the subsequent issue).

Fryer, M., and J. Greenman. *Optimisation Theory: Applications in OR and Economics*. London: Edward Arnold, 1987, Chaps. 6–7.

The Hotelling model is discussed in

Devarajan, S., and A.C. Fisher. "Hotelling's 'Economics of Exhaustible Resources': Fifty Years Later." *Journal of Economic Literature* 19, (March, 1981).

Solow, R.M. "The Economics of Resources or the Resources of Economics." *American Economic Review* 64 (May 1974).

Connections between the optimal extraction model and the value of resource endowments in an economy open to trade (with comparisons to the Boadway-Treddenick and Chambers-Gordon models) can be found in

Anderson, F.J. "Valuing a Depletable Resource in an Open Economy." *Canadian Journal of Economics* 19 (November, 1986).

The crucial role of expectations and the effectiveness of markets in allocating natural resource stocks over time are discussed in

Graham-Tomasi, T., C.F. Runge, and W.F. Hyde. "Foresight and Expectations in Models of Natural Resources Markets." *Land Economics* 62 (August, 1986).

CHAPTER THREE

ENVIRONMENTAL

IMPACTS OF

ECONOMIC ACTIVITY

▌ INTRODUCTION

Extraction of resource stocks from the natural environment is only one side of a materials balance relationship. On the opposite side of the relationship is the return of used products or unwanted by-products to the environment as part of the process of production and consumption. The present chapter looks at the economic issues associated with this return flow. When the return of materials to the environment lowers human welfare it is characterized as pollution. Pollution takes two forms: *flow* pollution and *stock* pollution. In the pure flow case, emissions lower welfare without causing adverse effects on the receiving medium: cessation of the flow immediately eliminates all adverse welfare effects. In the case of pure stock pollution, damage is caused entirely by the degradation of the medium into which emissions are discharged. Halting the flow of pollution in this case does not immediately reverse welfare losses since some lapse of time is required to renew the quality of the medium.

The first section of the present chapter looks at the economics of pure flow pollution. The flow model involves balancing the marginal benefits of pollution, measured in terms of the value of final products that additional pollution makes possible, against the marginal damages produced by pollution. Optimal control of pollution flows also requires marginal abatement costs to be set equal to marginal damage. In the second and third sections, public policy approaches to correct for damages in the flow model are examined. Regulation and taxation policy models are set out and compared. The regulatory approach sets permissible levels of emissions or effluent discharges with penalties for non-compliance used to enforce the regulated rates selected. The taxation approach penalizes polluters for each unit of discharge. Profit-maximizing polluters respond to pollution taxes by reducing the flow of pollution to the optimal level. In many cases, the locations of polluters relative to those affected by pollution is an important aspect of the policy problem.

Following the policy sections, the pure flow perspective is extended to allow for stock effects in the form of accumulation of pollutants and environmental irreversibilities. The Hotelling and modified Hotelling models of the previous chapter provide a useful background for considering the accumulation effects of pollution flows. Irreversibility occurs when current environmental decisions have an element of finality to them: even if future circumstances dictate greater attention to the environment, it may be too costly to undo the legacy of the present. Current policy decisions should recognize the presence of such irreversibilities.

Finally, the present chapter offers a brief overview of major environmental issues of the 1990s and Canada's approach to environmental policy, together with a discussion of some wider issues in the conflict between the operation of private markets and the environment. The expansion of industrial activity since the industrial revolution, and particularly since the turn of the century, has begun to generate long-term changes in the quality of the earth's environment. Many modern industrial processes produce emissions of hazardous new chemicals. These changes exemplify stock pollution: the discharge of gases, solid pollutants, and chemicals threaten to overwhelm the regenerative capacity of the earth's environment. Increased control over pollution will be needed to prevent further changes and to reverse changes that have already taken place. In common with other countries, the adequacy of Canada's environmental policy framework needs to be examined carefully.

∎ A PURE FLOW POLLUTION MODEL

The Basic Model

There are three distinguishing characteristics of pure flow models of pollution. First, an economic activity is being carried on that generates one or more by-products that are detrimental to human welfare. Second, the detrimental by-product is not included in the voluntary exchange process characteristic of markets. Third, the detrimental output is not of a character or level of severity to accumulate in the environment. Excessive noise levels can serve as a good example of pure flow pollution. It is certainly a by-product of other activities. Provided noise pollution does not reach levels high enough to produce psychological or auditory damage it is only an annoyance to those exposed to it. Cessation immediately transforms the auditory environment to its previous state. Noise abatement is seldom, if ever, the object of market exchange: those affected by noise rarely offer to pay the emitters to abate noise and emitters are not required to pay those affected to voluntarily tolerate uncomfortable noise levels.

From the economic point of view, the notion that noise is excessive turns critically on the lack of voluntary exchange. As described in chapter 1, an important property of a competitive market system is its ability to satisfy a number of efficiency conditions. The marginal cost pricing $(P = MC)$ efficiency condition will be satisfied by firms provided they produce output up to the point at which the value of the last unit, measured by the price paid by each consumer, equals the extra cost to each firm of producing the last unit.

Consider how this $P = MC$ condition might apply to the production of, say, widgets. Benefits from widget production are measured by the function $B = B(Q)$, where Q is the level of widget output. Since widgets are a marketable output, a good approximation to B can be obtained by consumers' expenditures on widgets plus consumers' surplus (CS) from widget consumption. The benefit level B is therefore measured by the shaded area under the widget demand curve DD in Figure 3.1. The cost to firms of producing widgets is $C = C(Q)$. The net benefit from widget production is therefore given by

$$W = B(Q) - C(Q) \qquad (1)$$

Maximizing net benefit from widget production requires that widgets be produced until the marginal benefit (MB) from an extra unit of widgets equals the marginal cost (MC) of widget production. The marginal benefit from widget production is $dB/dQ = B'(Q) = P$ where P is the price that consumers are willing to pay for an extra unit. The marginal cost of widgets is $dC/dQ = C'(Q) = MC$. Figure 3.1 illustrates the $P = MC$ condition with the shaded area equal to the difference between total benefit (B) and total

FIGURE 3.1

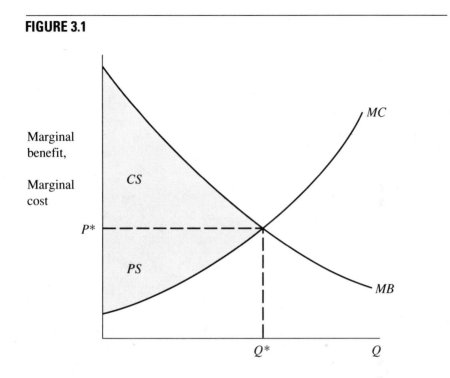

cost (C) at the optimum level of widget production Q^*. The price corresponding to Q^* is P^*. The portion of the shaded area below the demand curve and above P^* is consumers' surplus (CS) at Q^*. The portion of the shaded area below P^* and above the marginal cost curve is defined as producers' surplus (PS) equal to $P^*Q^* - C(Q^*)$. Competitive firms maximizing profits from widget production reach a market-clearing equilibrium that automatically maximizes net benefits (W) at P^*, Q^* since the MC curve in Figure 3.1 is the competitive industry supply curve for widgets.

Problems arise with this efficiency argument if widget production is accompanied by, say, noise emissions. Assume that noise emissions damage welfare by an amount that varies positively with the emission level. The loss of welfare caused by noise levels can be illustrated by the damage function $D = D(E)$ in Figure 3.2 where E measures the noise level in decibels and D is the amount of money that those affected by the noise level E would be willing to pay to eliminate E. Suppose, further, that noise is related in a simple way to the output of widgets such that $E = Q$ where Q is widget output. This simple relationship states that a zero level of output for widgets produces zero noise emission and that emissions rise linearly

FIGURE 3.2

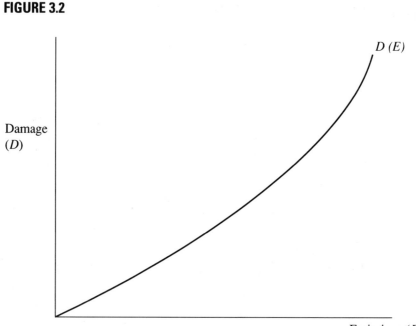

with widget output. Units for widget output have been chosen so that one extra unit of widget output leads to one extra unit of emissions.

The *social* net benefit function for widget production must now include the damage flowing from emissions and not just the net benefits from the widgets. The new social net benefit function, which replaces equation (1), is

$$W^* = B(Q) - C(Q) - D(E) \tag{2}$$

To maximize W^*, marginal benefit from widget production $B'(Q) = P$ must be equated to *all* marginal costs of widget production. In this case, the marginal costs of widget production are the marginal production cost $C'(Q) = MC$ *plus* the marginal damage cost from emissions. The latter is measured by $dD(E)/dQ = D'(E) \cdot dE/dQ$. The term $D'(E)$ is the marginal damage caused by an extra unit of emissions and dE/dQ is the additional emissions caused by an additional unit of widget output. We shall refer to the marginal damage cost $dD(E)/dQ$ as MC'. Since we are assuming that $E = Q$, $dE/dQ = 1$. Thus, maximization of social benefit requires

$$P = C'(Q) + D'(E) \cdot dE/dQ = MC + MC' \tag{3}$$

Figure 3.3 illustrates social net benefit maximization. As in Figure 3.1,

FIGURE 3.3

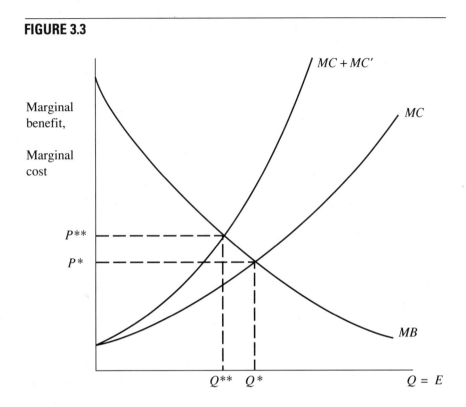

the marginal benefit is shown by the downward-sloping demand curve for widgets labelled MB. Marginal production cost for widgets is again shown as MC. The marginal *social* cost of widget production is shown by the $MC + MC'$ curve and includes both marginal production and marginal emission damage costs. The optimal social level of widget production is at Q^{**} where equation (3) is satisfied. Figure 3.3 also shows the production level Q^* where emission costs are ignored. Since emission damage raises the marginal cost of widget production, $Q^* > Q^{**}$ and $P^* < P^{**}$. Inclusion of emission damages in the optimization model reduces optimal widget output and raises the price of widgets to include marginal emission damage cost (MC') as well as marginal production cost (MC).

Pollution as an Externality

There are strong reasons to assume that competitive profit-maximizing widget producers will *not* take emission costs into account in their decisions and will produce at P^*, Q^* instead of at the social optimum point P^{**}, Q^{**}. The reason lies in the nature of the emission damages. Goods or services exchanged under market conditions are the property of the seller until transferred to the buyer for monetary consideration. The seller compares the monetary consideration (price) received against the marginal cost of producing the good and is willing to sell if $P \geqslant MC$. The buyer compares the marginal benefit (MB) to the price and is willing to purchase if $MB \geqslant P$. Gains from trade for both parties are exhausted when $MB = P = MC$.

Property rights must be well defined to ensure that the marginal cost pricing condition obtains. If the "buyer" can short-circuit the process by acquiring units of the good without compensating a "seller," then the "seller" has no incentive to produce the good. The market fails to operate and potential gains from trade are not realized. This type of situation can occur with *common property* goods or *open-access* goods. In the common property case, units of the good are owned jointly by a collective and no individual agent has been designated to exact compensation for units withdrawn from the common pool. In the open-access case, there are no property rights at all. In both cases, users are allowed to obtain units of the good without offering compensation. A pollution-free environment often falls into the common property or open-access category. Polluters are not required to pay compensation for environmental degradation since there are no effective private property rights to a pollution-free environment. Since no compensation is required, marginal damage costs are not taken into account by polluters. In the above example, polluters *internalize* only the marginal costs of producing widgets (MC) and leave the marginal damage cost (MC') as *external costs* to be borne by others. They choose to produce at P^*, Q^* rather than at the socially optimal level P^{**}, Q^{**}. The absence of property rights to a clean environment biases the economy toward excessive pollution. The situation is one of *market failure*.

The bias to excessive pollution could, hypothetically, be overcome if those damaged by pollution recognize that polluters can be bribed to reduce pollution flows and the appropriate size of such bribes can be ascertained and offered. What circumstances would be needed to achieve this result? First, those damaged must recognize the polluter's implied right to pollute and be willing to pay to reverse pollution flow levels. Second, the damage function $D(E)$ must be estimated. Third, those damaged must be willing to offer monetary consideration to polluters consistent with $D(E)$. With respect to the first condition, it is unlikely that those damaged will recognize that polluters have a right to degrade the environment. Instead of moving to a bribery solution, the affected parties may elect to wait for property rights to a clean environment to emerge from the political-legal system or may devote their actions to securing such a result. Second, the provision of a clean environment is a good that is not well suited to the market process even if the beneficiaries are willing to pay to secure it. Unlike widgets, for example, a clean environment is not a *private* good. An individual who purchases an additional unit of pollution abatement (a cleaner environment) purchases the unit on behalf of all those adversely affected by pollution. A cleaner environment is a *public* good: it is shared by a collectivity of individuals. The problems that this causes for market-based provision can be explored by looking more closely at the damage function in the widgets/emissions example.

Suppose there are n *identical* individuals affected by each unit of emissions. Each of the n individuals has his or her own damage function $D_i(E)$, $i = 1,2,\ldots, n$. Total damage is

$$D(E) = \sum_{i=1}^{n} D_i(E) = nD_i(E) \qquad (4)$$

Assuming, as before, that emissions are a linear function of widget output with $E = Q$, (4) can be written as

$$D(E) = \sum_{i=1}^{n} D_i(Q) = nD_i(Q) \qquad (5)$$

From equation (5), the overall marginal damage from emissions is $MC' = nD_i'(Q)$ where D_i' is the marginal damage to each of the n individuals affected. By definition, $D_i' = dD_i/dQ$. Rearranging equation (3), social efficiency requires that at the optimum level of output marginal damage equals marginal benefit from pollution, i.e.,

$$MC' = nD_i'(Q) = P - MC \qquad (6)$$

where, as before, MC' is the marginal emission damage, P is the price of widgets, and MC is the marginal production cost of widgets. Suppose each of the n individuals adversely affected by emissions decides to offer a bribe to polluters to abate emissions. If we assume that a competitive market in abatement is present, each affected individual faces a marginal cost of abatement of $P - MC$ which is the marginal value of widgets foregone, net of marginal production cost. This is the (minimum) amount that the affected individual must pay to polluters to get pollution reduced by an extra unit. Figure 3.4 illustrates this marginal cost of abatement $P - MC$. The individual's marginal benefit from abatement is D_i', also illustrated in Figure 3.4. The individual's optimal strategy is to pay for abatement as long as her or his own marginal benefit D_i' exceeds the cost of additional abatement $(P - MC)$. This produces an abatement level a^* at which $D_i' = P - MC$. Figure 3.4 also illustrates the optimal result a^{**} where the sum of marginal benefits to all the affected individuals (nD_i') is equated to the marginal cost of abatement $(P - MC)$ in accordance with equation (6).

Comparing these results reveals that the level of abatement resulting from individual actions (a^*) is less than the optimal level (a^{**}). This is so because the bribes offered by individuals are based on *individual* rather than *collective* benefits. Though a reduction in pollution benefits all those affected, individuals do not include the benefits experienced by others in

FIGURE 3.4

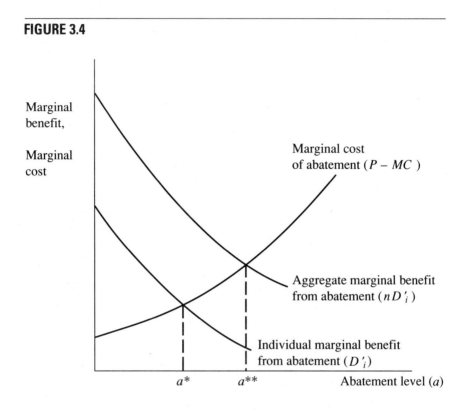

the abatement bribes they offer to polluters. This sharing of benefits defines *public* goods in contrast to private goods like widgets. Left to itself, a market approach to abatement virtually guarantees that insufficient abatement will emerge and pollution flows will be excessive when pollution affects a collection of individuals (i.e., $a^* < a^{**}$).

A second way of looking at the public good problem is to examine the difficulty of *sustaining* the optimal solution in equation (6) when individuals are free to decide on their own how much abatement expenditures to make. Suppose the optimal solution at a^{**} is somehow in effect in Figure 3.4. Since $D_i' < P - MC$ at a^{**}, the individual's marginal benefit from abatement is less than the marginal cost of abatement. It pays individuals to break away from the collectively optimal solution by purchasing a lower level of abatement than a^{**}. Since all individuals reason likewise, contributions decline and social welfare falls. The abatement level a^{**} depends on contributions from all the affected parties, yet each individual is motivated by self-interest to withdraw his or her own contribution. This is the *free-rider* problem inherent in sharing: individuals believe that they can benefit by leaving the commitment to provision of the shared good to others.

The likelihood that those affected by pollution will not enter into market-based abatement arrangements with polluters at all, combined with the failure of individuals to transmit true social preferences for a clean environment even if market-based transactions do occur (the free rider problem), implies that the optimal solution P^{**}, Q^{**} in Figure 3.3 (the optimal abatement level a^{**} in Figure 3.4) will not emerge in the absence of public policy. Instead, competitive widget producers ignore the social damages of emissions and produce at P^*, Q^*.

Adding Pollution Control Expenditures

Before examining the public policy instruments that are available to correct for the external pollution costs imposed on society by private decisions, it is worth extending the flow model to introduce expenditures explicitly designed to abate emissions. Such pollution control measures are an important component of a socially optimal approach to environmental management since pollution control can be used as a substitute for reduced output (lower production of widgets) to achieve the goal of a cleaner environment.

The introduction of abatement expenditures requires modification of the basic widgets/emissions model. The emission flow now depends not only on the flow of widget output but also on the amount of pollution control expenditures undertaken. Consider the simple model

$$E = Q - f(A) \qquad (7)$$

where, as before, E measures the emission flow and Q measures widget output. The new term A measures the size of pollution control expenditure. Provided $f(A)$ is increasing in A, equation (7) indicates that, for a given level of widget output, emissions decline as pollution control expenditure rises. It is assumed that $f(0) = 0$ such that emissions track output in the absence of abatement as in the previous model. Further assume that $E \geqslant 0$ which implies that f is defined over the interval $0 \leqslant f(A) \leqslant Q$. The new social welfare function is the sum of net benefits from widget production minus damages from emissions minus pollution control costs:

$$W^* = B(Q) - C(Q) - D(E) - A \qquad (8)$$

As in the previous model, if the level of pollution control is fixed, a one unit increase in widget output involves a one unit increase in emissions. The marginal net benefit of an extra unit of output is $(P - MC)$ and the marginal damage is $D'(E) \cdot dE/dQ = D'(E) = MC'$. Equating marginal net benefit and marginal damage, $P = MC + MC'$ (equation (3)). The present model also allows for W^* to be maximized with respect to pollution control spending. If the level of emissions is fixed, pollution control expenditure should be increased until the last dollar of expenditure produces an increase in the net value of widget output of one dollar. From equation (7), $Q = E + f(A)$. An increase in A (dA) with E fixed raises widget output by $f'(A)dA$. The value of the increased output is $(P - MC)f'(A)dA$. Equating the marginal cost (dA) to the marginal benefit $(P - MC)f'(A)dA$ implies

$$(P - MC)f'(A) = 1 \qquad (9)$$

as the condition for optimal pollution control. Notice that this condition can be combined with the condition $P - MC = MC' = D'(E)$ to produce the condition $D'(E)f'(A) = 1$. The latter states that pollution control spending should be carried out until the last dollar spent generates a one dollar reduction in damages from emissions.

When emissions are uncontrolled, there is no incentive for firms to introduce any form of pollution control. Widget output is carried on until $P = MC$. With $P - MC = 0$, equation (9) cannot be satisfied for any positive level of pollution control. When emissions are controlled such that $P = MC + MC'$, $(P - MC) > 0$ and it pays to control pollution in two ways: by reducing the output of widgets and by installing pollution control measures.

The next section examines the public policy approaches that can be used to nudge the pure flow pollution model from a private profit-maximizing equilibrium like P^*, Q^* in Figure 3.3, where emission damage costs are external to firms' calculations and pollution control is zero, to the socially optimal result (P^{**}, Q^{**}) in which the costs of emission damages and the costs and benefits of pollution control are accounted for explicitly.

■ PUBLIC POLICY FOR THE FLOW POLLUTION MODEL

Changes in levels of emissions flows can be brought about through several different kinds of public policy instruments. The effectiveness of these instruments can be judged by whether or not they lead producers to satisfy the socially optimal control conditions in equations (3) and (9). Equation (3) states that the policy package should lead to equality between the marginal benefit from additional emissions $(P - MC) \cdot dQ/dE$ and the marginal damage from emissions $D'(E)$. Equation (9) states that pollution control spending should be undertaken until the marginal cost of pollution control spending equals the marginal benefit from additional output made possible by pollution control such that $(P - MC)f'(A) = 1$. The policy instruments that we consider here are: a tax per unit of product output, subsidies on pollution control spending, a tax per unit of emissions, and regulation of emissions to a specified level.

Consider a *tax per unit of product output* first. Assume that widgets are produced under perfect competition so that widget suppliers accept the price of widgets (P) as fixed. Competitive producers will maximize the profit function

$$\pi = P \cdot Q - C(Q) - T \cdot Q - A \tag{10}$$

where P is the product price, Q is product output, T is the per unit tax on output, and A is the level of spending on pollution control. Ignoring pollution control spending for the moment, profit-maximizing firms produce until the product price net of the tax ($P - T$) equals marginal production cost $C'(Q) = MC$. In order to duplicate equation (3) the policymaker can set $T = MC'$ such that the profit-maximizing firms set $P - MC' = MC$. So far so good. But what about the level of pollution control? Profit is highest in (10) if $A = 0$. If $A = 0$, emissions (E) equal output (Q). But since there is no penalty on emissions under this policy, firms have no incentive to undertake pollution control measures. We can conclude that a simple tax on the product responsible for emissions will not be the right answer since it provides no incentives for firms to undertake potentially cost-effective expenditures (A) that reduce emissions relative to product output.

Turning to the case of a *tax per unit of emissions*, the profit function now becomes

$$\pi = P \cdot Q - C(Q) - T \cdot E - A \tag{11}$$

where $T \cdot E$ is the tax payment that firms must make on account of emissions. Again begin with the profit-maximizing choice of output and a fixed level of pollution control spending A. Since changes in emission flows equal changes in product output under the assumption of fixed A, the profit-maximizing choice of output requires $P - C'(Q) - T = 0$. With T set equal to MC', equation (3) results, as before. Now consider how the firms set A. For a fixed level of output Q, firms will want to choose a level of A that minimizes the term $T \cdot E + A$ in equation (11) in order to maximize π. The term $T \cdot E + A$ is the tax payment on account of emissions plus expenditures on pollution control. With output constant, an increase in A by the amount dA changes emissions by $-f'(A)dA$ leading to a change in tax payments of $-Tf'(A)dA$. Pollution control spending will be profitable to firms until the decline in tax payments from emission control equals the marginal cost of control (dA), i.e., until $Tf'(A)dA = dA$ or $Tf'(A) = 1$. Since $T = MC' = P - MC$, the optimum condition in equation (9) is met. The emission tax plan is successful in meeting both the required efficiency conditions. Comparing this result to the tax per unit of output policy reveals that it is best to correct for external costs by focusing the policy tool (taxation) on the activity (pollution) that is *directly* responsible for the problem. This conclusion is reinforced by examining the effect of *subsidies on pollution control costs*. Suppose that each dollar of pollution control

FIGURE 3.5

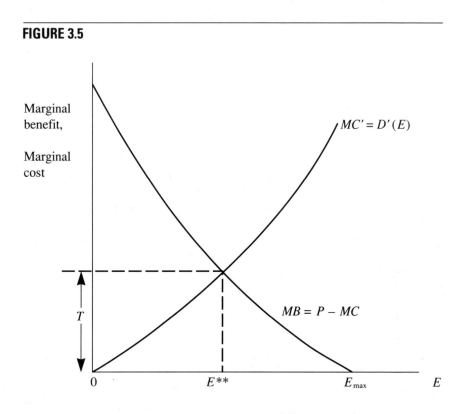

spending is subsidized at the rate s $(0 < s < 1)$. The firms' profit function is now

$$\pi = P \cdot Q - C(Q) - (1 - s)A \tag{12}$$

where $(1 - s)A$ is the unsubsidized portion of pollution control spending. At any level of output Q, firms will still maximize profits by setting $A = 0$ such that no pollution abatement takes place.

An efficient alternative to emissions taxes is direct *regulation* of the emission flow. Figure 3.5 illustrates the optimal level of emissions. As before, the marginal damage function is shown as MC' $(= D'(E))$. The marginal benefit from emissions is shown as MB where $MB = (P - MC) \cdot dQ/dE = (P - MC)$. In the absence of an emissions charge, firms maximize profits by ignoring pollution damages. They set $P - MC = 0$ and generate the emission level E_{max}. Installing the optimal pollution tax per unit of emissions $= T$ shifts the profit-maximizing equilibrium to E^{**} where $P - MC = MC'$. The emission level E^{**} can be achieved by regulating emissions to an amount less than or equal to E^{**}. Since firms observe marginal costs of emissions to be zero for $E < E^{**}$, they maximize profit by producing at E^{**}. Their pollution control decisions will also be optimal at the regulated level E^{**}. At E^{**}, an extra unit of output is worth $P - MC$ to the firms. Holding emissions constant at E^{**} implies $Q = E^{**} + f(A)$. Firms can increase output at the regulated level of emissions E^{**} by raising pollution control spending such that $dQ = f'(A)dA$. The marginal profit on the output from additional control expenditure dA is $(P - MC)f'(A)dA$. Since the marginal cost of control expenditure is dA, equating the marginal cost of control expenditure to the marginal profit on output generates the optimal pollution control condition in equation (9). Thus, regulation of emission flows can produce the same efficient result as taxation of emissions.

Up to this point it has been implicitly assumed that the damages generated by pollution depend only on the level of emissions that occur. The only ways to reduce damages are to cut back on emissions by reducing the product outputs of polluters or by undertaking pollution control expenditures. A third method is through the spatial separation of polluters and those affected. In this case, damage is reduced not because emissions are reduced but because damages from emissions are local and can be lowered by locating polluters at some distance from others.

Assume initially that polluting firms and those damaged by pollution are in close proximity and that the marginal benefits and marginal damages from emissions are as shown in Figure 3.5. If all parties remain in close proximity, the optimal level of pollution (achieved either through emissions taxes or regulation of emissions levels) is E^{**}. We can use the marginal benefit-cost curves in Figure 3.5 to measure the total benefits and costs implied by emissions at E^{**}. Figure 3.6 repeats Figure 3.5 and labels the total benefits and costs. The area *abcd* under the marginal benefits curve from $E = 0$ to $E = E^{**}$ measures total benefit. The area *acd* under the marginal damage curve from $E = 0$ to $E = E^{**}$ measures total emission damage. The difference between the two areas is the net benefit area *abc*.

What would happen if those affected by pollution were to be spatially separated from the polluters such that emissions do not produce *any* damage? With zero damage from emissions, firms can now produce at E_{max} in Figure 3.6 where $P = MC$. Everyone gains from such separation. Those previously affected by pollution no longer suffer the damage area *acd* and additional benefits of *dcf* are obtained from the expanded level of widget production. Should such a separation be made between the parties? This turns on a comparison between the gains from separation *acd* + *dcf* compared to the costs of separation. Assume that the extra minimum (annual) cost of separation is B. If $acd + dcf > B$, then it pays to replace the emission control at E^{**} with all parties in proximity by separation of the two parties with unrestricted emission at E_{max}. One could say that there are two *locally* optimal solutions to the emissions problem: one solution is proximity of the two parties with $E = E^{**}$ and the second is spatial separation of the two parties with $E = E_{max}$. Which of these two local

FIGURE 3.6

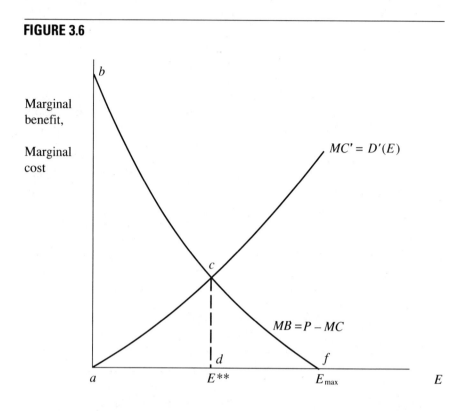

solutions is *globally* optimal depends on the comparison between $acd + dcf$ and B.[1]

The proximity/separation decision is also likely to exhibit market failure in the sense that private markets will be unable to make the right choice. To illustrate, suppose that it is least expensive to accomplish separation by moving firms. Suppose further that a single firm is involved and is regulated at E^{**}. If the firm moves it gains dcf and pays B. The firm will decide to stay put if $dcf < B$ yet it may be socially advantageous to move if, at the same time, $acd + dcf > B$. The private decision does not correspond to the socially optimal decision because the firm does not internalize the reduction in pollution damage costs to others when it calculates the gains from separation. In this situation, policymakers can intervene in the location decision to improve social welfare. An example is the location of pulpmills manufacturing kraft pulp relative to the communities from which their workers are drawn. The noxious odour of sulphur gases emanating from such mills would be costly to eliminate but dissipates over a fairly short distance (a few kilometres). Separation of community and mill makes sense in cases like this, particularly if the separation decision is undertaken at the time the mill is constructed and residential areas established.

Another case in which spatial characteristics can affect the outcome of pollution decisions occurs when polluters are located in one political jurisdiction and some of those harmed are located in another jurisdiction. Acid rain caused by fossil fuels consumed in thermal generating plants in the northeastern United States, for example, affects both Americans and Canadians. It is very difficult to reach efficient emission arrangements in this kind of cross-border problem. Balancing marginal damage costs to Americans with marginal benefits from cheaper power generation for Americans goes part way to the optimal solution but not all the way, since some of the acid-rain damage is external to the United States. From the Canadian viewpoint, very tight emission control seems optimal since Canadians tend not to internalize higher power costs to Americans in their calculations. Unequal division of emission costs and benefits across one or more jurisdictions adds considerably to the difficulty of formulating and carrying out efficient environmental policies.

■ STOCK-FLOW POLLUTION AND IRREVERSIBILITIES

A Stock-flow Model with Persistent Pollutants

The pure flow pollution model of the previous section is a reasonable framework when cessation of emissions immediately restores the environment to its previous state. An important class of environmental problems are not of this type at all, however. The opposite situation occurs with the disposal of non-biodegradable containers or emissions of heavy metals (such as lead or mercury) and persistent chemicals (such as PCBs and dioxin). The impact of the current flow is not as important as the inability of the receiving environment to absorb or neutralize these substances. A damaging stock build-up occurs as a result of the ongoing flow. A fraction of these stock pollutants may be taken up by organisms throughout the food chain, producing continuing damage up to the level of human health. It is therefore very important to modify the pure flow approach to take into account the accumulation of stocks of pollutants and the continuing damage that such stocks produce.

The nonrenewable resources models developed in chapter 2 turn out to be helpful in examining the welfare implications of stock pollutants. Consider the case in which the pollutant is persistent so that the stock of the pollutant in the environment (X) increases in each period by the amount of current pollution (E). The environment is nonrenewable and degradation is permanent. Analogously with the Hotelling model in chapter 2, the rate of change of the pollutant stock is

$$dX/dt = E \tag{13}$$

Assuming that one unit of output (say widgets) leads to one unit of pollution ($Q = E$), the marginal value of an extra unit of pollution is

$$p = P - MC - MC' \tag{14}$$

where P is the marginal value of widgets, MC is the marginal production cost of widgets, and MC' is the marginal damage cost of the *flow* of pollution emissions. As discussed in the previous section, if the only social damage from emissions is MC', it would be optimal to set $p = 0$. If, instead, we assume that emissions can also cause damage by increasing the stock X, then it may be advisable to further limit emissions below $E**$ in Figure 3.5 such that $p > 0$. The term p is analogous to the net price of nonrenewables as defined in chapter 2. It shows the increase in current net benefit from an extra unit of pollution.

To continue with the stock-flow model, assume that the damage each period caused by the pollutant stock depends on the size of the stock (X). Denoting this damage function by $D*$,

$$D* = D*(X) \tag{15}$$

We will assume that $D*(0) = 0$ and $D*'(X) > 0$: a zero stock of pollutants produces zero damage and an increase in the stock increases damage.

Equations (13), (14), and (15) can be used to derive an *asset equilibrium* condition describing optimal emissions behaviour. Just like the asset equilibrium analysis in chapter 2, the present one balances the marginal costs and benefits of stock changes. Consider two consecutive points in time, t and $t + \Delta t$. Since the marginal social value of emissions is measured by p, the decision to *add* a unit to the stock of pollution at time t leads to a return of $p(t)$. If, instead, the unit of pollution is added at time $t + \Delta t$, the discounted return is $p(t + \Delta t)/(1 + r\Delta t)$. If the unit is added at time t instead of at time $t + \Delta t$, social cost increases by $D*'(X)\Delta t$ during the time interval Δt since $D*'(X) = dD*/dX$ is the instantaneous increase in damage from an addition to the stock equal to dX and this increase persists over the interval Δt. The net benefit of adding dX to the stock at t rather than at $t + \Delta t$ is, therefore,

$$p(t) - D*'(X)\Delta t - p(t + \Delta t)/(1 + r\Delta t) \tag{16}$$

Equating the net benefit of the stock addition in (16) to zero and multiplying by $(1 + r\Delta t)$

$$p(t)(1 + r\Delta t) - D*'(X)\Delta t(1 + r\Delta t) - p(t + \Delta t) = 0 \tag{17}$$

Rearranging (17),

$$rp(t)\Delta t = p(t + \Delta t) - p(t) + D*'(X)\Delta t(1 + r\Delta t) \tag{18}$$

Dividing (18) through by Δt,

$$rp(t) = [p(t + \Delta t) - p(t)]/\Delta t + D^{*\prime}(X)(1 + r\Delta t) \qquad (19)$$

Shrinking the time interval by allowing Δt to approach zero, equation (19) becomes

$$rp = dp/dt + D^{*\prime}(X) \qquad (20)$$

This result is analogous to the modified Hotelling rule stated in equation (9) of chapter 2. In a real sense, pollution uses up "units" of the environment. Adding a "unit" to the environment by reducing pollution by one unit has a carrying cost of rp. The marginal benefits of doing so are captured by the increased benefit of polluting later (dp/dt) plus the stock damage that is avoided by deferring pollution ($D^{*\prime}$). The *terminal condition* in this problem obtains when the stock of the pollutant stabilizes. Since the environment is nonrenewable (pollutant stocks are persistent), this requires a zero emission flow. The zero flow condition defines the terminal net price $p_T = MB(0) - MC'(0)$ in Figure 3.5. With the emission flow at zero, $dp/dt = 0$ in equation (20) and the terminal requirement is $p_T = D^{*\prime}(X_T)/r$ where X_T is the terminal stock of the pollutant. This result is perfectly logical. When the pollutant stock stabilizes, the current marginal value of a slight rise in emissions above zero (p_T) must equal the present value of all the additional damage that would be caused if it were added to the (terminal) stock. Notice that along the optimal path to the terminal stock X_T, the flow of emissions is falling toward zero so p is increasing (i.e., $dp/dt > 0$). Equation (20) can be shown to be the result of a dynamic optimization problem for persistent pollutants with stock-flow damages. The optimization method is set out in the appendix to this chapter.

Adding stock damages to the flow pollution problem is an important modification since it offers a more realistic insight into the true level of difficulty involved in formulating optimal environmental policy. With stock pollutants present it is even less likely that private markets will be able to function efficiently than in the pure flow case. The discussion of the pure flow model in previous sections revealed that markets are unlikely to internalize flow pollution damage. The discussion of the nonrenewable resource problem in chapter 2 revealed that an absence of well-defined property rights and forward markets virtually precludes dynamic private market efficiency for nonrenewable resource stocks. In the present example, the environment is being treated as a nonrenewable resource. Like flow damage $D(E)$, environmental stock damage $D^{*}(X)$ will usually be shared by a collectivity of individuals, making it equally unlikely that the costs will be internalized by private decision makers.

Assuming that both $D(E)$ and $D^{*}(X)$ are external costs to firms, the optimal tax per unit of emissions in the stock-flow model must be designed to correct for *both* flow damages and stock damages. With profit-maximizing firms setting $P = MC$, the appropriate tax per unit of emissions to correct for the flow externality is $T = MC'$. To correct for *both* stock and flow externalities, the tax should be set so that $T = MC' + p = MC' + [dp/dt + D*'(X)]/r$.

In this simple model pollution control expenditures are absent and any positive level of widget production leads to positive emissions ($E = Q$). Thus the terminal result with zero emissions requires a zero output of widgets. This is not the case if optimal pollution control spending is added to the model. In this case, the terminal zero emission level ($E = 0$) is consistent with positive output of the product ($Q > 0$) because optimal pollution abatement is being undertaken.

The assumption that the environment is nonrenewable needs to be relaxed. In most cases, the environment actually has some absorptive or regenerative capacity so that zero growth of the pollutant stock in the steady-state terminal position is consistent with a positive emission flow equal to the environment's regenerative capacity. The basic principles of the model presented above are not changed by this realistic modification but the asset equilibrium condition (equation (20)) is affected. (See chapter 8.)

Irreversibility and Option Demand

The nonrenewable stock-flow model has a family resemblance to the problem of *irreversible* decisions. An example may help to explain the irreversibility problem. Consider an area of wilderness forest that is the result of hundreds of years of ecological succession. Suppose that the timber values from harvesting the forest now exceed the present value of wilderness benefits as currently calculated. If the forest *is* harvested now, any future reassessment of wilderness benefits will be pointless since the forest cannot be reproduced at any cost in the future. The decision to harvest today is an irreversible one: the future wilderness option is more or less permanently foreclosed. The issue is similar to the nonrenewable environment assumption: once a decision is made to transform the environment there is no going back.

Irreversibility does not occur with most types of goods and services. If society decides to sacrifice production of automobiles today in favour of housing, for example, this decision can be reversed tomorrow by using existing or new automobile plants to expand future automobile production at the expense of future housing. But the irreversibility problem inherent in certain environmental choices suggests that current decisions to expand production of goods and services at the expense of the environment should be taken with greater caution than current decisions about the automobiles/housing mix.

Consider a two-period approach to irreversibility. Society must choose a flow of environmental services in each of the two periods. Figure 3.7 shows the marginal benefits (MB) and marginal costs (MC) of alterna-

FIGURE 3.7

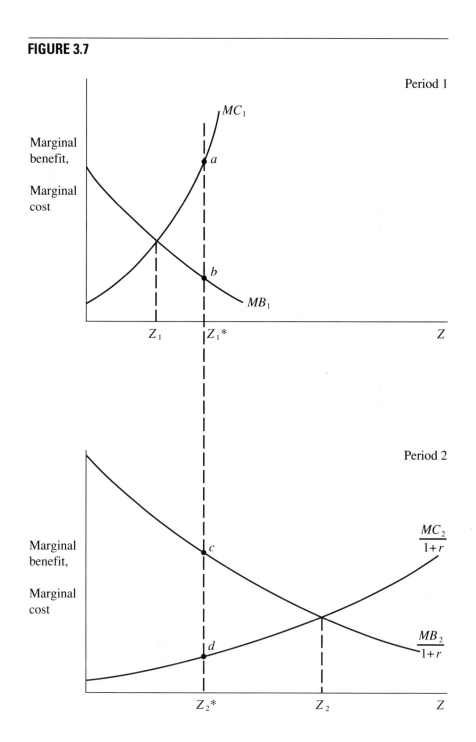

tive levels of environmental services (Z) in the two periods. Notice that the marginal benefits and costs in period 2 are discounted at the prevailing rate of interest (r). If *any* level of environmental services can be chosen in period 2, the appropriate strategy is to equate marginal benefit and marginal cost in each period, producing Z_1 in period 1 and Z_2 in period 2. Suppose that marginal benefit will be higher in period 2 than in period 1. This could be due to a taste change in favour of environmental amenities that raises the marginal benefit curve in period 2 compared to period 1, technical progress in goods production that lowers the marginal cost of producing environmental amenities in period 2, or a combination of these. In this case, optimum provision in each period implies $Z_2 > Z_1$ as shown. If irreversibility is present, however, then $Z_2 > Z_1$ is not feasible. The level of environmental amenities chosen in period 1 constrains the level in period 2 to $Z_2 \leqslant Z_1$. The optimal plan is to pick $Z_1^* = Z_2^*$ in Figure 3.7 such that the marginal loss from "overproducing" environmental amenities in period 1 (ab) equals the discounted marginal loss from "underproducing" environmental amenities in period 2 (cd). The irreversibility has introduced an element of conservation into current decisions: environmental amenities are produced currently that are worth less than the costs of their provision in order to preserve the underlying natural resource base so as to produce amenities with higher marginal benefits than marginal cost in the future.

To continue with the example, suppose that future benefits and costs are uncertain. To take the simplest case, imagine that the marginal benefit and marginal cost curves in period 2 will be the same as the marginal benefit and cost curves in period 1 with probability p ($0 \leqslant p \leqslant 1$). Alternatively, marginal benefits in period 2 will be higher than in period 1 (a taste change in favour of environmental amenities) and the marginal costs of providing them lower (technical progress in producing goods and services) as shown in Figure 3.7, with probability q ($0 \leqslant q \leqslant 1$). If these are the only possible outcomes, then $p + q = 1$. In this case, the optimal strategy is to equate the marginal loss (ab) from overproduction of amenities in period 1 to the (discounted) *expected* marginal gain $q \cdot cd$ on an extra unit of amenities in period 2. As illustrated in Figure 3.8, the optimal level of amenities production in period 1 is Z_1^{**} where $Z_1 \leqslant Z_1^{**} \leqslant Z_1^*$. In the special case in which $q = 1$, we have the model of the previous paragraph with $Z_1^{**} = Z_1^*$. In the special case of $q = 0$, marginal benefits and costs in period 2 are expected to be the same as in period 1 with certainty so that $Z_1^{**} = Z_1$. When $0 < q < 1$, the decision to hold extra units of the underlying natural resource equal to $Z_1^{**} - Z_1$ in period 1 can be described as an *option demand*. Extra units of the amenity flow are provided in the current period in order to permit society to exercise the option of producing additional units of the amenity flow in the future *if* it turns out to be advantageous to do so.

The option demand model reaches conclusions broadly similar to the nonrenewable stock-flow model. Irreversibility means that a more con-

FIGURE 3.8

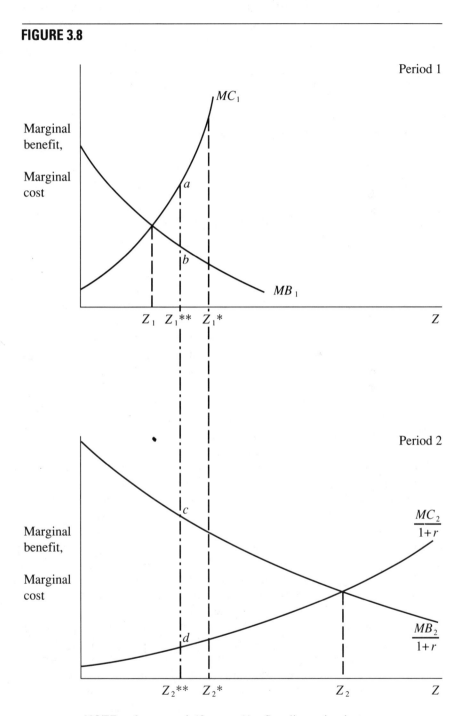

NOTE: $ab = q \cdot cd$ $(0 \le q \le 1)$.   See discussion in text.

servative approach to the use of the environment to produce current goods and services is optimal: we should keep our environmental options open. In the stock-flow model, an increase in the stock of pollutants caused by current flows means that future damages are an inevitable result of current pollution flows and current pollution flow levels should be reduced to take account of this. Like the Hotelling-style models of the previous chapter, restraining present levels of environmental depletion produces a positive net price for the resource. In the stock-flow model, the net price measures the user cost of pollution by the present value of damage caused by an increase in the pollutant stock. In the irreversibility model, the net price measures the expected loss of net benefits from restrictions on future amenity flows imposed by present decisions.

■ ENVIRONMENTAL ISSUES AND POLICIES: AN OVERVIEW

Global Issues

Canada is experiencing much the same set of environmental problems as other countries. Atmospheric and soil and water pollution have become areas of major worldwide concern in the 1980s. In both cases, flow by-products of manufacturing, resource extraction, and agricultural activities are altering the "stock" characteristics of the environment.

Fossil fuel combustion, particularly coal-burning, produces sulphur dioxide, nitrogen oxides, carbon dioxide, carbon particulates (soot), and methane. Smelting activities add further to sulphur dioxide emissions as well as chlorofluorocarbons (CFCs) and toxic metals. The burning of forests for agriculture or as a forest regeneration method releases carbon monoxide, nitrogen oxides, and methane. Animal husbandry adds to concentrations of methane. All of these gaseous emissions are implicated in atmospheric changes with local, regional, and global dimensions. The atmospheric conversion of nitrogen oxides and sulphur dioxide into nitric and sulphuric acids lies behind the acid rain problem associated with regional concentrations of fossil fuel-using industries. Acidification of lakes and soils is producing corrosion and destroying aquatic organisms and trees in the northeastern United States and central Canada. In this region, the acidity of precipitation has quadrupled during the present century (Graedel and Crutzen 1989). The interaction of solar radiation with nitrogen oxides and hydrocarbons is responsible for increased local ozone concentrations leading to smog. Smog reduces visibility and causes eye irritations and lung damage. In the upper atmosphere, the ozone problem is reversed. There, ozone concentrations have been reduced largely as a result of CFC emissions from aerosols and refrigerants. Reduced ozone in the upper atmosphere increases the amount of ultraviolet solar radiation reaching the earth and may increase the incidence of skin cancers.

Evidence is growing that emissions of carbon dioxide, methane, and other gases are helping to trap heat near the surface of the earth, producing the much-publicized "greenhouse effect" (Schneider 1989). Scientists also implicate carbon monoxide emissions in reducing the regenerative capacity of the atmosphere, making global warming more likely. Many scientists expect noticeable climatic changes by the middle of the twenty-first century as a result of the greenhouse effect with significant, but highly uncertain, effects on economic activity.

Water pollution is produced by direct discharges into watercourses or by deposition of atmospheric particles and gases through precipitation. Two kinds of waste are responsible for water quality problems: so-called "traditional" organic waste and the by-products of industrial operations (which include organic waste). Organic waste is biodegradable but the process of biodegradation causes oxygen depletion in receiving waters, measured by biological oxygen demand (BOD). In addition, organic waste in the form of human excrement contributes to waterborne disease such as typhoid fever and dysentery. Industrial waste includes heavy metals like mercury and lead along with a rapidly evolving collection of synthetic chemicals, including organochlorines. In some cases, pollutants enter the water cycle at *point sources* such as pulpmill effluent pipes and in other cases from diffuse sources (pesticides or fertilizers in runoff water, for example, or chemical wastes from toxic dumps). River bottoms can become the deposit sites for toxic chemicals and heavy metals. Traditional wastes are usually controlled through sedimentation and aeration. Contol of synthetic chemical discharges is more difficult and will require increasing efforts to substitute less-hazardous substances in industrial processes.

Canadian Environmental Policy

Extensive environmental regulation in Canada is a relatively recent phenomonon, dating to the mid-1960s. As with most other countries, the usual approach is to set permissable levels of pollution through regulations mandated by legislation. Individual polluters are expected to meet specified quantitative limits on their emissions. Both federal and provincial levels of government in Canada play roles in the environmental legislative process but most of the grassroots regulation and enforcement has taken place at the provincial level.

Virtually the only piece of environmental legislation of long standing is the federal *Fisheries Act*. As amended in 1960, the act makes it an offence to deposit substances harmful to fish into Canadian water resources without regulatory authorization. Under the *Fisheries Act* amendments, polluters can be required to monitor discharges, federal inspections are mandated, and fines and clean-up costs can be imposed on offenders. Though other regulations existed prior to 1960, it was not until the 1960s and 1970s that comprehensive environmental legislation began to appear and provincial and federal departments were created specifically to oversee the quality of Canadian air and water resources. Provincial governments passed air and water quality legislation in the 1960s and 1970s similar in general tone to the *Fisheries Act*. (Nemetz 1986; Webb 1988). The other major pieces of federal environmental control legislation are the *Canada Water Act* (1970), the *Clean Air Act* (1971), the *Environmental Contaminants Act* (1975), and the recent *Environmental Protection Act* (1988).

The *Canada Water Act* was designed to bring about federal-provincial co-operation in water resources management but has had little impact. The *Clean Air Act* has served as the basis for establishing national standards for air pollution control in specific industrial sectors. However, since the federal government has left most regulation activity on air pollution to the provinces, national standards are not always realized. The *Environmental Contaminants Act* was designed to deal with chemical pollutants not covered adequately under other federal legislation. In principle, the new *Environmental Protection Act*, dealing with toxic substances, represents a new beginning for federal involvement. The burden is to be placed on importers, manufacturers, and distributors to demonstrate that potentially harmful chemicals are being handled safely and provides for fines and jail sentences for contravention of the act.

An important role for federal policy lies in international negotiations and agreements on environmental quality. The Boundary Waters Treaty with the United States (1909) established the International Joint Commission (IJC). The IJC has undertaken several important studies of pollution in boundary waters and laid the foundation for a Canada–U.S. agreement on water quality in the Great Lakes (1972).

The traditional leading role of provincial governments in the regulatory process means that polluters must deal with both provincial and federal standards under provincial regulatory surveillance. At the provincial level, Ontario's legislation is the most comprehensive and sets the pattern for most other provinces. Given the large concentration and variety of industrial activities in Ontario, this is not surprising. The key pieces of Ontario legislation are the province's *Environmental Protection Act* (1980) and the *Ontario Water Resources Act* (1980). Under these acts no contaminant can be discharged into the air or into watercourses if the discharge exceeds the concentration allowed by specific regulations. When a discharge exceeds the regulated level, the Ontario Ministry of the Environment is empowered to issue a *control order* requiring the offender to comply with the regulations. The control order usually indicates what changes are needed (installation of pollution control equipment, modifications to the process causing pollution, or provision of a plan indicating the measures that will be taken to achieve compliance). In extreme cases, the Ministry may issue a *stop order* that requires immediate cessation of the discharge in excess of regulated amounts. The issue of a control order often initiates a process of negotiation involving an extended period of non-compliance with the regulations. Both control and stop orders can be appealed to a provincial Environmental Appeals Board.

Observers of the Canadian environmental regulation process have noted discrepancies between the language and presumed intent of legislation and the actual conduct of environmental policy. As Nemetz (1986) points out,

> . . .if one examines the maze of laws and regulations in Canada, one may be lulled into a misleading sense of security that Canadians and their environment are adequately protected; some may even argue overprotected. It is important to note that the Canadian system of government frequently produces strong enabling acts that form the basis for the tempered use of delegated powers by the administrative branches of government. In this system, there are two factors which determine the effective degree of protection from hazards: the nature of the regulation-making process itself, and the enforcement and extent of compliance.[2]

The actual environmental standards that form the basis of compliance with Canadian legislation have usually been determined only after discussion with the industries affected. Even when non-compliance is apparent, enforcement can be a slow process characterized by reluctance to invoke legislated penalties until a lengthy period of negotiation has elapsed. This time lag between the initial attempt by regulators to curb emissions and eventual compliance has been referred to as the "implementation gap" (Webb 1988). In many cases, prosecution has been a last resort enforcement mechanism. Even when prosecutions have been undertaken successfully, the resulting penalties (usually in the form of fines) have been too low to produce much of a deterrent effect.[3]

In one sense, co-operation between environmental enforcement agencies and polluters can be advantageous to the extent that it leads to solutions without confrontation and costly court actions. The negotiation process can also reveal new information concerning the costs and benefits associated with the emissions themselves. On the other hand, lengthy periods of non-compliance can amount to flouting the intent of the legislation itself. The latter interpretation has become prevalent in the late 1980s. Chappell (1988) quotes a senior official of the Ontario Ministry of the Environment:

> Prosecution is not the appropriate response to all situations, but I do think prosecution is under-utilized. This failure to prosecute in appropriate circumstances, in my opinion, leads to extensive delays in pollution abatement and erodes the credibility of law enforcement agencies. . .I have seen cases where requests by the Ministry of the Environment have fallen upon deaf

ears for years, but the steps requested were taken within a short time after laying charges.[4]

The interactions between firms in the Canadian pulp and paper industry and environmental regulators offers an interesting example of the slow process of negotiated compliance in the past and can serve as a case study of many of the issues involved in Canadian environmental policy formation. Amendments to the federal *Fisheries Act* in 1971 were accompanied by regulations applying to pulp and paper mill effluents flowing into watercourses. These standards were set following discussions with the industry but were only put into force for new or modernized mills. So-called "existing mills" were exempted and no date was set for the application of the 1971 effluent standards to these mills. Technically though, existing mills were still subject to the absolute prohibition of discharges harmful to fish in the unamended version of the *Fisheries Act*. This unrealistic prohibition guaranteed an "implementation gap" which has persisted to the present (Webb 1988). Federal prosecution of pulp and paper mills under the *Fisheries Act* have been rare despite violations. In Ontario, they are immune from federal prosecution provided they are in compliance with control orders issued by the Ontario Ministry of the Environment under the province's *Environmental Protection Act* (1980). Such immunity does not apply in other provinces however: a pulpmill complying with a negotiated British Columbia pollution control schedule was successfully prosecuted by the Environmental Protection Service (EPS), the administrative branch of Environment Canada, under the regulation provisions of the *Fisheries Act* in the 1970s (Webb 1988, 47). While there is, therefore, no absolute assurance that pulp and paper mills complying with provincial control schedules will be left alone by Environment Canada, the usual approach has been to rely on provincial initiatives.

In their dealings with provincial governments, pulp and paper firms have taken the position that federal or provincial regulations will require such costly pollution control expenditures as to cause exit from the industry and loss of jobs in communities almost entirely dependent on forest products employment. This "exit threat" strategy has proven to be a relatively effective bargaining tool from the early 1970s to the present, spinning out the negotiation process and forestalling prosecutions despite mounting evidence that more stringent pollution control would *not* have led to unmanageable cost increases for the industry (Muller 1976; Victor and Burrell 1981; Bonsor, McCubbin, and Sprague 1988). The "exit threat" strategy helped to win the industry pollution control subsidies as part of a shared federal-provincial modernization program that operated from 1979 to 1985.

Until recently, pulp and paper control regulations have centred on "traditional" pollution problems in the form of suspended solids, biological oxygen demand (BOD), and proven lethal chemicals. Levels of compliance and enforcement for these traditional pollutants remain variable across provinces as of the late 1980s.[5] Environmental concern has now shifted to toxic chemicals. The major concern of recent research has been the presence of certain organochlorines, principally dioxins and furans, in pulpmill effluents. These substances are released into watercourses by the industry's chlorine bleaching technology for pulp, and their concentrations in the ocean environment led to the closure of some fisheries in British Columbia in 1990. The scientific evidence on damage caused by toxic chemicals is certainly not conclusive. In high concentrations, they are known to cause skin problems. Popular opinion to the contrary, no clear scientific evidence of more serious health effects has yet been produced.[6] New regulations have now been developed to deal with the organochlorine problem. The industry's compliance costs appear to be small for moderate levels of abatement of these chemicals and the actual "exit threat" is minimal.[7] Some reductions in these chemicals in pulpmill effluents can actually be achieved profitably by moving from chlorine to oxygen bleaching. Very stringent abatement levels, though, would lead to significant cost increases for some firms.

Looking back at the 1970s and 1980s, environmental policy in Canada has a distinctive flavour. With the exception of environmental groups, most Canadians have left the regulatory process to the polluters and government officials. Quantitative pollution regulations for individual polluters have been promulgated by government but have typically been enforced less strictly than the legislative language might have led one to expect. But some changes are taking place. Canadians now seem more interested in participating in environmental decision making. One index of this interest is increasing citizen support for the use of environmental assessment procedures involving both experts and the public.

Both the federal government and some provincial governments in Canada now require such environmental assessment procedures as a condition of proceeding with large projects. The federal Environmental Assessment and Review Process (EARP) applies to projects initiated by federal government ministries or agencies and federal Crown corporations. EARP applies to the private sector projects as well if federal funding or the use of federal lands is involved. The Ontario *Environmental Assessment Act* applies to the province's ministries, agencies, and Crown corporations. Private projects can be designated by cabinet for review. In 1988, the Ontario government designated forest harvesting activities administered by the Ontario Ministry of Natural Resources for environmental assessment. Additional hydroelectric power capacity developed in the James Bay region will be subject to assessment by the federal Ministry of the Environment. Projects of this size generate significant changes in ecosystems as well as in the economic conditions facing resident groups, such as Native peoples. The purpose of assessment is to provide a public "fact-finding" forum in which a whole range of economic, cultural, social, and environmental impacts can be drawn together and subjected to systematic scrutiny at the project-planning stage so that modifications and constraints can be built in from the outset.

Another indication of changing attitudes is the willingness to contemplate stricter enforcement of existing regulations and stronger penalties for polluters. The existing system of sanctions on polluters has sometimes been referred to as "licences to pollute." The Law Reform Commission of Canada has been proposing stiffer penalties, including criminal sanctions for polluters, since the mid-1980s. Provided politicians and government officials sense public support, the negotiated gradual compliance model may yet change to a stricter enforcement mechanism. Businesses are increasingly finding that a pure public relations approach to the environment will not work as a substitute for action.

At the technical level, there appears to be little pressure to shift away from quantitative regulation of the emissions of individual polluters to any other scheme of limiting pollution. The use of emissions taxes in place of regulation has had little or no impact in Canada or elsewhere and does not seem likely to gain much support in the immediate future. The United States Environmental Protection Agency (EPA) is experimenting with pollution quotas, following an idea first proposed by Dales (1968). The quota idea takes the emphasis off emissions of the individual polluter and places it on the total level of emissions into a particular receiving environment. The overall quota is set and each polluter either receives or must purchase a share of the total. No one may discharge pollutants beyond the level of his or her quota. Quotas can be exchanged among polluters. In principle, a competitive market in quotas could establish a quota price and each polluter would discharge until the marginal benefit from pollution equalled the marginal cost as measured by the price of a unit of quota. The quota system thus minimizes the overall cost of achieving a specified quality level of the shared receiving medium. This could be a sensible alternative to discharge standards for individual polluters. (The approach is analogous to marketable fishing quotas discussed in chapter 7.) As yet, quota systems have not been introduced in Canada.

■ THE ENVIRONMENT AND THE MARKETPLACE

It is useful to summarize briefly the economic theory of environmental policy and its relationship to the real world of policy described in the preceding section. Economists begin with the premise that individual property rights to a clean and safe environment are not well established. The initial condition confronting policymakers is one in which industries possess the right to use the environment as a free disposal medium. The role of policy is to demonstrate the need to restrain industry's use of the environment as a dumping medium and to apply regulations and penalties to limit emissions to the point at which the demonstrated marginal social damage stemming from an additional unit of emissions equals the marginal benefit, measured in terms of the value of additional marketable output or pollution control expenditures saved. This general framework contains some hidden and significant biases.

The effectiveness of public policy is crucially conditioned by the need to demonstrate that the benefits of restraint outweigh the costs. As Schrecker (1984) points out in the Canadian context, the burden of proof of environmental damage lies with the public sector as a rule. Unless it can be shown that emissions are harmful, regulations are established that allow them to proceed. If the burden of proof were reversed, emissions would be prohibited unless they could be shown to be harmless. Standards of proof reflect the burden of proof. To accept the hypothesis that harm is being caused by emissions with 95 percent confidence, for example, one must show by experimental evidence that in over 95 cases out of 100, harm is caused. If the burden of proof were reversed, it would be necessary to accept the hypothesis that emissions are harmless as a condition of allowing them to occur. At the 95 percent confidence level this would require that they cause no harm in 95 cases out of 100. In the absence of certainty, placing the burden of proof on those affected by pollution rather than on polluters produces a lower quality environment than if the burden of proof were reversed. Reversal of the burden of proof may yet occur in Canada. The federal *Environmental Protection Act* (1988) may represent a move in this direction:

> The EPA emphasizes the anticipation and prevention of environmental contamination. This represents a major departure from the remedial approach taken by the current Environmental Contaminants Act, under which the onus is on the government to prove a chemical is harmful after it has been marketed. Under the new act, the onus will shift to the manufacturers who will be required to demonstrate, prior to marketing a chemical, that it is not harmful.[8]

A second problem inherent in the restraint approach to pollution relates to *equity* rather than efficiency. The decision to permit an "optimal" level of pollution in which marginal benefits from pollution equal marginal damage costs involves a decision to permit pollution damages to one group in society in exchange for gains to others in the form of lower product prices. Unless those damaged by emissions are explicitly compensated for damages, economists cannot make unqualified recommendations about optimal pollution levels. Efficiency in the sense of equality between marginal benefits and marginal damages is not a sufficient basis to proceed when the benefits and damages accrue to different groups. If property rights were reversed, such that pollution damage had to be paid for as a condition of pollution, then compensation would be paid to those damaged as a matter of right and the equity consequences of pollution would be the reverse of what usually happens.

Determination of the magnitudes of benefits and damages from pollution is a step that logically precedes determination of optimal pollution levels. But there are large elements of uncertainty in the measurement process. The benefits of reduced levels of pollution come in many forms, some of which virtually defy monetary valuation. In part this is due to the nature of pollution as an activity that takes place external to the market mechanism. In part it is simply due to the difficulty of assigning dollar values to aesthetic impacts, recreational opportunities, impacts on human life expectancy and other implications of pollution. In many cases, regulation of pollution must take place in the context of inadequate measurement and major uncertainties as to the actual effects of pollution on environmental characteristics. Reducing carbon dioxide emissions, for example, is expected to moderate climatic warming trends but scientists have not established precise connections between carbon dioxide and the greenhouse effect. Nor is it clear what the effects of global warming will be, what adaptations will be needed to cope with it, and how costly such adaptations will be. Moving to reduced levels of carbon dioxide emissions worldwide will change humankind's future in many ways but decisons to make such reductions can hardly proceed on the basis of precise marginal benefits from a cooler climate. The same problem occurs with the marginal costs of reducing pollution. In Canada, control orders placed on polluters is often the beginning of a process that reveals the costs of compliance rather than the result of a marginal-benefit–marginal-damage analysis in which compliance costs are already known. Efficient compliance technology may only emerge when the problem of emissions reduction is seriously addressed. In the case of stack scrubbers to reduce sulphur gas emissions, for example, attention to the problem by Union Carbide led to the development of a new scrubbing technology in the spring of 1990 which promises to be vastly cheaper than existing methods and will produce sulphuric acid as a useful by-product. This discovery may significantly change the benefit-cost balance surrounding acid rain. In general, an atmosphere of controversy and guesswork accompanies most environmental decisions. The real world of pollution regulation involves a complex set of interactions among self-interested industry participants, environmental control agencies, an ill-informed general public, voter-sensitive politicians, and environmental advocate groups, all of whom operate in a world of incomplete and evolving scientific evidence and technology. Recognition of these real world complications highlights the spurious precision inherent in marginal-benefit–marginal-damage models. As one observer points out, summarizing results of a number of Canadian environmental regulation studies,

...in particular cases it is extremely difficult and often impossible to quantify costs and benefits. This inability in particular instances to make a confident appraisal of whether a protection measure will confer benefits exceeding costs is the element that confounds environmental regulation more than any other. This uncertainty at the margin is the sum of scientific uncertainties about cause and effect relationships, technological uncertainties about alternate abatement and mitigation methods, and judgemental uncertainties about values and preferences.[9]

At a deeper level, the whole basis of marginal benefits and damages assumes that it is appropriate to incorporate environmental decisions into the monetary calculus of the marketplace. Treating uncontrolled pollution as *market failure* implies that policies that simulate outcomes that would occur if emissions *were* marketable is the right way to proceed. There are, however, some clear precedents for constraining the realm of the marketplace.[10] The buying and selling of votes in a democracy or the practice of indentured labour and slavery, for example, are transactions that are simply forbidden, in deference to overriding moral imperatives. The public provision of health care in Canada is a case in which an individual's access to the medical system is separated, as a matter of principle, from his or her personal ability to pay for goods and services. There is no question that social availability of medical care is constrained by costs but the prevailing principle is that each individual has the right to equal access to the overall level of medical care emerging from the political process.

The separation of market transactions from certain rights should act as a caution to economists attempting to reduce all decison making to simulated market measures. The potential conflict between market values (prices) and social values emerges sharply when pollution control costs can be incurred to save lives. Several studies have proposed that the marginal benefit of a life saved can be measured by discounted lifetime earnings. Application of the marginal benefit-cost framework suggests balancing the marginal cost of pollution control against the additional discounted lifetime earnings made possible by lives saved. An ethically sounder procedure is to use economics as an input to higher levels of decision making. Economists can indicate the market costs of alternative environmental actions and the projected effects on lives saved in each case. They can also inform society of the marginal cost of saving lives through other actions, such as expansion of public medical care expenditures. Where the marginal cost of saving lives through preventive environmental measures is less than the marginal cost of saving lives by health care expenditures, it can be pointed out that expansion of pollution control is the cheaper lifesaving method. But the final choice of how much sacrifice of goods and services is to be made to save lives must be left to the political system.

■ APPENDIX: DYNAMIC OPTIMIZATION WITH PERSISTENT POLLUTANTS

The appendix to chapter 2 developed a general framework for handling dynamic optimization problems in natural resources where the objective is to maximize the discounted sum of net benefits from resources use subject to the dynamics of the resource stock itself. The stock-flow pollution problem discussed in this chapter is a variant of this general problem. To illustrate the issues, we will assume that one unit of output of, say, widgets, denoted by Q, implies one unit of pollution emissions, E. The net benefit from the *flow* of widget production at time t is $B(Q) - C(Q) - D(E)$ from equation (2), where $B - C$ measures the flow benefits from widget production and D measures the flow damage from emissions associated with widget output. Since we are assuming that $Q = E$, the net benefit function is $B(E) - C(E) - D(E)$. Since we also want to include stock damage $D^*(X)$ in the model and maximize discounted net benefits over time, our continuous time maximization problem is

$$Maximize \quad V = \int_0^\infty \{B[E(t)] - C[E(t)] - D[E(t)] - D^*[X(t)]\}e^{-rt} \quad (A1)$$

$$Subject\ to \qquad\qquad dX/dt = E(t) \qquad\qquad (A2)$$

Equation (A2) states that the stock of the persistent pollutant grows each period by the amount of the current emission flow.

As the appendix to chapter 2 indicated, the solution method for this type of problem is derived from the Lagrange method and leads to the construction of the *Hamiltonian function*

$$H = \{B[E(t)] - C[E(t)] - D[E(t)] - D^*[X(t)]\}e^{-rt} + \mu(t)[E(t)] \quad (A3)$$

with necessary conditions for maximization given by

$$\partial H/\partial E = 0; \qquad d\mu/dt = -\partial H/\partial X; \qquad dX/dt = \partial H/\partial \mu \qquad (A4)$$

The costate variable $\mu(t)$ is interpreted as a present value such that $\mu(t) = \lambda(t)e^{-rt}$ and $d\mu/dt = d\lambda/dt \cdot e^{-rt} - r\lambda e^{-rt}$. The first two conditions in (A4) are then

$$B'(E) - C'(E) - D'(E) + \lambda = 0 \qquad\qquad (A5)$$

$$d\lambda/dt - r\lambda = D^*{}'(X) \qquad\qquad (A6)$$

Equation (A5) implies that the marginal flow value of an additional unit of emissions is $B'(E) - C'(E) - D'(E) = -\lambda$. In the text of the chapter we have denoted $B'(E) - C'(E) - D'(E)$ as $P - MC - MC'$ (see equation (14)).

Defining the net price of emissions as $p = -\lambda$ such that $dp/dt = -d\lambda/dt$, substituting into (A6) and rearranging produces

$$rp = dp/dt + D^{*\prime}(X) \qquad (A7)$$

which is the asset equilibrium condition given by equation (20) in the text of the chapter. The dynamics of the control variable (E) and the stock variable (X) can be obtained from (A5) and (A6) as well. Taking the time derivative of (A5),

$$d\lambda/dt = -[B''(E) - C''(E) - D''(E)]dE/dt \qquad (A8)$$

Substituting (A8) into (A6) and rearranging, the differential equation describing the motion of the control variable is

$$dE/dt = -\{D^{*\prime}(X) - r[B'(E) - C'(E) - D'(E)]\}/[B''(E)$$
$$- C''(E) - D''(E)] \quad (A9)$$

The differential equation describing the dynamic behaviour of the state variable is just $dX/dt = E$.

The end-points for the problem are obtained by setting the initial pollution stock at X_0 and requiring $dE/dt = dX/dt = 0$ for the terminal condition at $t = T$. Thus $E_T = 0$ and $D^{*\prime}(X_T) - r[B'(E_T) - C'(E_T) - D'(E_T)] = 0$. If $X_0 < X_T$, pollution flows are positive and declining toward the steady-state terminal condition. If $X_0 \geqslant X_T$, then the emission flow is immediately set equal to zero and held at zero.

■ NOTES

1. Further discussion of the local-global problem in the context of pollution control can be found in A.C. Fisher, *Resource and Environmental Economics* (New York: Cambridge University Press, 1981); and P. Dasgupta, *The Control of Resources* (Oxford: Basil Blackwell, 1982).
2. P. Nemetz, "Federal Environmental Regulation in Canada," *Natural Resources Journal* 26 (1986): 563.
3. Ibid., 570.
4. Quoted in D. Chappell, *From Sawdust to Toxic Blobs: A Consideration of Sanctioning Strategies to Combat Pollution in Canada* (Ottawa: Supply and Services, 1988), pp. 1–2.
5. N. Bonsor, N McCubbin, and J. Sprague, *Stopping Water Pollution at its Source: Kraft Mill Effluents in Ontario* (Toronto: Ontario Ministry of the Environment, 1988), p. 122.
6. Ibid., pp. 185ff.
7. Ibid., pp. 220ff.
8. E. Rovet, *The Canadian Business Guide to Environmental Law* (Vancouver: Self-Counsel Press, 1988), p. 13.

9. A. Thompson, *Environmental Regulation in Canada: An Assessment of the Regulatory Process* (Vancouver: Westwater Research Centre, 1980), p. 6.
10. See A. Okun, *Equality and Efficiency: The Big Tradeoff* (Washington: The Brookings Institute, 1975), Chap. 1, for a discussion of rights and the marketplace.

■ FURTHER READING

There is a wide literature in environmental economics. Specialist work appears in the *Journal of Environmental Economics and Management* and *Natural Resources Journal*. The following sources provide useful treatments complementary to the discussion in the present chapter.

Dasgupta, P. *The Control of Resources*. Oxford: Basil Blackwell, 1982, Chap. 8.

Fisher, A.C. *Resource and Environmental Economics*. New York: Cambridge University Press, 1981, Chaps. 5 and 6.

Fisher, A.C., and F. Peterson. "The Environment in Economics: A Survey." *Journal of Economic Literature* (March 1976).

Victor, P. *Economics of Pollution*. London: Macmillan, 1972.

Excellent discussions of Canadian environmental policy in the 1980s are

Nemetz, P. "Federal Environmental Regulation in Canada." *Natural Resources Journal* (Summer 1986).

Schrecker, T.F. *Political Economy of Environmental Hazards*. Ottawa: Law Reform Commission of Canada, Supply and Services, 1984.

An up-to-date survey of scientific views on environmental problems is provided by a collection of articles in the September 1989 issue of *Scientific American*.

SCARCITY

CONTROVERSIES

▎INTRODUCTION

Chapters 2 and 3 focused on the constraints that natural resource stocks and environmental quality considerations place on resource extraction activities and on production processes that involve environmental externalities. In both cases, efficient resource management requires recognition of scarcity through the pricing of resource stocks and environmental damages. In the nonrenewable resource utilization models of chapter 2, depletion acts to modify the optimal rate of exploitation of resource stocks. The present chapter confronts theoretical approaches to nonrenewable resources use with the available evidence bearing on resources scarcity.

We begin with a view of the scarcity issue from two perspectives: first, the physical (geological) perspective in which the adequacy of reserves and resources as the basis for future production is described and, second, the cost-price perspective in which scarcity signals are sought in the past and present behaviour of resources prices relative to the prices of other goods and services. Both points of view are important in any attempt to identify possible future shortages of resources.

Next, scarcity issues are examined from a Canadian perspective in which we distinguish between domestic resource scarcity and worldwide scarcity. These two types of scarcity have quite different implications for Canadian economic welfare. Then a more detailed analysis of depletion *versus* technological progress is set out. The final section describes ways of adapting to natural resources scarcity through substitution and recycling. An important theme that emerges from the scarcity discussion is the wide latitude for optimism or pessimism concerning the adequacy of existing and projected stocks of nonrenewables. Economic analysis can offer some assistance in evaluating and interpreting the wide range of views encountered here but a hard core of uncertainty inevitably remains.

■ PHYSICAL RESOURCE SCARCITY: RESERVES *VERSUS* RESOURCES

The adequacy of nonrenewable resources to support future production levels involves a great deal of speculation. Economic geologists approach mineral supplies by applying differing degrees of certainty to available stocks. Mineral supplies classified as reserves have the highest certainty of being converted into production economically—at marginal production costs less than the market prices of their products. Operating mines and mines that are on the verge of production are based on proven reserves and

> ...once sufficient economic volumes of ore are identified in an orebody to support development, it is unnecessary and unprofitable to identify further reserves until they are needed. In most major mines, new reserves are continually proven up at a rate capable of supporting 15 or 20 years' production.[1]

Proven reserves are available with virtual certainty at costs that allow profitable extraction using existing technologies. *Indicated* reserves are potentially available at costs that permit profitable extraction. Beyond proven and indicated reserves are *inferred* reserves that would be economic to extract if they were actually to materialize as expected. Other resources are known—sometimes with great certainty—but involve costs that cannot permit profitable production using existing techniques. These *subeconomic* resources may contribute to future supplies if new techniques become available or if product prices rise sufficiently to make their extraction profitable.

Resource supplies exist, therefore, as a spectrum from proven economic reserves to resources that may or may not turn out to be economically valuable as future exploration, technology, and market prices unfold.

FIGURE 4.1   Zwartendyk's box

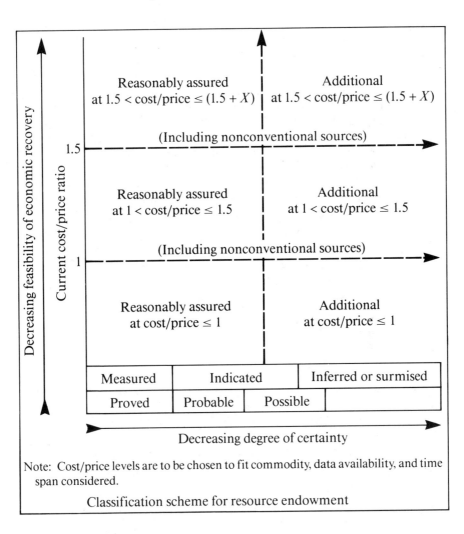

Note: Cost/price levels are to be chosen to fit commodity, data availability, and time span considered.

Classification scheme for resource endowment

Source: J. Zwartendyk, "Mineral Wealth—How Should It Be Expressed?," *Canadian Mining Journal*, April 1973, 44–52.

Figure 4.1 illustrates a classification approach due to Zwartendyk that classifies resources in accordance with the certainty of their availability and their projected costs of extraction.[2] The lower left-hand corner of Zwartendyk's box classification includes measured (known) reserves that are economic to extract. The upper right-hand corner classifies resources that are not easily measurable and are too costly to extract with presently known technologies. Horizontal movements within Zwartendyk's box bring in resources that are subject to less and less certainty in terms of physical volume. Vertical movements expand resource supplies by including those that are more and more costly to extract using existing technologies.

Even a cursory examination of Zwartendyk's box and similar classifications of resource availability leads to the conclusion that fixed stock models of availability, in which absolute limits to extraction are built into the analysis, are very difficult to interpret when actual resource supply measurements must be produced to support them. This difficulty was discussed in chapter 2 where it was noted that the resource stock limits in Hotelling-style models are easy enough to assume but hard to pin down in actual cases. The further into the future one goes, the less clear is the supply picture. On a global level, late 1970s and early 1980s estimates of non-fuel mineral supplies, for example, do classify resources into reserves (measured, indicated, and inferred), other resources (higher cost sources), resource potential (recoverable with existing or known technologies), and a much larger *base* resource which includes all sources of non-fuel minerals in the earth's crust. This information is shown in Table 4.1.

The high level of uncertainty implicit in estimates like those of Table 4.1 leaves a good deal of room for either optimism or pessimism when assessing the prospect of future physical scarcity. At the pessimistic extreme, some observers divide reserves by current production to generate a so-called *life index* which simply indicates how long existing known reserves would last at current production levels. The life-index can be shortened by allowing for a projected growth rate of production. If, for example, reserves alone are used as a measure of supply, the 1977 level of production of copper could have continued for less than sixty years. If copper production were to grow at historical rates (about 3 percent per annum), 1977 reserves would have only lasted for about thirty-five years. Note that copper has one of the shorter life indexes in Table 4.1.

Two studies undertaken in the early 1970s used the pessimistic life index approach to resource scarcity to predict impending resource exhaustion and economic collapse.[3] In both of these "doomsday" models, extraction costs were assumed to rise rapidly as resource exhaustion approached. Resource exhaustion, in turn, was predicted to occur when known and probable reserves (as of the early 1970s) had been used up. These models were subjected to sharp criticism from economists on a number of fronts but most particularly on the assumption that supplies of exhaustible resources can be measured by the reserves figures used in the studies. As measures of resource supply, reserve estimates are far too conservative. Future production will no doubt rely heavily on resources not

TABLE 4.1 World production and reserves in 1977 (estimated), other resources in 1973–77 (as data available), resources potential, and resource base of 17 elements (millions of tonnes)

	PRODUCTION	RESERVES	OTHER RESOURCES	RESOURCE POTENTIAL (RECOVERABLE)	BASE RESOURCE (CRUSTAL MASS)
Aluminum	17	5 200	2 800	3 519 000	1 990 000 000 000
Iron	495	93 100	143 000	2 035 000	1 392 000 000 000
Potassium	22	9 960	103 000	*	408 000 000 000
Manganese	10	2 200	1 100	42 000	31 200 000 000
Phosphorus	14	3 400	12 000	51 000	28 800 000 000
Fluorine	2	72	270	20 000	10 800 000 000
Sulphur	52	1 700	3 800	*	9 600 000 000
Chromium	3	780	6 000	3 260	2 600 000 000
Zinc	6	159	4 000	3 400	2 250 000 000
Nickel	0.7	54	103	2 590	2 130 000 000
Copper	8	456	1 770	2 120	1 510 000 000
Lead	4	123	1 250	550	290 000 000
Tin	0.2	10	27	68	40 000 000
Tungsten	0.04	1.8	3.4	51	26 400 000
Mercury	0.008	0.2	0.4	3.4	2 100 000
Silver	0.010	0.2	0.5	2.8	1 800 000
Platinum group	0.0002	0.02	0.05	1.2	1 100 000

*Not available

Source: G.O. Barney, *The Global 2000 Report to the President of the United States* (New York: Pergamon, 1980), p. 219. Resource potential refers to U.S. Geological Survey data and is subject to disagreement: see, for example, Trainer (1983), Table 1.

yet considered to fall into the reserves category and may even rely on minerals existing in very low concentrations in common rock.

On the side of extreme optimism, some observers are inclined to deny the existence of *any* fixed limits to the world's use of nonrenewable resources. In this view, the earth's crust provides a virtually inexhaustible source of most minerals. David Brooks, for example, argues that

> ...the notion of running out of mineral supplies is ridiculous...except for a few substances, notably crude oil and natural gas, which are discretely different from the rock masses that contain them, the quantities of mineral materials in even the upper few miles of the earth's crust approach the infinite.[4]

Using such optimistic measures, copper resources could last for several million years, which, as Brooks says, approaches the infinite. The truth lies somewhere between the pessimistic limits set by the "doomsday" models and the optimistic "cornucopian" approach favoured by Brooks and others.

Perhaps the most significant point to be made about estimates of resources supplies, apart from their uncertainty, is that continued production will almost inevitably involve resources of much lower quality than the quality of existing reserves. In the absence of technological progress, the costs of extracting much of the earth's mineral resource stock will be very high indeed, if not prohibitive. A second point of crucial significance is that future patterns of mineral and energy use will surely be different from the pattern of the 1980s.

Consider the world's future energy problem. Nordhaus' study of energy transitions has already been described in chapter 2.[5] The thrust of that study was that global energy requirements will be met in the future by shifts from present energy sources to what are now regarded as minor or unconventional sources: nuclear fission and (possibly) fusion, geothermal energy, and solar energy. The nature of such a series of transitions was illustrated in Figures 2.4 and 2.5. Research undertaken by the U.S. Geological Survey in the late 1970s concluded that recoverable nonrenewable energy resources (petroleum, natural gas, coal, shale oil, tar sands, and uranium) contain enough energy to sustain global requirements until the year 2110 if energy consumption grows at 2 percent per annum and until the year 2046 if energy consumption grows at 5 percent per annum.[6] Energy consumption growth rates will probably lie between these boundaries (2 to 5 percent). The Geological Survey estimates of nonrenewable energy resources are acknowledged to involve considerable uncertainty: reserves may err by as much as 10 to 25 percent with even larger errors possible in the case of undiscovered energy resources—those lying in the "inferred or surmised" regions of Figure 4.1.[7]

One of the key assumptions about energy use patterns in the twenty-

TABLE 4.2 World energy sources (quadrillion BTU)
(1 quadrillion or 1 quad = 1 million billion = 10^{15})

Recoverable nonrenewable sources:		
Petroleum	9 634	
Natural gas	8 663	
Solid fuels (coal)	120 854	
Shale Oil	20 130	
Tar sands	5 800	
Uranium (light water reactors)	1 960	
or (breeder reactors)	117 600–196 000*	
Hydraulic resources	33.1	
Solar energy	—**	
Total (light water reactors)		167 074
(breeder reactors)		282 714–361 114
1976 energy consumption	250	

*Not estimated.
**Energy content of uranium reserves 6 to 100 times for breeder technology.

Source: Adapted from G.O. Barney, *Global 2000 Report* (New York: Pergamon, 1980), Chap. 11.

first century in the Nordhaus study is a substantial shift, particularly in industrial energy generation, from petroleum to coal. Within the non-renewable energy resources category, coal is by far the largest component accounting for about 75 percent of the Geological Survey's estimate of recoverable energy (Table 4.2). Since large quantities of coal have already been located, very little coal exploration is taking place and some observers believe that its abundance could prove greater than current estimates if exploration efforts were resumed. The world's present reliance on petroleum resources relative to coal resources is far from proportional to the estimates of total energy available from these sources. In terms of energy content, coal is about twelve times as abundant as petroleum, yet with current patterns of use, conventional petroleum resources (excluding shale oil and oil from tar sands) might only last until the middle of the next century, while coal resources are large enough to sustain current coal production for approximately seventeen hundred years! The major problem of moving to greater reliance on coal as an energy source is the environmental impact of coal-burning technologies. Coal has been a major culprit in some of the pollution problems discussed in chapter 3. The impact of sulphur and soot emissions on the atmosphere means that stretching out energy resources by using coal means depletion of atmospheric resources.

An eventual shift away from nonrenewable energy sources of all kinds requires the development of alternative energy sources. Some of these sources are already here on a smaller scale. Employing present nuclear power generation technology,

...uranium reserves now represent a source of limited potential, comparable
in magnitude to that of the remaining recoverable resources of oil and gas.
The breeder reactor, if deployed, would increase the energy output from this
fuel by a factor of from 60–100 times.[8]

So uranium has real potential as an alternative energy source, prolonging
dependence on nonrenewable energy resources provided the breeder technology comes into use. Replacing fission (conventional or breeder)
sources of atomic energy with fusion would provide an unlimited source of
energy for industrial power. The difficulty with all nuclear power programs
lies with public attitudes to reactors. The minor radiation escape at Three
Mile Island and the serious contamination caused by the Chernobyl
disaster, combined with continuing difficulties in finding publicly acceptable locations for spent fuel storage, has significantly slowed nuclear power
programs in many countries.

Hydroelectric resources have the important quality of renewability.
The actual process of hydroelectric power generation has few, if any,
environmental side effects. Approximately 17 percent of the world's
technically exploitable hydroelectric power potential is currently being
used with the largest hydro "reserves" in Africa, Asia, and South America.
Notwithstanding the substantial room for hydroelectric development, even
full utilization of the world's falling water potential could not contribute a
large fraction of global energy requirements (Table 4.2). In the mid-1970s,
for example, world energy consumption was about 250 quadrillion BTU
and full development of world hydro resources could supply only 33
quadrillion BTU—only 13 percent of even mid-1970s levels of energy
consumption. Further, though the actual process of hydro power generation produces few, if any, adverse environmental effects, significant dis-
ruptions are caused by hydro power siting since large areas of land are
usually submerged to provide the reservoirs required to ensure continuous
operation of turbines.

Tidal power offers an even smaller potential for solving the world's
energy problems. The potential contribution of major tidal power sites
totals 90,000 megawatts of electrical capacity which is about 4 percent of
potential hydroelectric capacity from falling water. Other minor sources
include geothermal energy, based on the natural heat of the earth's core,
and wind power.

Allowing for all the minor energy sources, most of the replacement of
current conventional petroleum-based energy in the next century will have
to involve increased reliance on unconventional petroleum energy (shale
oil and tar sands), coal, and uranium, unless, of course, scientists can
master hydrogen fusion. Estimated shale oil resources are approximately
the same as remaining petroleum and natural gas supplies. Tar sands also
have substantial potential with world reserves estimated in the range of

1000 billion barrels compared to 1661 billion barrels of conventional petroleum.

The major problem in judging impending energy scarcity is the speed at which transitions from conventional sources to new sources must occur. Existing world reserves of recoverable nonrenewable sources could support recent energy consumption levels for several centuries, assuming a major transition to coal resources. If breeder power becomes important, the life index of existing and projected uranium reserves could be extended to 1100–1500 years. But if energy consumption is assumed to grow at historical rates, say even at a fairly modest rate of 3 percent per annum, existing recoverable nonrenewable sources could only last for a little over 100 years without the breeder technology and for only 120 to 130 years *with* breeder reactors! In this case technical advances by the year 2100 would be needed to make a final transition to some combination of fusion, solar, hydroelectric, and other energy forms.

All future energy sources, including coal, will involve increases in extraction costs measured at today's level of technical knowledge. With technology as the wild card, the response of future energy prices to future depletion remains hypothetical. In this respect, at least, the future will surely resemble the past.

Turning to global supplies of *non-fuel* minerals, Table 4.1 seems, at first sight, to support Brooks' contention that physical exhaustion is very remote if not completely implausible. This interpretation does seem to be sound for what geologists refer to as *geochemically abundant* minerals. For these minerals, the base resource (crustal mass) estimates of Table 4.1 suggest that the future will be similar to the past in that production will proceed to progressively lower quality deposits. Whether or not production costs rise depends, again, on the ability of technological progress to offset declining grades. While no one can predict the outcome of the race between technology and depletion for geochemically abundant minerals, there is certainly no evidence that technical progress will lose the race against depletion in the future. This guardedly optimistic conclusion does not apply to *geochemically scarce* minerals, however.

In several contributions on the question of long-term mineral supplies, the geologist Brian Skinner has developed the argument that a wide range of metallic minerals in current use must sooner or later be replaced by geologically abundant minerals.[9] These geochemically scarce metals— copper, lead, gold, mercury, nickel molybdenum, silver, tin, and uranium (to list the most important ones)—are currently being mined in ore concentrations that vastly exceed their concentrations in the surrounding earth's crust. Figure 4.2 shows the contrast between geochemically abundant metals, such as aluminum or iron, and the geochemically scarce metals. As Skinner points out,

FIGURE 4.2

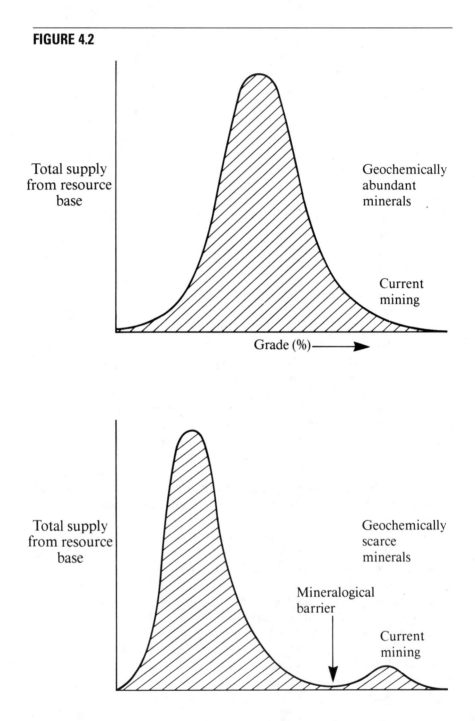

Source: B.J. Skinner, "A Second Iron Age Ahead?" *American Scientist* 64 (May/June 1976).

...the entire crust can be considered a potential resource of geochemically abundant minerals and...no major technological barriers, beyond the ability to mine steadily declining grades of ore, will have to be overcome. The smelting practices available today will also work in the future.[10]

For this group of metals, Skinner's view supports Brooks' contention that the crustal resource mass is the relevant physical concept for assessing long-run supply potential. For the geochemically scarce metals, however, crustal abundances, though large in relation to annual production, are very much lower than for iron and aluminum. As Table 4.1 indicates, chromium (the most common of the scarce metals in the earth's crust) occurs in a concentration that is 0.19 percent of the concentration of iron and 0.13 percent of the concentration of aluminum. Within common rock, iron is more than five hundred times as abundant as chromium by weight. Geochemically scarce metals are not only scarce in common rock compared to iron and aluminum, they are also prohibitively costly to isolate, since they occur as atomic substitutes in the more common minerals. Enormous amounts of energy would be required to separate scarce metal atoms from the atoms of the more abundant elements in these minerals. As Skinner puts it,

> Miners never consider common rocks when they are seeking ores of geochemically scarce metals. Instead they seek those rare and geologically limited volumes of the crust where special circumstances have produced marked local concentrations of geochemically scarce elements, and have done so in a manner that leads to the scarce elements being present in compounds of their own, not as atomic substitutes....These localized volumes (which we commonly call ore deposits) contain enrichments far above the average crustal abundance of an element—sometimes by as much as 100,000 times.... Lead, for example, has an average abundance in the continental crust of 0.0010% but lead ores usually contain at least 2% lead, and some are known to be as rich as 20% lead.[11]

It is clear, then, that for many economically important metals, the crustal resource base figures of Table 4.1 constitute a measure of supply potential that would be extremely expensive, if not prohibitively so. Skinner describes this in terms of a "mineralogical barrier" that exists between recoverable resources of geochemically scarce metals and their crustal mass. As Figures 4.2 and 4.3 illustrate, the mineralogical barrier lies between the mining of ore deposits and extraction of the same geochemically scarce metals from common rock.

The mineralogical barrier concept lends support to the use of fixed stock models of scarcity like the Hotelling model. For the geochemically scarce minerals, recoverable resources in mineral deposits appear to set a finite limit on cumulative future production unless some very substantial technological changes give us access to the crustal resource base.

From what has been said about energy resources and metallic mineral

FIGURE 4.3

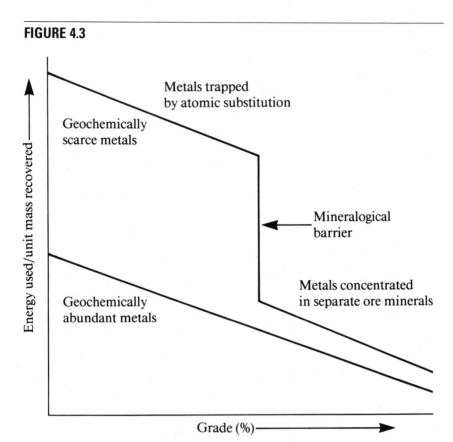

NOTE: The relationship between the grade of an ore and the energy input per unit mass of metal recovered is shown for both scarce and abundant metals. A steadily rising amount of energy will be needed to produce even geochemically abundant metals from the leaner ores of the future, but the amount of energy needed to produce scarce metals will take a tremendous jump when the mineralogical barrier is reached. At that point, when ore deposits are worked out, mineral concentrating processes can no longer be applied, and the silicate minerals in common rocks must be broken down chemically to separate the atoms of scarce metals from all the other atoms.

Source: B.J. Skinner, "A Second Iron Age Ahead?" *American Scientist* 64 (May/June 1976).

resources in this section, it can be concluded that the choice among the models of nonrenewable resources use examined in chapter 2 depends upon the type of resource being considered. For energy resources, present information suggests a series of transitions from petroleum and natural gas to coal and nuclear fuels and, possibly, fusion and solar energy. The cost of each energy source will be affected by future technological advances as and when they appear. This step-wise approach was illustrated in Figure 2.5 as an optimal path. For geochemically scarce metals, the presence of mineralogical barriers implies continued use of these minerals at declining ore concentrations with finite limits now in sight. Technological progress can hold costs down provided the world has access to ore deposits but cannot realistically be expected to overcome the barriers involved in extracting scarce metals from common rock. For geochemically abundant metals, finite limits to exploitable stocks cannot be identified. If technological progress can continue to offset declining ore grades, future production may be open-ended. For all practical purposes exhaustion is not inevitable in these cases.

■ COST-PRICE MEASURES OF SCARCITY

The foregoing discussion of resources scarcity in terms of physical supplies is obviously an important background to any scarcity analysis. But it does not exhaust the empirical evidence available. Not surprisingly, when confronted with questions of natural resource scarcity, economists have tended to supplement (often rough) estimates of physical supplies with an examination of long-run cost and price trends for natural resource commodities relative to other goods and services.

Three cost-price measures of scarcity have been proposed in the literature: the unit (capital plus labour) cost of producing natural resource output, the net price of the resource (p, as defined in chapter 2), and the price of resource products (π). Pioneering attempts to measure resource scarcity using cost and price measures were made by Herfindahl (1959) and by Barnett and Morse (1963).

Unit Cost and Net Price Measures

Barnett and Morse's *unit cost* approach examined the time trend in the amounts of labour and capital inputs required to produce a unit of natural resource output. They developed two hypotheses: a "strong scarcity hypothesis" that capital-labour inputs required per unit of resources output in the U.S. had been increasing in *absolute* terms over the period 1870– 1957 and a "weak scarcity hypothesis" that capital-labour inputs per unit of output of resources products had been rising *relative* to capital-labour inputs required per unit of nonextractive products. Barnett and Morse also examined the amount of labour input alone required to produce a unit of extractive resources goods (the inverse of labour productivity) relative to nonextractive goods and services. With the exception of forestry (discussed in chapter 6) the Barnett-Morse data led to the rejection of both the strong and weak scarcity hypotheses. Real unit capital-labour costs were found to decline over the whole period for extractive goods. Further, from 1910 to 1957 the weak hypothesis also failed to hold: real unit costs of resource products declined relative to the real unit costs of other products. As an alternative test of their weak hypothesis, Barnett and Morse examined the time trend of the prices of natural resource products relative to the prices of other products. Here again, relative scarcity could not be confirmed. Real resource product prices (except for forest products) were either level or declining over the test period extending from 1870 to 1957.

In explaining their results, Barnett and Morse distinguished between what they called Malthusian *versus* Ricardian scarcity. Malthusian scarcity implies definable resource stock limits while Ricardian scarcity is characterized by progressive movements to lower and lower quality resources (see Figure 2.3). The distinction between Malthusian and Ricardian scarcity closely parallels the distinction between *complete* and *incomplete* exhaustion models as discussed in chapter 2. Like Malthusian models, complete exhaustion models foresee fixed limits to the cumulative total of nonrenewable resource production flows sometime in the future. Ricardian movement to lower and lower grades of resources over time will lead to incomplete exhaustion *unless* technological change is present. When technological change is present, the upper limit on cumulative extraction becomes a moving limit that need never put an absolute end to extraction. Barnett and Morse strongly favoured the Ricardian concept of scarcity in which technological progress can reduce extraction costs as rapidly as, or more rapidly than, depletion tends to raise them, with the result that exhaustion can be forestalled for very lengthy periods of time. As they themselves concluded,

> The...Ricardian hypothesis...is that the character of the resource base presents man with a never-ending stream of problems,...that these will impose general scarcity—increasing cost—is not a legitimate corollary.[12]

Barnett and Morse's results have been extended beyond the late 1950s in subsequent contributions. Johnson and Bennett (1980) extended the test of the "strong scarcity hypothesis" to the late 1960s, finding that real capital-labour requirements per unit of extractive output continued to fall during the decade following the Barnett-Morse test period. Data on employment per unit of output in U.S. resource extraction sectors assembled by Manthy (1978) reveals that these series have continued to decline, again leading to rejection of a "strong scarcity hypothesis." Barnett (1979) concluded that the earlier Barnett-Morse results remained valid to the beginning of the 1970s.

As a measure of scarcity, capital-labour inputs per unit of resource output has been subject to criticism by several authors. Since unit cost is average cost, the Barnett-Morse approach may not capture the costs of inputs needed to produce resource products at the margin, using the lowest quality resources. Further, since the net price is excluded from the Barnett-Morse measure of cost, it can be claimed that the true cost of providing current resource output is understated by a unit cost measure that is restricted to capital and labour inputs. On this point, Brown and Field (1978) have argued that capital-labour costs per unit of output are likely to contain a *systematic* bias as a scarcity indicator. Recalling that the price of a resource product (π) in an optimal nonrenewable resource utilization model is the sum of marginal extraction costs (C) and net price (p), the following equation applies at each point during the extraction horizon:

$$\pi = C + p \tag{1}$$

If the net price is expressed per unit of the resource instead of per unit of final product and the amount of the resource used per unit of final product is denoted by Z, (1) becomes

$$\pi = C + p'Z \tag{2}$$

where p' is the net price per unit of the resource. Suppose p' is rising over time (as it is expected to do in the simple homogeneous fixed-stock Hotelling model, for example). Resources are becoming increasingly expensive relative to other inputs, the costs of which are included in C. As Figure 4.4 illustrates, cost-minimizing producers will be attempting to substitute capital and labour for resources along their isoquants. As a result, Z will be declining over time and capital-labour costs (C) will be subject to upward pressure as resource products become more capital-labour intensive and less resources intensive. This kind of substitution is a way of alleviating scarcity yet it causes C to rise *more* rapidly than if such substitutions could not be effected. It should also be noted that the net price per unit of final product ($p = p'Z$) will be rising less rapidly than the net price per unit of resources (p') as the substitution process goes on. In the simple Hotelling model, for example, with p' rising at a rate equal to the rate of interest (see chapter 2) p will be rising at a rate slower than the rate of interest if Z is falling through time.

Econometric studies have shown that substitution between capital-labour and resources in response to changes in their relative prices is an important way of moderating the effect of scarcity on product prices. If C is used as a scarcity measure, the substitution process is misinterpreted as contributing to scarcity rather than as alleviating it.

Examination of resource cost-price trends in the 1970s has moved away from use of the unit cost measure C. Increasingly, economists examine the other two measures mentioned above: net prices of resources (p) and final product prices (π).

The newer emphasis on *net price* coincided with the renewed development of optimal nonrenewable resources models in the 1960s and 1970s in the Hotelling tradition (chapter 2). There are several difficulties with the use of net prices as scarcity indicators, however. The really crucial problem

FIGURE 4.4

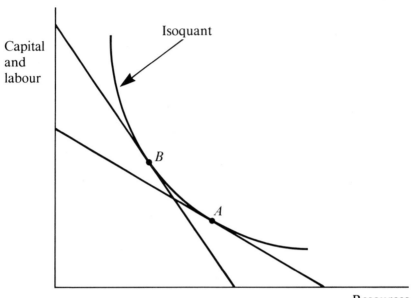

Cost-minimizing resource producers seek tangency positions between isoquants and isocosts. An increase in the net price of the resource (p^1) relative to the price of the capital–labour bundle causes a substitution of capital–labour for the resource as the cost-minimizing producer moves from A to B.

is that it is not clear whether impending exhaustion is to be signalled by *rising* or *falling* net prices. In the simple Hotelling model, net prices rise (at the rate of interest r), which signals eventual exhaustion of a homogeneous fixed stock. When the stock is low, the *level* of the net price is higher over the whole extraction horizon. But the *rate* at which the net price increases is the same (equal to r) no matter how small or large the stock of resources. To further complicate matters, when exhaustion occurs through rising extraction costs (incomplete exhaustion), the net price tends to *zero* as the last high-cost resources are used. The net price is, therefore, *falling* on average in the incomplete exhaustion model. When resource use involves transitions from one fixed stock resource to subsequent lower-quality fixed stock resources (Figures 2.4 and 2.5), the net price rises *within* each resource grade and falls as one resource grade *replaces* the previous grade. It is clear that, depending on how exhaustion is modelled, impending scarcity could be associated with rising or falling net prices!

There are further problems with the use of net prices as scarcity indicators. Net prices are seldom observable as statistical series. Whether or not such series can be estimated with any accuracy is a moot question. To do so, one must subtract marginal resource production costs (C) from resource product prices (π). Small percentage errors in the estimation of C or π could lead to large percentage errors in the estimation of p. It should also be noted that the use of net price as a scarcity indicator assumes that nonrenewable resources are being utilized in accordance with the optimal models described in chapter 2. If, instead, resources are simply brought into production whenever their product prices cover marginal production costs, net prices tend to approach zero, so that indications of scarcity under actual conditions of resource use must be sought elsewhere. The combination of theoretical and practical problems with the net price makes this measure virtually useless as a scarcity indicator.

The Product Price Measure

Partly as a result of the deficiencies of the net price approach, most recent studies of scarcity have placed the emphasis on *resource product prices* (π). The usual procedure here is to judge scarcity by examining the long-term trend of natural resources product prices relative to the prices of other goods and services. As previously mentioned, this was one of the methods used by Barnett and Morse to test their weak scarcity hypothesis. The approach was originated in an earlier study of deflated copper products prices undertaken by Herfindahl (1959).

Figures 4.5 through 4.8 illustrate long-run deflated resources products prices for four important metallic minerals. Each figure shows the price of the resource product in nominal terms (U.S. cents per pound) and in real terms (U.S. cents per pound divided by the U.S. wholesale price index). These series for copper, aluminum, nickel, and zinc are fairly typical of the behaviour of real prices of metallic minerals over the long term. There is a great deal of short-run volatility in all the series. In most cases long-run deflated mineral prices seem to have been declining or relatively constant for nearly a century. In some cases recent years show a slight tendency for real minerals prices to increase. As might be expected, different interpretations of the data have been advanced. Barnett and Morse concluded, on the basis of the data up to the late 1950s, that

> [s]hort-term movements aside, the trend of relative mineral prices has been level since the last quarter of the nineteenth century. This does not support the weak scarcity hypothesis. [13]

Subsequent investigations have questioned this conclusion. Some authors have preferred to take a neutral position, arguing that mineral prices data do not provide enough information to accept or reject a long-term scarcity hypothesis (Smith 1979). For some minerals such as alumi-

FIGURE 4.5

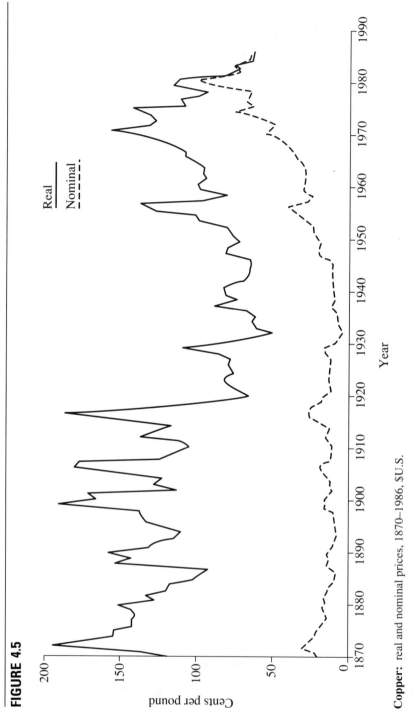

Copper: real and nominal prices, 1870–1986, $U.S.

Source: M. Slade, *Pricing of Metals* (Kingston: Queen's University Centre for Resource Studies, 1988).

FIGURE 4.6

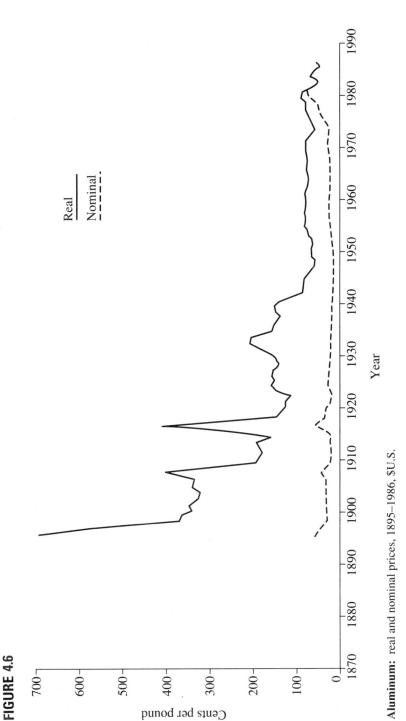

Aluminum: real and nominal prices, 1895–1986, $U.S.

Source: M. Slade, *Pricing of Metals* (Kingston: Queen's University Centre for Resource Studies, 1988).

FIGURE 4.7

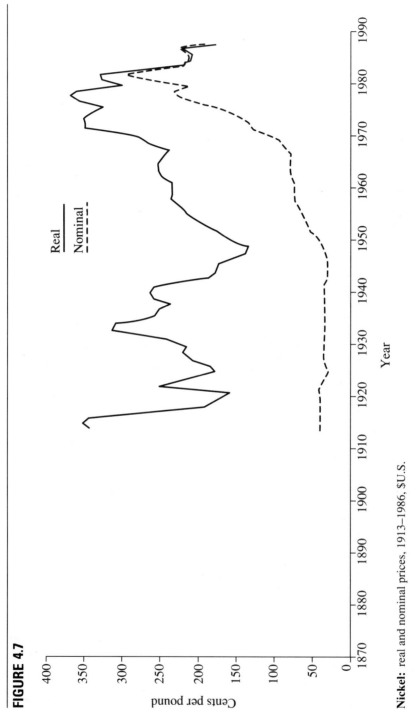

Nickel: real and nominal prices, 1913–1986, $U.S.

Source: M. Slade, *Pricing of Metals* (Kingston: Queen's University Centre for Resource Studies, 1988).

FIGURE 4.8

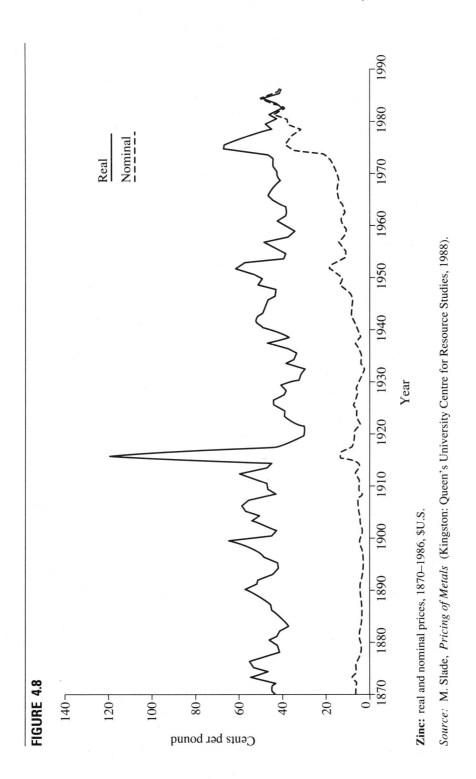

Zinc: real and nominal prices, 1870–1986, $U.S.

Source: M. Slade, *Pricing of Metals* (Kingston: Queen's University Centre for Resource Studies, 1988).

num, downward real price trends have become much weaker in the 1960s and 1970s. For others, such as copper and nickel, the data up to the mid-1970s seemed to suggest the onset of a rising trend in real product prices. This led to a new theory of real product price movements in which a U-shaped behaviour pattern was proposed (Slade 1982). This theory advances the argument that

> ...fitted linear-trend models underestimate relative prices of all the major metals and fuels in the last few years of the 1870–1978 period, because prices of all commodities have passed the minimum points on their fitted U-shaped curves and have begun to increase. Therefore, if scarcity is measured by relative prices, the evidence indicates that nonrenewable natural-resource commodities are becoming scarce. [14]

It is hard to judge the general validity of the U-shaped relative price hypothesis. Slade's ordinary least-squares (OLS) results revealed very little difference between linear and quadratic (U-shaped) relative price trends in terms of statistical goodness of fit. Rising real resource prices in the 1970s have turned into falling real prices in the 1980s for many commodities. On the other hand, for the geochemically scarce metals at least, there are reasons to believe that technological progress cannot permanently offset depletion. For energy resources, rising relative prices in the 1970s were so strongly affected by the success of the Organization of Petroleum Exporting Countries (OPEC) cartel in raising world oil prices that relative price trends cannot be used to infer true scarcity as opposed to artificial (monopolistic) scarcity over this period. In the 1980s, real oil prices have declined with the collapse of the OPEC cartel. The monopoly-cartel problem was recognized by Herfindahl (1959) in his study of real copper prices. He took pains to construct a copper price series from which periodic increases owing to cartel activities were removed.

The purpose of physical and cost-price scarcity measures is to attempt to predict the future availability of nonrenewable resources. Looking back at the theories of exhaustion discussed in chapter 2, how do product price measures relate to theories of nonrenewable resource use? If resource use is short-sighted such that the extraction sector does not factor user cost into current decisions, then net prices are expected to be zero. In this case, competitively determined product prices simply track marginal extraction costs and the deflated product price measure captures the movement of marginal extraction cost relative to marginal cost in non-resource sectors. Impending sudden resource limits will not show up. In the simple Hotelling model, for example, extraction cost and product price would remain constant right up to the moment of exhaustion. Gradual resource limits (the modified Hotelling model) will be revealed by rising product prices (if technological progress is unable to offset the impact of depletion on marginal cost). If the extraction sector is far-sighted and resources command optimal net prices, product price movements capture changes in marginal extraction cost and user cost (the net price). In this case, current (consumer) prices will be affected by both current extraction costs and impending scarcity. Resource product prices must rise in the latter stages of exhaustion to squeeze off demand at choke prices.

Evidence on the existence of physical supplies and recent cost-price trends constitute useful information—if scarcity looms, supplies should be getting tighter and real prices should be rising in anticipation of future shortages. Whether or not supplies really *are* running out or becoming more costly to locate and extract is a hard question to answer on the basis of the existing data, however. So much depends upon technological progress that scientific grounds cannot be found to support either an optimistic or a pessimistic conclusion on the scarcity issue.

▌ SCARCITY AND THE CANADIAN ECONOMY

Effects of Reduced Domestic Resource Supplies

The potential effect of resource scarcity on the Canadian economy depends on the adequacy of the Canadian resources base and on the future course of world resource products prices relative to prices in general. If, for example, the real prices of resource products on world markets remain relatively constant while Canada's marginal production costs increase, Canadian production of resources products can be expected to decline in the future. The long-term adverse results for Canada of declining resources production was discussed using the Boadway-Treddenick (BT) and the Chambers-Gordon (CG) models in chapter 1. A decline in natural resource production would involve the disappearance of economic rents that could have been realized with a more plentiful resource endowment (CG). The long-run structure of the Canadian economy would also shift from extractive production to non-extractive production. The changing structure of the economy involves reduced nonrenewable resources exports. This could produce a terms-of-trade effect on Canada by increasing prices of minerals on world markets.[15]

In order to examine the terms-of-trade and rent arguments more closely, assume that Canada produces resource commodities and manufactures using labour alone for manufacturing production (Y) and a combination of labour and natural resource endowments for the production of resource commodities (X). (Capital is completely mobile and earns a fixed rate of return on international markets.) This is the basic structure of the CG model. In chapter 1, the question posed was: what would happen if Canada lost its entire natural resource endowment? Referring to Figure 4.9, the loss of our entire resource endowment would shift the Canadian economy from point a to point c on the production possibilities frontier (PPF) just as in Figure 1.6. Suppose, however, that Canada's resource endowment falls but it does not fall to zero. In this case, the PPF shifts inward as shown in Figure 4.9 showing that if we used all our labour endowment to produce manufactures (Y) we could still produce the same amount of manufactures (point c) but if we used all our labour and the remaining stock of natural resources to produce natural resource goods (X) we would suffer a fall in resource commodity production from point d to point e. At point a, Canada is maximizing its national income at international prices P_x and P_y for the two goods (see the efficiency discussion in chapter 1). Provided international prices are unchanged, Canada maximizes its national income after the decline in its resource endowment by producing at point f. Analogously to Figure 1.6, the loss in moving from point a to point f is a loss of economic rent on the missing resources. Figure 4.10 illustrates the inward shift of the PPF as an increase in the marginal cost ($MC = -\Delta Y/\Delta X$) of producing natural resource goods. The economic rent area over the MC curve and under the price line (P_x/P_y) declines by the shaded amount.

Suppose, however, that the price ratio P_x/P_y is not independent of Canada's exports and imports on world markets, i.e., Canada is not a price-taker on world markets. Suppose, in particular, that the reduced supply of Canadian natural resource goods on world markets after the fall in our natural resource endowments leads to a rise in P_x so that the slope of the income line P_x/P_y becomes steeper in Figure 4.9. Canada's new production position is at point f' rather than at point f and Canadians can now consume along the income line $f'g$. Assuming that Canada exports resource commodities and imports manufactures, our old consumption combination was somewhere along ab (see also Figure 1.4). If our old consumption point was between g and a on the line ab, we will be worse off after the terms-of-trade change. But, surprisingly, if we had previously consumed along ab between b and g, the new situation is better than the old one. We have actually gained from losing some of our resource endowment! This seems strange. How is it possible?

The possibility that an economy could gain from losing some of its factor endowment or, conversely, could lose by an increase in its factor endowments, is actually a fairly well-known proposition in international trade theory and has a simple explanation.[16] At point a, the Canadian economy could have gained by withdrawing natural resource commodity output from world markets. Moving to a production point between a and c would have raised the world price of resource goods and enabled the Canadian economy as a whole to gain by exploiting its monopoly power over world resource commodity prices. But, by assumption, Canada is *not* exploiting its monopoly power at point a. When the country loses some of its natural resource endowment and goes to point f, the accompanying fall in Canadian resource commodity production acts like the exercise of monopoly power to improve Canada's terms of trade. Of course there is no guarantee that the "right" amount of natural resource stocks are being

FIGURE 4.9

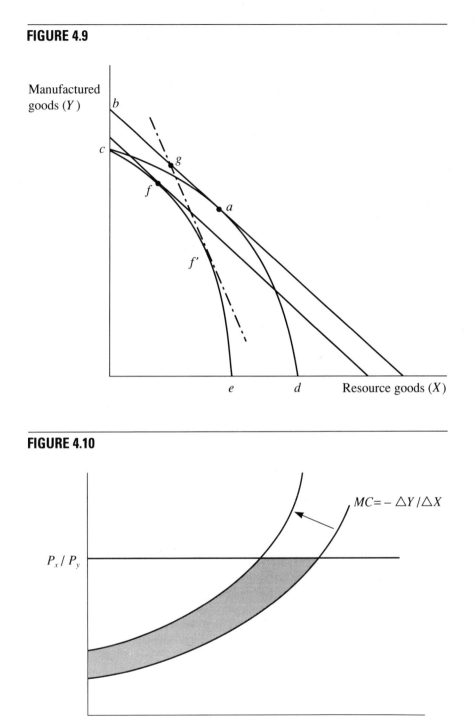

FIGURE 4.10

subtracted from our endowment so there is no guarantee that potential welfare will increase. But it will if the shift in the PPF is as shown in Figure 4.9 and the old consumption point was along bg. Allowing for the loss of rent, the terms-of-trade improvement resulting from Canada's decline in resource production can be welfare-improving.[17]

Does Canada have enough control over the world prices of at least some natural resources commodities to make the practice of supply restriction profitable for us? Could Canadians choose to exercise such monopoly power if it existed? For most resource commodities, Canada's market shares in world output are not large enough to confer significant monopolistic control over world prices (Caragata 1984). There are exceptions though. Until the 1970s, Canada's dominant role in nickel production conferred monopoly power on the International Nickel Company. This has been eroded by the appearance of new producers on the world nickel scene in the 1970s and 1980s. The Saskatchewan-based potash industry, the Saskatchewan government, and New Mexico producers were able to use supply management policies to raise potash prices for a period of time in the early 1970s. During the same period, the Canadian government participated in a cartel to raise prices of uranium exports to the U.S. Recent observers view these market-power episodes in minerals sectors as exceptional. For the most part, both industry and government oppose participation in cartels and international supply management schemes, partly because they seem unlikely to succeed and partly because they invite retaliation from foreign governments and minerals consumers (Webb and Zacher 1988). It has been claimed that the use of a lumber export tax by the federal government in response to U.S. protectionist demands in the late 1980s may have raised U.S. lumber prices and offered monopoly gains to Canada (Boyd and Krutilla 1987).

If world prices of most resource commodities cannot be influenced significantly by Canadian output levels then, in most cases the loss of Canadian resource endowments and output from world markets affects Canada through losses of economic rent, as predicted by the CG model of chapter 1. Whether or not such losses due to declining resource production in the Canadian economy are likely depends upon an assessment of Canada's ability to continue the process of discovering and developing resources at costs comparable to worldwide costs in the future.

Consider minerals as an example. The cost of minerals from new mines relative to minerals prices determines whether or not declining output from old mines can be economically replaced by output from new mines. Exploration costs, ore grades, the cost of capital, wage settlements, transportation, technical changes, and taxation, all enter into incentives to convert mineral resources into mineral products. The size of the physical resource base is just one of many influences on cost. The approach taken at Energy, Mines, and Resources Canada (EMR) is to examine the exploration cost of establishing new mineral reserves to replace depleted reserves and to measure the quality of mineral reserves from an extraction cost perspective. One way of measuring the effectiveness of exploration activity is by the (constant) dollar gross value of minerals discovered and produced per (constant) dollar of exploration spending. Using this measure for the post–World War II period, Cranstone (1988) has found that exceptional exploration successes characterized the 1950s and that there may have been a slight decline in success rates in the late 1970s and early 1980s:

> ...it is reasonable to conclude...that after the remarkable exploration successes of the mid-1950s, the value of metals discovered per dollar of exploration expenditure was fairly steady from then on, certainly until the end of 1977. It would be premature to conclude that the lower values since 1978 are clear evidence of a permanent long-term increase in Canadian ore discovery costs.[18]

In an article that challenges the assumption of declining ore grades over time, Martin and Jen (1988) find that most Canadian minerals are not subject to serious depletion effects at all. For many minerals, average ore grades have not declined significantly and where lower grade ores are being used, it is often the case that these lower grades exist in larger and more accessible deposits than ores extracted earlier in time and are therefore cheaper to mine. In a number of cases, exploration results simply do not turn up ore deposits in descending order of grade as assumed in the modified Hotelling model of chapter 2. Referring to Canadian mining experience up to 1980, EMR researchers stated that

> ...sufficient geological evidence exists to justify confidence that Canada's extensive landmass will continue to offer many opportunities for discovering new deposits and developing new reserves of metals. Certainly within this century, no fundamental metal supply problems are in sight that would be the result of a lack of resources of these metals. ... Any questions concerning metal supply adequacy in the foreseeable future are related not to the physical limits of mineral resources, but to economic incentives that would maintain the flow of metal supplies from those resources through the creation of new reserves and production capability.[19]

This optimistic assessment of Canada's mineral potential appears to be valid a decade later. Martin and Jen conclude their more recent analysis of Canada's mineral prospects with the following observations:

> For Canada, the record of mining since 1939, rounded off with what can be expected in 1989, forms a fifty-year overview which suggests that exploration geologists have managed to continue discovering deposits comparable in quality to previous discoveries. Thus, the question of "when Canada will run out of good ores" seems premature and can safely be set aside until some time in the twenty-first century.[20]

FIGURE 4.11

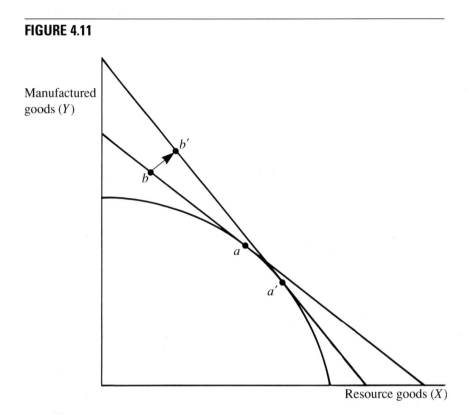

Effects of Rising World Resource Prices

A second way in which resource scarcity can affect Canada is if other countries experience higher resource extraction costs. This type of scarcity would lead to rising real (deflated) prices of world mineral products as discussed in the previous section. What effects would rising real mineral products prices have on the Canadian economy? The answer to this question depends upon whether the mineral products experiencing real price increases are exported or imported by Canada. If exported minerals experience a price increase, there is an improvement in Canada's terms of trade. Referring to Figure 4.11, before the increased price of the exported resource product (X), Canada produces at point a on its PPF and consumes at point b. The increase in the world price of the resource product alters Canada's production point to a' and opens up new consumption opportunities beyond—to the northeast of—point b. Rising real prices of exported resource commodities would, therefore, be beneficial to Canada. Of course the reverse would be true for imported resource commodities. Continuing domestic resources abundance combined with rising relative prices for resource goods on world markets would improve the potential welfare of Canadians unless global scarcities are focused on specific resource goods that Canada imports.

■ TECHNOLOGICAL PROGRESS *VERSUS* DEPLETION

In both chapter 2 and the present chapter, the history and prospects of nonrenewable resources use have been viewed as a contest between technological progress and depletion. Declining real minerals prices over most of the twentieth century seem to suggest that technological progress has prevailed over depletion in the past. The chances of this trend continuing are hard to assess, though it now seems clear that the geochemically scarce metals present technological barriers that are likely to prevent the transition to resources with very low concentrations of these minerals.

Depletion is a complex phenomenon involving at least three factors that can contribute to cost increases:

1. As individual deposits are exhausted, the process of discovery may become more costly if the larger and more accessible ore bodies tend to be found first.
2. Once located, deposits tend to show declining ore grades over time. Richer deposits are usually utilized before poorer deposits.
3. New deposits may exhibit different basic characteristics relative to old deposits that involve higher extraction costs (oil from tar sands as opposed to conventional reservoirs, for example).

In each of these cases, technological change can come to the rescue, holding costs down over time. Consider exploration first. In the late nineteenth century, most discoveries were made by individual prospectors relying on surface features to identify ore bodies. Modern exploration techniques involve geochemical and geophysical approaches previously unknown. In the 1950s Canadian mineral exploration produced many important discoveries as a result of the first serious use of modern exploration methods (Cranstone 1988). Ground and airborne electromagnetic geophysical methods permitted a much more thorough examination of Canadian mineral potential and represented a key technological advance in the discovery process with resulting reductions in the average amount of exploration expenditure needed for a new discovery. Between 1957 and 1962, Canadian minerals exploration was somewhat less successful than in the early and mid-1950s and depletion effects—reduced discoveries per dollar of exploration expenditure—tended to outweigh technological advances. Since 1963 the economics of exploration has improved again owing to the application of geological models for the selection of promising areas and the systematic ranking of potential mineral-bearing locations. The results of Cranstone's (1988) study of exploration costs, referred to in the previous section, noted the unusually successful performance of the 1950s and slightly lower values of minerals per dollar of exploration in the 1980s along with the overall conclusion that improving exploration methods have been important in maintaining Canadian mineral supplies. It should also be noted that over the period from 1960 to 1980, each dollar of exploration expenditure was responsible for about $150 in gross value of metals discovered. Even allowing for a required rate of return on exploration spending, exploration is a relatively small fraction of the price of minerals products.

The most important effect of depletion on minerals costs involves extraction rather than discovery costs. A decline in ore grades means that mining and concentrating costs rise. If, for example, ore grades decline to half their previous values, unchanged mining methods means that the same factor inputs will produce about half the previous quantity of metal at the pithead. Some mineral resources have experienced large historical declines in grade. Taking copper as an example, typical ores in 1700 were about 13 percent copper. By 1900, world copper ore grades had fallen to 2.5–5.0 percent copper content. Current world grades have declined to less than 1 percent copper as a world average with lower grades in use where co-products and by-products are recovered along with copper. From 1960 to 1976, average world copper grades fell by approximately one-half (Table 2.1). Real copper prices fell more or less continuously from 1900 to 1940 (Figure 4.5) despite declining grades.

Two key technical changes were responsible for real price declines despite falling copper grades. First, underground vein mining of copper was replaced by open-pit mining of large copper sulphide (porphyry) deposits. Open-pit mining requires excavation rather than the sinking of shafts, and excavation technology has improved rapidly with the use of larger shovels, bigger trucks, and other advances in earth-moving equipment. Second, the development of froth flotation permitted increased metallic copper recovery from sulphide ores in the concentration process. These two technological advances were substantially complete by the 1940s. Further declines in copper ore grades will require additional technical advances. Whether or not such advances can offset the effect of depletion in the immediate future is hard to tell. The presence of a mineralogical barrier at a copper grade of 0.1 percent seems to ensure that depletion must eventually triumph over technical progress in this industry. With a fixed technology, there is an inverse relationship between mineral product prices and cutoff grades. At higher prices profitable extraction can proceed with poorer deposits. Cessation of technical change would lead to rising real mineral prices as the cutoff grade is extended to poorer and poorer deposits. But the rate of increase of mineral products prices would not be as rapid as the rate of decline in cutoff grades over time. This is so because

...lower ore grades impinge mostly on mining and concentrating costs, and only marginally on smelting, refining, and marketing costs when expressed per unit of weight of metal.[21]

The third aspect of depletion involves transitions, not to lower grades of deposits that are otherwise similar, but to mineral products sources that are different in kind from previously used resources. Such transitions were noted in the context of the Nordhaus energy model in chapter 2. In the case of transitions to new types of resource deposits, technical progress involves something different from learning how to deal with deposits with gradually diminishing mineral concentration. New methods have to be found to keep the costs of entirely new sources comparable to the costs of existing sources if real product prices are not to increase. Over the past decade, the extraction of petroleum products from tar sands has been viewed as a method of supplementing reservoirs of conventional crude oil. Most world resources of oil in tar sands are in Canada, and two extraction plants (Syncrude Canada and Suncor Oil Sands) operating on the Athabaska field are the only two producers in the world. Despite tax concessions, faltering world oil prices in the early 1980s prevented the appearance of a third producer (Alsands). An increase in world oil prices or cost-reducing technical changes in oil sands extraction in the 1990s will be required to make new tar sands production competitive with conventional petroleum sources.

■ ADAPTING TO SCARCITY

A Link Between Scarcity and Demand?

When assessing the future outcome of the race between depletion and technical progress, it is important to recognize that depletion rates depend upon the rate of growth of production of the resource. In chapter 2 equation (11) showed the effect on unit production cost of the joint action of depletion and technological progress. Repeating that relationship,

$$dC/dt = -C_x q + \partial C/\partial t \tag{3}$$

If the entire equation is divided through by the current cost level,

$$(dC/dt)/C = (-C_x q)/C + (\partial C/\partial t)/C \tag{4}$$

Suppose technological progress proceeds so that unit production costs at constant grade decline at a steady rate of (say) 3 percent per annum. In that case, $(\partial C/\partial t)/C = -0.03$. Suppose further that each 1 million tonnes of the mineral produced increases unit production cost by a constant percentage, say 0.025 percent. Then $-C_x/C = 0.00025$. If current production is 200 million tonnes of metal, the depletion term $(-C_x q)/C = 0.05$ and the rate of current cost increase $(dC/dt)/C$ is $0.05 - 0.03 = 0.02$ or 2 percent in equation (4). Depletion is outpacing technical progress and causing a 2 percent (annual) rate of unit cost increase. This will be reflected in rising real product prices. Depending upon the elasticity of demand for the mineral product, consumption should decline over time. If the production rate declines, technical progress may be able to keep pace with depletion. If production (q) drops to 120 million tonnes per year, the same values for the depletion term $(-C_x/C = 0.00025)$ and the same rate of cost reduction through technological progress lead to a stable trend in unit costs: $(dC/dt)/C = 0$ in equations (3) and (4). The inverse relationship between product price and consumption (= depletion) means that the race between technical change and depletion contains an equilibrating feature which tends to slow down depletion when unit costs rise and *vice versa*.

There is some evidence that mineral commodities experiencing the most rapid increases in real prices exhibit the slowest rates of growth of consumption. Petersen and Maxwell (1979) have observed that

> ...there is generally an inverse relation between the growth rates of production and of mineral prices expressed in constant dollars...if a commodity is geologically scarce or technologically costly to obtain, its price rise will spur substitution and reduce consumption.[22]

The rate of depletion is thereby reduced so that technological progress has a better chance of holding down cost increases. New discoveries need not be made as rapidly, resort to poorer deposit grades is delayed, and the use of less familiar kinds of resources can be postponed.

Demand Responses to Scarcity

The preceding observation that depletion can be reduced by slowing down consumption of mineral products leads naturally to a discussion of various methods of adjusting to resources scarcity. In general, resource depletion can be expected to slow down if economic growth slows down, if substitutes for depletable resources can be found in the production of capital goods, intermediate, and final products, and if larger quantities of previously extracted resources can be recycled. The gradual shift in Western economies toward increased consumption of services relative to goods means that demands for nonrenewable resources tend to grow more slowly than GNP. It remains true, of course, that declining GNP growth rates will reduce the growth rates of resources demands and slow down depletion. Reduced depletion is one of the advantages claimed by advocates of slower economic growth along with the benefits of reduced population increases and reduced environmental costs. Resource scarcities, signalled by increasing real prices for mineral products, could have the effect of slowing economic growth and moderating depletion though the exact mechanisms are difficult to specify. Substitution effects are likely to be more important. One of the criticisms of the "doomsday" models was that they failed to account for the effects of rising relative prices of resource products on the quantities of resources demanded. As the observations of Petersen and Maxwell (1979) mentioned in the previous section imply, resources experiencing above-average increases in real product prices over time are also likely to experience the slowest rates of consumption growth. Among renewable resources, lumber is a product that has experienced continuous real price increases throughout the twentieth century. As a result, the consumption of lumber has been held down to an important extent by the substitution of other building products. Similar kinds of substitution effects in consumption followed the sharp increases in world oil prices in the 1970s.

A great deal of resource consumption is concentrated in specific industries. Kay and Mirrlees (1975) used an input-output approach to identify the major industrial users of major mineral resources. They discovered that the construction and motor vehicle industries in the U.K. were the most intensive users of mineral resources, being responsible for 50 percent of British steel consumption, 45 percent of zinc consumption, 40 percent of lead consumption, and 38 percent of aluminum and copper use. Economies in mineral resource use seem to focus on particular products. Thus, for example, rising real prices for lead could significantly reduce consumption of lead if cars come to be designed without lead batteries. These kinds of substitution effects are highly specific to the design of particular products. The more extensive are substitution possibilities, the greater will be the elasticity of demand for mineral products and for the underlying resources. Real price increases for resources also promote the recycling of old materials. In some cases, used commodities and materials are relatively high-grade sources of resources. For example,

[c]urrently junked automobiles weigh about 4,000 pounds (1,800 kilograms) and contain about 80 percent iron and steel. Certainly the discovery of a deposit of iron ore...yielding half that value in metallic iron would be welcomed. Instead, taconite containing 30 percent or less iron is mined and beneficiated.[23]

Increasing costs for newly mined material will promote the substitution of old material such as the junked automobiles for new ore deposits with an accompanying decline in depletion. The demand curve for newly mined resources becomes more elastic, since it is a *net* demand curve, consisting of the quantity of metal demanded at each price minus the quantity of metal supplied from recycled products (Figure 4.12). Since recycling can never involve 100 percent recovery of metals contained in the old products, the position of SS tends to shift to the left over time in Figure 4.12 relative to DD at a constant price level and technology. Still, with large stocks of recyclable materials and high recovery rates, SS can make a significant long-run contribution to total mineral supplies. In the

FIGURE 4.12

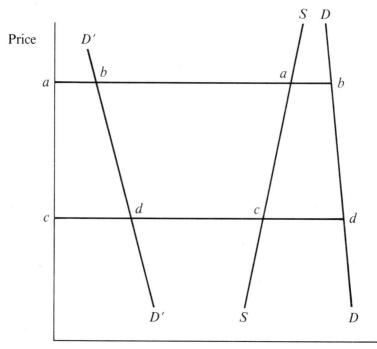

DD = Total quantity of metal demanded.
SS = Total recycled supply of metal.
$D'D'$ = Net demand for newly mined metal (DD minus SS).

extreme case of 100 percent recycling—a goal comparable to producing a frictionless machine—a constant level of consumption would require no newly mined material, while increasing consumption levels would require only enough new mining to make up the difference between each period's consumption and the consumption of the previous period.

   When discussing substitution and recycling, it is important to include the effects of technological change. In the previous section, the impact of technological change was stressed as a mechanism holding down exploration and extraction costs as depletion proceeds. But depletion rates can also be reduced if technological progress brings forth substitutes for resource-intensive products that were previously unknown or brings in new methods of recycling previously mined materials. These kinds of changes will shift the net demand curve for mineral products in Figure 4.12 ($D'D'$) to the left, reducing requirements for newly mined resources at each price level. Though technological change is usually modelled as an exogenous force in economic models (see chapter 2), new cost-reducing discoveries may also be induced by changing relative scarcities. If the real price of a mineral product increases, for example, this will initiate research and development directed to reducing costs of providing newly mined resources, locating products that can be used as substitutes for the resource product, and expanding the role of recycled materials. Successful research on these fronts will reduce the impact of depletion on the real prices of minerals and slow the rate of depletion itself.

■ CONCLUSIONS

The attempt to anticipate the adequacy of nonrenewable resources over future decades (and even centuries) is partly an extrapolation of the past and partly a collation of the best possible information about the future. Past trends in scarcity indicators, possibly weighted to stress recent developments, suggest that technological progress combined with substitution and recycling have allowed the real costs of mineral products to decline, though the rate of decline may have slowed down over the past decade or two. Slade (1982) has extended this observation to a U-shaped hypothesis in which the cost-increasing effects of depletion may be starting to overwhelm technological progress, leading to real price increase. As discussed earlier, the evidence to support a conclusion that real mineral prices have begun an upward trend is still tentative, but it is clear that some of the earlier optimism of Barnett and Morse (1963) has been tempered by subsequent developments.

Direct evidence on the future adequacy of nonrenewable resources rests chiefly on available geological information. The fixed stock or finite world assumption that produces *inevitable* shortages has been undercut by geological estimates of huge quantities of nonrenewable resources in the earth's crustal mass (Table 4.1). The optimism that is engendered by those estimates is, in turn, undercut by the arguments advanced by Skinner and others that a large fraction of resources in the crustal mass—particularly resources of geochemically scarce metals—will remain permanently inaccessible to the mining industry. For some metals of great current economic importance, finite limits (or mineralogical barriers) must enter into our calculations. For the abundant metals, large ultimate resources still do not guarantee future adequacy: important technological advances will still be necessary to deal with inevitable grade declines. For energy resources, fixed stock assumptions apply to oil and gas resources (Table 4.2) and other fossil fuels, though the potential for coal is very large. Transition to more abundant nonrenewable fuel sources, such as uranium, as breeder fuel and to the virtually unlimited energy potential of hydrogen fusion and solar power, will be events of the next century. The breeder technology is in the experimental stage and fusion remains elusive. Again, technological breakthroughs are the key.

There is no reason to believe that any future increases in real non-renewable resources prices will occur suddenly. If technological progress proves unable to deal with declining grades and transitions to new resources at constant or declining real prices, the resulting scarcities will certainly be signalled by the price system as the problems unfold, allowing adaptations to be undertaken. Resources scarcity is a matter of problems and challenges, not a matter of impending disaster.

▮ NOTES

1. Energy, Mines and Resources, *Mineral Policy: A Discussion Paper* (Ottawa: 1981), p. 21.
2. J. Zwartendyk, "Mineral Wealth—How Should It Be Expressed?," *Canadian Mining Journal* (April 1973): 44–52. Other resource classifications and their relationships are discussed in A. Hussain, "The Reserve-Resource Spectrum," *CIM Bulletin* (February 1979): 31–37.
3. J. Forrester, *World Dynamics* (Cambridge, Mass.: Wright-Allen, 1971); D.H. Meadows, et al., *The Limits to Growth* (New York: Universe Books, 1972).
4. D. Brooks, "Minerals: An Expanding or a Dwindling Resource," *Energy, Mines and Resources Mineral Bulletin* 134 (1973): 4.
5. W. Nordhaus, *The Efficient Use of Energy Resources* (New Haven: Yale University Press, 1979).
6. G.O. Barney (Study Director), *The Global 2000 Report to the President of the United States* (New York: Pergamon, 1980), p. 187
7. Ibid., 189.
8. Ibid., pp. 193–94. The breeder technology generates additional nuclear fuel as a by-product of power generation.
9. B.J. Skinner, "A Second Iron Age Ahead?," *American Scientist* 64 (May/June 1976); D. P. Harris and B.J. Skinner, "The Assessment of Long-term Supplies of Minerals," in V.K. Smith and J. Krutilla, eds., *Explorations in Natural Resource Economics* (Baltimore: Johns Hopkins, 1982); R.B. Gordon, et al., *Toward a New Iron Age?* (Cambridge, Mass.: Harvard University Press, 1987).
10. Skinner, "A Second Iron Age": 26. Reprinted by permission of *American Scientist*, journal of Sigma Xi, The Scientific Research Society.
11. Ibid.
12. H.J. Barnett and C. Morse, *Scarcity and Growth: The Economics of Natural Resource Availability* (Baltimore: Johns Hopkins, 1963), p. 244.
13. Ibid., 212–13.
14. M.E. Slade, "Trends in Natural Resource Commodity Prices: An Analysis of the Time Domain," *Journal of Environmental Economics and Management* 9 (1982): 136.
15. In what follows, we will ignore the factor proportions effect discussed in chapter 1 on the assumption that capital is perfectly mobile internationally.

16. J. Bhagwati, "Immiserizing Growth: A Geometrical Note," *Review of Economic Studies* 25 (1958): 201–5.
17. There are income distribution issues to be considered here as well. The increase in resource commodity prices raises profits in the resources extraction process in Canada while, at the same time, increasing prices to Canadian consumers of resources products. The net gain is positive because the increases in profits are larger than the losses to Canadian consumers.
18. D. Cranstone, "The Canadian Mineral Discovery Process since World War II," in J. Tilton, R. Eggert, and H. Landsberg, eds., *World Mineral Exploration: Trends and Economic Issues* (Washington: Resources for the Future, 1988), p. 295. See also B. Mackenzie and R. Woodall, "Economic Productivity of Base Metal Exploration in Australia and Canada," in Tilton, et al., eds., *World Mineral Exploration*.
19. H. Martin, J. McIntosh, and J. Zwartendyk, "Monitoring Canada's Mine Production," *CIM Bulletin* (July 1979): 44.
20. H. Martin and L.S. Jen, "Are Ore Grades Declining? The Canadian Experience, 1939–89," in Tilton, et al., eds., *World Mineral Exploration*, p. 444.
21. U. Petersen and R. Maxwell, "Historical Mineral Production and Price Trends," *Mining Engineering* (January 1979): 32.
22. Ibid.: 33.
23. D. Brobst, "Fundamental Concepts for the Analysis of Resource Availability," in V.K. Smith, ed., *Scarcity and Growth Reconsidered* (Baltimore: Johns Hopkins, 1979), pp. 129–30.

∎ FURTHER READING

Readings on the future availability of resources include

Barney, G.O. (Study Director). *The Global 2000 Report to the President of the United States*. New York: Pergamon, 1980, Chap. 11 on fuel minerals and Chap. 12 on nonfuel minerals.

Brobst, D.A. "Fundamental Concepts for the Analysis of Resource Availability." In V.K. Smith, ed., *Scarcity and Growth Reconsidered*. Baltimore: Johns Hopkins, 1979.

Harris, D.P., and B.J. Skinner. "The Assessment of Long-Term Supplies of Minerals." In V.K. Smith and J. Krutilla, eds., *Explorations in Natural Resource Economics*. Baltimore: Johns Hopkins, 1982.

Skinner, B.J. "A Second Iron Age Ahead?" *American Scientist* 64 (May–June 1976).

Tilton, J.E., R.G. Eggert, and H. Landsberg, eds. *World Mineral Exploration: Trends and Economic Issues*. Washington: Resources for the Future, 1988. This volume contains very useful studies of Canadian mineral supply by Cranstone; Martin and Jen; and Mackenzie and Woodall.

Important articles on cost-price indicators of scarcity and the race between depletion and technical progress are

Brown, G.M., and B. Field. "Implications of Alternative Measures of Natural Resource Scarcity." *Journal of Political Economy* (April 1978).

Mackenzie, B.W. "Looking for the Improbable Needle in a Haystack: The Economics of Base Metal Exploration in Canada." *Canadian Institute of Mining and Metallurgy Bulletin (CIM Bulletin)* (May 1981). Reprinted in F. Anderson, ed., *Selected Readings in Mineral Economics*. New York: Pergamon, 1987.

Petersen, U., and R.S. Maxwell. "Historical Mineral Production and Price Trends." *Mining Engineering* (January 1979).

Slade, M.E. "Trends in Natural-Resource Commodity Prices: An Analysis of the Time Domain." *Journal of Environmental Economics and Management* 9 (June 1982).

A valuable survey of scarcity issues with a large bibliography is

Peterson, F., and A.C. Fisher. "The Exploitation of Extractive Resources: A Survey." *Economic Journal* 87 (December 1977). The issues discussed in this chapter are treated by Peterson and Fisher on pp. 704–10.

The September 1990 issue of *Scientific American* contains a valuable collection of articles on energy alternatives for the future in which environmental issues are integrated with supply issues.

CHAPTER FIVE

RENT CAPTURE

AND RESOURCE

TAXATION

∎ INTRODUCTION

The possibility that natural resources can yield surpluses to society over and above the costs required to extract them from the natural environment is an important determinant of the way we value resource endowments. In chapters 1 and 4, economic rent formed an important component of any losses that Canada would sustain in the long run in the absence of resource endowments. Indeed, the Chambers-Gordon (CG) model proposes that, in the absence of terms-of-trade effects (Canada assumed to be a price taker on world markets) and in the absence of a factor proportions effect (due to international capital mobility), economic rent under competitive conditions measures the full value of natural resource endowments to the Canadian economy.

The *Constitution Act* (1982) confirms that provincial resources are owned by the provinces to the extent that they have not been transferred to private owners. The provinces explicitly assume exclusive responsibility for nonrenewable resources exploration, management of nonrenewable resources, forests, and electrical energy together with the making of (non-discriminatory) laws concerning the provincial export of resource products. The provinces have the right to "make laws in relation to the raising of money by any mode or system of taxation" for their resources. In addition to these provisions, however, the federal government can enact its own laws affecting natural resources and can prevail in the case of conflict with the provinces. So Ottawa's right to set domestic oil and gas prices, for example, remains in the *Constitution Act* even though exercise of that right reduces the revenues that provinces can obtain from natural resources.

Thus, under the Canadian constitution, and subject to existing private ownership patterns and federal pricing policies, provincial resource endowments and the revenues accruing from them belong to the provincial governments as Crown owners of the resources within their respective jurisdictions. Natural resources outside the provinces and lying in the Yukon and Northwest Territories or offshore, are owned and managed by the federal government. The nature and size of economic rents accruing to these natural resource endowments, the methods that can be used to transfer rents from the private sector to Crown owners, and the impact of corporate taxation on resources sectors are the subjects of this chapter. We shall focus on the Canadian minerals sector, leaving aspects of rent capture and taxation in the renewables sectors (forestry and fisheries) for later chapters.

■ CONCEPTS OF ECONOMIC RENT

Natural resources commanding positive net prices (p) can be said to produce *scarcity rents*. The difference between product price (π) and marginal production cost (C) is the scarcity rent per unit of output. If marginal production cost exceeds average production cost, then there is a further component of rent that can be referred to as *differential* or *Ricardian* rent.[1]

These two concepts of rent are illustrated in Figure 5.1. Along the horizontal axis, we measure the number of units of a natural resource extracted and converted to final products. In panel A, we assume that scarcity rent is equal to zero: product price π^* is equal to marginal extraction cost C^* on the last unit of resources extracted q^*. If, as shown in panel A, resources are of differing quality and are ranked in ascending

FIGURE 5.1   Economic rents

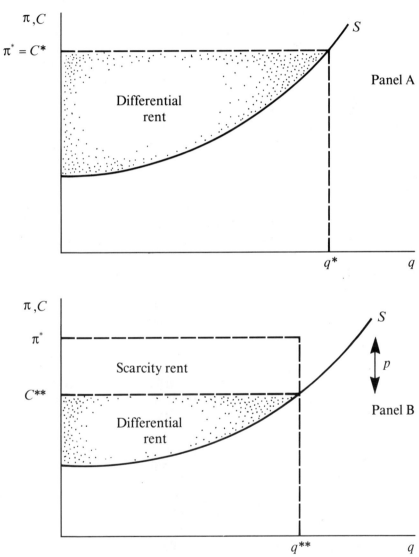

order of marginal production cost, all units of the resource extracted from zero to q^* incur lower extraction cost than the price received for them. The difference between total revenue (π^*q^*) and the total cost of extraction (the area under the marginal extraction cost curve S) constitutes economic rent (the shaded area). This version of economic rent is differential rent since it emerges entirely as a result of differences in the quality of the underlying units of the resource endowment. In panel B, both scarcity and differential rent concepts are present. Resource extraction is restricted to a level q^{**} less than q^* so that all units of the resource earn scarcity rent of $p = \pi^* - C^{**}$ and total scarcity rent is $(\pi^* - C^{**})q^{**}$. In addition to scarcity rent in panel B, the shaded area measures differential rent.

In the nonrenewable resources models discussed in chapter 2, resources were assumed to be homogeneous *during each extraction period*. This assumption does not mean that nonrenewable resources are all of the same quality. In the modified Hotelling model, in particular, resource quality is assumed to decline as a result of cumulative production. So marginal extraction costs rise *over time* as more and more of the stock is removed. But, in a single short period (dt), units of the resource extracted are of the same quality so that differential rent does not appear within each period. In this case, rent is entirely of the scarcity variety. If, on the other hand, resources extracted within a single period are of different qualities, then rent accruing during the period can take the form of *both* scarcity and differential rents as shown in panel B.

An important characteristic of rents as surpluses is the theoretical possibility that they can be transferred from the extractive sectors in which they arise to the owners of the resources. This transfer process is referred to as *rent capture*. In panel A, for example, each unit of resources extracted to the left of q^* generates a price π that exceeds the cost C of extracting that particular unit. Indeed, the economic incentive for the extraction decision on all units $q \leqslant q^*$ is that $\pi^* \geqslant C$. If the differential rent on a unit extracted is appropriated—captured—by the owner of the resource in the amount R, the private sector will still find it profitable to extract that unit provided that $R \leqslant \pi^* - C$. Thus, in principle, virtually all the differential rent indicated by the shaded area in panel A can be transferred to the owners if an appropriate transfer mechanism can be found. The exact mechanisms that might be used to effect the rent transfer will be discussed below. The same argument concerning rent capture applies to panel B: provided a transfer mechanism can be found that leaves $\pi^* \geqslant C$ on all units up to q^{**}, virtually all the scarcity and differential rents generated at q^{**} can be captured by the owners of the resource deposits.

In cases of private ownership, the transfer (capture) mechanism could work automatically under competitive conditions. Consider a mining company that wants to purchase a unit of the (unextracted) resource to convert it to final products. The private owner of the resource deposit can accept bids from mining companies. Acceptance of a bid means that, in consideration of payment equal to the bid, the resource owner transfers ownership (extraction rights) to the mining company. With a large number of mining companies bidding on any owner's deposit, the winning bidder will be forced by competition to pay an amount approximating $\pi^* - C$ and thus transfer essentially the full rent to the owner. If the payment to the owner is made in advance of extraction it is an up-front or *ex-ante* payment that becomes a sunk cost for the mining company once extraction begins. If the rent payment to the owner is made as extraction proceeds, then it becomes an *ex-post* payment. When the resource is publicly owned, *ex-post* rent payments take the form of *resource taxes* levied on mining companies as the revenues and costs of extraction are realized.

The assumption that the mining of deposits with different cost characteristics in a given period leads to differential rents depends crucially on the assumption that all mining costs can be attributed to specific deposits. This characteristic is implicit in the construction of Figure 5.1. Suppose, by contrast, that only a fraction of mining costs can be allocated to specific deposits (mines). The remaining costs are *joint costs* that can be attributed to mining output in general but not to specific deposits. The costs of developing known mineral deposits, extraction of the deposits, and processing to the level of the resource commodity are costs that are specific to each deposit. Exploration costs, on the other hand, are joint costs that cannot be so attributed. Suppose, for example, that a $100 million exploration budget gives rise to a collection of variable quality deposits, a subset of which is economic to extract. Looking at a single one of the economic deposits, it is impossible to say what part of the exploration budget led to the existence of the deposit. Referring to Figure 5.2, assume that resource owners receive a scarcity rent equal to p, as before. Since exploration costs are assumed *not* to be assignable to particular deposits, marginal production cost for deposits (C) includes only development and extraction/processing costs once the deposits have been located. Exploration costs are measured by the shaded rectangle which is not assignable to particular deposits, and include unsuccessful tries involved in producing the output q^{**} from the successful discoveries. Assuming that the scarcity rents are being transferred to the owners, the remaining surplus from producing at q^{**} is area A minus the shaded exploration cost rectangle. Suppose a public resource owner—say a provincial government—identifies area A as "differential rent" and attempts to use taxation to transfer it from the private to the public sector. Since private producers are incurring exploration costs that are not deducted in the calculation of rent, they now fail to cover all costs with this type of transfer mechanism. Output in subsequent periods will decline as the mining industry refuses to continue its uncompensated exploration efforts. Area A therefore overestimates the true surplus from mining and its transfer to the public sector leads, over time, to the elimination of mining.

The true total surplus from the mining sector is, therefore, the scarcity

FIGURE 5.2

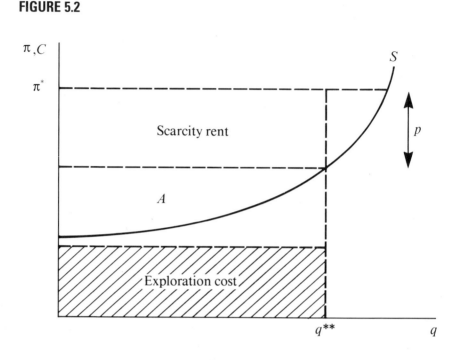

rent area plus area *A* minus total exploration cost. The attempt to capture scarcity rent plus area *A* ignores the fact that costs must be incurred to find the underlying deposits. The exploration component has been likened to a lottery in which

> ...top prizes are needed to compensate investors for the losses or low returns on other occasions and to produce a rate of return that is normal in the light of the risks taken, just as big lottery prizes are needed to compensate for the many tickets with zero or low winnings.[2]

The big winners are those deposits close to the vertical axis in Figure 5.2 for which there is a substantial excess of product price net of scarcity rent $(\pi^* - p)$ over extraction cost C. The low winners are those deposits further to the right for which the excess of $(\pi^* - p)$ over extraction cost is small. The losing tickets (deposits) are those for which extraction cost exceeds $(\pi^* - p)$ and includes unsuccessful trials. Clearly the presence of differences in the quality of mineral deposits does not guarantee the presence of differential rent when some of the costs of resource exploitation cannot be assigned to specific deposits.

Suppose mining companies anticipate that a $100 million exploration budget applied to a particular land area under provincial control will give rise to the results shown in Figure 5.2. It is also known that the provincial owner will levy a tax of p per unit of the resource extracted. In this case, mining companies competing to acquire the right to spend $100 million to explore the area and produce all resulting economical deposits at a (net) selling price of $\pi^* - p$ will be willing to bid up to area A minus the $100 million exploration budget. Alternatively, the provincial government could restrict production to q^{**} and expect a winning bid equal to scarcity rent plus area A minus $100 million. In both cases, all of the expected rent is captured by the *ex-ante* bidding process. If producers do acquire resource rights through a well-functioning competitive bidding process, and *they assume that this is the only method of rent capture that is to be applied*, any subsequent application of rent taxes is unexpected and is simply a double impost—a misguided attempt to transfer the same rent twice.   The use of an *ex-ante* bidding process to capture rents should not be taken as an argument against *ex-post* methods of rent capture (taxation) though. If mining companies anticipate at the time they make their bids that rent taxes will be collected later as extraction takes place, they can adjust their bids accordingly. In the foregoing example, the initial bid will include scarcity rent if it is known in advance that production is to be restricted t. q^{**} but will exclude it if it is known that subsequent extraction will attract a scarcity rent tax per unit of output equal to p.

It is also important to realize that the bids entered *ex-ante* have to be based on expectations of success rates from the exploration budget and on expected costs and revenues at the time that extraction and processing takes place. If there is an unexpected change in costs and revenues, *ex-post* (realized) rent will differ from *ex-ante* (expected) rent. The difference between expected and realized rent is a windfall. If government resource owners use the tax system to transfer windfalls from the private to the public sector, this is not a double impost, *provided the windfalls are truly unexpected*. It might be argued, for example, that sharp increases in world oil prices in 1973–74 and again in 1979 were the results of unexpected political developments in the Middle East and were not incorporated in previous bidding levels for Alberta's petroleum resources. The appearance of special taxes to capture the windfalls for the provincial Crown would then not represent an attempt to secure surpluses that had already been incorporated in prior bidding activity for oil leases in Alberta. By the same token, however, falling world oil prices after 1982 may have been equally surprising to the industry. It is quite clear from the reactions of governments to windfalls in the oil industry that governments are eager to capture positive windfalls. As Watkins (1987) points out,

> Up-front single-payment bids on development and production rights can normally capture...rents as long as knowledge about the biddable prospects

is well established and competition is sufficiently genuine and intense. Under such conditions, bonus bids tend to be the least distortionary and least avoidable of mechanisms. However, bids cannot handle rents associated with unanticipated prices (and costs). And in the case of oil it is differences between realized and expected prices that have dominated rent generation (or attrition) over the past decade or more.[3]

It should be noted as well that competitive bidding for resource development and extraction rights is not standard rent capture procedure for Canadian minerals. With the exception of oil and gas resources in western Canada, payments for mineral rights do not take place on an *ex-ante* basis. Perhaps the bidding process could and should be extended to other minerals but most provinces will probably continue to derive their resources revenues from *ex-post* rent taxation systems. If most mineral sector rent capture does continue to be done *ex-post*, it is important to try to develop rent taxation systems that are efficient. An efficient system, in turn, is one that captures a "reasonably large" fraction of rent without introducing distortions into the extraction process. Distortions are introduced whenever the rent tax on a particular deposit exceeds the revenue generated by the deposit net of all costs ($R > \pi^* - C$). The subsequent section on efficient rent capture models addresses this question.

Two additional points can be made before examining some recent rent estimates in Canada. First, rent capture as a transfer of economic surplus from the private to the public sector is an income distribution issue. The judgement is being made that such surpluses *ought* to be so transferred as a consequence of public ownership of resources under the *Constitution Act* (1982). Second, it is not *always* the case that rent capture should avoid changing the nature of private sector resource extraction behaviour. As discussed in chapter 2, we must also deal with the issue of divergence between private resource exploitation decisions and the socially optimal rate of use of nonrenewables. When current extraction decisions raise the costs of extraction in the future, there is an efficiency case for holding back on current output to generate a positive net price ($q^{**} < q^*$ in Figure 5.1). If extraction rights are limited to q^{**} in Figure 5.2 and exploration costs and extraction costs are minimized at q^{**}, then economic rent equals the scarcity rent area plus area A minus exploration cost. The positive net price (p) is slowing down current rates of extraction to reflect the future costs of using up resources today and is acting as a "depletion tax." If some economic rent is not captured but is left with the private sector, it may be necessary to control the rate of exploration as well, to ensure that search does not become a way of accessing rents before someone else does. The public owner can control the rate of exploration and prevent excessive search by controlling the rate at which exploration leases are granted on Crown lands and by ensuring that leases offer exclusive rights to the winning bidders.

■ ACTUAL AND POTENTIAL RENTS ON CANADIAN RESOURCES

A recent study by the Economic Council of Canada (1982) attempted to estimate the actual size of economic rents on Canadian natural resources in 1980.[4] Table 5.1 reproduces the main results of that study. The Council defined rents as existing in two categories: natural resources revenues actually collected by the provinces on their resources and resource revenues that could have been collected but were actually passed forward to the consumers of resources products in the form of low prices. In the latter case, the Council's reasoning was that an increase in some resource commodity prices to reflect world prices would have led to increased rents on resource extraction. The major commodities marketed at prices less than world prices were petroleum products and hydroelectric power.

In the case of oil and gas, the below-market price in 1980 reflected the federal government's policy of domestic pricing. From 1973 to 1982, the period in which the Organization of Petroleum Exporting Countries (OPEC) enforced large increases in world oil prices, Canadian oil and natural gas prices were set below international prices. In the case of oil, the price differential was enforced through an export tax collected by the federal government. The federal proceeds of the oil export tax on western Canadian shipments to U.S. markets were directed to the cost of maintaining the domestic oil price below the cost of imported oil in Quebec and the Atlantic region. The price of natural gas exports to the U.S. was set by the National Energy Board (NEB) above the domestic price with the extra revenues on export sales shared by the producing companies and provinces and the federal government. Had Canadian oil and gas prices been set at international levels, the oil-producing provinces, principally Alberta, would have been able to collect much larger oil and gas revenues by capturing the wellhead or field price increases in the form of higher royalties.

Artificially low prices for hydroelectric power also transfers rents from hydro producing provinces to power consumers. In this case, the transfer to consumers reflects an interesting interaction between the costs of resource extraction (hydroelectric power costs) and principles of public utility regulation. Figure 5.3 illustrates the main issues in this interaction. The supply curve (SS) shows the marginal cost of obtaining electric power from two alternative sources: hydro or thermal (coal, oil, or nuclear) generation. The low-cost sources, corresponding to the initial rising portion of SS, are hydro sources. The high-cost sources, corresponding to the horizontal section of SS, are assumed to be the thermal sources. The demand curve for electrical power is DD. Under marginal-cost pricing principles, the equilibrium price is shown as P_m. At this price, the hydro

TABLE 5.1 Estimates of the magnitude and distribution of natural resource rents, Canada, by province or territory, 1980

	NFLD.	P.E.I.	N.S.	N.B.	QUE.	ONT.	MAN.	SASK.	ALTA.	B.C.	YUKON AND N.W.T.	CANADA
					(millions of current dollars)							
Provincial natural resource revenues (excl. water power rentals)	27.9	0.2	9.8	13.4	114.1	138.4	43.2	695.2	5 089.3	874.7	—	7 006.4
Rents not collected on Crude oil	—	—	—	—	—	13.8	83.3	1 296.3	10 305.9	315.8	23.5	12 038.6
Natural gas and LPG*	—	—	—	0.3	—	45.3	—	183.6	5 242.8	521.7	54.9	6 048.5
Hydroelectricity	736.7	—	26.4	70.5	1 514.4	758.1	455.8	29.0	6.7	139.7	—	3 737.3
Total rents, by province of production	764.7	0.2	36.3	84.2	1 628.5	955.6	582.3	2 204.1	20 644.6	1 851.9	78.4	28 830.8
Hydro rents lost on exports	−73.5	—	−0.1	−9.1	−175.0	−92.4	−55.6	−0.1	—	−6.3	—	−412.1

Rent Capture and Resource Taxation **153**

Total redistribution of rents to other provinces	−194.9	77.6	776.0	787.9	4 544.9	5 899.6	589.4	−635.0	−12 716.5	857.5	13.4	—
Net distribution of rents	496.2	77.8	812.1	862.9	5 998.4	6 762.9	1 116.1	1 569.0	7 928.1	2 703.2	91.8	28 418.6
					(dollars per capita)							
Resource rents, by province of production	1 318.6	1.9	42.5	119.0	258.4	111.5	566.2	2 274.1	9 932.5	702.4	1 217.5	1 205.6
Redistribution of rents to other provinces	−336.1	624.1	910.2	1 114.3	721.0	688.4	573.2	−655.2	−6 118.1	325.3	208.5	—
Net distributed rents	855.7	626.0	952.7	1 220.4	951.6	789.1	1 085.3	1 618.9	3 814.4	1 025.3	1 426.0	1 188.3

*LPG = liquefied petroleum gases.

Source: Economic Council of Canada, *Financing Confederation Today and Tomorrow* (Ottawa: Supply and Services, 1982), p. 42. Reproduced with the permission of the Minister of Supply and Services Canada, 1990.

FIGURE 5.3

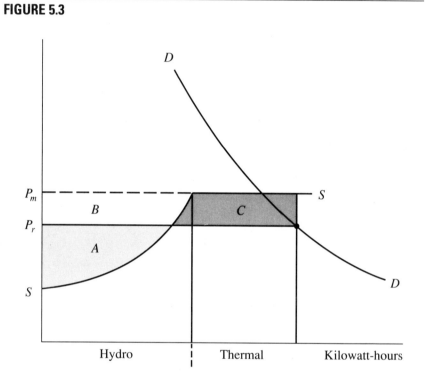

sources would earn economic rent equal to the area between the rising
section of *SS* and the price line P_m shown as areas $A + B$. Under public
utility regulation, however, consumers must be charged the average cost of
power in order to prevent "excess profits" (rents) from being earned by
power companies. In Figure 5.3 the regulated average cost price is shown
as P_r. Assuming that power companies meet the demand at P_r, the overall
surplus is zero. On some of the hydro generation, rents are earned equal to
area A. On the remaining hydro sources and all of the thermal sources,
power producers lose area C. Provided P_r is set "correctly," area A = area
C and no "excess profits" are earned on power generation. All the
economic rent to low-cost hydro generation has been dissipated in the form
of low regulated-power prices. Instead of paying a price equal to the cost of
generating electricity from the high-cost (thermal) sources, consumers end
up paying the lower price that corresponds to the cost of delivery from all
sources. Adding further to the problem, some of the average costs of
generation in the regulated pricing scenario are low historical costs that

tend to reduce regulated prices below the replacement cost of generating facilities. The way to estimate the rent that would accrue to hydro resources under efficient pricing is to establish a price equal to the marginal cost of new thermal power (P_m in Figure 5.3) and to use this price to measure the true rent to hydro power sources as area $A + B$. Bernard, Bridges, and Scott (1982) and Zuker and Jenkins (1984) have undertaken such studies. Their true hydro rent estimates (for 1979) were not in full agreement but were both quite large.

The Table 5.1 rent estimates include not only provincial natural resource revenues (about $7 billion) and rents that would have been collected on petroleum resources and hydro power (about $22 billion) at international prices, but also subtracts rents transferred to foreign consumers of hydroelectric power as a result of low regulated prices in Canada (about $400 million). The hydro power rent estimates are based on Zuker and Jenkins (1984). The overall size of Canadian resource rents—over $28 billion in 1980—was impressive and amounted to about 10 percent of GNP. As a long-term estimate, this is misleading, however, since the Council's estimates were made just after the appearance of the large oil price windfalls of the 1970s (and immediately after the 1979 increases due to the revolution in Iran) and therefore contained a large "windfall effect." Clearly a significant proportion of the nearly $22 billion in resource rents passed forward to domestic consumers of petroleum products in Table 5.1 were destined to disappear when world oil prices declined after 1982 and domestic prices returned to equality with international prices. Of total rents in Table 5.1, the amounts actually collected by provincial governments ($7 billion) amounted to 2.5 percent of GNP or approximately $300 per capita. In the western provinces, resource revenues form a significant share of provincial budgets. Almost half of Alberta's provincial expenditures in 1983 were financed out of resource revenues.

Since three-quarters of economic rents were passed forward in reduced product prices in Table 5.1, a large proportion of the benefits of Canadian resources production in 1980 were received outside the provinces in which the rents were actually generated. Of the $21 billion in economic rent (about 75 percent of the Canadian total) generated on oil and gas resources in Alberta, only $8 billion was retained by residents of Alberta in the form of oil and gas revenues or reduced prices for Alberta consumers of petroleum products. Most of the benefits of reduced oil and gas prices flowed to other provinces. Newfoundland's hydroelectric power industry generated $.737 billion in economic rent, of which $.603 billion (82 percent) was transferred to other provinces or to U.S. consumers. The major reason for this particular transfer has been the relatively low long-term contract prices on power sold by the Churchill Falls Labrador Corporation to Hydro Quebec. As the Economic Council observed in another study, the loss of resource rents amounted to about $1200 per Newfoundlander in 1980.[5] The patriation of the Canadian constitution (the former *British North America Act*) in 1982 did little to alter the issues of rent distribution between the provinces (in the form of direct resource revenues) and the federal government and consumers (in the form of regulated domestic prices). The provinces continue to be recognized as the owners and managers of their resources and are entitled to resource revenues. But the federal government did not give up the right to make national laws that impinge on provincial resource revenues (Anderson and Bonsor 1986). If the federal government *had* permitted oil and gas prices to rise to international levels prior to 1982, the producing provinces (mainly Alberta) could have collected much larger resources revenues and interprovincial rent redistribution would have declined significantly. From the provincial viewpoint, it is noteworthy that the 1989 Canada–U.S. Free Trade Agreement (FTA) prohibits the use of government intervention to set prices that discriminate against U.S. consumers of Canadian exports. Export taxes are explicitly prohibited (with the exception of the negotiated Canadian export tax on lumber).[6]   The rent estimation approach used by the Economic Council has quite a number of problems apart from the "windfall effect" noted above. The Council's use of provincial natural resources revenues to estimate economic rents produced by differences between producers' revenues evaluated at domestic selling prices and their costs can be questioned. First, as discussed later in this chapter, provincial resources taxation may actually *reduce* the size of potential rents in resources industries by distorting extraction decisions. Alberta's royalties on wellhead oil revenues, for example, means that producers will produce only up to the point at which marginal cost equals wellhead price minus the royalty (their after-tax price). Rents on oil output that has a marginal cost less than the wellhead price but greater than the wellhead price minus the royalty are lost. Second, and more important, natural resources revenues will only measure the size of potential rents at domestic prices if the provinces succeed in transferring 100 percent of potential rents from the private sector to their own coffers. The design of existing provincial resources revenue systems certainly does not permit 100 percent rent capture. Even very carefully designed rent capture models could not aim for total rent capture. The Economic Council recognized that actual resource revenues were a low estimate of total rent. Estimating the rents left with the private sector would be very difficult since it would require detailed knowledge of revenues and costs over time in the whole range of Canada's resources sectors. It is precisely this kind of detailed knowledge of revenues and costs that forms the basis of the efficient rent capture models discussed in the next section.

TABLE 5.2   Hypothetical mining project.

1 YEAR	2 ASSESSABLE RECEIPTS	3 DEDUCTIBLE PAYMENTS	4 NAR*	5 ACCUMULATED NAR ($r = .10$)	6 TAX AT 50%
1	0	100	−100	−100	0
2	0	300	−300	−410	0
3	50	100	−50	−501	0
4	200	50	150	−401	0
5	200	50	150	−291	0
6	200	50	150	−170	0
7	200	50	150	−37	0
8	200	50	150	109	54.5
9	200	50	150	0	75
10	200	50	150	0	75
11	200	250	−50	−50	0
12	200	50	150	95	47.5
13	200	50	150	0	75
14	200	50	150	0	75
15	200	50	150	0	75

*NAR = net assessable receipts
Source: R. Garnaut and A. Clunies Ross, "Uncertainty, Risk Aversion, and the Taxing of Natural Resource Projects," *Economic Journal* 85 (1975): 272–87.

∎ EFFICIENT RENT CAPTURE METHODS

The Resource Rent Tax (RRT)

Efficient rent capture requires at the outset that the rent magnitude be located and measured in any particular case. Once this has been done, an efficient rent capture mechanism needs to be worked out to shift part of the rent magnitude from the private to the public sector. An extremely useful and influential approach to these issues has been worked out by Garnaut and Clunies Ross (1975;1979). We use their own numerical illustration in Table 5.2 to show the costs and revenues of a hypothetical mineral project that is to be subject to rent capture. Column 1 of Table 5.2 shows the years in which the project generates its costs and revenues. Under the receipts column, the project generates no revenue in years 1 and 2, comes into partial production in year 3, and generates revenues of $200 million in each subsequent year until termination of the project at the end of year 15. In the costs column, exploration occurs in year 1 to the extent of $100 million. Development of the mine, including capital costs, amounts to $300 million in year 2, and additional development and operating costs of $100 million

FIGURE 5.4

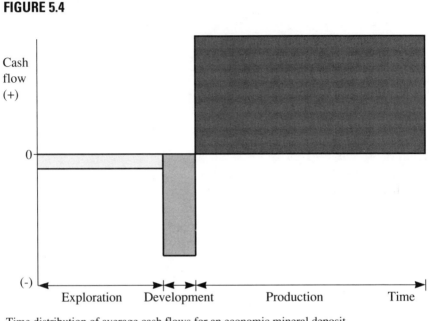

Time distribution of average cash flows for an economic mineral deposit.

☐ Exploration expenditure

▨ Development capital cost

■ Revenue – production cost

Source: B. Mackenzie and R. Woodall, "Economic Productivity of Base Metal
Exploration in Australia and Canada," in J. Tilton, R. Eggert, and H. Landsberg,
eds., *World Mineral Exploration: Trends and Economic Issues* (Washington:
Resources for the Future, 1988).

appear in year 3. From year 4 to year 10 annual costs are level at $50
million per year. In year 11 an extension of the mine adds a further $200
million above operating costs, after which annual cost remains level to the
end of year 15. With the exception of the extension of the mine in year 11,
the general pattern of expenditures and revenues in Table 5.2 models the
typical cash-flow pattern for mining projects as illustrated in Figure 5.4.
Column 4 of Table 5.2 is obtained by subtracting column 3 from 2 and is
referred to by Garnaut and Clunies Ross as net assessable receipts (NAR).
The project shown is an *economic* project in the sense that the present
value of receipts minus the present value of costs is positive.[7]

Note that the exploration costs assigned are somewhat arbitrary and are assumed to be "representative" for an economic project. Each economic project discovered involves a single exploration success accompanied by exploration costs that lead to no discovery at all or to the discovery of uneconomic deposits. Suppose the success rate on exploration trials is 1:50 and a single trial costs $2 million. In that case, on average, each discovery of an economic project involves forty-nine failures, so that the expected exploration cost associated with an economic discovery is $100 million as shown in Table 5.2. The hypothetical project has enough exploration costs loaded on to it in year 1 to cover the *expected* exploration budget associated with its discovery. This feature is necessary to avoid a rent capture approach that confiscates the prizes of the winners without recognizing the losses of the unsuccessful participants (Grubel 1979; Campbell and Lindner 1983). With an appropriate exploration budget taken into account, it is now possible to calculate economic rent on the hypothetical project.

Since costs and revenues appear in different periods, reducing them to a single measure requires the use of an acceptable discount rate. The net present value of the project is

$$NPV = \sum_{i=1}^{15} (R_t - C_t)/(1 + r)^t \tag{1}$$

where R_t = receipts in year t from column 2, C_t = payments in year t from column 3, and r = the discount rate taken at .10 (10 percent) for illustration. Applying equation (1) to the figures in Table 5.2, net present value (NPV) equals $321 million. This is the present value of the surplus of all receipts over payments during the fifteen-year project horizon and is, therefore, the economic rent attached to the project.

The rent capture model proposed by Garnaut and Clunies Ross involves what they refer to as a resource rent tax (RRT) which is designed to transfer a specified fraction of the $321 million from the private sector to the public sector. The RRT approach operates by levying the resource rent tax on economic projects only after receipts are sufficient to cover costs including a rate or return on capital invested. Once all costs, including the 10 percent return on capital, have been recovered out of receipts, the RRT appropriates a fraction of the surplus (50 percent in this example).

Columns 5 and 6 of the table show how the RRT mechanism works. In year 1 the project's invested capital is $100 million equal to exploration outlays. In year 2 mine development expenditures add up to $300 million. Allowing the mining company to earn 10 percent on the previous year's invested capital, invested capital in year 2 is $410 million (= (100)(1.1) + 300). This is shown as accumulated NAR in column 5. In year 3 the firm invests an additional $50 million in the project on the basis of receipts minus payments. Allowing for the 10 percent return on capital invested in year 2, its total invested capital (or accumulated NAR) in year 3 is $501 million ($= 410(1.1) + 50$). This procedure carries on to year 8, at which point the project has recovered all its capital costs, including the 10 percent annual return allowed on capital and shows a surplus of $109 million. With the RRT set at 50 percent, $54.5 million is assessed as the RRT. Since it has been taxed, the surplus no longer enters accumulated NAR. In years 9 and 10, annual surpluses of $150 million appear, half of which are captured by the RRT. In year 11 the capital expenditure that is not covered by operating surplus is added to invested capital. In year 12 the invested capital of $50 million from year 11 is recovered along with its 10 percent rate of return out of net receipts of $150 million. The surplus in year 12 is $95 million ($150 - (1.1)50$) producing an RRT of $47.5 million in column 6. During the final three years of the project, the rent tax amounts to $75 million annually on annual surpluses of $150 million.

The rent taxes shown in column 6 are exactly 50 percent of the economic rents generated in those years, allowing for the 10 percent return on capital. The net present value of the project can, therefore, be calculated from column 6 as

$$NPV = 2[54.5/(1.1)^8 + 75/(1.1)^9 + 75/(1.1)^{10} + 47.5/(1.1)^{12} + 75/(1.1)^{13}$$
$$+ 75/(1.1)^{14} + 75/(1.1)^{15}] = \$321 \text{ million}$$

The present value of economic rent transferred to the public sector is, therefore, $160.5 million using the RRT approach with a 50 percent tax rate. Higher rates of RRT transfer larger fractions of the $321 million to the public sector. The receipts and costs in columns 2 and 3 are defined specifically for the assessment of the RRT on economic rent. The authors refer to them as "assessable receipts" and "deductible costs" to draw attention to their definitions. Deductible costs do *not* include interest payments on debt associated with the project since returns to capital are already being allowed for in the rent calculation. Also, *all* tax payments (other than the RRT) are allowed as deductible costs in the calculation since the 10 percent rate of return is taken on an after-tax basis.

The key feature of the Garnaut–Clunies Ross model is that rent is isolated and measured in a theoretically satisfactory way and the resulting rent magnitude is used as the tax base for calculating the RRT. When exploration costs are assigned to particular projects, some care has to be taken with projects that have negative NPVs because of the assigned exploration costs, however. Since exploration costs are not truly assignable to individual projects, some projects may turn up that do not cover their assigned exploration "cost," yet when the exploration cost is excluded, NPV becomes positive. These projects will be undertaken by the private sector once they have been discovered. An example will help to show how such projects should be handled. Suppose a total exploration budget of $200 million turns up two projects. Assigning exploration costs of $100 million to each, assume that project 1 is as shown in Table 5.2. Suppose further that the government applies a 100 percent RRT and collects all the present-valued rent on project 1 equal to $321 million. Assume project 2 has NPV = $–60 million with the assigned exploration cost included and the government sets its RRT = 0 on project 2. Once the exploration budget is spent, project 2 will be undertaken since exclusion of its assigned exploration cost gives an NPV = $40 million. But mining firms will *not* undertake the $200 million in exploration leading to the 2 projects under these conditions since the private surplus on project 1 is zero due to the 100 percent RRT rate and the private surplus on project 2 is $–60 million. To get the process to work with the assigned exploration costs, the government must subsidize the negative NPV of project 2 at the chosen RRT rate. In this case, the subsidy is $60 million and the present value of rent captured is $321 million – $60 million = $261 million which is all the rent that is actually available on the 2 projects together. If this arrangement is not followed, the RRT does not truly fall on economic rent, since the surpluses on projects that more than cover their assigned exploration costs are taxed while the deficits on projects that fail to meet their assigned exploration costs are borne entirely by the private sector.

Ex-ante, *Ex-post*, and Participation Methods

There are a number of variations on *ex-post* rent-based resource taxation in addition to the Garnaut–Clunies Ross RRT model. One of these is *rate-of-return taxation*.[8] Under this approach projects do not attract rent taxes until they meet a threshold rate of return on capital r^*. The rent capture formula takes the form

$$R = a[1-(r^*/r)] \qquad (2)$$

where R is the tax rate as a percentage of annual operating profit (assessable receipts minus deductible payments), a is a positive constant, r^* is the allowed rate of return on capital (10 percent in the present example), and r is the internal rate of return on capital (IROR). The IROR in any year is the rate of discount that produces a zero net present value (NPV) of assessable receipts minus deductible payments over all years including the year of the calculation. For example, consider year 7 in Table 5.2. The IROR for year 7 is calculated as follows:

$$NPV = 150/(1 + r)^7 + 150/(1 + r)^6 + 150/(1 + r)^5 + 150/(1 + r)^4$$
$$- 50/(1 + r)^3 - 300/(1 + r)^2 - 100/(1 + r) = 0$$

The calculated value for r is approximately 9 percent. Setting $r = .09$ and $r^* = .10$ in equation (2), $r^*/r > 1$ and $R < 0$. When $R < 0$, no rent taxes are collected because the project has not yet reached its 10 percent threshold return. In year 8, r rises above 10 percent, $r*/r < 1$ and R > 0 so rent taxes begin to be collected in year 8 just as in Table 5.2. Though it is not as easy to calculate as the Garnaut and Clunies Ross RRT and is not as clearly related to the actual size of economic rent as the RRT, the rate-of-return taxation method does transfer rent from the private to the public sector without impinging on economic costs. Just as with the RRT, care has to be taken to share losses with the private sector on economic projects that do not recover assigned exploration costs. A version of the rate-of-return taxation model has been used by the federal government to capture rents on petroleum resources on the Canada Lands.

A *participation* approach to rent capture is also feasible. Under this method, all revenues associated with the project are taxed at rate T and all costs are subsidized at rate T. The government enters as a partner in all costs and revenues. Taking the 50 percent rent capture objective, the government could pay half of all exploration, development, and production costs while receiving half of all receipts. In this case, dividing the entries of columns 2 and 3 by two, the government receives half the net present value of the project, and the private operator obtains the other half. The government becomes a *pro-rata* player in mineral development activities. If the participation rate is set at 100 percent, then the entire project is undertaken by the public sector—possibly by a Crown corporation—with the entire economic rent accruing to the public sector as well. Saskatchewan has used a combination of RRT taxation and participation to capture rents in its uranium industry. The RRT portion of the Saskatchewan scheme was not efficient, owing to excessively generous capital recovery provisions which allowed uranium firms to recover more than the actual value of capital invested prior to payment of a graduated RRT.[9] The province's participation approach allowed a provincial Crown corporation (the Saskatchewan Mining Development Corporation) to participate in any mining project to the extent of 50 percent of all costs and revenues.

A *de-facto* participation result can be achieved easily by applying the rent capture rate T to all operating income (revenue less variable costs) and permitting mining companies an immediate 100 percent write-off of all capital expenditures (including exploration and development) against current operating income. Provided current operating income is large enough, the immediate write-off of capital costs saves the company an amount equal to the tax rate T multiplied by the capital costs, thus subsidizing capital costs at rate T, as required by the participation approach.[10] If current operating income is *not* sufficient to absorb capital costs, one solution would be to allow the company to claim capital costs up to operating income and simply subsidize the unclaimed balance of capital costs at rate T. Alternatively, the government could use *carry-backs* or *carry-forwards*. With carry-backs, the unclaimed balance of capital costs over current operating income would entitle the firm to a refund of taxes paid in previous years equal to the unclaimed capital costs at rate T. With carry-forwards, the unclaimed capital costs could be used to reduce operating income and taxes in subsequent years. If carry-forwards are used, however, the unclaimed capital costs must be compounded forward at the rate of interest r^* to ensure that the firm earns a normal return on capital invested (carried forward). The project taxation model in Figure 5.2 involves carry forwards at rate r^*. An alternative to capital subsidies or carry-backs and carry-forwards would be the use of *marketable tax credits*. Under this system the firm's unclaimed capital costs are assigned a tax credit at rate T. The firm can then sell the tax credit to other firms who use them to reduce their own current tax liabilities. In a perfectly competitive market for tax credits, the selling firm should receive the full tax value of tax credits sold to other firms. A slightly more complex version of marketable tax credits are *flow-through shares* discussed below in the corporate taxation section of this chapter.   The project characteristics in Table 5.2 can also be used to illustrate some of the issues of *ex-ante* rent capture. Suppose that the receipts and payments shown in the table represent the expected values of those variables, so that the project represents the average results to be anticipated from a $100 million exploration budget. If exploration rights are auctioned off to the private sector, the expected net present value of the $100 million exploration package is $321 million. If competition is intense and bidders are not averse to the risks involved (or attracted by those risks), the winning bid should approach $321 million, leaving the winning bidder with an expected normal rate of return on capital invested. If the average results of exploration are actually the same as the expected results, full economic rent will be captured by the bidding method. If the government is doubtful about the degree of competition in the bidding process, it may enter its own *appraisal* of the net present value of the project as an *upset price*, refusing to transfer exploration rights to the private sector for less than the upset price. The effectiveness of the *ex-ante* approach depends almost entirely on the assumption that expected future returns from exploration activities can be reasonably accurately estimated. This assumption is the principal weakness of the approach. *Ex-ante* methods of rent capture require that rents be predicted independently of actual rents that materialize subsequently. Since firms have to absorb all subsequent changes in net revenue themselves, strong incentives to economic efficiency are present in this kind of rent transfer approach.

Various combinations of *ex-ante* and *ex-post* approaches to rent capture are possible. For example, the government could apply a 50 percent RRT to resource projects and place the exploration rights up for auction. Half the economic rents (including windfalls) would be captured with the RRT (as described above), and part of the remaining half would be captured through the auction process (depending on information and competition). Some observers favour such a combined method:

A combination of bonus bids with a resource rent tax offers the best hope for the accurate collection of economic rents without introducing distortions. The bonus bids can extract *ex ante* rents and provide governments or other resource owners with an early cash flow from the provision of mineral rights to investors. The resource rent tax can collect *ex post* economic rents and provide a cash flow to governments in subsequent years.[11]

Another two-part rent capture mechanism might combine participation with an RRT, as was the intention in the Saskatchewan uranium rent capture system. Participation could also be used in the early stages of the mineral supply process with an RRT taking over in the later stages. The government could, for example, share exploration costs on a 50:50 basis with private operators who initiate projects. The 50 percent RRT could then be applied to the payments and receipts of the project, *excluding* exploration costs. This method captures half of economic rent without the need to assign exploration costs to particular projects. A third combination could see governments participating in (or even assuming entirely) exploration costs and then auctioning off the rights to develop and produce the resulting deposits. An advantage that could be claimed for this rent capture combination is that the auction should work better when information concerning deposits is already known by the bidders.

■ MANAGING THE RATE OF DEPLETION

The rent capture models discussed in the previous section assume that a fixed total of economic rent (equal to the net present value of the project) originates in the private sector, that a correct accounting of revenues and costs can measure this rent, and that a fraction of it can then be transferred to the public resource owner without distorting private production decisions. There are two important reservations about these rent capture procedures. First, we have not so far recognized that there is any limit, short of 100 percent, on the fraction of rent that can be transferred. With *ex-ante* approaches, a highly competitive bidding process (or very accurate appraisal) could, in fact, lead to 100 percent capture. With *ex-post* capture, it is much harder to believe that all of resource rent could be transferred to the public owners. If total economic rent originating with private sector projects *ex post* were actually insensitive to the capture rate, rent transfer to the public sector would be purely a matter of redistributing a fixed total from the private to the public sector. This is the case illustrated in Table 5.2: private decision makers are maximizing rents and these maximizing decisions are not altered by the transfer process. When rent-maximizing decisions are not affected by rent capture, this is called *neutrality*. An RRT and the other rent-based *ex-post* methods described in the previous section are neutral provided private sector decision makers are willing to maximize total rent no matter how little of total rent they themselves receive. It is unlikely, in fact, that individuals will be willing to maximize rent for a very small share of the proceeds. We will return to this problem later in the chapter. The second reservation turns on the magnitude of rent generated in the private sector prior to transfer. It may be the case that the rent generated in the private sector is not as large as it could be under optimal decision making. Expansion of total economic rent available to be shared between the public and private sectors is possible, for example, if private resource depletion rates diverge from optimal rates. Suppose that trends in receipts and payments are such that postponing the project for one year would raise its starting net present value from $321 million to $360 million, an increase of about 12 percent. If the opportunity cost of capital is 10 percent, postponement is worthwhile, since economic rent is growing more rapidly than the rate of interest: its present value is higher in the next period than it is today. This, of course, is the message of the Hotelling framework: if net prices are rising faster than the rate of discount, resource production should be delayed. With declining deposit grades and deteriorating exploration results over time, postponement can also be justified by the resulting reduction in costs on future resource production. In this case the resource manager attributes cost declines (rent increases) on the outputs of future periods to delays in the present rate of exploitation. Referring back to equation (11) in chapter 2, the cost of delaying the receipt of net price (rp) is justified by the increase in net price over time (dp/dt), and by the rent increases obtained by postponing the transition to higher cost projects ($-C_xq$).

When timing considerations are brought into the discussion, efficient resource managers must be involved not only in transferring a fraction of economic rent to the public sector but also in adjusting the rate of resource exploitation—the rate at which new projects are brought forward—so that the net present value of rents from all projects, present and future, is maximized. Maximizing the present value of economic rent maximizes the total amount of surplus jointly available to both private and public claimants. As in the case of environmental resources, the issue of property rights plays an important role in securing efficiency. If the public owner refuses to transfer secure mineral rights to the private sector in exchange for a share of rents, private operators will not have the incentives needed to maximize the value of mineral rights. If, for example, rights to produce minerals are given to those who first locate them, then exploration of mineral-bearing properties can occur too soon and by too many competing explorers. The public owner could counter by licensing a limited amount of exploration on an exclusive basis. This would slow down the discovery process and prevent inefficient open-access exploration. Rents would be transferred either through bidding on the exploration licences or by subsequent (*ex-post*) capture. Once reserves are established following exploration, the holders of the exploration rights must be able to lease the property for production. Leases should be long enough to ensure that producers can choose the optimal time to invest in mining infrastructure and to extract and process the minerals. If production leases are too short, the private sector may be forced to invest and extract too soon. All of these property rights constraints affect the present value of the underlying mineral deposits.   Slowing depletion to a rate lower than the rate at which marginal cost equals product price produces a positive net price (p) and scarcity rents on the resource. Rearranging equation (9) from chapter 2, the net price of the depleting resource should be

$$p = (dp/dt - C_x q)/r \tag{3}$$

in order to maximize the present value of economic rent. The private individual can only obtain the benefits of deferred exploration ($dp/dt - C_x q$) if he owns the mineral rights and can exercise them at a later date. In this case, the private owner has an incentive to form predictions on future prices and extraction costs in the industry and to defer his own exploration, development, and extraction activities in accordance with equation (2). If potential resources can be appropriated by others or leases are too short, private operators have reduced incentive to weigh the future in their decisions. Present costs and revenues dominate, depletion is too high, and the net price is too low, perhaps zero. If mineral prospects are to command a positive scarcity value in addition to any differential rents or windfalls that may emerge in the supply process (see Figure 5.1), the public owner must become involved in depletion decisions. As indicated above, the public owner can ration (exclusive) exploration licences. Or the public owner could use a tax on exploitation activities to slow down depletion. A tax of T per unit of production could, in principle, be set to equal p in equation (2), assuming that the private sector would otherwise exploit the resource until p = 0. Such a "depletion tax" would both slow depletion and transfer scarcity rents to the public owner. To ensure that the exploitation process is moderated right from the exploration stage, the depletion tax could be levied on exploration itself. This would also have the advantage that the tax would not discourage production from high-cost deposits once they have been discovered.[12]

The use of "depletion taxes" to control the rate of exploitation of resources is a subject to which we return in chapter 7 in the discussion of optimal exploitation of renewables such as fish stocks. We have already noted in chapter 3 that optimal taxes on pollution activities can be motivated not only by current (flow) damages but also by (stock) depletion effects on environmental quality.

■ MINERALS TAXATION AND THE EFFECTIVE TAX RATE CONCEPT

Canadian Minerals Taxation: Background

The Canadian mining industry pays corporation income taxes levied at the federal and provincial levels as well as provincial mining taxes and royalties. Originally conceived as devices to raise revenues for the provincial resource owners under the old *British North America Act*, mining taxes and royalties have come to be viewed as rent capture devices since the early 1970s. The present section begins by examining corporation income taxes in the mining sector and then examines the effectiveness of mining taxes and royalties as methods of transferring economic rent from the private to the public sector.[13] The rent capture framework described above acts as a benchmark against which existing rent capture regimes can be judged.

The Canadian corporate tax system is a continuously evolving structure. Corporate tax reforms in the late 1980s introduced quite a number of changes. The basic structure involves taxation of the net income of Canadian corporations by both the federal and provincial governments. The federal corporate tax rate for 1990–91 was 28 percent of net income with slightly lower rates applied to manufacturing corporations (23 percent) and smaller corporations (12 percent). Since 1976, the federal government has permitted a 25 percent resource allowance for resource corporations to "make room" for provincial mining taxes and royalties which ceased to be deductible as a cost of production for federal corporation tax calculations in 1974. The federal resource allowance, therefore, reduces the basic federal tax rate from 28 percent to 21 percent for mining companies compared to 23 percent for manufacturing companies. Provincial corporate tax rates vary from 11 percent in Alberta to 16 percent in British Columbia, Newfoundland, and Manitoba. Thus, the overall (federal and provincial) corporate tax rate after deduction of the resource allowance ranges from 32 percent to 37 percent for resource corporations.

The overall impact of the Canadian corporation tax system depends importantly on the nature of various deductions allowed in the calculation of net income to which the above tax rates apply. In addition to operating costs, including costs of materials and labour, expenditures on capital equipment can be deducted according to specific capital cost allowance (CCA) rules. For example, as of 1991, investments in manufacturing and processing machinery and equipment, referred to as Class 29 assets in the tax code, can be deducted on a 25 percent declining-balance basis (each year, 25 percent of the remaining balance is deducted in calculating net income). Mining equipment and structures (Classes 10 and 28) are also entitled to a 25 percent declining-balance CCA. Canadian exploration expenditures can be deducted at 100 percent in the year they are incurred. Canadian development expenditures that prove up resource properties can be deducted at 30 percent declining-balance. Prior to 1990, mining companies received additional federal deductions for exploration and development spending, referred to as "earned depletion" but this deduction has been eliminated. Some provinces allow various forms of depletion allowances and some permit the deduction of provincial mining taxes and royalties in lieu of the resource allowance in calculating net income for provincial corporation taxes. Companies also used to receive "investment tax credits" at the federal level. These have also been eliminated, except for research expenditures and capital expenditures in designated regions (Atlantic Canada).

The tax code CCAs on capital expenditures and the write-offs for exploration and development are more generous than one might expect on the basis of actual rates of depreciation or depletion of the assets involved. For example, the actual physical rates of depreciation for buildings and equipment are probably in the range of 8 to 10 percent per year, compared to the 25 percent rate in the tax code. The tax system, therefore, permits *accelerated depreciation* of capital assets. Exploration and development spending generates assets in the form of mineral reserves. The actual "depreciation" of reserves takes the form of depletion as they are extracted. The 100 percent and 30 percent deduction rules applied to exploration and development allow the costs of reserves to be recovered more rapidly than actual (cost) depletion. Accelerated depreciation (or accelerated depletion) rules are advantageous to taxpaying companies because they shift after-tax income from later to earlier periods. With a positive interest rate, a dollar of income today is worth more now than a dollar tomorrow.

The Effective Tax Rate Approach

To examine the impact of corporate taxation on investment decisions in the mining industry (or any other industry), we need a theoretical model of the way taxation affects returns to capital. We will use the *neoclassical* theory of investment to do this. Suppose we assume that capital investors can borrow on international capital markets at a fixed rate of interest r. Investors are deciding whether or not to hold a particular capital good with price p_k. Assume that the capital good offers a current return of MRP, consisting of marginal sales revenue net of marginal operating cost.[14] Actual depreciation is assumed to take the form of a specified rate of decline in the value of the capital asset to the investor and is δp_k so that, for example, 8 percent of the capital asset's value is lost during the current period if $\delta = .08$. We assume that the current rate of change of p_k is zero.[15] Investors will be just willing to hold capital goods of this type if

$$MRP = rp_k + \delta p_k \qquad (4)$$

since *MRP* is the current return from holding the capital asset, rp_k is the current interest cost of holding the asset, and δp_k is the depreciation cost of holding the asset. If $MRP > rp_k + \delta p_k$ then investors will be eager to hold capital and will bid up p_k until (4) is satisfied and *vice versa*.

Now introduce corporate taxation at rate T. The corporation is taxed on its income flow with actual depreciation deducted. The current after-tax return from holding the capital asset is $(1 - T)MRP$ and the after-tax cost of depreciation is $(1 - T)\delta p_k$. After-tax asset equilibrium is achieved when

$$(1 - T)MRP = rp_k + (1 - T)\delta p_k \qquad (5)$$

Using the concepts in equation (4), the pre-tax net return on the capital asset in (5) is $(MRP - \delta p_k)$ and the pre-tax *rate* of return is $r^* = (MRP - \delta p_k)/p_k$. Substituting into (5),

$$r^* = r/(1 - T) \qquad (6)$$

Thus, the effect of the tax system with actual depreciation allowed as a deduction is simply to raise the pre-tax rate of return on capital (r^*) relative to the after-tax rate set by the required international rate of return (r). For example, if the federal/provincial corporate tax rate is 35 percent and the international borrowing rate is 10 percent, then the pre-tax rate of return is $r^* = 10$ percent$/(1-.35) = 15.38$ percent. The *effective* tax rate is $(r^* - r)/r$ $= (15.38 - 10.00)/10.00 = .538$ or 53.8 percent. The effective tax rate measures the percentage by which the tax system raises the pre-tax rate of return on capital relative to the after-tax rate of return on capital. In this case, $(r^* - r)/r = [r/(1 - T) - r]/r = T/(1 - T) = .35/.65 = .538$. Clearly the corporate tax system is discouraging capital investment. In order to achieve a 10 percent after-tax return, investors will only hold capital up to the point at which it yields 15.38 percent. The effective tax rate measures the distortion that the tax system is imposing on investment decisions in the corporate sector. Figure 5.5 illustrates the effects of corporate taxation on the capital-holding decision. The inversely sloped *DD* and $D_t D_t$ curves show the marginal revenue product of capital (MRP) net of actual depreciation (δp_k) in the pre-tax and after-tax situations. MRP declines as capital held increases because projects are ranked in descending order of their operating surpluses net of actual depreciation. At point A, equation (5) is satisfied and marginal rent is zero. The pre-tax rate of return on the amount of capital held at point A corresponds to point B. In the absence of corporate taxes, the amount of capital held would expand to point C. The effective tax rate $(r^* - r)/r$ is therefore responsible for reducing capital held from C to A. This distortion leads to the loss of economic rent shown by the shaded area.

Canada's corporate tax system (and the systems of most other countries) makes no attempt to identify actual depreciation. Instead, actual

FIGURE 5.5

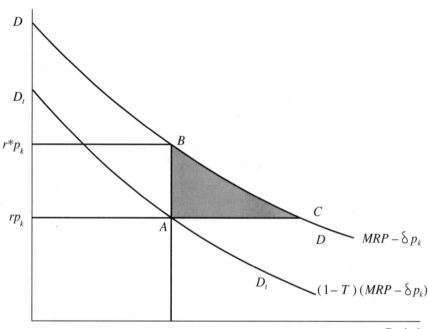

depreciation is ignored in favour of granting capital assets accelerated capital consumption allowances (CCAs) of the sort described above. The presence of accelerated depreciation tends to lower the effective tax rate below the rate implied by the statutory tax rate (35 percent in the example). To see how this works in the neoclassical investment model, assume that the capital asset is granted a declining balance CCA of 25 percent. Using the assumed 10 percent discount rate, an asset purchased for p_k = $1.00 has a present-valued stream of CCAs equal to $.79.[16] If each item in the CCA stream is deductible from operating income at a 35 percent corporate tax rate, the present value of all the tax deductions is .35($.79) = $.28. The (after-tax) cost of the capital asset to the investor is actually $1.00 – $.28 = $.72. Let us reconsider the after-tax asset equilibrium condition in equation (5) in the light of this. The return on holding the capital asset is $(1 - T)MRP$. Since the after-tax price of the capital asset is reduced by the present value of tax deductions ($.28 in the example), the interest cost of holding capital is $(1 - A)rp_k$ and the depreciation cost is $(1 - A)\delta p_k$, where, in this example, A = .28. Equality between the after-tax return on capital and its holding cost implies

$$(1 - T)MRP = (1 - A)rp_k + (1 - A)\delta p_k \tag{7}$$

As before, the pre-tax rate of return on capital is $r^* = (MRP - \delta p_k)/p_k$ which implies that $MRP = r^*p_k + \delta p_k$. Substituting for MRP in equation (7) and solving for r^*,

$$r^* = [(1 - A)r + (T - A)\delta]/(1 - T) \qquad (8)$$

With $T=.35$, $A=.28$, and an actual depreciation rate of 8 percent ($\delta=.08$), $r^* = 1.11r + .009$. If $r = .10$, $r^* = .12$ or 12 percent. The effective tax rate $(r^*-r)/r$ is 20 percent. This compares with the effective tax rate of 53.8 percent with actual depreciation rather than accelerated depreciation deducted. The effective tax rate does not have to be positive. For example, the Canadian system permits deduction of interest payments on bond-financed projects in calculating net income. This increases the present value of tax deductions A. If $A > T$, then $r^* < r$, and the effective tax rate is negative. In this case, the tax system actually encourages corporate investment. Corporations are induced to undertake projects that yield a lower social rate of return than the rate of return that could be earned by buying financial instruments on world markets. As discussed below in connection with the work of Boadway, McKenzie, and Mintz (1989), negative effective tax rates are typical in the Canadian mining sector. With negative effective tax rates, Figure 5.5 would have to be redrawn to show the $D_t D_t$ curve above the DD curve so that the corporate tax system reduces economic rent by causing more capital to be held than is optimal.

Notice in equation (8) that if the tax rate equals the present value of tax deductions per dollar of capital invested, i.e., $T = A$, then $r^* = r$. In this case, the effective tax rate is zero and the corporate tax system is *neutral*. Corporations undertake the same set of investments with the tax system as they do without it. This is exactly what happens with the ideal rent tax model discussed in the previous section: capital expenditures are being subsidized at the same rate (A) as net incomes are being taxed (T) so that corporate decisions are the same before and after taxation (rent capture).

In the corporate tax analysis described above, the effective tax rate depends importantly on the present value of allowed tax deductions that flow from up-front expenditures in mining (A). For firms with substantial profits and taxes on a whole range of mining activities from exploration to extraction and processing (fully integrated firms), there will be no problem in calculating A since these firms will have large enough tax liabilities in any period to permit them to take full advantage of all tax deductions as soon as they are allowed to make them. For a firm engaged in the exploration phase only (junior companies), the allowable tax deductions are likely to exceed the firm's current tax liability. This, in turn, reduces the value of A and increases the effective tax rate for the firm. One method of dealing with the problem is the *flow-through share* introduced in the early 1980s. Under the flow-through share scheme, a junior mining firm can sell shares to investors that permit the investors to claim the exploration expenditures immediately against their own tax liabilities. If the market for the firm's shares is highly competitive, flowing the deduction through to the investor should raise the value of shares issued by the amount of the tax credit flowed through. So the firm receives the exploration tax credits after all in the form of increased share prices. The size of the tax credit depends on the investor's tax bracket rather than on the corporate tax rate so, in principle, the shares tend to be worth the most to investors in high personal tax brackets. Since 1987, the flow-through mechanism has been enriched by allowing firms issuing such shares to claim additional grants.

Effective Taxation with Resource Rents

Equation (8) provides a way of judging the effect of the corporate tax system on investment decisions. Notice that the marginal project yields a return after-tax $(1-T)MRP$ that just covers holding costs of capital after the accelerated depreciation subsidy on capital $(1-A)(r+\delta)p_k$ in equation (7). If this project were *also* subject to an RRT, the RRT would equal zero since there are no (after corporate tax) rents to the marginal project. In this case, the corporate effective tax rate of 20 percent is also the effective tax rate for the system *including both corporate and resource rent taxes*. In practice, however, provinces do not collect revenues from natural resources using an RRT-type framework. When resource taxes are added to the corporate tax system, the effective tax rate changes. To appreciate why provincial resource taxes are non-neutral, we need to examine their general characteristics. Since the early 1970s, provincial governments have become increasingly conscious of the role of natural resource revenues as transfers of economic rent on provincially owned resources from the private sector to the public sector. At the same time, the provinces' resource revenue mechanisms reflect an earlier historical perspective under which natural resource taxation was viewed largely as a device to raise provincial revenue in the context of encouraging resource development rather than as a deliberate attempt to transfer rents to the provincial Crown. In the metallic minerals sector, which is the focus of discussion in this section, provincial revenues have typically been collected through mining taxes levied on profits of minerals companies. For oil and gas, provincial revenues have been collected through royalties levied on production values (wellhead oil prices and field price of natural gas) and through bidding on production leases.

Table 5.3 illustrates the steps involved in a representative provincial mining tax calculation. Total revenue is the quantity of mineral production evaluated at actual selling prices for concentrates, smelter products, or refined products. Net income is derived by subtracting operating costs. Though the specific rules vary from province to province, each province allows depreciation allowances on capital involved in extraction. Exploration and development activities undertaken within the province can be written off immediately in the mining tax calculation. Since most mines are

TABLE 5.3   Representative mining tax calculation.

Revenue
- Operating cost

= Net income before allowances
- Depreciation allowances
- Exploration and development expenditures

= Income for processing allowance
- Processing allowance

= Income for provincial mining tax
Provincial mining tax

---

integrated forward into concentrating and/or smelting-refining activities, not all net revenue from the company's final product sales can be attributed to mining itself. As a result, part of profits represent a return on processing assets. The processing allowance subtracts an estimate of profit at the processing stages in order to isolate profit subject to the mining tax. The latter is then assessed as a percentage of income for provincial mining taxes. Table 5.3 is a prototypical provincial mining tax system. Individual provinces vary slightly from the prototype. Some provinces assess mining taxes as a flat rate percentage of income for provincial mining tax in Table 5.3., some have graduated systems, and some permit an initial exemption before any mining taxes are collected (see, e.g., Boadway, McKenzie, and Mintz 1989, 44).

The key question addressed in this section is the effectiveness of Canadian mining tax systems of the type shown in Table 5.3 as rent capture devices. The basis for assessment is the efficient RRT-style framework set out in the previous section. Assume for the time being that processing allowances effectively remove the returns to capital beyond the extraction stage from mining company incomes so that mining taxes are being levied on income at the extraction stage.

An initial criticism of the mining tax as a rent capture device is that corporation income taxes paid to the federal and provincial governments have not been deducted in calculating income subject to mining taxes, as required by the RRT framework. These taxes are to be taken as net of tax deductions obtained through CCAs and other project deductions. A second criticism is that no explicit attempt is being made to guarantee the mining firm's required rate of return on capital.[17] A simple method of dealing with this problem would be to allow firms to deduct capital expenditures for extraction immediately in calculating income for provincial mining taxes. If all expenditures (deductible payments) including capital expenditures could be set against revenue (assessable receipts) immediately, the mining tax system would begin to approximate the RRT framework. (It would then be necessary to eliminate all depreciation deductions, since an immediate write-off of capital costs means that capitalization is not being applied to the acquisition of new assets.) If a firm does not have enough income to claim its investment spending immediately, subsidization, carry-back, or carry-forward with interest arrangements should be put in place as discussed in the previous section. Finally, the assumption that processing allowances do no more than remove income beyond the extraction stage from the tax base is not generally correct. They are usually more generous than this.

In summary, existing provincial mining tax systems of the type illustrated in Table 5.3 fail to identify the correct base for *ex-post* rent capture. If a true rent-capture regime is to be instituted, the following changes are required: corporation taxes should be allowed as a deductible payment; all extraction capital costs, not just exploration and development outlays, should be allowed as deductible payments; the present capital depreciation system should be eliminated; any unrecovered capital costs should be carried forward at a rate of interest corresponding to the industry's required rate of return on capital; and the processing allowance should be adjusted to reflect required returns on capital in processing. These changes would result in an RRT-style system.

Effective Mining Tax Rates in Canada

In order to judge the impact of both federal/provincial corporate taxes and mining taxes on the minerals sector, Boadway, McKenzie, and Mintz (1989) have conducted an analysis of the overall effective tax rate on marginal investments in mining. The methodology is the same as the approach outlined above for the calculation of an effective tax rate for corporate taxes except that mining tax rates are included in T and the present value of mining tax deductions are included in A. With the exception of investments in inventories, their analysis revealed that investment expenditures in the minerals sector produced *negative* effective tax rates using the post-1987 corporate and mining tax structure:

> ...corporate income and mining taxes are generally favourable to the mining industry. In fact, investment is subsidized at the margin rather than taxed for most types of capital expenditures. Although mining firms are paying on their inframarginal and marginal profits, the negative effective tax rates suggest that current corporate and mining taxes are poor collectors of resource rents....In some provinces, tax systems have also encouraged firms to process concentrates in the province in which they are produced through further processing allowances.[18]

What types of reforms can be proposed? First, with respect to provincial rent collection, reform of mining taxes along the lines proposed above could be used to convert mining tax systems into RRT-style rent taxes that are neutral in concept. If strict neutrality was the goal, corporate tax systems could also be changed so that $A = T$ in equation (8). With RRT-style rent collection and a zero effective corporate tax rate, taxation policy would no longer subsidize mining investments relative to the international cost of capital. Boadway, McKenzie, and Mintz do recommend an RRT-style approach to rent collection but they do not recommend moving to a zero effective corporate tax rate. The reason for avoiding strict neutrality in the corporate tax system, the authors argue, lies in the nature of the way governments handle foreign taxes paid on repatriated profits. Profits earned on U.S.-owned capital in Canada and repatriated to the U.S. receive a tax credit against U.S. corporation taxes if taxes have already been paid on these profits in Canada. Thus, with limitations, Canadian corporation taxes levied on the profits of U.S.-owned capital are a transfer to Revenue Canada from the U.S. Treasury. With a zero effective corporate tax rate in Canada, this transfer would disappear. It would therefore pay to have a *positive* effective corporate tax rate in Canada. This causes some distortion of Canadian investment decisions against holding capital but leads to a compensating gain in the form of foreign tax credits.

In the Canadian oil and gas sector, both production royalties and *ex-ante* bids are used to transfer rents to provincial governments. Royalties are calculated on wellhead or field prices and are even less efficient than provincial mining taxes as a rent transfer device. At least mining taxes are calculated on net revenue after the deduction of operating costs, while royalties take gross revenue as the tax base. Taxes are, therefore, being levied on operating costs, returns to capital, and other (corporation) taxes. Some projects earning positive economic rent before the imposition of royalties fail to do so after royalties are assessed. Alberta's experience with royalties is an interesting one. The province's initial response to the rapid rise in oil prices after 1973 was to increase its royalty rates on wellhead production values from 16 percent in the early 1970s to 30 to 50 percent in the early 1980s. The discouraging effect of such high royalty rates on petroleum projects led to a complex set of adjustments to Alberta's rent capture system. Alberta introduced generous drilling incentives to offset the impact of high royalty rates on exploration activity. Investments in recovery of oil from existing reservoirs were encouraged through deferrals of royalties and a variety of allowances designed to accommodate extraction from high-cost wells. Alberta policymakers seem to have recognized the inefficiency of revenue-based royalties as a method of shifting rents from the private sector to the public sector without, at the same time, being willing to move to discard the royalty system altogether in favour of an RRT-style rent capture mechanism. In a recent study of Alberta's royalty system, Kemp (1987) states that

[a] noteworthy feature of the whole scheme applied to Alberta, with its proliferation of deductions and allowances, is its great complexity. The allowances may be required to ensure that the basic structure does not produce economic distortions, but the cost is the additional complexity. The compliance costs are higher as a result. The exploration incentives may work well, but it is probable that a scheme which was more directly linked to economic rents could meet all the required objectives with less complexity and frequency of discretionary changes.[19]

■ HOW MUCH RENT CAN REALLY BE CAPTURED?

Resource rent capture systems in Canada stop far short of transferring all the available rent to public resource owners. In part, this is due to the fact that mining tax and petroleum bidding and royalty regimes are not neutral in their design. The very act of collecting rents reduces the overall rent surplus available to be shared between the private and the public sector by changing the revenue and cost conditions confronting private resource developers on marginal projects. But even neutral rent collection mechanisms like the RRT that use the appropriate rent base cannot be designed to transfer 100 percent of economic rent to the public owners. The reason lies in the effects that *ex-post* rent transfer has on incentives to maximize net returns in the private sector. If 100 percent of rent is subject to transfer, an extra dollar of costs incurred by the private sector simply reduces public sector revenue by one dollar with no effect on private sector returns. Why, then, should private operators bother minimizing costs and maximizing net revenues from rent-yielding projects? Any extra costs that are incurred in the private sector can be passed over to the public sector in the form of reduced rent. The private sector has no incentive to avoid incurring costs that have little or no chance of being recovered in increased revenues, a process sometimes referred to as "gold plating."

The "gold plating" problem implies that there is an inevitable tradeoff between efficiency and rent transfer, even when the correct rent base has been identified. When the rate of rent capture is low, private optimization incentives remain strong, efficient private decisions are being taken, and total rent (what is captured by the public sector plus what is left behind in the private sector) is high. The public sector receives a low level of resource revenue, however, precisely because the capture rate is low. At the opposite extreme, a very high rate of capture produces low total rent, because the private sector has little incentive to maximize total rent. The public sector again receives a low level of resource revenue, since it is capturing a large share of a small total. The likely behaviour of total rent and public resource revenue in response to different capture rates is illustrated in Figure 5.6.

Figure 5.6 assumes that an *ex-post* RRT-type capture mechanism is in place. The curves would be lower if less effective mechanisms (royalties or

FIGURE 5.6

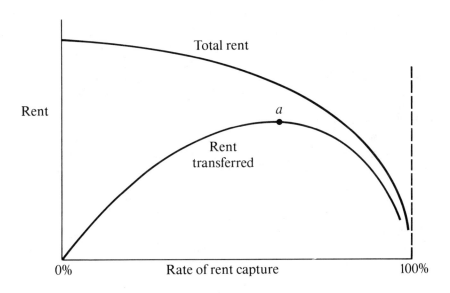

conventional mining taxes, for example) were being used. Point *a* in Figure 5.6 maximizes the resource revenue received by the public resource owner. The rate of rent capture at which this maximum is achieved is open to speculation, but it is obviously some finite distance short of 100 percent. An efficiency-revenue tradeoff is likely to characterize participation as well. Once public participation in projects reaches a high level, the remaining costs and revenues to the private sector will be too small to promote efficient private decisions. In the limit, if a Crown corporation undertakes the projects (100 percent public participation), optimization incentives obviously have to be embedded entirely within the public sector. There is no reason to believe that the optimization incentives needed to motivate efficient behaviour by the managers of Crown corporations would be less that the incentives needed to motivate private sector managers. Indeed, the managerial expertise required to operate Crown corporations is presumably drawn from the same group of individuals as is private sector management.

Ex-ante rent transfer via bidding and/or appraisals can eliminate the tradeoff illustrated in Figure 5.5. With the rent transfer set at the beginning of the project, every dollar saved or earned by the private operator in the subsequent management of the project is his or hers alone. Whether or not this advantage is decisive, however, is not clear. The amount of rent collected by *ex-ante* methods depends upon the strength of competition in the bidding process (or the accuracy of appraisals). And *ex-ante* methods capture expected rent, not realized rent. These will differ if there are unexpected windfalls that appear after the *ex-ante* rent transfer.

So no rent capture process is perfect. Those that operate on realized rents (the *ex-post* methods) cannot hope to transfer rent to the public sector without reducing the total amount of rent to be transferred, even if they are rent-based RRT-style systems. Those that operate by predicting rents (the *ex-ante* models) can, at best, transfer all of expected rents with no guarantee that realized rents are being captured in the process.

▌CONCLUSIONS

A great deal of ground at the intersection between resource economics and public finance has been covered in this chapter. The crucial issue has been one of attempting to translate theoretical rent concepts into models of rent capture that can work. The minerals sector is subjected to both corporate tax measures and resource revenue mechanisms. If the corporate tax system is given, rent available on the resource is most efficiently captured *ex-post* by using an RRT-style approach with corporate taxes and tax deductions included in the costs and revenues of the project for purposes of mining taxes.

If we look at the corporate tax system itself, we might initially think that neutrality $(A = T)$ would be the best approach. A zero corporate effective tax rate plus an RRT rent collection mechanism looks like the ideal way of securing the optimal social rent-maximizing amount of capital investment in mining. If it were not for the foreign tax credit argument for a positive (economy-wide) corporate effective tax rate, this rent-maximizing argument might suffice. If the effective corporate tax rate is to be positive to balance off some loss of rent at the margin against foreign tax credits, then the RRT-type rent collection mechanism is still the right approach. But corporate taxes have to be taken into account in the RRT to avoid any further marginal distortion. We can also think of *ex-ante* rent capture as an alternative approach and a blend of both *ex-ante* and *ex-post* models could also be useful.

An examination of the existing corporate tax structure and various resource revenue systems has revealed that we are a good distance away from an optimal tax system for minerals. Negative effective tax rates on mineral projects have been calculated by Boadway, McKenzie, and Mintz (1989) using late 1980s federal/provincial corporate tax and resources revenue regimes. Efficiency requires that we move to a positive effective corporate tax rate economy-wide and that we move to a zero effective resource tax model so that projects attract resource revenues only when their rents are positive.

None of Canada's existing resource taxation mechanisms comes to grips with the issue of optimal depletion in an explicit way. The negative effective tax rates that characterize existing systems tend to promote minerals depletion. Under a system with a positive effective tax rate, depletion would be slower. Whether or not it would be optimal from the viewpoint of maximizing the *present value* of economic rents on Canadian minerals is an open question.

■ APPENDIX: RESOURCE TAXES AND DEPLETION

Chapter 2 developed a framework for optimal depletion of nonrenewables. In the present chapter, we have examined a range of resource taxation and rent capture models. It seems natural to ask what effects the different types of resource taxation and rent capture models have on depletion decisions. The issue is put the following way: if depletion is optimal in the absence of taxes or rent capture devices, what effects do such devices have on these decisions? We consider four cases.

1. Proportional Taxes on Rent

In this case, a fraction of the net price or scarcity rent is to be transferred to the Crown owner using an RRT-style model. The pre-tax extraction pattern is assumed to be optimal and to follow the modified Hotelling rule from chapter 2:

$$rp = dp/dt - C_x q \qquad (A1)$$

A proportional tax on the net price multiplies each term in (A1) by $(1 - T)$ to give the after-tax results. The net price, the change in the net price, and the change in cost due to depletion are all "shared" to the extent of $(1 - T)$ for the private sector and T for the public sector. The set of outputs over time that satisfy (A1) also satisfy

$$(1 - T)rp = (1 - T)dp/dt - (1 - T)C_x q \qquad (A2)$$

so that the after-tax extraction pattern is the same as the pre-tax extraction pattern. Therefore, a proportional RRT is neutral with respect to depletion.

2. Progressive Taxes on Rent

Here, the net price is still the tax base but the rate of rent capture is graduated so that the marginal capture rate T' exceeds the average capture rate T''. Now the optimal pre-tax extraction pattern defined in (A1) leads to

$$(1 - T'')rp > (1 - T')dp/dt - (1 - T')C_x q \qquad (A3)$$

for $T' > T''$. The progressive RRT is non-neutral with respect to depletion. The after-tax marginal benefits of holding resources falls relative to the after-tax carrying cost so that there is an incentive to raise the rate of depletion.

3. *Ex-ante* Rent Capture

In this case, net prices along the extraction path are collected by bidding or by appraisals carried out by the owner. Payments are up-front and are unaffected by the subsequent extraction path followed. They are, therefore, sunk costs. Equation (A1) is unaffected so the *ex-ante* method is neutral regarding depletion decisions.

4. Royalties

Consider a tax rate T that is levied as a fraction of product price π. Since the tax does not allow for cost deductions, it is not a rent tax. The after-tax net price is $p^* = (1 - T)\pi - C = p - T\pi$, where p is the pre-tax net price $(\pi - C)$. The rate of change of the after-tax net price is $dp^*/dt = dp/dt - T(d\pi/dt)$. Write equation (A1) as

$$rp - dp/dt = -C_x q \qquad (A4)$$

At the pre-tax extraction pattern, we will show that,

$$rp^* - dp^*/dt < -C_x q \qquad (A5)$$

so that the royalty is non-neutral and causes extraction to be deferred, thus slowing down the rate of depletion. The proof is as follows. Substituting the definitions of the after-tax net price and its rate of change into the left-hand side of (A5),

$$rp^* - dp^*/dt = r(p - T\pi) - dp/dt + T(d\pi/dt)$$
$$= rp - dp/dt - T(r\pi - d\pi/dt) \qquad (A6)$$

Provided that $(d\pi/dt)/\pi < r$, the term $(r\pi - d\pi/dt) > 0$. For products to be sold in the current period rather than held for capital appreciation, it must be true that $(d\pi/dt)/\pi < r$. From (A6), it follows that $rp^* - dp^*/dt < rp - dp/dt$. Since, in the pre-tax equilibrium, $rp - dp/dt = -C_x q$, it follows that $rp^* - dp^*/dt < -C_x q$ in accordance with (A5) and extraction is deferred.

If the royalty is *constant* per unit of output, then $p^* = p - T$ and $dp^*/dt = dp/dt$ so that, again, $rp^* - dp^*/dt < rp - dp/dt$ and extraction is deferred in this case as well. These results are expected since a tax on output acts as a "depletion tax" as discussed earlier in the chapter.

■ NOTES

1. D. Ricardo, *Principles of Political Economy and Taxation* (London: J.M. Dent, 1933; originally published 1817).
2. H. Grubel, "Ricardian Rent and the Minerals Industry—The Debate Concludes," *Canadian Tax Journal* 28 (1980): 774.
3. G.C. Watkins, "Postscript: Canadian Policy Perspectives," in A. Kemp, *Petroleum Rent Collection Around the World* (Montreal: Institute for Research on Public Policy, 1987), p. 326.
4. Economic Council of Canada, *Financing Confederation Today and Tomorrow* (Ottawa: Supply and Services, 1982), Chap. 4.
5. Economic Council of Canada, *Newfoundland: From Dependency to Self-Reliance* (Ottawa: Supply and Services, 1980).
6. Article 408 of the Canada-U.S. Free Trade Agreement (FTA) prohibits export taxes. Article 409 permits export restrictions under circumstances consistent with the General Agreement on Tariffs and Trade (GATT), provided such restrictions are also applied to the domestic market. Controls on log exports and unprocessed fish exports are consistent with the FTA but not with GATT.
7. Projects that are economic even though they make little or no contribution to exploration costs are discussed below.
8. Rate-of-return taxation is discussed in Centre for Resource Studies, *Rate of Return Taxation of Minerals* (Kingston: Queen's University, 1977); and B. Mackenzie and M. Bilodeau, *Effects of Taxation on Base Metal Mining in Canada* (Kingston: Queen's University Centre for Resource Studies, 1979).
9. See O.Y. Kwon, "Neutral Taxation and Provincial Mineral Royalties: The Manitoba Metallic Minerals and Saskatchewan Uranium Royalties," *Canadian Public Policy* 9 (1983): 189–99; D.L. Anderson, "Innovation in Public Rent Capture: The Saskatchewan Uranium Industry," in T. Gunton and J. Richards, eds., *Resource Rents and Public Policy in Western Canada* (Montreal: Institute for Research on Public Policy, 1987).
10. See E.C. Brown, "Business-income Taxation and Investment Incentives," in *Income, Employment, and Public Policy* (New York: Norton, 1948).
11. Kemp, *Petroleum Rent Collection*, p. 324.
12. If resources extracted in each period are taken as homogeneous, as in the Hotelling and modified Hotelling models of chapter 2, then a depletion tax can just as well be levied at the extraction stage.
13. The description of tax systems and effective tax rate concepts follows the general methodology set out in R.W. Boadway, K.J. McKenzie, and J.M. Mintz, *Federal and Provincial Taxation of the Canadian Mining Industry* (Kingston: Queen's University Centre for Resource Studies, 1989).
14. *MRP* is the marginal revenue product of capital. Consider a simple case in which the production function is $Q = Q(K, L)$ where Q = output, K = capital inputs, and L = labour inputs. Totally differentiating, $dQ/dK = \partial Q/\partial K + (\partial Q/\partial L)(dL/dQ)$. Multiplying by product price P, $P(dQ/dK) = P(\partial Q/\partial K) + P(\partial Q/\partial L)(dL/dK)$. Assuming price-taking behaviour with labour hired until its marginal revenue product equals the wage (w), $P(\partial Q/\partial L) = w$. Thus, $P(dQ/dK) = P(\partial Q/\partial K) + w(dL/dK)$. Rearranging, $P(\partial Q/\partial K) = MRP =$

$P(dQ/dK) - w(dL/dK)$. Thus the marginal revenue product of capital equals marginal sales revenue minus marginal operating cost.

15. If the price of the capital good is changing, then the equilibrium condition is $MRP + dp_k/dt = rp_k + \delta p_k$. If the capital good offers a zero return in the form of revenue net of operating cost then $MRP = 0$. If it does not depreciate then $\delta = 0$. In this case, price appreciation would be required to provide a competitive yield on the asset and the equilibrium asset-holding condition follows the Hotelling rule: $(dp_k/dt)/p_k = r$.

16. If depreciation is claimed at the declining balance rate of a, then the undepreciated sequence of capital stock values for a \$1 investment is: \$1, \$$(1-a)$, \$$(1-a)^2$, \$$(1-a)^3$... The sum of all the depreciation allowances is: \$$a$ + \$$a(1-a)$ + \$$a(1-a)^2$ + \$$a(1-a)^3$... The discounted sum of the depreciation allowances is therefore \$$a$ + \$$a(1-a)/(1+r)$ + \$$a(1-a)^2/(1+r)^2$ + \$$a(1-a)^3/(1+r)^3$... The sum of this (convergent) geometric series is given by: $S = \$a/[1 - (1 - a)/(1 + r)]$. For $a = .25$ and $r = .10$, $S = .786$.

17. While it is true that graduated-rate mining tax systems with basic exemptions do shield income from taxes within a range, this range is not related systematically to the firm's rate of return requirement.

18. Boadway, McKenzie, and Mintz, *Federal and Provincial Taxation*, pp. 93–94.

19. Kemp, *Petroleum Rent Collection*, pp. 322–23.

▌ FURTHER READING

An interesting debate on concepts of economic rent in the mineral supply context is (in chronological order)

Cairns, R.D., "Ricardian Rent and Manitoba's Mining Royalty." *Canadian Tax Journal* 25 (September–October 1977).

Grubel, H.G. "Ricardian Rent and the Minerals Industry: A Comment." *Canadian Tax Journal* 27 (November–December 1979).

Cairns, R.D., and H.G. Grubel. "Ricardian Rent and the Minerals Industry—The Debate Concludes." *Canadian Tax Journal* 28 (November–December 1980).

The Economic Council of Canada's rent estimates for the Canadian economy in 1980 are contained in

Economic Council of Canada. *Financing Confederation: Today and Tomorrow*. Ottawa: Supply and Services, 1982.

The hydroelectricity rent estimates are in

Zuker, R., and G.P. Jenkins. *Blue Gold—Hydroelectric Rent in Canada*. Ottawa: Economic Council of Canada, Supply and Services, 1984, which includes comparisons with the rent estimates made by J.T. Bernard, G.E. Bridges, and A.D. Scott in "An Evaluation of Potential Canadian Hydroelectric Rents," Resource Paper 78, Department of Economics, University of British Columbia.

On the RRT-style approach to rent collection, see

Bradley, P.G., and G.C. Watkins. "Net Value Royalties—Practical Tool or Economist's Illusion?" *Resources Policy* (December 1987).

Garnaut, R., and A. Clunies Ross. "Uncertainty, Risk Aversion and the Taxing of Natural Resource Projects." *Economic Journal* 85 (June 1975).

Kemp, A. *Petroleum Rent Collection Around the World*. Montreal: Institute for Research on Public Policy, 1987.

An excellent case study of the Saskatchewan uranium royalty is

Anderson, D.L. "Innovation in Public Rent Capture: The Saskatchewan Uranium Industry." In T. Gunton and J. Richards, eds. *Resource Rents and Public Policy in Western Canada*. Montreal: Institute for Research on Public Policy, 1987.

Description of the Canadian corporate tax system in the late 1980s and the effective tax rate methodology and calculations are from

Boadway, R.W., K.J. McKenzie, and J.M. Mintz. *Federal and Provincial Taxation of the Canadian Mining Industry*. Kingston: Queen's University Centre for Resource Studies, 1989.

CHAPTER SIX

MANAGING

CANADA'S FOREST

RESOURCES

▌INTRODUCTION

This chapter and the next shift attention away from nonrenewable resources to Canada's renewable resources, focusing on forestry and fisheries. Unlike hydraulic power, for which flows and regeneration are automatic and based on physical processes essentially beyond man's control, biological processes lie behind the availability of timber and fish, and these biological production functions can be influenced by deliberate management strategies. Renewable resources can be replenished through regeneration. This distinction cannot be pushed too far, however. As discussed in chapter 2, exploration efforts are capable of "regenerating" nonrenewable resources—perhaps indefinitely in the case of geochemically abundant minerals—at unit costs that may or may not increase over time, depending on rates of technical progress. Even in the absence of technical progress, regeneration of renewable resources is not necessarily accompanied by increasing costs provided the biological environment is stable. In some cases, regeneration is completely natural. The hydrological cycle (precipitation and evaporation), for example, ensures regeneration of hydro potential. In other cases, regeneration is costly, and decisions not to incur those costs will result in depletion (mining) of the resource. Most forest resources regenerate naturally (though not necessarily to desired species) and others require costly (artificial) regeneration.

In the case of forests, current supplies of timber depend on the rate at which existing growing stocks of timber are drawn down. As with non-renewable resources, stocks are much larger than flows and economic theory can be applied to determine an optimal rate of stock utilization or depletion. In forestry the optimal rate of stock utilization is referred to as the *rotation decision*: to what age should trees be allowed to grow before they are harvested. Rotation theory and the management of forests to provide ongoing supplies of timber for the forest products sector occupies the first two sections of the present chapter.

Forests provide not only timber inputs for forest products, they also provide special environments that contribute directly to human welfare. The aesthetic pleasures of a forest and the ecological system that it supports are influenced by timber harvesting and the rotation decision is (or should be) affected by these nontimber values. The third section brings these considerations into the calculus of harvesting.

Chapter 4 examined the question of long-run scarcity applied to nonrenewable resources—minerals and energy. The fourth section of the present chapter extends the framework of that discussion to forest resources. The discussion in chapter 4 concluded that there is no definite evidence of past upward trends in the real prices of most mineral resources. One might suppose that scarcity would be even less apparent for a renewable resource such as timber. Surprisingly, the opposite is true. Forests have undergone significant depletion in North America during this century. They have been harvested more rapidly than they have been regenerated to desired species through natural and artificial processes. The presence of this "regeneration gap" in the forestry sector leads naturally to a consideration of the costs and benefits of reforestation.

To this end, a benefit-cost framework suitable to regeneration decisions is developed and the framework applied to reforestation in Canada. Professional foresters have been warning us of the depletion of forest resources for many years. This concern has become much stronger in the last ten years or so, partly as a result of improving physical data on the condition of Canada's forest resources. Federal and provincial regeneration initiatives are now being undertaken with greater urgency than before. It is important that these efforts be informed to a greater extent by economic criteria.

The final section of the chapter briefly takes up the question of rent capture in forestry. Unlike the minerals sector, rent capture has not been a prominent issue for renewable resources. With the exception of British Columbia, existing methods in forestry are rudimentary and the B.C. system itself (*ex-ante* appraisal) has been altered under the influence of international trade actions in the United States.

■ THE HARVEST TIMING DECISION: ROTATION THEORY

A General Rotation Framework

The theoretical approach used to develop the Hotelling model (chapter 2) can be carried over with some modifications to decisions in the forestry sector. A stand of timber differs in three important economic respects from a mineral prospect, however. First, unlike mineral deposits, trees experience growth, so that a decision *not* to harvest in the present means that a larger timber volume will be available in the stand for later use. (If stands are allowed to become too old, volume may decline due to death and rot.) With minerals, a decision not to extract in the present does not alter the size of the deposit left for the future. Second, trees occupy potentially valuable land that can be used either for non-forestry purposes or for starting a new crop of timber. By contrast, the space occupied by mineral deposits has little or no economic value. The third major distinction between trees and minerals is that forests can provide social benefits so that harvesting leads to the transformation of a valuable social asset into an industrial input. Mineral deposits, by contrast, provide no benefits other than those derived from their eventual extraction.[1] This third distinction is not dealt with in this section, but rather reserved to a following section in which nontimber values are integrated into the harvesting decision model.

Just as with mineral resources, renewable resources possess a net price (p) equal to the difference between the price of the product (π) and its marginal extraction cost (C). The net price of a stand of timber is the value of the products—lumber and pulp—that can be obtained from the timber minus the marginal cost of harvesting the trees and converting them into these final products. In forest economics, the net price of timber is referred to as the *stumpage price*. It is the value per cunit or per cubic metre of trees in the forest or "on the stump."[2]

A wealth-maximizing owner of a timber stand has, as his objective, choosing the correct time in the stand's growth cycle to convert his timber into a manufacturing input (logs). Throughout this chapter, we will assume that all trees in a stand are of equal age. This means that the decision to harvest the stand is a decision to harvest all the trees in the stand. We do not consider the possibility of thinning. When trees in a stand are of equal age, foresters refer to this type of management regime as *even-aged* management. (The case of *uneven-aged* management occurs when the stand consists of trees of many ages such that harvesting of stands proceeds as a selection harvest.)

The wealth-maximizing timing decision under even-aged management without thinning involves comparing returns available to the owner from harvesting the stand at different times in much the same way that the owner of mineral deposits must decide to extract now or later. If the timber owner harvests *now* he receives the stumpage value of his resource, provided he can sell the timber in the stand at a price corresponding to the difference between its product value and marginal cost of harvesting and manufacturing $(\pi - C)$. He can also sell the land on which the timber has been growing for its market value as bare land. If he waits and harvests in the *future*, the return he receives *now* is the discounted present value of the future stumpage return plus the discounted value of the future bare land.

Suppose the volume of merchantable timber in the owner's stand is $x(t)$ at time t and $x(t + \Delta t)$ at time $t + \Delta t$. The stumpage price per unit of volume is $p(t)$ at time t and $p(t + \Delta t)$ at $t + \Delta t$. The bare land occupied by the stand can be sold for an amount $A(t)$ at t and at $A(t + \Delta t)$ at time $t + \Delta t$. If the forest owner cuts the stand and sells the land it occupies at time t, he or she receives a return of $p(t) \cdot x(t) + A(t)$. If the owner holds the timber until the next time period $(t + \Delta t)$, at which time he harvests it and sells the bare land, he receives $p(t + \Delta t) \cdot x(t + \Delta t) + A(t + \Delta t)$. Which of these strategies dominates in his wealth-maximizing decision is determined by comparing their present values. He will hold the stand for future harvest if

$$p(t) \cdot x(t) + A(t) < [p(t + \Delta t) \cdot x(t + \Delta t) + A(t + \Delta t)]/(1 + r\Delta t) \quad (1)$$

where r is the continuous discount rate and $(1 + r\Delta t)$ is the usual discounting factor (see chapter 2). If the forest owner is postponing harvesting according to equation (1), then the same comparison of present values must be applied to future time periods. Provided the return from immediate harvesting equals the return from harvesting one period later at some point in the forest stand's growth cycle, wealth is maximized at that point by harvesting since

$$p(t) \cdot x(t) + A(t) = [p(t + \Delta t) \cdot x(t + \Delta t) + A(t + \Delta t)]/(1 + r\Delta t) \quad (2)$$

If equation (2) is rearranged, it can be written as

$$\begin{aligned}[p(t + \Delta t) \cdot x(t + \Delta t) - p(t) \cdot x(t) + A(t + \Delta t) - A(t)]/\Delta t \\ = r[p(t) \cdot x(t) + A(t)]\end{aligned} \quad (3)$$

Equation (3) states that the increase in the value of the timber stand plus the increase in the value of the land occupied by the timber during the current period has to be just large enough to cover the costs of capital tied up in timber and the land it occupies. If the value of timber and land is increasing by more than its holding costs, harvesting should be postponed. If it is increasing by an amount insufficient to cover holding costs, harvesting should have taken place earlier in the timber growth cycle.

Defining $x(t + \Delta t) = x(t) + \Delta x$ and $p(t + \Delta t) = p(t) + \Delta p$, the term $p(t + \Delta t) \cdot x(t + \Delta t) - p(t) \cdot x(t) = x(t)\Delta p + p(t)\Delta x + \Delta p\Delta x$ in equation (3). Similarly, $A(t + t) - A(t) = \Delta A$. Making these substitutions and allowing the time interval Δt to shrink to dt, equation (3) becomes

$$x(t) \cdot dp/dt + p(t) \cdot dx/dt + dA/dt = r[p(t) \cdot x(t) + A(t)] \qquad (3A)$$

or

$$(dp/dt)/p + (dx/dt)/x + (dA/dt)/px = r(1 + A/px) \qquad (4)$$

The harvest timing rule now states that the rate of change of net price or stumpage price $(dp/dt)/p$ plus the rate of growth of timber volume $(dx/dt)/x$ plus the change in the value of occupied land per dollar of timber must equal the opportunity cost of capital (r) adjusted for the carrying cost of bare land (rA/px). Following rule (4) implies cutting timber such as to maximize the private owner's wealth. Provided timber values and land values correctly reflect social values, it can be shown that equation (4) is also the socially optimal harvesting rule.[3]

Equation (4) can be compared to the Hotelling rule for mineral resources given by equation (4) in chapter 2. If the resource volume is not growing through time, as is the case for a nonrenewable resource, then $dx/dt = 0$. If, at the same time, the resource does not occupy land (space) with a positive value in its own right, then $A = 0$ and $dA/dt = 0$. Under these circumstances, optimal extraction (harvesting) takes place when the rate of change of the net price $(dp/dt)/p$ equals the rate of interest r (the Hotelling rule).

The role of equation (4) in setting the optimal forest rotation is shown in Figure 6.1. The *yield curve* in Figure 6.1 illustrates the behaviour of timber volume in a hypothetical stand. The slope of the yield curve at any point in the stand's growth cycle is dx/dt. At a particular point in the stand's growth cycle—say 75 years after planting—equation (4) is satisfied. The optimal or wealth-maximizing rotation period is, therefore, 75 years. If economic and biological conditions remain unchanged over the very long run and regeneration is undertaken immediately following cutting, the bare land produces a new timber harvest of $x*$ at the end of each 75-year period.

If 75 hectares of forest land are subjected to the 75-year rotation with one hectare planted and harvested each year, the flow of timber will remain constant through time. The 75-hectare forest produces an *even flow* of wood equal to $x*$ per year. A forest that produces an even flow of wood annually with a constant rotation has stands at each stage of the growth cycle represented by equal areas of land. Foresters call it a *normal* or *fully regulated forest*.[4] The total volume of timber in the fully regulated forest is represented by area X in Figure 6.1: it is the sum of all the stand volumes

FIGURE 6.1   The forest rotation decision

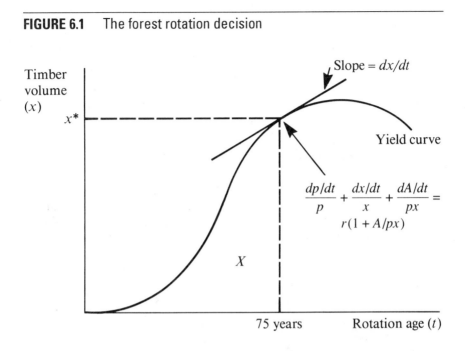

from planting to harvest. Area X is usually called the *normal growing stock*. A stylized diagram of a fully regulated even-aged forest is shown in Figure 6.2.

If the annual harvest from a fully regulated forest is 140 cubic metres per hectare (20 cunits/acre), a modern newsprint mill producing 160 000 tonnes of newsprint per year would harvest approximately 480 000 cubic metres of wood per year, or 3400 hectares of forest. Over 13 square miles of forest are being cut over every year by a mill of this size.[5] With a 75-year rotation, perpetual operation of the mill would require a normal forest occupying nearly 1000 square miles! Such a huge area, referred to as the mill's *timbershed*, reflects the large size required for the economical manufacture of pulp and paper products. Timbersheds for economical sawmills are much smaller.

There is really nothing normal about a "normal" or fully regulated forest: it requires a very special distribution of the land area over timber age-classes. Nevertheless, the concept of the even-flow fully regulated forest is an important one in forestry practice and often serves as a goal for long-term management. The implications of this goal in the context of economic optimization will be taken up in the following section.

FIGURE 6.2

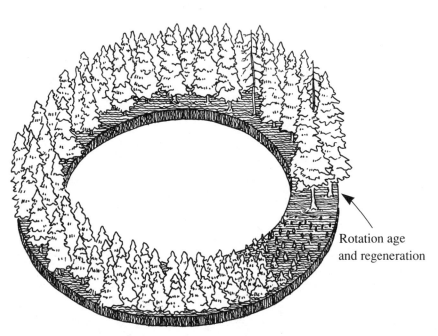

Rotation age
and regeneration

Source: M.L. Hunter, *Wildlife, Forests, and Forestry* (Englewood Cliffs, N.J.:
Prentice-Hall, 1990).

Specific Rotation Models

Equation (4) provides a very general statement of the optimal time to
harvest a growing timber stand. By making additional assumptions about
the discount rate (r), the rate of change of stumpage prices $[(dp/dt)/p]$, or
the value of bare land (A), it is possible to generate more specific rotation
rules that have been advocated at one time or another in the economics and
forestry literature.[6]

A simple rotation rule that is sometimes proposed assumes that (real)
stumpage prices are constant and the value of bare land is zero. Setting
$(dp/dt)/p$ and A equal to zero in equation (4),

$$(dx/dt)/x = r \qquad (5)$$

is the harvest timing rule in this case. In a land-abundant economy, such as
Canada's, there is some plausibility in setting a low value on bare land in
forested regions. Setting a zero value for real rates of stumpage price

increase may be less realistic, however, since long historical series compiled for the United States suggest that a trend rate of 2 to 3 percent per year for sawtimber stumpage prices is likely based on past experience.[7] Sawtimber owners should take this source of appreciation of sawtimber values into their calculations of the optimal time to harvest.

A more complex rotation rule emerges if real stumpage prices are assumed constant (as above), while the value of bare land is derived from the value of growing timber on it. The resulting rotation rule owes its existence to the nineteenth-century forest economist Martin Faustmann. The Faustmann rotation values bare land in accordance with the present value of an endless series of stands that can be grown on it. Faustmann's present value approach works as follows.

Consider bare land that is capable of growing future timber supplies. If trees are planted on it, the cost of regeneration is c. After a full rotation, the stand will be harvested, yielding revenue to the owner of px. If the rotation period is t years and the annual discount rate is r, the present value of the harvest is $(px)/(l + r)^t$. So the present value of the bare land on *one* rotation, and after initial regeneration cost, is $(px)/(l + r)^t - c$. If this process is repeated for an endless series of rotations of t years in duration, the present value of the land will be

$$A = px/(1 + r)^t - c + [px/(1 + r)^t - c]/(1 + r)^t +$$
$$[px/(1 + r)^t - c]/(1 + r)^{2t}..... \qquad (6)$$

Equation (6) is a converging infinite geometric series much like a multiplier series. Its first term is $(px)/(1 + r)^t - c$ and each subsequent term in the series is obtained by multiplying the preceding term by $1/(1 + r)^t$ (the geometric ratio). The sum of such a series can be written as

$$A = [px/(1 + r)^t - c]/[1 - 1/(1 + r)^t] \qquad (7)$$

which is its first term divided by one minus its geometric ratio. Now that the value of the bare land in the Faustmann model has been derived, one small step remains before returning to equation (4). Since the time interval Δt is being taken to be very short ($= dt$), discounting does not proceed annually but, rather, continuously. In this case the discounting term $(1 + r)^t$ has to be replaced by e^{rt} where e is the base of natural logarithms (2.718).[8] Equation (7) becomes

$$A = (pxe^{-rt} - c)/(1 - e^{-rt}) \qquad (8)$$

The optimal rotation according to Faustmann is then obtained by replacing A in equation (4) by the bare-land value term in equation (8) with stumpage prices (and bare-land value) constant so that,

$$(dx/dt)/x = r + r(pxe^{-rt} - c)/px(1 - e^{-rt})$$
$$= r(1 - c/px)/(1 - e^{-rt}) \qquad (9)$$

The effects of changes in the stumpage price (p), regeneration cost (c), and the rate of discount (r) on the Faustmann rotation can be found easily from (9). An increase in c/p lowers the right-hand side of (9). To restore equality, the left-hand side must also decline, implying a lower rate of growth of timber at harvest and, therefore, a longer rotation period. Thus the Faustmann rotation is longer with higher regeneration cost and lower stumpage prices. If regeneration cost (c) is zero, then changes in the stumpage price have no effect on the rotation period. An increase in the discount rate raises the right-hand side of (9). Restoring equality requires a shorter rotation period as a result.

Even with the assumption of stable stumpage prices (and bare-land values), the Faustmann rule is sufficiently comprehensive to incorporate other rotation rules as special cases. For example, if bare land has zero value, then $A = (pxe^{-rt} - c)/(1 - e^{-rt}) = 0$, implying that $c/(px) = e^{-rt}$. Replacing $c/(px)$ in equation (9) by e^{-rt} simply reproduces equation (5). When $A > 0$, $c/(px) < e^{-rt}$ so that the square-bracketed term in equation (9) is greater than one. The presence of valuable land *shortens* the optimal rotation, since the growth rate of the stand $[(dx/dt)/x]$ must be greater at the moment of harvesting than if land has zero value. The forest owner following the Faustmann rule harvests before $(dx/dt)/x = r$ in order to free up land for subsequent timber rotations.

The presence of a positive rate of discount (r), representing the opportunity cost of tying up capital in the form of timber and land is often, but wrongly, ignored in actual forest management decisions. If $r = 0$ in the Faustmann rule, it can be shown that the term $r/(l - e^{-rt})$ in equation (9) equals $1/t$.[9] Equation (9) then becomes

$$(dx/dt)/x = (1 - c/px)/t \tag{10}$$

If regeneration cost (c) is also set equal to zero in (10), then

$$(dx/dt)/x = 1/t \tag{11}$$

Equation (11) is a very popular forest management rule with policymakers and is usually referred to as a *maximum sustained yield* (MSY) rule of harvesting. Figure 6.3 should help to put this MSY rule into perspective. The curve x/t shows the stand volume from Figure 6.1 divided by the growing period and is defined by foresters as the mean annual increment or MAI of the stand. The curve dx/dt graphs the slope of the yield curve in Figure 6.1 showing the addition to volume during each (short) time period dt. This is the current annual increment or CAI in forestry terminology.

As usual with average and marginal relationships, the CAI curve cuts the MAI curve at the latter's maximum point. So, selecting CAI = MAI means $dx/dt = x/t$ or $(dx/dt)/x = 1/t$ as in equation (11). Satisfying equation (11) therefore maximizes sustained yield *per unit of land area*. The timber stand is cut as soon as its CAI threatens to fall below the MAI that could be obtained from the hectare on the next rotation (point a in Figure

FIGURE 6.3   MSY in forestry

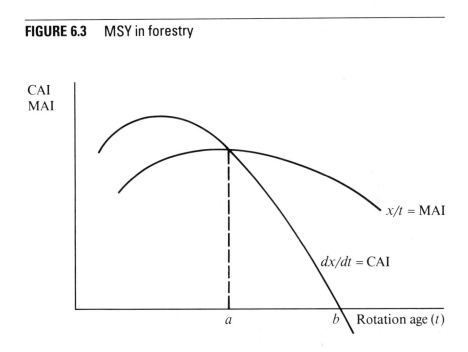

6.3). This ensures that each hectare of forest land is producing the largest possible average yield of wood sustainable over an indefinite sequence of rotations.

It should be noted that the forestry concept of MSY differs from the MSY concept discussed in chapter 7 for fisheries resources. The CAl = MAI harvesting rule maximizes yield per hectare of forested land. In the fishery there is no implicit scarcity attached to the space occupied by the resource itself. In this case MSY means maximizing the resources harvest volume (x) which implies dx/dt = CAI = 0. Applying this rule to forest stands would produce a longer rotation period equal to b in Figure 6.3.

Our examination of special cases in rotation theory can be summarized with reference to equations (5), (9), and (11). All three special cases neglect the rate of change of real stumpage prices and land value incorporated in equation (4). Of the three special cases, the Faustmann rule in equation (9) is the most general and also produces the *shortest* rotation, since it recognizes the costs of tying capital up in timber and in bare land. When bare land is a "free good" $(A = 0)$, only the cost of capital tied up in timber is relevant, and equation (5) emerges as a special version of the Faustmann rule for this case. If bare land is scarce and the discount rate is arbitrarily set equal to zero, the MSY rule of equation (11) can be derived as above.[10] Since capital tied up in timber stands—and in bare land if

$A > 0$—has a definite opportunity cost measured by the rate of interest, there is no economic justification for setting $r = 0$ in harvest timing models despite the frequent preference of forest managers for the MSY framework. One consequence of ignoring the opportunity cost of capital in forest management decisions is that rotation periods selected in the MSY framework are *too long* when judged by economic optimization objectives.

■ ECONOMIC ROTATIONS AND TIMBER SUPPLY POLICY

Timber management policies in Canada have been heavily influenced by both the maximum sustained yield (MSY) approach to harvest timing and the even-flow characteristic that would be present in a fully regulated or normal forest. Both Canada and the U.S. have large volumes of old-growth timber experiencing low or even negative rates of growth. Forest managers in both countries favour the MSY approach to selecting the rotation period. Timber stands beyond the MSY rotation period are harvested gradually, usually with the intention of establishing a fully regulated forest in the future.

Despite their frequent association in the minds of policymakers, the MSY rotation concept and the fully regulated forest are analytically distinct concepts. To see this, consider a forest manager selecting an MSY rotation rule, say 50 years. Suppose the manager is endowed with 3000 hectares. The 3000-hectare endowment consists of 1000 hectares at age-class 60, 1000 hectares at age-class 45, and 1000 hectares at age-class 20. If the manager sticks to his MSY rule for each stand, he immediately harvests the over-mature (beyond rotation age) timber in age-class 60, waits for 5 years and harvests another 1000 hectares, and harvests the remaining 1000 hectares 30 years hence. The timber flow is very uneven with long periods of zero harvesting. Enter an economist favouring a Faustmann rotation of (say) 40 years. The economist regards the age-class 45 and 60 areas as over-mature by her rotation rule and harvests both immediately, waiting for 20 years to harvest the remaining 1000 hectares. The economist's timber flow is also highly uneven but because she is using a shorter (optimal) rotation, she classifies more timber into the over-mature category at the outset and therefore begins the harvesting program with a larger harvest than the manager.

If the manager favours not only MSY rotations but also has a preference for even-flow results, he may temporarily override his own rotation rule at the stand level in order to regulate the forest for the future. An extreme method of doing this is to adopt strict *area control*. The manager uses his MSY rotation to divide the 3000 hectare endowment into fifty 60-hectare units. One 60-hectare unit is harvested and replanted every year. At the end of 50 years—referred to as the *conversion period*—he has a fully regulated forest. It is impossible to achieve full regulation any faster than this: the conversion period cannot be shorter than the rotation period. This strict area-control approach reduces the harvest in the first period below the harvest without regulation and "smears" it out over several subsequent periods. So the harvest in the initial period is lower than the economist's both because the manager is choosing to regulate the forest (over one rotation) *and* because he is choosing to regulate the forest using a longer rotation than the economist's (if he chose the economist's shorter rotation he would harvest 75 hectares in each period on strict area control).

Forest regulation practice is rarely as inflexible as the strict area-control approach described above. The manager can introduce some flexibility by setting the conversion period to be longer than the rotation period. Suppose, for example, the manager remains with his 50-year MSY rule but gives himself "one degree of freedom" by choosing a 51-year conversion period. This allows him to choose the land area to be harvested in the first period and then forces him to harvest 60 hectares per year thereafter. If the volume of timber per hectare in age-class 60 is large relative to subsequent flows and is being harvested first, the manager might use his one degree of freedom to reduce the area harvested in the first period below 60 hectares. This "saves" some of the age-class 60 volume for the subsequent area-control period. By lengthening the conversion period relative to the rotation period, more and more degrees of freedom are introduced into the volume flow during the conversion period. The manager is using a mixture of area control and *volume control* in converting the initial age-class mixture to the target regulated forest.

The economist can now object to the whole management scheme on two grounds. First, of course, the selection of the rotation period itself reflects the MSY model rather than the Faustmann model. Second, the economist would ask why any attempt is being made to regulate the forest *at all*. If the forest manager is a price taker, an uneven harvest based on cutting each stand in accordance with its Faustmann rotation maximizes the net present value of each stand. Since the forest is just a collection of stands, the NPV of the forest is also being maximized. Conversion to a regulated forest simply involves cutting most stands at the wrong age and reduces net present value below its maximum value. Focusing on the overmature categories of timber, the economist recommends much more rapid liquidation of these stocks than the MSY rule combined with regulation produces. The Faustmann rule classifies both age-class 60 and age-class 45 timber as beyond rotation age while the MSY rule classifies only age-class 60 as beyond rotation age. The economist is recommending that both age-classes be removed as rapidly as possible to make way for new stands instead of being left to grow at rates that are too low to provide a competitive rate of return on the timber and bare land tied up in slow-growing timber. The flow of wood to lumber and pulp and paper mills diverges further from "even-flow" under economic criteria than under the

FIGURE 6.4

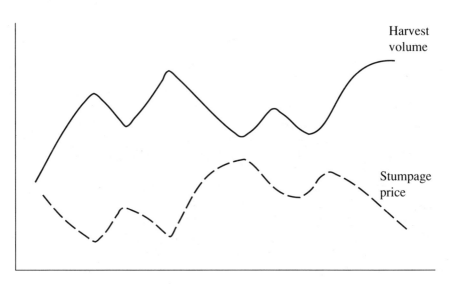

slow liquidation–MSY regime that characterizes present timber management policy.

Are there circumstances in which economic analysis might favour a shift toward a fully regulated forest in the long run? The answer to this question turns on the impact of variations in harvest volume on stumpage prices. The preceding discussion assumed that the forest manager accepts stumpage prices as given in formulating harvest decisions. This may not be the correct assumption to make in all cases. Recall that the stumpage price is the net price of timber obtained by subtracting marginal harvesting and processing cost (C) from the price of forest products (π). An increase in harvest volume can lead to lower stumpage prices if the increased harvest leads to lower forest products prices or increased marginal harvesting and processing costs. This produces an inverse relationship between the harvest volume and the net price. Referring to Figure 6.4, variation in harvest volume over time produces inverse variation in stumpage prices: when harvest volume is increasing from one period to the next, stumpage prices are falling and *vice versa*. Equation (4) indicates that, other things equal, a period of rising stumpage prices tends to lengthen economic rotations. The logic is that if stumpage prices are rising, the wealth-maximizing forest manager will want to delay timber harvests to take advantage of higher timber values in the future. By the same token, if stumpage prices are falling, the wealth-maximizing manager will want to accelerate harvests by cutting stands sooner to take advantage of higher timber values. If this optimizing behaviour is followed, there is a tendency for harvests to even out somewhat: larger areas of timber are harvested during periods of high stumpage prices and smaller areas are harvested during low price intervals relative to a harvesting pattern that ignores the time variations in stumpage prices.

How does this behaviour affect long-run timber supply? Consider two adjacent decades. Suppose managers adopt the same rotation (say 50 years) for all timber so that the harvest yield *per hectare* is the same in both decades. Suppose further that the land areas are such that this rule leads to harvesting 60 hectares in the first decade and 30 hectares in the second. The harvest volume falls by 100 percent between the two decades, causing, say, a rise of 15 percent in the stumpage price. If managers react to the rising stumpage price, they may decide to postpone some of the first decade's harvesting and shift harvesting into the second decade. If they harvest 50 hectares in the first decade and 40 in the second, this not only evens out the current harvest somewhat, it also leads to a different and more even distribution of land areas for future rotations. Assuming that they regenerate each hectare immediately, 5 decades later they will encounter 50 hectares of maturing timber and 6 decades later they encounter 40 hectares. Again, the harvest volume is declining between the two adjacent decades (following the 50-year rotation rule) but only by 20 percent this time. Again, they may decide to postpone some harvesting from the fifth to the sixth decade in reponse to rising stumpage returns, leading to further smoothing of harvests and land areas in adjacent age-classes.[11]

Obviously the foregoing example is only suggestive but it does imply that gradual movement to a regulated forest may turn out to be optimal over a sequence of rotations. If this is so, an optimal harvesting regime in which stumpage prices are inversely related to harvest volumes will probably involve a conversion period that is much longer than a single rotation. It should also be pointed out that a strategy of gradual conversion to a regulated forest may not involve serious losses of net present value even when stumpage prices are independent of harvest volume, provided net present value is maximized over the conversion period *and* the correct economic rotation is chosen for the final regulated forest.[12]

∎ BRINGING NONTIMBER VALUES INTO THE MODEL

Until the late 1970s, the harvest timing decision framework assigned value to forests solely for the timber that they could produce as an industrial input to lumber and pulp and paper firms. It had always been recognized informally that forests are capable of providing a range of nontimber benefits as well, but rotation theory had always focused on stumpage values as described in the previous section. In a sense, it seems obvious that forests managed for timber supplies can also produce other benefits to society simply as a by-product of their existence as growing timber inventories. What has changed dramatically over the past decade or so is the extent to which nontimber benefits have been promoted from the status of by-products to equal partners in optimal forest management models.

The concept of *multiple-use* recognizes that forests produce benefits in the form of soil and water control, wildlife stocking, and recreational/aesthetic features along with flows of harvestable timber. Optimum multiple-use forest management has to integrate all these uses of forests into harvesting decisions. Different solutions are possible. In some cases the provision of one kind of benefit appears to negate the provision of another. Preservation of forests for wilderness recreation or as examples of wild habitats outside the influence of man's activities preclude commercial harvesting, for example. In this case a separate facilities or *dominant-use* solution is called for with wilderness areas set aside and completely exempted from the provision of timber supplies. The size and number of such wilderness areas inevitably provokes lively discussion. The benefits of wilderness forests are not amenable to market solutions since prices are not usually paid for access to these areas. In both Canada and the U.S., most wild forests are publicly owned. The public ownership feature, combined with incomplete markets for many nontimber benefits, means that decisions concerning tradeoffs between timber management and other forest uses will be channeled through the political process, much the way environmental concerns have worked their way into legislation (chapter 3). Forests are now perceived as resources that should be subject to *integrated management* designed to optimize overall benefits and costs associated with Canada's forest resources.

Apart from wild habitats, most forests are capable of producing both commercial timber volumes and other nontimber benefits during their growth cycles. Harvest timing models have been developed that incorporate both timber and nontimber values into the rotation decision (Hartman 1976; Calish, Fight, and Teeguarden 1978; Bowes and Krutilla 1989). A modified version of equation (3A) can be used to show how multiple-use affects harvesting decisions. For simplicity, assume that stumpage prices and bare land values are constant with respect to time. Nontimber value is incorporated by assuming that the standing timber volume $[x(t)]$ provides a flow of benefits each period denoted by $Z[x(t)]$. There are now two advantages to holding a timber stand during the current period: the increase in stumpage value caused by the growth of forest volume and the flow of nontimber benefits. The cost of holding the stand is, as before, the carrying cost of the timber and occupied land. The optimal harvesting point occurs when

$$p \cdot dx/dt + Z[x(t)] = r[p \cdot x(t) + A(t)] \qquad (12)$$

At first glance, equation (12) seems to imply that the addition of the nontimber benefit term on the left-hand side of (3A) must lengthen the

optimal rotation under multiple-use management by making it advantageous to hold the timber stand for a longer time before harvesting. This
interpretation overlooks the fact that the value of bare land (A) on the right-
hand side of (12) must now include both the value of future timber harvests
from bare land *and* the value of future nontimber benefits that will be
provided by the future sequence of forests. In some cases, it turns out that
the addition of nontimber benefits will make very little difference to the
harvesting period selected (Calish, Fight, and Teeguarden 1978). To see
this, assume as a simple case, that the flow of nontimber benefits over the
forest growth cycle is constant at $Z[x(t)] = Z^*$. Suppose a forest manager
simply adopts the Faustmann rule and chooses a rotation period of t^*
which maximizes the present value of timber benefits alone. The value of
bare land solely due to timber benefits is $A'(t^*)$. So the timber manager is
satisfying the condition

$$p \cdot dx/dt = r[p \cdot x(t^*) + A'(t^*)] \qquad (13)$$

where dx/dt refers to the growth of timber volume at age t^*. Now suppose
that the timber manager moves to a multiple-use framework and decides to
include nontimber benefits in the rotation decision. Since land involved in
the rotation of timber provides a constant flow of nontimber benefits
forever, the value of bare land due to nontimber benefits is the present
value of a perpetual periodic flow Z^* and is equal to Z^*/r. Denote the value
of bare land due to nontimber benefits as $A'' = Z^*/r$. Adding the nontimber
benefit flow Z^* to the left-hand side of (13) and the nontimber value of the
bare land to the right-hand side yields

$$p \cdot dx/dt + Z^* = r[p \cdot x(t^*) + A'(t^*) + A'']$$
$$= r[p \cdot x(t^*) + A'(t^*) + Z^*/r] \qquad (14)$$

The terms involving Z^* simply cancel so that the optimal rotation is
unaffected by adding nontimber benefits to the timber optimization framework because $Z^* = rA''$. What this result implies is that it is *variation* in
nontimber benefits over the forest growth cycle that causes multiple-use
harvest timing to diverge from harvest timing for timber alone. If nontimber benefits depend *positively* on the stage of the forest growth cycle,
then forests containing larger timber volumes provide a larger stream of
benefits to users. In this case, the current flow of nontimber benefits at any
rotation length t^*, given by $Z[x(t^*)]$, always exceeds the carrying cost of
bare land valued by its nontimber benefit flow, i.e., $Z[x(t^*)] > rA''(t^*)$,
provided the timber growth rate is positive.[13] In this case, adding nontimber benefits to the timber-alone rotation model will lengthen the
optimal rotation and may even eliminate harvesting of the stands altogether (Hartman 1976). The elimination of harvesting is a dominant-use
case in which the forest area is managed exclusively for nontimber

benefits. The wilderness regime mentioned above is an example of dominant-use. Even where wilderness proper is not the target, capital investments in campgrounds, trails, scenic lookouts, and other facilities that derive much of their justification from the existence of a surrounding mature forest can raise the nontimber benefits from the mature forest to the point at which timber harvesting cannot compete with these other uses. Even though wilderness is a relatively small component of many national and provincial parks, exclusion of commercial harvesting from these areas reflects dominant-use policy.

Multiple-use management of forest stands, therefore, has two identifiable effects on the model of the preceding section. First, the addition of nontimber benefits has the potential to alter the optimal rotation period and, second, the value of bare land increases under multiple-use management. In their study of Pacific coast Douglas-fir forests, Calish, Fight, and Teeguarden (1978) found that, while multiple-use management had relatively minor effects on optimal rotation periods, the inclusion of benefits due to fish and game, nongame wildlife diversity, visual aesthetics, soil movement (erosion) control, and water yields, led to such a large increase in forest land value that up to 75 percent of land value could be attributed to nontimber benefits under multiple-use management.

Since the optimal timber rotation is generally shorter than the maximum sustained yield (MSY) rotation, it is not obvious that a longer rotation that might be caused by inclusion of nontimber benefits in the harvesting decision will lower annual flows of timber to the forest products sector from a fixed land base and a fully regulated forest. Suppose, for example, that 1000 hectares are subject to a 50-year timber rotation with 20 hectares harvested each year. Each hectare harvested produces 150 cubic metres of wood for an annual even-flow timber supply of 3000 cubic metres. Suppose that nontimber benefits are an increasing function of timber volume and inclusion of these benefits leads to a 75-year rotation so that 13.3 hectares are harvested annually. Provided the timber yield per hectare rises to at least 225 cubic metres as a result of the longer growth cycle, the annual harvest remains at or above 3000 cubic metres. While there *may* be a tradeoff between nontimber benefits and timber flows under some management regimes (such as dominant-use), such a tradeoff is not the inevitable result of incorporating nontimber values into the forest management regime. Further, as discussed below, inclusion of nontimber benefits in the valuation of forest land may make it socially optimal to expand the amount of land devoted to continuous management, resulting in increases in both timber and nontimber benefits.

Relative to multiple-use of all areas, the dominant-use model has the advantage of minimizing conflicts among users. The locational characteristics of Canada's forest resources may make dominant-use a more logical solution to the provision of timber and nontimber benefits than multiple-use. In the Ontario case, for example, much of the recreational demand for forested areas is concentrated in the populous southern region of the province. This will give dominance to recreational values over timber values in the area stretching north to Algonquin Park. In northern Ontario, recreational demands are much lighter due to lower population concentrations. In this region, large areas of forested land can be set aside exclusively for timber production without significant adverse effects on other forest users. Since wilderness areas must be free both of development for timber harvesting *and* intensive recreational use, many northern Ontario locations are also logical for this purpose since they are sufficiently remote from population concentrations and developed transportation facilities to minimize pressures for intensive recreation and commercial timber production. Habitat preservation may require relatively large wilderness preserves which would be hard to maintain close to large concentrations of population or forest industry activity.

Bringing both timber and nontimber benefits into the economic-optimization framework means that all benefits and costs are *internalized* (see also chapter 3). Public ownership of forest land can secure internalization of all costs and benefits provided the public owner adopts a comprehensive framework for benefit-cost measurement and regulates the rate of harvesting by private firms in accordance with equation (14).

∎ SCARCITY ISSUES IN THE FOREST SECTOR

Chapter 4 discussed resources scarcity in the context of nonrenewable mineral and energy supplies. Two general types of scarcity measure were proposed and examined: cost-price indicators and physical abundance indicators. The same approach can be applied to the availability of timber inputs.

Cost-price Indicators

The most common cost-price measures used to examine timber scarcity are real prices of forest products and real stumpage prices. The longest historical series of prices available are for the U.S. economy. U.S. experience in this matter is broadly applicable to the Canadian forest industry, since forest products markets in the two countries are closely linked through large Canadian exports of lumber and pulp and paper to the U.S. Further, U.S. stumpage prices on public lands are determined by market processes rather than through administrative formulae as they are in Canada. Scarcity, if present, should show up more clearly with market-determined prices.

A study of real resource prices undertaken by Manthy (1978) showed a rising trend for real forest products prices of about 1.4 percent per year from 1870 to the mid-1970s. Within the overall forest products category, real pulp and paper prices have been stable, while lumber and plywood prices have been responsible for the overall uptrend. The deflated price of lumber has been increasing at an average annual rate of 1.7 percent for over a century in North America. Stability of real pulp and paper prices is correlated with stability in the real price of pulpwood. Most of the increases in real lumber prices are reflected in rising real sawlog prices which increased at just over 2 percent per annum over Manthy's study period. As expected from the other price series, real prices for pulpwood stumpage have been stable, while sawtimber stumpage prices have been rising. Douglas-fir stumpage prices have risen rapidly relative to Douglas-fir lumber prices since the 1930s (Brown and Field 1979).

In contrast to the cost-price indicators for minerals, in which it was difficult to pick up clear scarcity trends (chapter 4), evidence of sawtimber scarcity seems unmistakable on the real price evidence. Pulpwood stumpage supplies, on the other hand, show no signs of economic scarcity on the basis of historical price evidence for North America.

Physical Supplies of Timber

What of the future? Here, physical evidence is of considerable importance though, as usual, it is more complicated to interpret than the past cost-price evidence. At the world level, North America usually emerges as the region with the most favourable balance between timber growth and timber harvest. Measures of current timber growth—the CAI or MAI—provide somewhat ambiguous supply measures. If the world consisted of normal forests on fixed rotations with an unvarying amount of land devoted to each forest type, current timber growth would give a measure of the amount of wood fibre available *inelastically* each year in perpetuity, provided forest regeneration follows harvesting without delay and reproduces previous growth behaviour. None of these assumptions accurately reflects the state of the world's forests. Forests are not typically normal. For example, the boreal forests of Canada and the Soviet Union contain large numbers of old trees. As removals proceed, these old-growth areas may come to be occupied by faster growing stands of lower average age so that the CAI per hectare is increased in the long run. Policies to accelerate old-growth removal can increase *current* timber supplies sharply, since old stands frequently contain very large timber volumes. Supplies will then decline later as harvests focus on smaller diameter timber. This is the so-called *falldown* effect. A decision to change the rotation period, therefore, alters the long-run CAI and affects short-run supplies through acceleration or postponement of harvests. Afforestation of new areas can expand long-run timber supplies, while deforestation has the opposite effect. All these influences mean that current timber growth figures must be interpreted with extreme caution as supply measures.

Reservations aside, what can be inferred from existing data on growth *versus* removals of timber? First, for the world as a whole, and for less developed countries in particular, deforestation has been occurring for some time and will continue. The *Global 2000 Report* (Barney 1980) cited studies showing that forested land declined from 25 percent of the world's land surface in the 1950s to 20 percent in the 1970s.[14] Second, in most areas of the world, harvests are nearly equal to or exceed the annual growth of wood net of losses through death, decay, insects, and fire. While it is true that harvests in excess of annual growth can be justified in many regions by the need to remove old timber stands and adopt shorter and more economical rotations, a period of lower harvests will have to follow adjustments of this kind.

In North America the *Global 2000 Report* showed harvests equal to about 70 percent of net annual growth in the early 1970s. Over the last decade, however, harvests have increased relative to growth. Canada, once considered a country possessed of almost unlimited wood resources, is now experiencing a very close balance between growth and harvest. Until the late 1970s, the Canadian forest products industry appeared to be operating virtually without resource constraints. Net annual growth, measured as an Annual Allowable Cut (AAC), was always in excess of annual harvest removals. During the 1970s, however, Canadian lumber production increased by 65 percent. Wood pulp production increased by 20 percent. Plywood and particle board output increased by 75 percent. Table 6.1 reports Canada's regional harvests versus AACs for the late 1980s, based on a study prepared for the Canadian Forestry Service. The softwood harvest is nearly 90 percent of the total and Figure 6.5 shows the narrowing gap between softwood AACs and harvests since 1960.

In some cases, provinces are in the process of redefining their AACs, usually downward. British Columbia's AAC, for example, has recently been reduced to reflect accessibility and other factors. In some regions large forested areas have been withdrawn from timber production as wilderness or environmental protection areas. Timber stocks have been destroyed by fire and by insect infestations of which the damage caused by the spruce budworm to forests in the Atlantic region is the best-known example. In some provinces, past AAC calculations have exceeded annual growth to allow for the removal of high-volume stands in older age-classes. As these old-growth stands are exhausted, AACs have to be revised downward. This falldown effect is another reason for current and expected reductions in provincial timber availability in the 1990s and beyond. Regeneration of cutover land has been incomplete as well, so that the land area occupied by productive forest in Canada, as in other areas of the world, has been shrinking over time. The authors of the report to the Canadian Forestry Service in which Table 6.1 appears comment that

> ...Canada's ability to continue to expand production of traditional commodities such as softwood dimension lumber and bleached softwood kraft

TABLE 6.1: Canada—allowable annual cut, estimated current demand, and apparent timber surplus (million m³ per year)

	AAC			1988 DEMAND ESTIMATE			APPARENT SURPLUS OR (DEFICIT)		
	Softwood	Hardwood	Total	Softwood	Hardwood	Total	Softwood	Hardwood	Total
British Columbia									
Coast	30.9	0.5	31.4	33.5[2]	0.3	33.8	(2.6)[4]	0.2	(2.4)
Interior	47.8	4.7	52.5	46.4[3]	0.7	47.1	1.4[5]	4.0	5.4
Prairies	20.8	14.9	35.7	11.0	3.0	14.0	9.8	11.9	21.7
Ontario	27.0	16.9	43.9	21.2	7.8	29.0	5.8	9.1	14.9
Quebec	32.5	15.0	47.5	34.5[6]	5.9	40.4	(2.0)	9.1	7.1
Atlantic	15.7	6.5	22.2	14.8	3.7	18.5	0.9	2.8	3.7
Canada[1]	174.7	58.5	233.2	161.4	21.4	182.8	13.3	37.1	50.4

1. Excluding Yukon and NWT.
2. Includes approx. 4.0 million m³ of chip/log transfers from the Interior to the Coast and 2.5 million m³ of log exports from Coastal forests.
3. Excluding the 4.0 million m³ of chip/log transfers to the Coast.
4. The apparent deficit is more than covered by the 4.0 million m³ fibre transfers from the Interior and 2.5 million m³ of log exports.
5. Not including 2.5 million m³ of chip exports to Japan and the USA.
6. Including 3.6 million m³ of fibre imports.

Source: Woodbridge, Reed and Associates, *Canada's Forest Industry* (Prepared for Forestry Canada, Ottawa, 1988). Reproduced with the permission of the Minister of Supply and Servies Canada, 1991.

FIGURE 6.5 Trends in AAC and harvest: Canada's softwoods

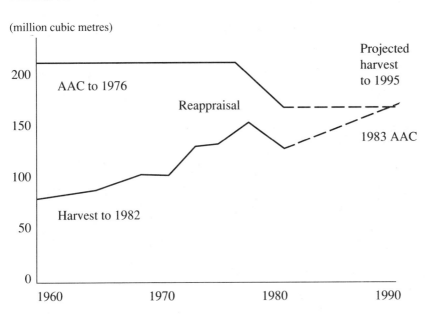

(million cubic metres)

Timber requirements 1979/80 vs. 1995

Based on a 1983 Annual Allowable Cut of 175 million cubic metres, and projections for a 1995 harvest of 186 million cubic metres, Canada will be experiencing a shortage of softwood fibre within a relatively short time.

An alternative does exist: to increase the AAC by reducing the volume of timber lost to fire, disease and insects; reducing the amount of forest land removed from timber production; utilizing to a better degree existing fibre resources; and increasing the amount of silviculture practised.

Source: Canadian Pulp and Paper Association, *Forest Resource Update,* September 1985.

pulps will be severely limited....The timber supply analysis...demonstrates that the timber harvest cannot continue to grow at historic trends. As a result, the opportunities for new primary manufacturing facilities are limited and the key to future expansion lies in making better use of the fibre supply through more complete utilization, application of higher yield processing technologies and further integration into value-added manufacturing.[15]

With the exception of northern Alberta (which is in the process of allocating its unassigned AAC to new forest products complexes), softwood production in Canada has now reached, and in some provinces surpassed, available net growth. Forest policy in the 1980s is no longer a matter of promoting industrial growth. Unless relative prices of pulp and paper products and lumber rise faster than historical trends, economically inaccessible areas are likely to remain inaccessible in the near future. (In some provinces AACs attributed to economically inaccessible areas may be needed to sustain present levels of forest products output.)

The close of Canada's "forest frontier" not only means the end of a long expansionary phase in forest products production, it is also causing both federal and provincial policymakers to focus their attention on the sustainability of the existing resource base. Despite an ideological commitment to sustained yield, Canadian forest policy has failed to produce a level of regeneration sufficient to maintain timber supplies for the future. Combined natural and costly artificial regeneration has simply not kept pace with the annual harvested area. Expanded reforestation programs are either in place or being implemented by provincial governments with the assistance of the federal government. In large measure, the "regeneration gap" reflects low economic returns from regeneration expenditures. The next section examines the economics of capital investments designed to produce yields of wood and nontimber forest outputs in the future.

▌ THE BENEFIT-COST BALANCE IN REGENERATION DECISIONS

A length of time equal to the optimal rotation separates initial regeneration expenditures (c) from harvest returns (px). For this reason, capital investments in initial regeneration are sometimes called *point-input, point-output* problems in capital theory (Hirshleifer 1970): capital costs occur at one point in time, benefits occur at a specified later point in time. More complex versions of the regeneration problem include forest management expenditures (such as fertilization and weeding) that are undertaken during the forest's growth cycle. When these types of management expenditures are undertaken, the term c should include both initial (stand-establishment) expenditure and the present value of management expenditures made during the growth cycle. If, for example, planting costs of $200 per hectare are incurred at the beginning of the rotation and fertilization costing $150 per hectare is incurred 20 years after planting, then $c = \$200 + \$150/(1 + r)^{20}$. Similar present valuation applies to any benefits that appear prior to the end of the rotation. These benefits could be derived from the standing forest (nontimber benefits as discussed earlier) or from stumpage returns due to thinning harvests that precede the main end-of-rotation removal.

If timber production *alone* is the objective of management expenditures, the value of bare land under a projected infinite series of timber rotations with stable stumpage prices is given by the Faustmann valuation formula derived in equations (7) and (8). If bare land has no alternative use outside forestry, the Faustmann valuation formula implies that it will remain under continuous forestry, provided that the present values of all future harvests is at least equal to the present value of the management expenditures required to generate those harvests, i.e., provided $A \geq 0$ in equation (7) or (8). If bare land has a value outside forestry of A^*, then it will remain in forest production only so long as $A \geq A^*$.   Assuming that forest land has no alternative use ($A^* = 0$), land remains in continuous forestry provided

$$(px)/(1 + r)^t - c \geq 0 \tag{15}$$

which is the condition for $A \geq 0$ in equation (7). Whether or not (15) can be satisfied in any particular forest region depends on management cost per hectare, the rate of discount employed (r), the length of the rotation period (t), the assumed stumpage price (p), and the timber yield (x). Referring to the discussion of rents in chapter 1, the criteron $A \geq 0$ in (15) corresponds to the Chambers-Gordon criterion under which expanded resources pro-duction is welfare-improving provided it increases economic rent. In the present context, economic rent is *positive* on stands that are already in existence but can be *negative* when such stands must be planted and managed. Where natural regeneration works ($c = 0$), rents are positive on all areas for which stumpage returns are positive ($p > 0$).

Benson (1988) has calculated net present values (rents) for regenera-tion and management of high and low productivity sites in Ontario using 1983–84 costs of reforestation and management and real discount rates varying from 4 to 8 percent. "Intensive management"—consisting of artificial regeneration, weeding, and fertilization—returns negative net present values in nearly all cases. When the real discount is low, end-of-rotation stumpage prices are high, and high productivity sites are used, positive net present values can be achieved. For all other sites Benson concluded that "extensive management" (natural regeneration) would be a more appropriate management approach. Depending upon the treatment of administrative overheads in forest management, positive (or only slightly negative) NPVs can be obtained from extensive management. It is appar-ent that over large forest areas currently being harvested or for which harvests are planned, returns to forestry investments are low. Based on the results for Ontario, this is likely to be so for much of the boreal region extending from Newfoundland and Labrador west to northern Alberta and British Columbia, which is forested by major commercial species used primarily for the manufacture of pulp and paper (spruce, jack pine, and balsam fir). There are some sites for which above-average timber growth *can* permit equation (15) to be satisfied but it is also clear that timber benefits alone will not justify artificial regeneration costs on a large proportion of land currently providing wood inputs to the Canadian forest products sector. Referring to the same problem in the U.S., Manthy (1977) pointed out that

> [o]n a significant portion of what is identified as commercial forest land, perhaps as much as a third, trees grow too slowly to earn acceptable rates of return on management expenses and hence are not economically renewable (Clawson 1975). Harvesting wood on such lands is the economic equivalent of mining a stock resource.[16]

A map of North America that distinguished existing forested areas from those areas for which continuous timber production returns positive rents at existing costs and prices would show the latter as a relatively small fraction of the former. Large areas on the Pacific coast and in the southeastern U.S. are viable areas for economical timber production but, outside these regions, costs of artificial regeneration more often than not exceed the timber benefits derived from them.[17] If forest products prices rise relative to harvesting and processing costs in the future, net prices (p) will rise (as has been the case for lumber in the past). This, in turn, will expand the area over which intensive management yields positive rents and will dampen the original increase in net prices through long-run timber supply increases.

Evidently, the application of economic criteria to the process of timber growing would lead to the abandonment of such investment activities over large areas of Canadian forest land at present prices and costs. Even when secure tenure over future harvests can be guaranteed, private operators seldom evince much interest in commercial timber growing, unless regeneration outlays are heavily subsidized. As Benson points out, one answer to the "regeneration gap" is to adopt modified harvesting techniques to secure more natural regeneration. Reducing the size of clear-cut areas and cutting in strips, for example, would permit greater reliance on natural reseeding of cutovers. Greater reliance on extensive management appears to be the only cost-effective approach to maintaining long-run timber supplies over much of Canada's productive forest land base.

How is reforestation policy affected when nontimber benefits enter the model? When forest land is managed exclusively for timber returns, any nontimber benefits from regeneration activity appear as external benefits. Markets are capable of capturing timber benefits in the form of stumpage returns, but this is rarely true of nontimber benefits:

> ...in an unregulated market environment nontimber values would not influence the market evaluation of the resource base nor the timing of harvesting. ...The purpose of regulation under these circumstances would be to ensure that these nontimber benefits of the forest base were explicitly incorporated into decisions regarding the pricing of timber and the timing of harvests.[18]

The Calish-Fight-Teeguarden (1978) approach indicated that, in their west coast Douglas-fir models, the present value of nontimber returns accruing to society during the stand's rotation period could contribute more value to reforested land than the present value of timber production. When forests produce both timber and nontimber values, the net present value of the forest may be increased to the point at which the returns to regeneration are attractive even if management for timber alone does not produce adequate returns. It is not clear, though, that nontimber benefits are large enough to make much difference to the value of bare land in most Canadian regions. Vast tracts of unoccupied forest in the boreal regions of northern Canada provide little or no return in the form of nontimber benefits. Most Canadians are quite unaware of the extent of such forests. While it is true that most nontimber benefits are not valued in any market process and are extremely difficult to estimate, it appears that national and provincial parks and wilderness areas, which are relatively accessible and free from logging activity, supply virtually all the nontimber forest outputs that most Canadians want to consume. There are some hunting and fishing benefits to be had from timberlands, but their value per hectare must surely be small.

Traditional forest management has been heavily committed to automatic regeneration of harvested areas without regard to economic criteria. Many foresters still view reforestation as a cost of harvesting existing stands. Private sector managers who would not consider an investment in plant and equipment that failed to yield "normal" after-tax returns are willing to advocate such investments in timber growing provided the forest management costs are funded by the public sector. Companies engaged in forest regeneration on Crown land expect either immediate increases in their AACs or government compensation for reforestation expenditures undertaken out of corporate funds if they are to engage in significant reforestation activity.

Both federal and provincial levels of government are expanding the financing of forest management, in many cases through agreements with forest products companies in which the latter are reimbursed for timber management expenditures and are offered secure long-term supplies of timber for their plants. Despite the federal Treasury Board's own benefit-cost policy that requires positive NPVs at discount rates in the 5–10 percent range on public projects, this criterion is not being applied to intensive management expenditures in the forestry sector. Instead, the thrust of public policy in forestry tends to be directed to preserving output and employment opportunities in the forest products sector rather than to the achievement of positive rents to Canada as a whole from forest regeneration policy. It is in this latter context that the advantages of extensive management and modified harvesting techniques over intensive management should be judged.

▌ RENT CAPTURE IN THE FORESTRY SECTOR

Canadian forest policy has not been nearly as preoccupied with rent capture as has policy in the minerals sector, even though rent capture issues follow similar theoretical lines in both. All provinces levy stumpage charges on the extraction of timber from Crown forests. Regeneration costs are usually borne by the Crown owner. Unlike mining taxes and royalties, stumpage payments are treated as costs for the calculation of provincial and federal corporate taxes. The corporate tax system does not contain the generous incentives that apply to mining. Indeed, timber harvesting is treated as part of the manufacturing process except that capital expenditures for harvesting capital receive less generous rates of depreciation for tax purposes than capital expenditures for sawmills and pulp and paper plants.

The provinces do not make a systematic attempt to isolate and capture forest rents using the techniques described in chapter 5. Stumpage charges are set per cubic metre of wood harvested and are usually indexed to the selling prices of forest products to prevent erosion of the real value of stumpage revenues with inflation. In some forest regions it is likely that the value of harvested wood minus harvesting cost fails to cover assessed stumpage, so that wood that is capable of producing economic rent is not utilized.[19] In other areas, economic rent exceeds stumpage charges and remains in the private sector. The relative magnitudes of rent lost or left with the private sector have not been measured.

Until the late 1980s, the British Columbia Ministry of Forests made the most comprehensive (and administratively expensive) effort to isolate and transfer economic rent from private operators to the public purse. Though bidding for standing timber was once important in B.C. (as well as in other provinces), the B.C. method for capturing rents was an *ex-ante* appraisal system. The ministry used private sector data (pertaining to the "operator of average efficiency") to estimate harvesting costs. For the coastal areas of B.C., estimated harvesting costs plus an allowed profit margin was subtracted from the value of the resulting logs in the Vancouver log market to arrive at stumpage assessments. In the B.C. interior, product values were calculated by subtracting estimated lumber and pulp and paper manufacturing costs from lumber and pulp and paper revenues received by manufacturers. These product values replaced the log market price for B.C. interior stumpage price calculations. The B.C. appraisal system deducted costs (including required profit) from revenue to establish standing timber values.

The practical aspects of timber appraisal systems have been criticized on a number of grounds. First, the calculation of an appropriate profit margin for producers has usually not been theoretically sound.[20] This is a problem that also plagues rent collection mechanisms in the mining sector (chapter 5). Second, it has been argued that industry-wide collective bargaining may increase wage costs in the forestry sector at the expense of provincial rents. The appraisal system, deducting the "operator of average efficiency" costs in calculating rent, contains no mechanism to resist industry-wide encroachment on rent through high wage settlements.[21] Third, Vancouver log market prices have tended to be held down by log export restrictions (see chapter 1), and may provide too few arm's-length price observations to be truly representative of product values even in the absence of export controls.[22]

In 1988, the B.C. appraisal system was radically altered by Canada's agreement to levy export taxes on lumber shipped to the United States. U.S. sawmillers competing against Canadian lumber had argued during the 1980s that Canada's stumpage revenue systems involved much lower payments to provincial governments than payments made by American lumber producers on timber purchases in the U.S. In response to their argument that Canadian lumber exports were being subsidized by Canadian stumpage systems, the federal government agreed to levy a 15 percent export tax on Canadian shipments of lumber to the U.S. in order to forestall trade action by the U.S. in the form of a countervailing duty. Part of the agreement was that Canadian shipments would be freed from the export tax if stumpage payments were raised in Canada.[23] British Columbia opted to raise its stumpage revenues to eliminate the export tax. As a result, the B.C. stumpage revenue system is no longer an appraisal model. Instead, variations in harvesting cost are taken into consideration in determining stumpage but the province-wide level of payments is determined by the requirement that not less than 15 percent of export values be collected as timber revenue.

While no one seems to have advocated an *ex-post* RRT-style approach to collecting rents on Canadian forests, bidding *has* been advocated as a superior alternative (or supplement) to appraisals. Bidding is mandatory for the disposition of publicly owned timber in the U.S. In some regions the large timbersheds required to support individual manufacturing operations restricts the number of effective bidders to such an extent that bid prices would probably fall substantially short of economic rent on the resource. Further, security of wood supply to manufacturing plants seems to require purchasers to secure their inputs three to five years in advance of actual use, if U.S. practice is used as a guide. Bids will then reflect expected prices and costs. Over-optimistic expectations held by U.S. sawmillers in the late 1970s produced large increases in winning bids on Douglas-fir stumpage from U.S. national forests. The recession of 1981 and 1982 saw these lumber producers locked into excessively costly wood-supply agreements. Some operators were forced to shut down, and demands for renegotiated stumpage prices reached the U.S. Congress in the early 1980s. As discussed above, U.S. lumber producers also argued for a substantial tariff on Canadian lumber exports to compensate them for alleged differentials between Canadian and U.S. stumpage charges on public timber. The resulting countervailing duty case led to the 15 percent export tax and increased stumpage in Canada.

∎ CONCLUSIONS

Forest management policy requires optimal decisions to be taken on the timing of harvests from existing stands and on the regeneration of forest land after harvest. As with nonrenewables, these decisions draw on capital theory. In the case of harvest timing, the optimal rotation is obtained by balancing the benefits of an additional period of forest growth against the holding costs of timber and bare land. Benefits include the value of timber growth, stumpage price appreciation on standing timber volumes, and nontimber or amenity benefits flowing from the standing forest. Capital tied up in standing forests and land occupied by forests should earn a marginal return equal to the return available in other sectors. When timber flows affect stumpage prices, an economic argument can be made for gradual smoothing of harvest volumes in the direction of a regulated forest. Optimal regeneration decisions should also be directed to maximizing the net present value of decisions taken. The present value of the the benefits from regeneration, assuming an optimal harvest timing decision, has to be compared with the present value of the costs of establishing and managing the stand until the moment of harvest.

The use of optimal rules in harvesting are often at variance with the rules applied by public forest managers based on other criteria such as MSY or gradual liquidation of old-growth timber. Similarly, regeneration decisions are often pursued without due attention to the benefits and costs to be obtained from them. If Canadians are to obtain maximum returns (rents) from forest resources, it is essential that existing management models be replaced by economic optimization.

∎ NOTES

1. An exception (not discussed in the literature) would be the case of a deposit worked by open-pit or strip-mining methods for which the continued existence of the deposit implies the continued existence of the natural area associated with it.
2. One cunit is 100 cubic feet of solid wood and equals 2.8 cubic metres. For simplicity, it is assumed in this chapter that the net price (stumpage price) is independent of the sizes of the trees in the stand and of the volume of the stand itself. In some cases, increased tree size means that more valuable final products can be obtained. In this case, the stumpage price rises with stand age. See T. Heaps, "An Analysis of the Present Value of Stumpage under a Variety of Economic and Management Conditions," *Discussion Paper 284* (Ottawa: Economic Council of Canada, 1985).

3. F. Anderson, "Optimal Timber Harvesting: Generalizing the Faustmann Rule," *Discussion Paper 89–01* (Thunder Bay: Department of Economics, Lakehead University, 1989).
4. See, for example, J. Buongiorno and J.K. Gilless, *Forest Management and Economics* (New York: Macmillan, 1987); L. Davis and K.N. Johnson, *Forest Management* (New York: McGraw-Hill. 1987).
5. The conversions are as follows: 1 square mile = 259 hectares; 1 metric ton of newsprint = (approximately) 3 cubic metres of wood.
6. An excellent modern treatment that parallels the discussion here is P.A. Samuelson, "Economics of Forestry in an Evolving Society," *Economic Inquiry* 14 (1976): 466–92. See also S.J. Chang, "Determination of the Optimal Rotation Age: A Theoretical Analysis," *Forest Ecology and Management* 8 (1984): 137–47.
7. R. Manthy, "Scarcity, Renewability, and Forest Policy," *Journal of Forestry* 75 (1977): 201–5. Real price trends in forestry are described below.
8. The McLaurin expansion of e^r is $1 + r + r^2/2! + r^3/3! + \ldots$ Since r is small, with continuous compounding e^{rt} is approximately equal to $(1 + r)^t$.
9. This demonstration requires another short mathematical excursion. Setting $r = 0$ means that $r/(1 - e^{-rt}) = 0/0$ which is undefined. L'Hopital's Rule, however, states that the limit as r approaches zero of an expression $f(r)/g(r)$ is the same as the limit as r approaches zero of the expression $f'(r)/g'(r)$, where the primes indicate derivatives. Treating $r/(1 - e^{-rt})$ this way involves finding the limit of $1/te^{-rt}$ as r approaches zero which is $1/t$.
10. Recall that equation (11) also rests on the assumption of zero regeneration cost ($c = 0$). If $c > 0$ is assumed instead, the rotation period lengthens relative to the MSY model. This reduces the frequency of regeneration costs and is referred to by Samuelson, "Economics of Forestry," as a maximum sustained net yield rotation.
11. Optimal movement toward a fully regulated forest when stumpage prices vary inversely with harvest volumes is not fully established in the literature. Simulation results reported by J.L. Walker in "ECHO: Solution Technique for a Nonlinear Economic Harvest Optimization Model," in J. Meadows, et. al., eds., *Systems Analysis and Forest Resource Management* (Washington: Society of American Foresters, 1976), and by M. Kemp and E. Moore, "Biological Capital Theory: A Question and a Conjecture," *Economics Letters* 4 (1979): 141–44, imply that regulation will occur over time. T. Heaps and P. Neher, in their "The Economics of Forestry when the Rate of Harvest is Constrained," *Journal of Environmental Economics and Management* 6 (1979): 297–319, show that harvesting costs rising with harvest volume leads to optimal diversification of forest age-classes over time. T. Mitra and H.Y. Wan, in "Some Theoretical Results on the Economics of Forestry," *Review of Economic Studies* 52 (1985): 263–82, have provided a mathematical proof for regulation when the discount rate is zero.
12. See Buongiorno and Gilless, *Forest Management*, Chap. 7.
13. The term A'' is the discounted value of nontimber benefits in perpetuity. The requirement of a positive growth rate is an overly strong condition.
14. G.O. Barney (Study Director), *The Global 2000 Report to the President of the United States* (New York: Pergamon, 1980), Vol. 2, p. 117.
15. Woodbridge, Reed and Associates, *Canada's Forest Industry* (prepared for

Forestry Canada, 1988), Volume 5: "Fibre Assumptions." Reproduced with the permission of the Minister of Supply and Services Canada, 1991.

16. Manthy, "Scarcity": 204. There is a very good introduction to theory and policy issues in the United States in M. Clawson, *Forests for Whom and for What?* (Baltimore: Johns Hopkins, 1975).

17. An early 1970s evaluation for the U.S. is contained in R. Marty, "Economic Effectiveness of Silvicultural Investments for Softwood Timber Production," Appendix D in *Report of the President's Advisory Panel on Timber and the Environment* (Washington: USGPO, 1973). It is Marty's work that is referred to in Clawson, *Forests for Whom and for What?*, Chap. 7.

18. M.B. Percy, *Forest Management and Economic Growth in British Columbia* (Ottawa: Economic Council of Canada, 1986), p. 19.

19. J. Nautiyal, "Forest Tenure Structure in Ontario," *The Forestry Chronicle* 53 (1977): 23–24.

20. P.H. Pearse, *Timber Appraisal—Second Report of the Task Force on Crown Timber Disposal* (Vancouver: British Columbia Forest Service, 1974), Chap. 3.

21. L. Copithorne, *Natural Resources and Regional Disparities* (Ottawa: Economic Council of Canada, 1979), Chap. 4. Copithorne raises the point that economic rents in the forestry sector may accrue partly to labour to the extent that forestry and mill workers earn higher wages than they could in other sectors.

22. A.D. Scott, "The Cost of Compulsory Log Trading," in W. McKillop and W. Mead, eds., *Timber Policy Issues in British Columbia* (Vancouver: University of British Columbia Press, 1976).

23. Treatments of the U.S. lumber duty case can be found in F. Anderson and R.D. Cairns, "The Softwood Lumber Agreement and Resource Politics," *Canadian Public Policy* 14 (1988): 186–96; and M.B. Percy and C. Yoder, *The Softwood Lumber Dispute and Canada-U.S. Trade in Natural Resources* (Halifax: The Institute for Research on Public Policy, 1988).

■ FURTHER READING

A modern classic in rotation theory is

Samuelson, P.A. "Economics of Forestry in an Evolving Society." *Economic Inquiry* 14 (1976).

The use of area and volume control to even out harvests from unregulated forests is a topic of importance in forest economics. An excellent discussion with linear programming models of forest regulation appears in

Buongiorno, J., and J.K. Gilless. *Forest Management and Economics*. New York: Macmillan, 1987, Chaps. 1–8.

The most important articles extending rotation theory to include nontimber benefit flows from the forest are

Calish, S., R. Fight, and D. Teeguarden. "How Do Nontimber Values Affect Douglas-fir Rotations?" *Journal of Forestry* 76 (1978).

Hartman, R. "The Harvest Decision when a Standing Forest has Value." *Economic Inquiry* 14 (1976).

Excellent treatments of Canadian forestry issues can be found in

Economic Council of Canada . *Western Transition*. Ottawa: Supply and Services, 1984, Chap. 5.

Percy, M.B. *Forest Management and Economic Growth in British Columbia*. Ottawa: Economic Council of Canada, 1986, Chaps. 1–4.

CHAPTER SEVEN

OCEAN FISHERIES:

FROM OPEN-ACCESS TO

EFFICIENT MANAGEMENT

∎ INTRODUCTION

The previous chapter examined renewable resources management rules for forestry. In fact, most of the economic theory of renewable resources management in the last decade or so has centred on fisheries resources, the subject of the present chapter. Unlike forests, ocean fisheries have often been exploited as open-access or common property resources: harvesting firms (fishermen) cannot claim ownership of units of the stock until they have actually caught them. This *rule of capture* feature of fisheries is the background for the analysis of the first section of this chapter in which a simple fisheries exploitation model is used to show how the rule of capture regime leads to the dissipation of economic rent.

The second section explores an optimal management strategy for fisheries still utilizing the basic biological and economic framework of the first section. As with the nonrenewable resources discussion in chapter 2 and the forestry models of the previous chapter, a capital theoretic approach is the basis for the optimal management strategy. Explicit comparisons are then made between the fisheries management model and optimal forest management.

The policy section of the chapter describes the effectiveness of alternative instruments for converting the open-access result to an optimal management regime. These instruments include restrictions on fishing inputs (effort), determination of the total allowable catch (TAC), catch quotas applied to individual fishermen, and depletion taxes. Finally, models of population behaviour are introduced for which steady-state equilibria may not apply. These models usually involve lags in population biomass adjustments that lead to a greater variety in dynamic behaviour than the simpler models of earlier sections. Both stable and unstable equilibria can be identified in these models and, in some cases, relatively simple dynamic models can produce seemingly erratic population behaviour.

The appendix provides mathematical background on optimal steady-state management of renewable resources.

■ OPEN-ACCESS RESOURCE EQUILIBRIUM

An open-access or common property fishery tends to produce a level of exploitation that eliminates the resource's economic rent (Gordon 1954; Scott 1955). Most open-access fishing models, including the one described in this section, examine a *steady-state equilibrium* in which the harvest and the underlying resource stock take on unchanging values from period to period. The steady state model is sometimes called a *bionomic equilibrium* which stresses that specific biological and economic conditions have to be satisfied simultaneously for the steady state to persist. For the fishery, biological equilibrium requires that the periodic growth increment of the fish stock equal the rate of harvest. Economic equilibrium requires that fishermen earn zero long-run pure profit so that the revenue from the harvest is exactly equal to fishermen's costs, including a normal rate of return on capital tied up in boats and gear. Biological behaviour can be expressed as follows:

$$dX/dt = f(X) - q \qquad (1)$$

where X is the size or *biomass* of the resource stock, $f(X)$ is the current natural increase in the biomass, and q is the harvest rate. Equation (1) conveys the idea that the growth of the stock during the interval dt is a function of the stock size itself. When the rate of harvest (q) equals natural stock growth $f(X)$, the stock X is neither increasing nor decreasing in size from one period to the next and the harvest q is *sustainable*. In the fisheries literature, equation (1) often takes on the *logistic* form (Schaefer 1957) in which

$$f(X) = aX - aX^2/b \qquad (1A)$$

where a and b are constants. The idea behind the logistic model is that the population biomass tends to grow at a constant proportional rate a in the absence of environmental constraints (exponential growth). When a fixed environmental constraint is introduced, the maximum biomass is limited to a size equal to b (the environment's carrying capacity). The logistic equation says that the population growth rate slows down and approaches zero as the population size approaches environmental carrying capacity. In this model, $f(X) = 0$ when $X = 0$ and when $X = b$. When the resource stock lies between 0 and b, $f(X) > 0$ with a maximum value at $X = b/2$.[1] At $X = b/2$, the steady harvest is maximized so this is the MSY (maximum sustained yield) point in the logistic fishery model. As discussed in chapter 6, the MSY concept differs in fishing and forestry models. In the latter, MSY maximizes sustainable harvest per unit of space (land area) occupied by the resource (see the discussion in chapter 6). Figure 7.1 illustrates biological equilibrium for a fishery resource following the logistic growth rule. Each harvest level (q) below MSY can be achieved at two different steady-state values for the resource stock (X).

Turning to economic equilibrium, the fishery *production function* relates the size of the sustainable harvest to the number of fishing inputs in the industry and the size of the resource stock:

$$q = q(E, X) \qquad (2)$$

where, once again, q is the harvest rate and X is the resource stock. E stands for the quantity of inputs devoted to fishing and is usually treated as a composite of boats, gear, and manpower—E for "effort." A simple and convenient form for (2) which has been used by Munro (1981, 1982) is

$$q = e \cdot E \cdot X \qquad (2A)$$

where e is a "catchability coefficient" which is assigned a constant value in the production function.[2] The rationale for (2A) is quite simple. It states that the catch per unit of effort (q/E) depends on the density of the fish stock (X) in a fixed fishery environment. If density doubles, each unit of fishing effort tends to encounter twice as many fish. An increase in the catchability coefficient (e) implies an increase in the productivity of fishing inputs for a fixed density of fish (X). For a fixed catchability coefficient, a fall in fish density lowers the productivity of effort.

If fishing inputs can be attracted in the long run from the rest of the economy (or returned to the rest of the economy) at constant prices, each unit of effort in (2A) costs w, where w is the constant cost (including normal profit) of the package of inputs making up one unit of effort. Total fishing cost (TC) is, therefore,

FIGURE 7.1

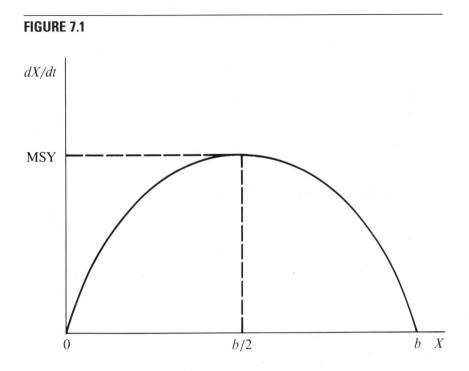

$$TC = w \cdot E \qquad (3)$$

Suppose, following Munro, we want to construct the total cost of harvesting the sustainable yields associated with different levels of the fish stock (X). The first step is to substitute (2A) into (3) so that $TC = (w \cdot q)/(E \cdot X)$. Next, using the logistic rule (1A), eliminate q by substituting $q = aX - (aX^2/b)$. The result is

$$TC = w[aX - (aX^2)/b]/eX = aw[1 - (X/b)]/e \qquad (4)$$

Equation (4) shows a linear relationship between TC and X. The steady-state fraction of the stock caught is $q/X = a(1 - X/b)$. As X approaches zero, this catch fraction approaches a, such that the required effort is $E = q/eX = a/e$ and $TC = wE = wa/e$. When X approaches b, q/X approaches 0 which requires $E = 0$ and $TC = 0$.

Economic equilibrium occurs when total cost (TC) equals total harvest revenue (TR). At this point, fishermen are making zero economic profit so that there is no incentive for fishing effort to increase (entry) or decrease (exit). Total harvest revenue for different levels of the resource stock can be derived from (1A) and Figure 7.1. Suppose the output from an individual fishery is a small fraction of the total market for fish products. In

FIGURE 7.2

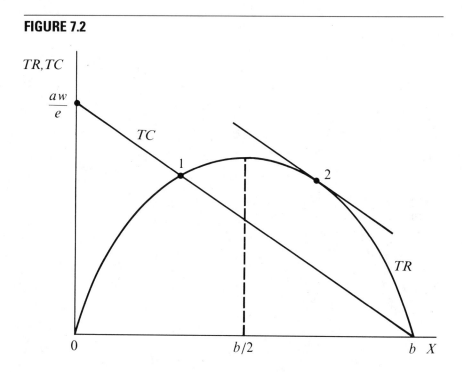

that case, the landed price of fish (π) for the individual fishery is independent of its harvest rate (the fishery is a price taker). The total revenue
function for the fishery is then

$$TR = \pi \cdot q = \pi \cdot f(X) = \pi[aX - (aX^2/b)] \tag{5}$$

The total revenue relationship is obtained from Figure 7.1 by simply
multiplying the harvest on the vertical axis by the constant landed price of
fish (π). Total revenue is zero at $X = 0$ and at $X = b$ and is maximized at
$X = b/2$.

Figure 7.2 illustrates the total cost relationship (4) and the total
revenue relationship (5) for the fishery. At point 1, bionomic equilibrium is
achieved. The fishery is producing a harvest in accordance with equation
(1A). At the same time $TR = TC$, so that fishermen are earning zero pure
profits. To the left of point 1, $TC > TR$ and fishermen exit from the
industry, reducing the harvest level so the stock grows until $TC = TR$. To
the right of point 1, the reverse occurs: $TR > TC$, so fishermen enter the
industry in response to super-normal profit, the resource stock declines,
and TC and TR move to equality.[3]

Two observations can be made about point 1. First, point 1 illustrates
an equilibrium fish stock less than the MSY stock at $b/2$. Though this is

commonly the case, the open-access equilibrium point *may* occur to the right of $b/2$ as well. So, although in practice common property renewable resource equilibrium tends to produce a resource stock below the MSY stock, this is not logically necessary: if the TC line is rotated upward around b, $TC = TR$ approaches and then passes through the MSY stock.

Unlike minerals and forests, no real attempt has been made in the past to capture potential rents from Canadian fisheries. One approach to correcting the zero-rent open-access fishery equilibrium to produce a positive level of rent would simply be to adjust the size of the stock to maximize the steady-state "profit" from the fishery defined as $TR - TC$. In Figure 7.2 this involves selecting a stock at point 2 where the slope of the TR curve equals the slope of the TC curve. While it is true that point 2 maximizes the excess of the value of the catch over harvesting cost, capital theory approaches in the early 1970s conclusively revealed the deficiency in this approach. The difficulty involves the carrying cost of capital embodied in the resource stock at point 2. Once units of the stock acquire a positive value equal to the net price $(\pi - C)$, holding these units sacrifices the return that could be obtained by harvesting them and investing the proceeds at the ruling rate of return on capital (r). Just as with nonrenewable resources, an optimal extraction policy for renewable resources involves comparison of the present value of resource units extracted in the future with the returns obtainable through immediate extraction. Unlike nonrenewables though, units of the stock that are carried forward in time *grow* as a result of biological processes. The following section develops a framework for optimal renewable resources use using capital theory principles. The results of this framework will then be compared with the forest management (rotation) rules discussed in chapter 6.

■ AN OPTIMAL FISHERY MANAGEMENT MODEL

The contrast between open-access management leading to point 1 in Figure 7.2 and optimal management can be brought out by imagining the fishery under private ownership with the owner attempting to maximize the present value of his resource. The owner is considering whether or not to expand the number of units of the resource held.

Suppose the open-access equilibrium (point 1 in Figure 7.2) occurs at $X = X_o$. Following the same line of reasoning used in chapters 2 and 3, we can compare the benefits and costs of adding a marginal unit to the resource stock. The current return sacrificed by adding a unit to the resource stock is the net price. In the present model, the net price is $p = \pi - C(X)$ where π is the fixed product price and $C(X)$ is marginal extraction cost which depends on the stock size X. From equations (2A) and (3), $C(X) = TC/q = w/eX$. With an interest rate r, the cost of holding an additional unit of the stock is, therefore, rp. What are the benefits of holding an extra unit of stock? There are three types of benefits. First, the unit of stock may appreciate in value by an amount equal to dp/dt. Second, the unit of stock lowers harvesting cost $C(X)$. Since $C(X) = w/eX$, $dC/dX = C_x = -w/eX^2 < 0$. The reduction in unit harvesting cost applies to all units produced, so the total current gain from holding an extra unit of stock is $-C_x q$. Finally, since we are dealing with a renewable resource, the additional unit of stock will grow. The growth function is $f(X)$ so an addition to the stock will increase growth by $df(X)/dX = f_x$. The value of the additional growth is $f_x p$. The present-value maximizing owner wants to add units to the resource stock provided

$$rp < dp/dt - C_x q + f_x p \qquad (6)$$

that is, provided the carrying cost of an extra unit is less than the sum of its current capital appreciation, harvesting cost benefits, and growth benefits. Now consider the open-access equilibrium at $X = X_0$. This is a steady-state position for the fishery in the sense that $dX/dt = f(X) - q = 0$. Since the net price is given by $p = \pi - C(X)$ and the product price π is fixed, it follows that $dp/dt = -C_x dX/dt$. Since $dX/dt = 0$ in the steady state, $dp/dt = 0$ as well. We know that any steady-state equilibrium fish stock less than the optimal stock offers a net benefit from expanding the stock, i.e.,

$$rp < -C_x f(X_0) + f_x p \qquad (7)$$

This relationship follows from (6) with $dp/dt = 0$ and $q = f(X)$ in steady-state equilibrium. The inequality in (7) simply indicates that the open-access equilibrium is one in which the resource owner will want to increase the stock. The way to raise the stock is to reduce output q below $f(X)$ so that $dX/dt > 0$. Note that the net price (p), the change in unit harvesting cost due to a change in stock (C_x), and the marginal growth rate (f_x) are all evaluated at $X = X_0$ in (7).

The resource owner has to ask the question: how low should output q be set to build the stock up to its optimal steady-state value? In the present model, the answer to this question is a simple one: set $q = 0$ until the stock rises to its optimal steady-state value. To see this, assume that the owner decides to reduce output from $f(X_0)$ in the open-access equilibrium to some lower level $q > 0$ where the size of the output reduction is $\Delta q = f(X_0) - q = dX/dt$. We have now moved out of the steady state. The net price is no longer constant and, in fact, $dp/dt = -C_x dX/dt = -C_x \Delta q > 0$. Since the output level selected is q, the marginal decline in total harvesting cost from a marginal addition to the stock is $-C_x q = -C_x [f(X_0) - \Delta q]$.

Applying inequality (6), the owner will *still* want to add units to the stock X_0 at output q if,

$$rp < -C_x \Delta q - C_x [f(X_0) - \Delta q] + f_x p \qquad (8)$$

where, as before, p, C_x, and f_x are evaluated at $X = X_0$. However, (8) *must* hold provided (7) holds, i.e., provided $rp < -C_x f(X_0) + f_x p$, since the terms in $C_x \Delta q$ cancel in (8). We have shown, therefore, that no matter how large the reduction in output (Δq) contemplated at stock size X_0, the owner will still want to reduce output further (build up the stock faster) with the logical constraint being that output q cannot fall below zero. The owner's optimal plan then is to set $q = 0$ until the stock size has grown to its optimum level at X_T. Once the stock equals X_T, the owner abruptly raises harvesting output to the optimal steady-state solution $q = f(X_T)$. The characteristic of the optimal steady-state is that

$$rp = -C_x f(X_T) + f_x p \qquad (9)$$

where p, C_x, and f_x are evaluated at $X = X_T$. At X_T the marginal holding cost of an extra unit of the stock equals the marginal harvesting cost and growth benefits provided by the extra unit. The adjustment process with $q = 0$ when $X < X_T$ and $q = f(X)$ when $X = X_T$ is sometimes called a "bang-bang" strategy. Since this strategy leads to the fastest possible growth of the stock to its optimum value X_T, it is also referred to as a *most rapid approach path* or MRAP.

The reason why the "bang-bang" or MRAP strategy is correct in this model is because the net price does *not* depend on the rate of harvest. Since product price π is fixed by assumption and unit harvesting cost C depends on stock size X but not on the harvesting rate, $p = \pi - C(X)$ does not change at a given stock size when the harvest rate changes. This is a crucial assumption. If a reduction in the harvesting rate q raises the product price, i.e., $\pi = \pi(q)$ with $d\pi/dq = \pi_q < 0$, or if unit harvesting cost increases with q, then the net price becomes an inverse function of q, i.e., $p = p(q)$ with $dp/dq = p_q < 0$. If $p_q < 0$, the reduction in the harvesting rate below $f(X_0)$ in the steady-state (open-access) equilibrium *raises* the net price and it will not usually be optimal to follow an MRAP strategy by lowering q to zero. At a positive output rate with stock size $X < X_T$ the owner's optimal strategy is to satisfy the asset-equilibrium condition:

$$rp = dp/dt - C_x q + f_x p \qquad (10)$$

such that the holding cost of a marginal addition to the stock equals appreciation of the stock unit plus the harvesting cost and growth benefits of the additional unit. Equation (10) implies a gradual approach to the optimum steady-state X_T described by equation (9). As discussed in the appendix, the initial harvesting rate starts below $f(X)$ and then moves smoothly toward $q = f(X_T)$.

Comparing the present results with the nonrenewable asset-equilibrium result from the modified Hotelling model, equation (10) differs from equation (11) in chapter 2. The difference is the appearance of $f_x p$ in the present result. If a resource is nonrenewable, holding an additional unit of stock does not lead to any increase in the total available supply (the growth effect is zero) so $f_x = 0$. Equation (11) in chapter 2 can, therefore, be thought of as a *special case* of optimal natural resource use in which units of the stock have a zero growth rate.

Since nonrenewable resource models focus on the optimal rate of depletion of a fixed (economic) stock, they are nonsteady-state models ($dp/dt \neq 0$). The steady state arrives only when the stock is exhausted. By contrast, renewable resources models often examine steady states in which the rate of harvest equals the rate of stock growth and $dp/dt = 0$. The assumption of a zero rate of change in the net price has already been made in chapter 6 for some of the forest rotation models discussed there. In the steady-state fishery case, equation (10) is replaced by equation (9).

The optimal steady-state result in (9) can now be compared with the open-access result (point 1 in Figure 7.2), the MSY rule (with the stock set at $b/2$ in Figure 7.2), and the "profit"-maximizing rule (point 2 in Figure 7.2). Since the net price (p) is positive in (9), the optimal steady-state result obviously occurs to the right of point 1 in Figure 7.2 where total revenue (*TR*) exceeds total cost (*TC*). So, as assumed above, the *optimal* renewable resource stock (X_T) is larger than the open-access stock (X_0).

If the rate of interest (r) is set equal to zero in equation (9), then $C_x q = C_x f(X) = f_x p$. Since $p = \pi - C$, this means that $\pi f_x = C f_x + C_x q$. It is easy to show that this is the condition for maximizing revenue net of harvesting cost and is obtained from Figure 7.2 by choosing X where the slope of *TR* equals the slope of *TC*.[4] This demonstrates that the "profit"-maximizing rule at point 2 neglects the carrying costs on capital tied up in the unharvested resource. Once carrying costs are included, optimal management implies that the resource owner chooses a point to the *left* of point 2 in Figure 7.2 to reduce holding costs on capital tied up in the resource stock. So the optimal steady state resource stock is *lower* than the stock in the profit-maximizing position, for any positive rate of interest.

The foregoing discussion has shown that the optimal steady state resource stock lies *between* points 1 and 2 in Figure 7.2. Can anything be said about its relationship to the MSY stock at $b/2$? Like the forest rotation cases in the previous chapter, the MSY rule *does* emerge as a particular (and rather unrealistic) case of equation (9) under special assumptions. If the rate of interest is zero *and* unit extraction cost (C) is independent of stock size so that $C_x = 0$, then equation (9) implies that $rp = f_x p$ and, therefore, $f_x = 0$ if r = 0. The condition $f_x = 0$ means that an increase in stock size has a zero effect on the growth of the stock and this occurs at the MSY point with stock equal to $b/2$. So the MSY rule is correct for a zero rate of interest and harvesting costs independent of stock size. Not surprisingly, a positive rate of interest, which leads resource owners to economize on resource stocks, pulls the optimal stock to the left of $b/2$ toward point 1 while a favourable effect on extraction cost exerted by the resource stock ($C_x < 0$) pulls the optimal stock to the right of $b/2$ toward point 2. With these two forces pulling in opposite directions, an optimal steady-state fish stock of $b/2$ *could* occur, but only as a very special (accidental) result.

Realizing the full value of the economic surplus from fisheries requires a movement to the right of point 1 in Figure 7.2. When the fishery operates as a common property resource in which fishermen freely capture all fish for which $\pi > C$, the resource stock is too low—low enough, in fact, to drive economic rent to zero, as we have seen. Building the stock up above the open-access equilibrium requires a temporary reduction in harvesting rates so that $f(X) > q$ for a period of time. The increase in the stock simulates the decisions that would be undertaken by an owner desiring to maximize the present value of the fishery. This is the conclusion reached from the application of capital theory principles to a common property renewable resource. In chapter 2, we noticed that open-access produced analogous problems for mineral resources: when existing mineral deposits can be exploited by anyone, there is a strong tendency to extract resources as soon as revenues exceed extraction (harvesting) costs. Over-exploitation and zero net prices go hand in hand.

■ FISH *VERSUS* FORESTS: SOME COMPARISONS

There are some basic differences between the fisheries models discussed in the previous two sections and the forest management (rotation) models described in chapter 6. The forest management models involve selective harvesting: stands of trees are identified within the resource stock and their individual growth paths followed until they are selectively harvested as even-aged stands at the end of the rotation period. By contrast, the usual approach to the fishery is not to identify different age-classes of the resource for selective harvesting but rather to treat the entire resource population as eligible for extraction in each time interval.

One way of exploring the contrast between fish and trees is to imagine a fish stock that *can* be harvested selectively like a forest. Such an imaginary fishery might have the following characteristics. First, like forest stands, average extraction cost might be thought of as independent of the resource volume. Like trees, this kind of fish does not have to be searched for so a large resource stock does not lower extraction cost. In this case, $C_x = 0$ in equation (9) which now reads:

$$rp = f_x \cdot p \qquad \text{or} \qquad r = f_x \qquad (11)$$

Since we are assuming the individual age classes of this kind of fish can be selectively extracted by using, for example, nets with adjustable mesh sizes which permit all individuals smaller than the selected size to escape, a *steady-state* fishery with a constant harvest flow is being managed like a *fully regulated* even-flow forest. So equation (11) *should* be recognizable in terms of the rotation rules discussed in chapter 6.

The steady-state harvest in this selectively managed fishery is q and is equal to the growth of the entire stock $f(X)$. Since only the largest age-class is being harvested, q equals the biomass of this largest age-class which was denoted by x in chapter 6. So, in the steady state, $x = q = f(X)$. From this it follows that $dx/dt = d[f(X)]/dt = f_x \cdot dX/dt = f_x \cdot x$. Therefore, $f_x = (dx/dt)/x$. Substituting this result into (11) gives

$$(dx/dt)/x = r \tag{12}$$

which is the forest rotation rule given by equation (5) in chapter 6. That rotation rule is appropriate to timber occupying land with a zero opportunity cost ($A = 0$) with the net price of timber (the stumpage price) assumed constant ($dp/dt = 0$). So, our imaginary fishery is being optimally managed like a fully regulated forest.

Real fisheries differ considerably from this imaginary fishery. In many fisheries it is technologically difficult or impossible to use a selective harvesting regime to focus the entire catch on the largest age-class in the population. The use of trawls and lines, for example, permits little in the way of age-class selectivity. Gillnetting, however, offers an element of selectivity absent with other kinds of gear. When age-class selection cannot be accomplished, rotation-style rules like (12) are not relevant to resource management.

Even where age-class selection *is* possible, it may not be economic. This conclusion emerges when the assumption that extraction cost is independent of stock size is dropped. With $C_x < 0$, the elusive nature of the resource receives recognition. It may be very costly in terms of effort per unit of harvest (E/q) to confine harvesting activity to one or a few age-classes in the population. Broadening the number of age-classes targeted for harvesting increases the size of the targeted population and therefore increases the productivity of harvesting effort. A lower value for unit harvesting cost (C) increases the net price ($\pi - C$).

Even if an extraction cost argument for expanding the target population into younger age-classes is ignored, there is another reason for expanding the target population. If harvesting is confined to the oldest individuals in the population, it is unlikely that any economic level of effort will succeed in capturing *all* the (elusive) individuals in the target age-class. Individuals that escape into older age-classes before being captured will have slower growth rates when (and if) they are caught. Thus, even though selective harvesting *begins* when the individuals are growing at the rate of interest (equation (12)), many, and perhaps most, individuals are harvested at lower growth rates. This means that the *average* rate of growth of individuals harvested falls below r. It is then optimal, on rotation theory principles, to lower the target age-class until the average rate of growth of the harvested individuals satisfies equation (12). Again, the elusive nature of the fish resource provides an argument for expanding the target population into younger age-classes.   In summary, a combination of technical problems in adjusting fishing gear for age-class selection together with the elusiveness of individuals comprising the resource has generated a different *theoretical* structure for the optimal management of fisheries compared with forests. In addition, at the level of practical realism, there are many more age-classes of individuals in forests than in fisheries. So, in contrast to forests, the usual assumption is that all (or most) of the fish resource population is assumed to be the target population for harvesting efforts. The choice of a target age-class ("rotation period") for fishing is usually ignored as it has been in the previous sections of this chapter.[5]

From the standpoint of existing resource stocks, fisheries and forests often present contrasting management problems. Stressing the MSY principle and the gradual removal of old-growth, North American forest managers have allowed large and uneconomic volumes of timber to occupy forest lands. As a result, there have been arguments for increased timber harvests over the next few decades. As noted above, the policy problem for fisheries is essentially the reverse. The prevalence of open-access to fish populations has tended to reduce fish stocks below their optimal levels. In this case, the central focus is on reducing fishing pressure to allow stocks to recover.

With respect to the open-access issue, it is also worth noting that it is precisely the elusive nature of renewable fish populations that makes possible an open-access harvesting equilibrium with a positive resource stock such as point 1 in Figure 7.2. As the fish population shrinks under the influence of harvesting, extraction cost increases ($C_x < 0$) until harvesting is no longer profitable. Profit disappears before the resource does, so that the resource is actually protected from annihilation by the elusiveness of its members. If elusiveness is absent or slight so that unit extraction costs do not rise, or rise very little, as the population stock is reduced, the results may be very different. Referring back to equation (2A), if harvesting productivity is independent of stock size (X), then the production function is simply $q = e \cdot E$. It is always profitable to enter the industry if $TR - TC > 0$, i.e., if $\pi q - wE > 0$ or $\pi > w/e$, and the resource stock is driven to extinction by open-access entry. If a forest area were opened to all comers with $\pi > w/e$, nothing would prevent a wave of logging activity followed by years of zero harvesting. No costly regeneration activities would seem worthwhile to individual users given the uncontrolled access to the regenerated resource. Even if natural regeneration could take place following harvesting, loggers would harvest the area again as soon as the trees had reached minimum economic size. Deforestation is virtually guaranteed by the absence of effective property rights over the resource just as environmental degradation is the outcome of an absence of property rights in the environment (chapter 3). The effective extinction of the passenger pigeon in the 1890s is another example of management failure leading to the elimination of a resource stock. In this case the passenger pigeon population was lowered through open-access hunting to a point at which successful natural regeneration (reproduction) could not take place. Among ocean species, blue whale stocks have been severely threatened by open-access exploitation. Agreements to control harvesting through the aegis of the International Whaling Commission have been relatively ineffective.

It is also important to realize, when comparing the economic literature on fisheries and forests, that multiple-use issues have been much less prominent in fisheries modelling. When fish stocks or stocks of ocean mammals are threatened with extinction, however, multiple-use issues *do* surface in the form of perceptions and efforts by environmentalists to reduce harvesting activities in the interests of maintaining the benefits of the remaining population. The resource stock begins to acquire significance other than as a source of commercial harvests. If, like the nontimber benefits of standing forests, benefits of ocean resource stocks can be integrated into future management plans for these resources, costs of extraction will then have to include the loss of benefits from having a smaller population available to provide non-commercial benefits to humankind and to serve as a reproductive reservoir for the future of the species. The forestry literature on nontimber benefits (chapter 6) is at least suggestive of ways to integrate stock-related benefits into the management of renewable resources.

∎ POLICY INSTRUMENTS AND POLICY OPTIONS

Policy Background

As we have seen above, one way of dealing with the open-access or common property problem is through effective sole ownership of fisheries. If the sole owner acts as a net present value maximizer, he will adopt equation (9) in determining his optimal steady-state harvest and population stock level. What prevents this optimal result from emerging for open-access fisheries is precisely the lack of a single decision maker committed to maximization of the NPV of the resource.

Examining the ownership issue more closely, the situation in Canada is that the federal government has jurisdiction over the management of ocean fish stocks within Canada's control. Canada's control over ocean fish stocks was greatly enhanced by the establishment of extended fisheries jurisdictions (EFJs) in 1977 as a result of the United Nations Third Law of the Sea Conference.[6] In 1982, most United Nations countries adopted the EFJ. The EFJs assign control of fisheries and their economic benefits to coastal nations insofar as these fisheries lie within two hundred miles (three hundred and twenty kilometres) of national coastlines, replacing the older twelve-mile (approximately nineteen-kilometre) limit. The "two-hundred-mile" concept is not without problems, though. In some cases, EFJs overlap (Canada-U.S. in the region between Nova Scotia and Maine, for example, or Canada-France in the region south of Newfoundland surrounding St. Pierre and Miquelon). In other cases, fisheries extend beyond Canada's EFJ into international waters. Subject to these limitations, part of the open-access problem has been resolved by the EFJs. Whether or not the federal government, through the Department of Fisheries and Oceans (DFO), intends to maximize the NPV associated with ocean fisheries under its control is, as yet, uncertain though.

Suppose that the Canadian government chooses the NPV maximization objective for fisheries management. What policies might be used by the DFO to produce this result? Several instruments might be considered, including controls over fishing effort, catch quotas, and fees levied on harvest volumes (Scott and Neher 1981). Since open-access involves excessive fishing effort, the most obvious approach is to strengthen existing controls over the number of boats and types of gear used to extract the resource. In his examination of the Pacific fishery, Pearse noted that catches of salmon and roe-herring on the west coast in the early 1980s could have been taken with fleets and costs equal to about half their actual magnitudes.[7] Active attempts to reduce the number of fishermen and boats has been a common approach to reducing harvesting effort. One basic problem can be identified, however, that tends to cause these kinds of restrictions to fail. Quantitative restrictions on fishing inputs have to be comprehensive and detailed. Fishermen can respond to selective input controls by expanding catching power in other ways. If, for example, the boat is the basis for entry licensing, fishermen may be able to increase effort by increasing the size and/or speed of boats or by utilizing a higher ratio of gear and crew to vessel capacity. This is sometimes referred to as "capital stuffing." In addition, inefficient types of boats and gear may be used. Effort units have indeed turned out to be very pliable in the Pacific salmon fishery. As Pearse explains,

> . . . when one or more inputs in the fishing process are restricted, the capacity of the fleet can continue to expand by adding other, unrestricted inputs. . . . In the Pacific salmon fishery, the initial restriction on the number of vessels led to their being replaced with larger vessels. Then, in an effort to control vessel size, restrictions on tonnage and length were added. These led to further investment in new gear and vessel improvements. In the roe-herring fishery, restricting the number of persons permitted to fish has not prevented expansion of the fishing power of their vessels.[8]

FIGURE 7.3

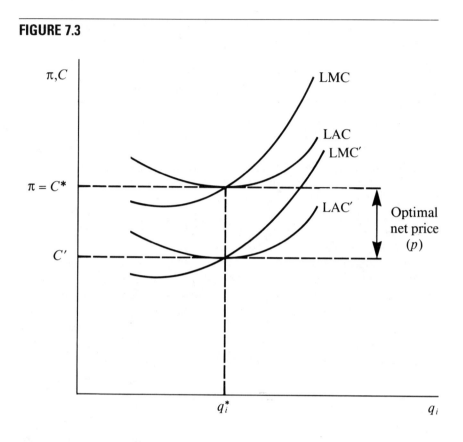

Analysis of Policy Instruments

Figure 7.3 illustrates the effect of effort licensing (entry restriction) on the fisherman's choice of inputs. When fishermen choose their inputs entirely in response to cost-minimizing criteria, the minimum long-run average cost of harvesting is C^* in Figure 7.3. The optimal-sized fishing "firm" catches q_i^* tonnes of fish each season. A "firm" consists of a single boat with accompanying crew and gear. In the open-access case, net price is zero so $C^* = \pi$ (where π is the landed price of fish). To reach the optimal solution, the licensing plan is to reduce the number of boats while each boat (firm) continues to minimize costs by harvesting at rate q_i^*. This occurs at C' in Figure 7.3.[9] The fall in the number of firms has reduced the total catch and the population biomass (X) has expanded as a result. So each firm's costs are lower ($C' < C^*$). At C', the net price is $p = \pi - C'$. The problem here is that each fishing firm has an incentive to expand

FIGURE 7.4

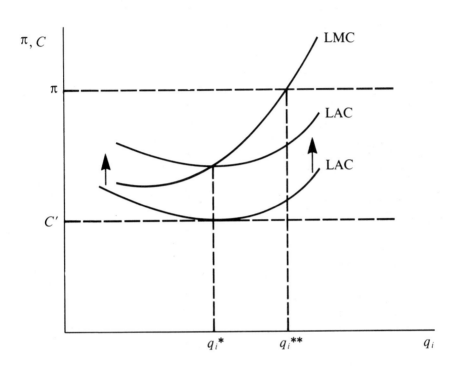

harvesting to the right along LMC′ until LMC′ = π. This can be accomplished by changing the size and speed of each licensed boat, its crew size, and the amount and type of gear deployed. The total catch now rises above its optimal level, the fish stock (X) falls, and, in final equilibrium, fishing firms end up in the position shown in Figure 7.4. Cost curves have been pulled up above their optimal level in Figure 7.3 owing to sub-optimal fish stock size and each fishing firm produces too much output $(q_i{}^{**})$ at an average cost per unit that is too high. Since the landed price (π) exceeds average cost in Figure 7.4, the resource does yield *some* rent, but the net price is below its optimum value. Things are not as bad as in the open-access case, but restrictions on entry of boats is still a failure when compared to the optimal solution.

An alternative to licensing that has turned out to be an even more dramatic failure from the standpoint of generating economic rent is a simple *global quota* on the annual harvest without the assignment of shares in the global quota to individual fishing firms. This too has been a common approach to management of Canadian fisheries. Suppose the optimal stock is known in Figure 7.5 (point 2). If the fishery is currently operating at the

FIGURE 7.5

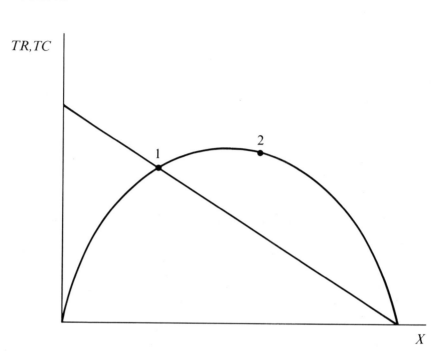

open-access equilibrium (point 1), the global harvest must be reduced temporarily until the stock rises to point 2. The harvest is then raised to its steady-state value at point 2, so the fishery will remain at that point year in and year out. Since no attempt is made to allocate the total quota at point 2 to individual fishermen, there is nothing to prevent the number of fishing firms from expanding until $C = \pi$ and economic rents are eliminated. Since the global harvest is fixed, each fisherman ends up taking a small enough fraction of the total stock to raise his average cost up to the landed price (π) as illustrated in Figure 7.6. Instead of taking the optimal catch per firm of $q_i{}^*$, each fisherman takes only $q_i{}'$. The industry suffers from excess capacity in the sense that the global quota could be caught at lower cost with a fraction of the number of fishermen. One way in which this kind of excess capacity shows up is through reduced fishing seasons: large numbers of fishermen fish until the global quota is reached, then the fishery is closed for the season leaving people, boats, and gear idle for the rest of the year. Economic rent is completely dissipated.

The mechanism by which the global quota fails suggests the ingredients that would be required for a successful quota policy. The optimal global quota has to be assigned to individual firms, so that each

FIGURE 7.6

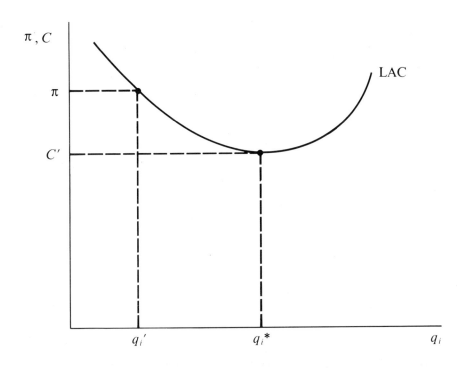

firm ends up at q_i^* instead of at q_i'. The optimal total catch is q^* at point 2 in Figure 7.5. Suppose that this global quota can be sold in the form of *quota licences* to individual fishermen. Fishermen are allowed to take fish only to the extent that they hold quota licences. The lower the cost of fishing, the more each firm can afford to pay for a unit of licensed quota. At point C' in Figure 7.4 the firm can afford to pay the most for a unit of licensed quota. Under competitive conditions, the price of each unit of quota will, therefore, equal $\pi - C'$, which is the most that an efficient operator can afford to pay and is equal to the optimal net price (at q_i^* in Figure 7.3).[10] Suppose a fishing firm produces to the left of q_i^*. In that case, the price it can afford to bid for quota units and survive is less than $\pi - C'$ and firms producing at q_i^* will outbid it.

As an instrument of optimal fisheries management then, the quota scheme will work under the following circumstances. First, a global quota q^* has to be set to establish resource equilibrium at point 2 in Figure 7.5. This will require reductions in total harvests during the period in which the resource stock is being built up from the depressed open-access equilibrium. Second, units of the global quota have to be assigned to individuals, who will then want to minimize the cost of extracting them. Assignment through the market mechanism (bidding) will ensure that only the lowest cost fishermen use the resource.

The alternative to an efficiently run quota licence scheme is the imposition of *landing fees*. The quota licence scheme establishes the net price $p = \pi - C'$ by marketing a global quota to individual operators. The landing fee approach simply sets a tax of $T = \pi - C'$ on each tonne of fish landed at processing plants. The landing fee ensures that cost-minimizing firms end up at C' in Figure 7.3. The level of the firms' cost curves at C', in turn, implies a particular (optimal) stock appropriate to point 2 in Figure 7.5.

Landing fees are essentially *depletion taxes* (see chapter 5). For the public owner of a fishery, depletion taxes are one method of capturing the potential economic rent from the resource. Provided the depletion tax is set at the correct level, it can be used to capture the rents to the resource that arise under optimal management. Can an efficiently run quota system also be used to capture fishery rents? The answer to this question is certainly in the affirmative. The public owner can auction individual quota licences to fishermen. The resulting competitively determined quota prices (net prices) not only secure an efficient solution to the fishery management problem, they also transfer the rents to the Crown. It can be noted that revenues raised through quota auctions would represent *ex-ante* rent capture while landing fees represent *ex-post* rent capture (chapter 5).

Canadian Fisheries Policy

Following the establishment of EFJs, new recommendations and management policies for Canadian ocean fisheries have appeared. Issues surrounding the management of Atlantic fish stocks and the Atlantic fish-processing sector were discussed in the Kirby Report.[11] The Pearse Report dealt with the problems of Pacific fisheries.[12] In 1990, the Harris Report examined the stock problems and management options for the cod fishery off the the northern coast of Newfoundland.[13] Each of these studies drew attention to different aspects of fisheries management in Canada.

The anticipation of increased domestic fish landings with the two-hundred-mile EFJ caused considerable expansion of fish-processing capacity on the Atlantic coast. Costs rose rapidly at a time when fish prices were not increasing. These factors created a financial crisis in 1980 and 1981 in which Atlantic processors were threatened with bankruptcy. Much of the Kirby Report dealt with the financial problems of the processors rather than with questions of resource management as such. The report's discussion of fisheries management recognized the open-access nature of the problem and recommended *quota licences* to be allocated to individual fishing enterprises with the sum of such quota licences adding up to the global quota or total allowable catch (TAC). For the smaller inshore vessels operating in the cod fishery, the Kirby task force did not recommend quota licences since

> [g]iven the present system of monitoring landings, it would be impossible to keep accurate track of the individual catches of the more than 8000 craft under 35 feet. Even if that were possible, the relatively large year-to-year variations in catch per vessel in many inshore fisheries would make a system of individual boat quotas impractical, unless means were devised to permit the easy transfer of quota between fishermen as the season progressed and as the luck of individual fishermen waxed and waned.[14]

Instead, smaller boats would require capacity licences to control effort applied to harvesting by specifying the use of a certain number of hooks on a long liner or the number of fathoms of gillnet permitted each fisherman. The task force understood clearly that such effort licences are second-best alternatives to quota licences, since fishermen can still increase their catches by inefficiently substituting uncontrolled harvesting inputs for controlled inputs as previously described.

The Kirby Report was strongly committed to the idea that quota and effort licences be marketable through licence exchanges operated at the major Atlantic ports. The TAC for each Atlantic fish stock was to be divided into allowable catches for the inshore and offshore portions of the fishery. Beginning in 1982, most of the offshore TAC was divided into quota licences, referred to as *enterprise allocations*, held by the major trawler operators. Quota licences are not transferable between the inshore and offshore sectors, nor from one geographical sector to another in which fish stocks are being independently managed with their own TACs. The Kirby Report did *not* recommend the use of licence auctions or landing fees to capture potential economic rent in the Atlantic fisheries.

The Pearse Report was a comprehensive examination of management methods on the Pacific coast. In common with other studies, Pearse considered landing taxes and quota licences to be efficient solutions to the problems produced by past reliance on effort licences and global quotas but with some important exceptions.

In fisheries where stable annual TACs could be identified, the Pearse Report favoured the use of quota licences similar to the Kirby recommendations. Initially, ten-year quota licences would be allocated to existing fishermen by the DFO. In each subsequent year, one-tenth of these licences would be replaced by new ten-year licences. These replacement quota licences were to be allocated to existing holders through an auction process with each winning bidder retiring an equivalent amount of his previously held quota. After ten years, new quota licences would be placed on sale in each year to equal one-tenth of the TAC and all quota licences would be awarded through a bidding process. Further, after the ten-year transitional period, anyone, not just existing quota holders, would be allowed to enter the annual quota auction. The reason for the initial quota allocation being transformed into an auction reflected commitment to capturing fisheries rents for the Crown:

> ...my terms of reference provide guidance; after allowing fair and reasonable returns to commercial fishing enterprises the surplus should accrue to the Crown....resource rents...should be captured by the government through levies that are consistent with the value of resources recovered....[15]

Provided competition is strong—and Pearse intended to guarantee strong competition by restricting any single quota holder to 5 percent or less of all licences—the bidding process should ensure that an *ex-ante* estimate of economic rent is transferred through the auction process to the Crown once the transition period is complete. During the transition period, rent captured by the Crown would increase gradually to its full value as the initial licences are replaced by those acquired at auction. The strong rent capture component of the Pearse Report differed from the approach of the Kirby task force.

In addition to the bidding mechanism, Pearse proposed that economic rent be transferred to the Crown through landing fees or royalties levied per kilogram or per tonne of landings. Landing fees were to be set at approximately 10 percent of landed values. This approach would permit some rent to be collected on the initial allocation of quota licences. Once the ten-year transition period was complete, the landing fees would simply substitute for bids on quota licences in the sense that, in principle, a ten cent per kilogram landing fee would simply lower the bid-price for a quota licence by ten cents per kilogram.

Pearse acknowledged an important difficulty with the use of the licensed quota system in the important salmon and roe-herring fisheries, the two most important fisheries on the Pacific Coast. The quota model assumes that the annual TAC can be fixed with a fair degree of precision in advance of the allocation of individual quota licences. In Pearse's view, however,

> ...any system of individual catch quotas would...be difficult for these fleets to adjust to and probably beyond the capability of the Department... [of Fisheries and Oceans]...to administer. The stocks and available catch of these species are notorious for their wide and unpredictable year-to-year fluctuations, making it impossible to allocate individual quotas in advance with any degree of certainty.[16]

This difficulty has to be confronted whenever a TAC is to be set in the context of fluctuating population sizes. The fluctuating behaviour of landings (see Figures 7.7 and 7.8 for Northern cod and Pacific salmon data) indicates the nature of the problem. It is clear, however, that control over harvest rates must be effected. As the Pearse Report pointed out, effort licences have tended not to be very effective in the past for the reasons previously discussed.

To work effectively, effort licences would have to specify the particu-

FIGURE 7.7   British Columbia sockeye salmon landings

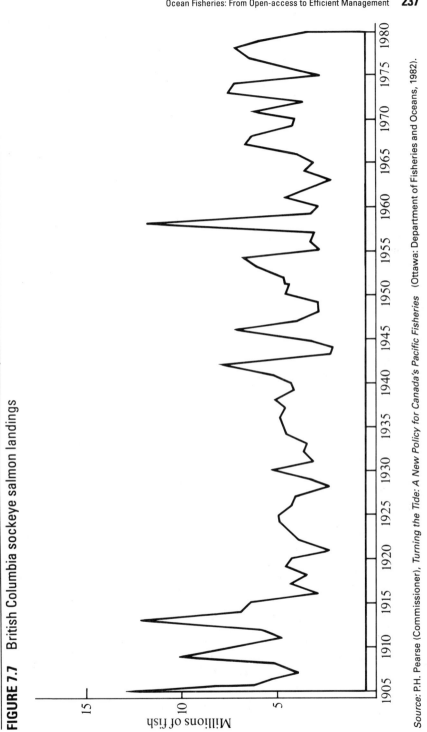

Source: P.H. Pearse (Commissioner), *Turning the Tide: A New Policy for Canada's Pacific Fisheries*   (Ottawa: Department of Fisheries and Oceans, 1982).

FIGURE 7.8 Newfoundland Northern Cod Landings

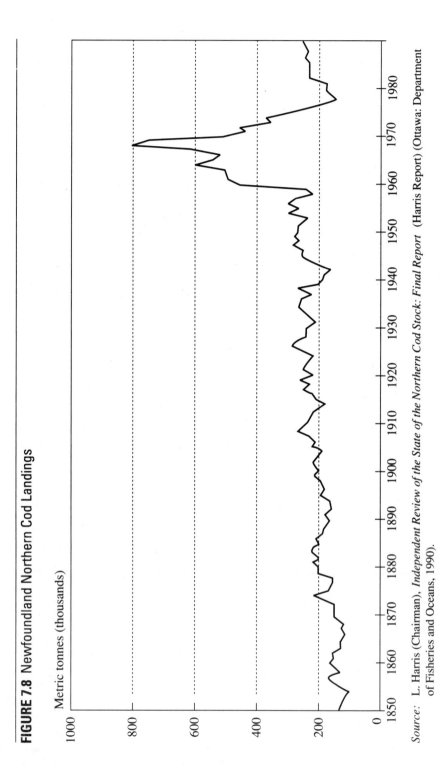

Source: L. Harris (Chairman), *Independent Review of the State of the Northern Cod Stock: Final Report* (Harris Report) (Ottawa: Department of Fisheries and Oceans, 1990).

lar vessel licensed (with stringent vessel-replacement restrictions) and the type of gear that the vessel is permitted to deploy. Input substitution must be sealed off as much as possible for effort licences to accomplish their goal. Second, a systematic attempt has to be made to retire licences so that fishing capacity actually disappears from the harvesting sector. Again, a ten-year licence was recommended. Existing licences were to be replaced with a set of initial (carefully specified) effort licences. In each year of the transition period, new ten-year effort licences were to be issued equal to one-tenth of the size of the target fleet. The new licences were to be sold at auction like the quota licences for other Pacific fisheries, with the bidders restricted to holders of initial licences during the transition period. In each year the size of the fleet would drop by about 5 percent as successful bidders for new licences relinquished their initial licences. After the transition period, anyone would be allowed to bid at the annual licence auction. The proposed ten-year reduction in the number of effort licences in the salmon and roe-herring sectors was to be accomplished by "buy-back" provisions allowing fishermen to sell their existing licences to the DFO with these purchases financed by the proposed landing taxes levied during the transition period.

Pacific fishermen have expressed support for the "buy-back" arrangements but have opposed landing taxes and licence auctions. "Buy-back" provisions have been attempted in the past with only modest success. Once rents begin to appear in fisheries, there are strong entry pressures. Indeed, all attempts to restrict harvest rates produce opposition.

The primary commitment of the DFO has been the preservation of fish stocks rather than to the collection of economic rent from fisheries. In part, this reflects closer attention to biological than economic principles within the Department. As one observer points out,

> [t]hirty-five years have passed since the publication of H. Scott Gordon's. . . seminal article describing rent dissipation in open-access fisheries. During this time, the Canadian government. . .[has]. . .tried to solve the problem by adopting quantitative input restrictions. . . .By controlling the number of vessels. . .and. . .inputs per vessel. . ., regulators have created restricted access fisheries theoretically capable of generating rent. What regulators did not anticipate was the ability of fishermen to continue dissipating rent. This is not surprising, since regulators. . .have been concerned more with biological than with economic objectives.[17]

The difficulty of controlling fishery inputs also reflects the problem of reducing fishing pressure when the incomes of fishermen are relatively low and their opportunities outside the fishery are limited. Most importantly, though, the whole issue of economic rent has been dwarfed in the 1980s by the much more serious problem of declining population stocks on the east coast. Rapid advances in fishing technology in the 1960s led to large increases in harvests (see Figure 7.8 for the Northern cod case), followed by falling harvests in the 1970s. Adoption of EFJs in 1977 was expected to control the harvest rate and stabilize fish biomasses. Instead, the 1980s brought further stock declines, even after harvest rates stabilized at levels well below those of the 1960s and early 1970s. The Harris Report addressed the stock problem in the context of Northern cod. It became apparent in 1988 that one of the major methods of estimating stocks by the DFO at that time, using catch per unit of effort (CPUE), resulted in a considerable overestimation of stocks.

The CPUE approach uses the ratio q/E to make inferences about population size. In our simple model, for example, CPUE $= q/E = eX$, from equation (2A). Provided the catchability coefficient e remains constant over time, variations in measured q/E can be used to infer variations in the stock size X. During a period of rapid technological change, e will be increasing, however. If this is not taken into consideration, CPUE tends to overestimate the underlying stock size. This, along with lags in acquiring independent survey data on stock sizes and a general mood of optimism following the establishment of EFJs, resulted in unexpected depletion of east coast fish stocks in the mid-1980s. It also became apparent that the new fish-seeking methods employed in the offshore fishery allowed fishermen to deplete spawning stocks and thus reduce recruitment to the future resource. As Harris explained with reference to the Northern cod stock,

> We have underestimated our own capacity to find, to pursue, and to kill. . . .
> Modern electronics tell the fishermen exactly where the fish are and they
> fish on concentrations of spawning fish. If the fish are concentrated, then the
> catch will be as high as ever—and it will remain high until the last fish is
> caught.[18]

All other aspects of fisheries management in the Atlantic region faded into the background in the late 1980s in the face of the depletion problem. The TAC for Northern cod, for example, fell by 25 percent from 266 000 tonnes in 1988 to 197 000 tonnes in 1990. Similar reductions in TACs in other east coast fisheries meant declining incomes and employment in Atlantic coast communities dependent on fishing and fish processing. Residents of these communities are not concerned at all with maximizing the present value of economic rents from the fisheries but are vitally interested in the future size of TACs and the total amount of income that future harvests will provide to fishermen and those engaged in fish processing.

■ MODELS OF FLUCTUATING POPULATIONS

The open-access and optimal management models of the previous sections as well as the discussion of policy instruments have assumed that fish

populations have a tendency to move over time to a steady-state equilibrium within their natural environments. A constant level of harvesting
activity essentially adds an additional stress on the population and reduces
its steady-state level below the maximum/m carrying capacity of the natural
environment to some lower level.

The long-run behaviour of fish stocks gives only qualified support to a
steady-state model. While stocks cannot be measured directly, year-to-year
harvest flows for many marine species show significant fluctuations
which, in turn, suggests that the underlying stocks are also fluctuating over
time. Figures 7.7 and 7.8 show the behaviour of Northern cod landings on
the Atlantic coast and British Columbia sockeye salmon landings on the
Pacific coast. The volatility of these series over long periods of time
suggests that the steady-state model is an oversimplified approach to the
exploitation problem for these species.

In essence, two causes of volatility are possible. The first lies in
environmental shocks. Natural fluctuations in food supplies or water
conditions, for example, may lie behind fluctuations in stocks. Part of the
environment includes commercial harvesting itself. If harvesting becomes
more efficient (an increase in the catchability coefficient e), for example,
harvests may rise for a while and then decline as the population base is
depleted.

The second possible cause of population fluctuation may lie in the
way the stock dynamic itself works. To see this in a simple way, we can
reformulate equation (1) to introduce a lag in the response of the *current*
population to the *past* population. (A more complicated continuous adjustment model can also be used with higher order terms in X than in our
simple open-access model.) With the one-period lag, equation (1) takes the
discrete form

$$X_{t+1} - X_t = f(X_t) - q_t \qquad (13)$$

where t refers to population biomass in the current period and $t + 1$ refers
to the biomass in the subsequent period (Conrad and Clark 1987). Thus the
current stock leads to growth equal to $f(X_t)$ from which the current harvest
q_t has to be subtracted in calculating the biomass change for the next
season. To keep the model simple, assume that a fixed fraction c of the
current stock is harvested so that $q_t = c \cdot X_t$. Suppose we further assume
that the logistic relationship in equation (1A) describes the natural growth
of the current stock $f(X_t)$. Substituting into (13),

$$X_{t+1} = aX_t - aX_t^2/b - cX_t + X_t$$
$$= (1 + a - c)X_t - aX_t^2/b \qquad (14)$$

which is a first-order nonlinear difference equation in X. Equation (14) has
three parameters, $a > 0$, $b > 0$, and $c > 0$ with $(1 + a - c) > 0$. To keep our
example as simple as possible, we will reduce the three parameters to a

single parameter k by assuming that $k = 1/(1 + a - c)$ with the further restriction that $a/[b(1 + a - c)] = 1$. We can then write (14) as the very simple equation

$$X_{t+1} = kX_t(1 - X_t) \tag{15}$$

The dynamic behaviour of equation (15) has been explored in detail by mathematicians and this behaviour depends entirely on the specification of k. In the present model, we restrict the values of the biomass so that $0 \leqslant X_t \leqslant 1$ which are the lower and upper stationary points for the population. This implies, in turn, that k is restricted to the values $0 \leqslant k \leqslant 4$.[19] If we are to believe in the steady-state model, then X should *converge* on the upper stationary point $X = 1$ in this model as time passes. But what is the actual dynamic behaviour of (15)?

It turns out that the dynamic behaviour of equation (15) is much more complicated than simple convergence to $X = 1$. Figure 7.9 graphs equation (15) with X_t on the horizontal axis and X_{t+1} on the vertical axis. A 45° line is used to transfer the value of X_{t+1} back to X_t so that dynamic behaviour can be followed on a single diagram. The four panels of Figure 7.9 illustrate the range of dynamics for different assumed values of k. In Panel A, $0 \leqslant k < 1$ and successive values of X approach zero. Panel A is not very interesting from our viewpoint since the only stable equilibrium point or *attractor* occurs at a zero stock size and zero harvest. In Panel B, $1 < k < 2$. This is a conventional steady-state case with two equibria. The zero population equilibrium is now an unstable equilibrium or *repellor* while $X = 1$ becomes an attractor. Population equilibrium moves directly to the attractor in Panel B. In Panel C, $2 < k < 3$ and, again, there are two equilibria: a repellor at $X = 0$ and an attractor at $X = 1$. The population stock approaches the attractor in Panel C by a series of convergent oscillations. Panel D shows the case of $3 < k \leqslant 4$. Here, *both* the $X = 0$ and the $X = 1$ equilibria are repellors. Dynamic behaviour now becomes more complicated.

As k passes through the value 3, the attractor at $X = 1$ splits or *bifurcates* into two second-order attractors on either side of $X = 1$. The second-order attractors have $X_t = X_{t+2}$ and $X_{t+1} = X_{t+3}$ instead of $X_t = X_{t+1}$. The result is convergence to an oscillatory pattern in the population stock with a two-period cycle. When k reaches a value of 3.45 (approximately), each of the second-order attractors bifurcates again to form a four-period cycle.

As k increases further, bifurcations become more frequent until, by the time k has reached a value of 3.57 (approximately), an infinite number of bifurcations has taken place and the fluctuating behaviour of X has become completely irregular and unpredictable. This region of unpredictable fluctuation is referred to as *chaos*.[20] Once the chaos region has occurred, it is essentially impossible to distinguish the movements of X from random behaviour. Figure 7.10 shows the two-period cycle that appears as k passes

FIGURE 7.9

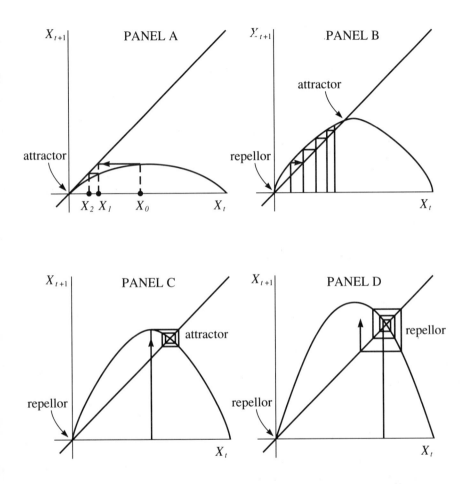

through 3, the four-period cycle as k passes through 3.45, and an example of chaotic behaviour ($k = 3.94$). As biologist Robert May has pointed out,

> The fact that...[a]...simple and deterministic equation...can possess dynamical trajectories which look like some sort of random noise has disturbing practical implications. It means, for example, that apparently erratic fluctuations in the census data for an animal population need not necessarily betoken either the vagaries of an unpredictable environment or sampling errors: they may simply derive from a rigidly deterministic population growth relationship. ...[21]

This short excursion into population dynamics with a one-period lag

FIGURE 7.10

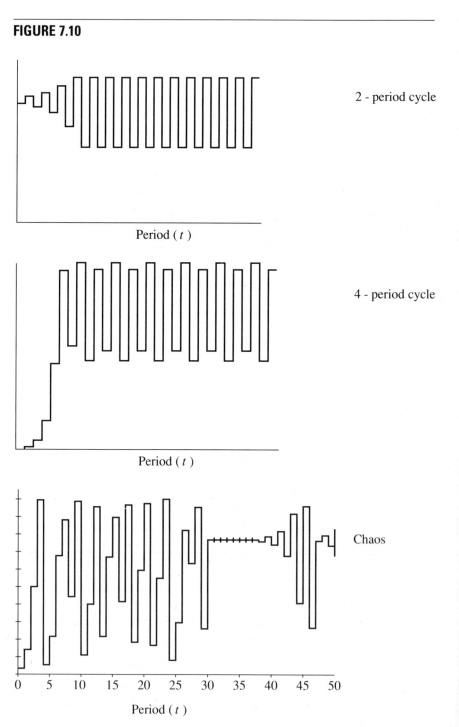

2 - period cycle

Period (*t*)

4 - period cycle

Period (*t*)

Chaos

Period (*t*)

Source: W. Baumol and J. Benhabib, "Chaos: Significance, Mechanism, and Economic Applications," *Journal of Economic Perspectives* 3 (1989): 77-105.

establishes the notion that regularly or irregularly fluctuating populations are entirely possible, even when the population dynamic is as simple as equation (15). We have a number of choices when observing actual fluctuations in renewable resource stocks. We may have a simple stable steady state (Figure 7.9, Panel B) or an oscillatory stable steady state (Figure 7.9, Panel C) disturbed by irregular shocks. Or we might have chaotic population behaviour with or without shocks. Changing the level of harvesting effort in this type of model can change not only the average level of harvests but also the underlying dynamic behaviour of the population model itself (by changing k in the present example).

Life is obviously much simpler with steady-state models. But it is increasingly clear that complex and even unpredictable behaviour may be characteristic of some biological populations. We cannot automatically assume that steady-state open-access or optimal management models are the right approach to the fishery problem. In fact, some fisheries biologists have constructed models with multiple steady-state equilibria, some of which are stable and some unstable (e.g., Steele and Henderson 1984). Models of this kind react to exogenous shocks in interesting ways. For small shocks, the population tends to return to its previous equilibrium state (local stability). When larger shocks are applied to such models, the population stock can move to a new higher or lower (stable) equilibrium, depending on the direction of the shock.

■ CONCLUSIONS

The first two sections of the present chapter were used to develop the comparison between inefficient open-access exploitation of fisheries and an efficient approach that maximizes the net present value of harvests associated with a naturally regenerating fish population.

The policy section examined alternative tools available to the federal government to accomplish the transition from inefficient to efficient fisheries management and the analyses and some of the recommendations made by studies conducted of Canada's Atlantic and Pacific fisheries in the 1980s. Quotas assigned to individual fishermen that add up to an optimal global quota of fish harvested or landing taxes were both identified as effective policy instruments that could allow Canada's fisheries to be managed for maximum returns. Global quotas alone can achieve the optimum harvest but lead to dissipation of returns to the resource through excessive entry. Effort licensing to control entry tends to produce inefficiency as fishermen substitute uncontrolled for controlled inputs. Assigned individual quotas that add up to the optimum global quota will minimize extraction costs and transfer returns to the resource to the federal Crown if the assignment process takes place through competitive markets (bidding on quotas). Appropriately chosen landing taxes can do the same thing.

The technical feasibility of managing Canadian fisheries for maximum returns does not mean that an immediate transition from inefficient to efficient management is likely or even desirable. Reducing the number of fishermen, particularly in the inshore fisheries of the Atlantic region, would involve difficult adjustment problems for low-income communities with few alternative local job opportunities. The problem of efficient stock management of some species, such as Northern cod, has recently been dwarfed by the problems of preventing further stock declines and providing economic alternatives for fishermen and fish-processing workers severely affected by declining catches. In addition, the steady-state model on which much of the current theory and policy of fisheries management relies may need to be modified to deal with stock fluctuations that are due either to environmental shocks or nonsteady-state behaviour endogenous to fish populations.

■ APPENDIX: DYNAMIC OPTIMIZATION AND FISHERY MANAGEMENT

The optimal fishery management framework follows from the general resources management model set out in detail in the appendix to chapter 2. Referring back to that discussion, equations (A19) and (A20) set out the structure of the problem: the present value of the net benefits of fish harvests (q) are to be maximized over an infinite time-horizon, subject to a state equation describing the growth of the fish stock (dX/dt) as a function of stock size (X) and the current harvest (q). Repeating the Hamiltonian function (equation (A21) in the appendix to chapter 2) we have

$$H = \{B[X(t), q(t)] - C[X(t)] \cdot q(t)\}e^{-rt} + \mu(t)\{f[X(t)] - q(t)\}$$

where $\mu(t)$ is the present value of the Lagrange multiplier such that $\mu(t) = \lambda(t)e^{-rt}$.

The Most Rapid Approach Path (MRAP) Model

If the landed price of fish (π) is a constant and benefits do not depend on stock size, the benefit function B is $B = \pi \cdot q(t)$. In this case, the Hamiltonian becomes

$$H = \{\pi \cdot q(t) - C[X(t)] \cdot q(t)\}e^{-rt} + \mu(t)\{f[X(t)] - q(t)\} \quad \text{(A1)}$$

Since the Hamiltonian is linear in $q(t)$, the necessary condition $\partial H/\partial q = 0$ cannot usually be satisfied and is replaced by the corner conditions

$$q = q_{max} \quad \text{if} \quad \pi - C(X) > \lambda \quad \text{(A2)}$$

$$q = q_{min} \quad \text{if} \quad \pi - C(X) < \lambda \qquad (A3)$$

Condition (A2) applies if the existing stock X is larger than the optimal steady-state stock. In this case, current output (q) is set as high as possible to reduce the stock as rapidly as possible to its optimal steady-state value. Condition (A3) applies in the opposite case when the existing stock is less than the optimal stock. In this case, the usual restriction is $q_{min} = 0$: extraction ceases until the stock is built up to its optimal size. The size of the optimal steady-state stock (X_T) is obtained by setting $\pi - C(X) = \lambda$ and using the second necessary condition $d\mu/dt = d\lambda/dt \cdot e^{-rt} - r\lambda e^{-rt} = -\partial H/\partial X = [C_x q - \mu f_x]e^{-rt}$. Cancelling the terms in e^{-rt} and setting $dX/dt = f(X_T) - q = 0$ and $d\mu/dt = 0$ in the steady state,

$$r\lambda = -C_x f(X_T) + f_x \lambda \qquad (A4)$$

Substituting $\lambda = \pi - C(X_T) = p$ (the net price), equation (A4) becomes

$$rp = -C_x f(X_T) + f_x p \qquad (A5)$$

which was equation (9) in the body of the chapter. Thus, the most rapid approach path (MRAP) if the initial stock $X < X_T$ is $q = 0$ until $X = X_T$ at which point $q = f(X_T)$.

Net Price Dependent on the Harvesting Rate

Suppose the net price p depends inversely on the harvest rate. This could be due to a downward-sloping demand function for landed fish. In this case, the benefit function is $B[q(t)]$ with marginal benefit $dB/dq = \pi(q)$ where $d\pi/dq = \pi_q < 0$. The Hamiltonian is

$$H = \{B[q(t)] - C[X(t)] \cdot q(t)\}e^{-rt} + \mu(t)\{f[X(t)] - q(t)\} \qquad (A6)$$

From (A22) in the appendix to chapter 2, the necessary conditions for maximization are

$$\partial H/\partial q = 0; \quad d\mu/dt = -\partial H/\partial X; \quad dX/dt = \partial H/\partial \mu$$

Using the first two of these conditions,

$$\partial H/\partial q = [\pi(q) - C(X)]e^{-rt} - \lambda e^{-rt} = 0$$

such that

$$\lambda = \pi(q) - C(X) = p(X,q) \qquad (A7)$$

where, as usual, the net price is symbolized by p. The costate equation is

$$d\mu/dt = (d\lambda/dt - r\lambda)e^{-rt} = -\partial H/\partial X = -(-C_x + \lambda f_x)e^{-rt}$$

such that

$$d\lambda/dt - r\lambda = C_x q - \lambda f_x \qquad (A8)$$

Substituting $p = \lambda$ from equation (A7) into (A8) gives the asset equilibrium condition

$$rp = dp/dt - C_x q + pf_x \qquad (A9)$$

which is equation (10) in this chapter. Equation (A9) is a special case of equation (A18) in the appendix to chapter 2 with $B_x = 0$ (the stock does not enter the benefit function). If we want to explore the dynamics of the control and state variables (q and X), we begin by taking the time derivative of (A7) such that

$$d\lambda/dt = dp/dt = p_x dX/dt + p_q dq/dt = \pi_q dq/dt - C_x dX/dt \qquad (A10)$$

Substituting into the costate equation (A8),

$$\pi_q dq/dt - C_x dX/dt - r[\pi(q) - C(X)] = C_x q - f_x[\pi(q) - C(X)] \qquad (A11)$$

Since $dX/dt = f(X) - q$, (A11) can be written as

$$\pi_q dq/dt - C_x[f(X) - q] - r[\pi(q) - C(X)] = C_x q - f_x[\pi(q) - C(X)]$$

or

$$dq/dt = \{C_x f(X) + r[\pi(q) - C(X)] - f_x[\pi(q) - C(X)]\}/\pi_q \qquad (A12)$$

which, together with the state equation $dX/dt = f(X) - q$, describes the motion of the system. The end-point conditions specify an initial stock X_0 and the terminal steady-state values q_T and X_T such that $dq/dt = 0$; $dX/dt = 0$. When $X < X_T$ (the open-access case) the control variable (q) will be set at $q < f(X)$ to allow the stock to grow toward X_T. As dq/dt approaches zero, equation (A11) approaches the terminal steady state given by equation (9) in the body of the chapter.

■ NOTES

1. Maximizing dX/dt requires $d^2X/dXdt = 2 - 2aX/b = 0$ which implies $X = b/2$.
2. In equation (2A), catch per unit of effort (q/E) is simply a constant fraction of the population available to be caught (X). Equation (2A) can be thought of as a special case of the Cobb-Douglas production function $q = e \cdot E^\alpha X^\beta$ with $\alpha = \beta = 1$.
3. The stability of bionomic equilibrium is dealt with in V.L. Smith, "Economics of Production from Natural Resources," *American Economic Review* 58 (1968): 409–31.
4. The total catch cost is $C(X)q$ where C is average catch cost as a function of the stock and q is the harvest rate. In the steady state, $q = f(X)$ so total cost is $TC = C(X)f(X)$. The slope of TC is, therefore, $d(TC)/dX = C_x f(X) + f_x C(X) = C_x q + f_x C$.
5. See, however, C. Clark, *Mathematical Bioeconomics* (New York: Wiley, 1976), Chap. 8.

6. E. Borgese, in "The Law of the Sea," *Scientific American* 248 (1983): 42–49, describes the history and accomplishments of the United Nations Law of the Sea Conferences.

7. The potential rent available in the B.C. salmon fishery has been estimated to be in the \$70–75 million range in 1982, equal to about half the value of salmon landings. See R. Schwindt, "Public Policy and the Pacific Salmon Fishery's Harvesting Crisis," in T. Gunton and J. Richards, eds., *Resource Rents and Public Policy in Western Canada* (Halifax: Institute for Research on Public Policy, 1987); D. Dupont, "Rent Dissipation in Restricted Access Fisheries," *Journal of Environmental Economics and Management* 19 (1990): 26–44.

8. P.H. Pearse (Commissioner), *Timber Rights and Forest Policy in British Columbia*, 2 vols. (Victoria: 1976), p. 83.

9. In our present example, average cost ($=TC/q$) is given by w/eX and so is inversely related to stock size X. If each firm produces at minimum average cost, then TC/q is minimized. It is not necessarily true that $q_i^* = q_i'$ as illustrated here though.

10. This result is discussed and proven in D. Moloney and P. Pearse, "Quantitative Rights as an Instrument for Regulating Commercial Fisheries," *Journal of the Fisheries Research Board of Canada* 36 (1979): 859–66.

11. Task Force on Atlantic Fisheries, *Report: Navigating Troubled Waters—A New Policy for the Atlantic Fisheries* (Kirby Report) (Ottawa: Supply and Services, 1982).

12. Commission on Pacific Fisheries Policy, *Final Report: Turning the Tide—A New Policy for Canada's Pacific Fisheries* (Pearse Report) (Ottawa: Department of Fisheries and Oceans, 1982).

13. Minister of Fisheries, *Final Report: Independent Review of the State of the Northern Cod Stock* (Harris Report) (Ottawa: Department of Fisheries and Oceans, 1990).

14. Task Force on Atlantic Fisheries, *Report*, p. 79. The Atlantic inshore fishery is defined as lying within twelve miles (nineteen kilometres) of the coast.

15. Commission on Pacific Fisheries Policy, *Final Report*, p. 77.

16. Ibid., p. 105.

17. Dupont, "Rent Dissipation": 26. The reference is to H.S. Gordon, "The Economic Theory of a Common Property Resource," *Journal of Political Economy* 62 (1954): 124–42.

18. Quoted in S.D. Cameron, "Net Losses: The Sorry State of our Atlantic Fishery," *Canadian Geographic*, April-May 1990: 29, 33–35.

19. The maximum value for $X_t(1 - X_t)$, $0 \leqslant X_t \leqslant 1$ occurs at $X_t = .5$ such that $X_t(1 - X_t) = .25$. To ensure that $X_{t+1} \leqslant 1$ requires $k \leqslant 4$. For all other values of X_t in the interval, $0 \leqslant k \leqslant 4$ will suffice to satisfy the condition $X_{t+1} \leqslant 1$.

20. See W. Baumol and J. Benhabib, "Chaos: Significance, Mechanism, and Economic Applications," *Journal of Economic Perspectives* 3 (1989): 77–105. Readable full-length treatments of chaos are in J. Gleick, *Chaos: Making a New Science* (New York: Viking Press, 1987); and I. Stewart, *Does God Play Dice? The New Mathematics of Chaos* (New York: Penguin, 1989).

21. R.M. May, "Simple Mathematical Models with Very Complicated Dynamics," *Nature* 261 (1976): 466.

■ FURTHER READING

The dissipation of economic rent under common property exploitation of a fishery was demonstrated in

Gordon H.S. "The Economic Theory of a Common Property Resource." *Journal of Political Economy* 62 (April 1954).

The role of sole ownership in maximizing the annual flow of rent from a renewable resource first appeared in

Scott, A.D. "The Fishery: The Objectives of Sole Ownership." *Journal of Political Economy* 63 (April 1955).

Further insight into the problem of maximizing the present value of returns from a renewable resource assuming a positive discount rate waited upon applications of optimal control theory in the early 1970s. Two recent companion articles that provide the basic model used in this chapter as well as further references to the originating literature are

Munro, G. "The Economics of Fishing: An Introduction." In J.A. Butlin, ed., *The Economics of Environmental and Natural Resources Policy*. Boulder: Westview Press, 1981.

———"Fisheries, Extended Jurisdiction and the Economics of Common Property Resources." *The Canadian Journal of Economics* 15 (August 1982).

Both the above articles are outstanding for their expository skill. The latter is at a more advanced level than the former. The literature in fisheries management grew by leaps and bounds in the 1970s. Many relevant contributions are discussed in

Peterson, E.M., and A.C. Fisher "The Exploitation of Extractive Resources: A Survey." *Economic Journal* 87 (December 1977). Pages 682–91 correspond to the material discussed here.

An excellent treatment of renewable resources management using the optimal control techniques used in the appendix to this chapter can be found in

Conrad, J.M., and C.W. Clark. *Natural Resource Economics: Notes and Problems*. New York: Cambridge University Press, 1987, Chap. 2.

The principal public policy documents on Canadian fisheries management discussed in this chapter are

Task Force on Atlantic Fisheries. *Report: Navigating Trouble Waters—A New Policy for the Atlantic Fisheries* (Kirby Report). Ottawa: Supply and Services, 1982, especially Chap. 10.

Commission on Pacific Fisheries Policy. *Final Report: Turning the Tide—A New Policy for Canada's Pacific Fisheries* (Pearse Report). Ottawa: Department of Fisheries and Oceans, 1982, especially Chaps. 5, 8, 9, and 10.

Minister of Fisheries. *Final Report: Independent Review of the State of the Northern Cod Stock* (Harris Report). Ottawa: Department of Fisheries and Oceans, 1990.

CHAPTER EIGHT

NATURAL RESOURCES

MANAGEMENT AND

PUBLIC POLICY

■ INTRODUCTION

The concept of natural resources stocks as capital assets, the role of property rights and externalities in resource management, and the problem of transmitting future resource values to resource managers responsible for current extraction decisions are themes that recur in preceding chapters. In this chapter, we will look at these themes more closely, making comparisons among different types of renewable and nonrenewable resource situations and extending the analysis in some new directions.

Capital theory has been a central focus for natural resources economists since the 1970s surge of interest in the intertemporal stock allocation problem first formalized for the nonrenewables case by Hotelling in 1931. Within this framework, society is thought of as having capital stock endowments that include both renewable and nonrenewable resources.

Economic activity uses up these resource stocks, and their value to society from current use is equal to the difference between the current marginal social benefit obtained from resource products and the marginal extraction and processing cost of these products. This difference is usually measured by the competitive price of resource products (π) minus the marginal cost of extraction and processing (C) and can be referred to as the net price (p).[1] We can justify using up units of resources or the environment on efficiency grounds when the net price is greater than or equal to the marginal "user cost" of resources. The marginal user cost measures the value of a unit of the resource if it is left for future use.

User cost has many facets. In some cases, marginal user cost simply measures the present value of future extraction opportunities that are sacrificed by the decision to extract today or by the increased extraction costs on lower quality resources that must be used when better quality resources are extracted for current use. In other cases, reducing resource or environmental stocks today leads to a fall in the future flow of benefits that such stocks can provide. The decision to add to the stock of a persistent pollutant, for example, means that the benefits of a marginally cleaner environment in all future periods are being sacrificed. Efficient resource use means that *all* benefits and costs, both present and future, are being weighed in the current decision to use up some of society's existing resource or environmental stocks. When all costs and benefits are considered, current extraction decisions lead to optimal (efficient) changes in the size of society's resource capital stock. By the same token, when resources can be regenerated, current investment decisions must be taken in the light of the increased future social values from a larger capital stock in the form of natural resources. The first section of this chapter pulls together previously discussed models within a general capital theory framework.

The second section focuses on property rights issues in natural resources management. The capital theory framework proposes that society's objective is to utilize its extractive and environmental resource assets so as to maximize their net present value. Markets for resource stocks can only operate effectively to maximize the net present value that society obtains from its present and future resource stocks if private buyers, sellers, and resource holders receive *all* the social returns from their transactions and from the resource stocks they hold. If all net social returns do accrue to those making resource-use decisions, then property rights are adequate and we can say that property rights are *well defined*.

In many cases, we have seen that existing social arrangements do not provide well-defined property rights in natural resources. For example, property rights over environmental stocks are frequently not present at all and producers are motivated to reduce society's environmental resource stocks without taking account of environmental costs in their private wealth-maximizing calculations. It is useful to compare the range of property rights problems that have emerged in the resource management discussions of the previous chapters since well-defined property rights are a *precondition* for efficient resource management using markets.

The third section of the chapter goes on to examine the problem of how current expectations about future resource scarcity and resource values depends both upon the amount of information about the future that exists and how that information is processed by individuals making current extraction decisions. In this section, we assume that markets are competitive and property rights are well defined.

As noted in chapter 2, obtaining a correct allocation of a nonrenewable resource stock to present and future social needs, under full information concerning available stocks, extraction technologies, and demand conditions, requires that forward markets exist to transmit this information to the present. Since forward markets typically do not exist very far into the future, the absence of these markets makes it difficult for individual decision makers to adjust their extraction plans to the plans of others. This is a *co-ordination problem*. The co-ordination problem forces market participants to fall back on their own expectations of future resource prices to establish the assumed user costs of current supply decisions. In addition to the absence of a co-ordinating function provided by forward markets, society's information on resource stocks, future extraction costs, and future demand conditions on which current resource use decisions must be based may be incomplete or highly uncertain. This produces an *incomplete information problem*.

The final section offers a perspective on public policy. Four policy areas are identified: general initiatives such as competition and trade policy, rent capture and resource taxation policy, policies to improve the definition of property rights, and policies to assist private markets in co-ordinating resource use over time and in gathering and processing information on future resource stocks, technology, and demand conditions.

■ RESOURCE STOCKS AS CAPITAL ASSETS

The Capital Theory Framework

A strong unifying theme in earlier chapters has been the use of capital theory concepts to identify optimal management regimes for natural resources. In the nonrenewables, environment, and fisheries chapters, natural resource stocks are held at levels that satisfy *asset-equilibrium conditions*. In the forestry chapter, rotation decisions and forest regeneration decisions were also viewed as capital theory problems. In chapter 5, the effects of corporate and natural resource taxes on capital-asset-holding decisions in the mineral sector were examined.

The present section offers some generalizations to support the idea that optimal capital-holding decisions in the economy as a whole can be approached in terms of a unified asset equilibrium framework that includes various types of natural resource capital stocks as special cases. Consider the following relationship that describes optimal capital-holding behaviour:

$$F_k \cdot p_c = MRP = \delta p_k + r p_k - dp_k/dt \qquad (1)$$

where F_k is the marginal productivity of any particular capital good in terms of consumption goods, p_c is the (dollar) price of a unit of the consumption good, p_k is the (dollar) price of a unit of the capital good, δ is the rate of depreciation of the capital good, and r is the real rate of interest.[2] The left-hand side of equation (1) measures the value of additional output obtained by holding an extra unit of the capital good. It is the marginal revenue product of capital, denoted as MRP. The right-hand side of (1) measures the marginal costs of holding an extra unit of capital. The first term on the right-hand side is the current decline in the value of a unit of capital that is the result of depreciation. The second term is the interest cost of holding the unit of capital. The third term subtracts capital appreciation of the unit of capital from the depreciation and interest costs. If dp_k/dt is negative, the value of the unit of capital is falling and this adds to the cost of holding a unit of it.

Provided the holders of capital assets adjust immediately to any differences between MRP and the cost of capital, the equilibrium price of the capital stock (p_k) has to satisfy equation (1). Suppose, for example, that capital's MRP exceeds capital cost. In this case, demand for capital assets is greater than the existing stock and p_k increases until equation (1) is satisfied. The equilibrium price of capital p_k can then serve as an incentive to increase or decrease the capital stock, depending upon the supply curve for new capital goods.

When capital goods take the form of natural resource stocks, the details of equation (1) must reflect the peculiar characteristics of natural resource assets. First, since the resource stock itself is the same thing as the good it produces (extracted units), it is usual not to distinguish their prices. Since a unit of the natural resource extracted has a net price p, this net price is used to determine the value of units of the resource held in stock. Thus, $p = p_k = p_c$. Since natural resource stocks do not depreciate through wear and tear or obsolescence, we will also set $\delta = 0$ in moving from capital assets in general to consideration of resource stocks.

The MRP of capital held in resource stocks can involve several components. First, holding an extra unit of resource capital can raise the flow of net benefits by lowering the unit cost of extraction. This effect has been denoted by $-C_x q$ in the earlier chapters, where $-C_x$ is the reduction in unit cost caused by holding an extra unit of the stock and q is the rate of extraction.

Second, holding additional units of resources can change the direct benefits that society gets from its resource endowments. This feature was a part of the environmental resources management model in chapter 3 where direct consumption (amenity) benefits flow to members of society from resource holdings. The amenity aspect was explored there by assigning a marginal damage function to increases in pollution stocks. For simplicity in notation, we will say that an addition to the stock of pollution is an equivalent subtraction from the environmental stock (X). So the marginal damage $D^{*\prime}(X)$ from pollution equals the marginal benefit from an addition to the environmental stock. The same idea applies to an increase in nontimber benefits from an increase in the forest stock (see chapter 6).

Third, when resources are renewable, units of the stock may grow. Adopting the growth notation from the treatment of fisheries in chapter 7, the *marginal growth* effect is $df(X)/dX = f_x$ where $f(X)$ is the stock's growth rate. The value of the additional growth is $f_x p$. With extraction cost, amenity, and growth effects present, the MRP term on the left-hand side of equation (1) should be replaced by $f_x p + D^{*\prime}(X) - C_x q$.

Making all of these indicated substitutions, equation (1) becomes

$$f_x p + D^{*\prime}(X) - C_x q = rp - dp/dt$$

or

$$rp = dp/dt - C_x q + f_x p + D^{*\prime}(X) \tag{2}$$

When we ignore the amenity aspects of the resource stock $(D^{*\prime} = 0)$, equation (2) just reproduces the asset-equilibrium condition obtained for the fishery (see equation (10) in chapter 7 and the mathematical appendix to chapter 7).

If the resource stock is nonrenewable, then $f_x = 0$ in equation (2) and we obtain the asset-equilibrium condition for the modified Hotelling model (see equation (9) in chapter 2 and the appendix to chapter 2). The simple Hotelling Rule for nonrenewables $(rp = dp/dt)$ emerges as a further special case when unit extraction cost is independent of stock size $(C_x = 0)$.

All of the capital theory models in the preceding chapters can be formulated for steady-state equilibria. The steady-state results emerge when both the rate of extraction from the stock is constant and the stock level itself is constant over time. Denoting the extraction by q and the rate of growth of the stock X by $f(X)$, the steady-state conditions are $dq/dt = 0$ and $dX/dt = f(X) - q = 0$. Since the net price is $p = \pi(q) - C(X)$, $dp/dt = \pi_q dq/dt - C_x dX/dt = 0$ in the steady state. Using equation (2), the asset-equilibrium requirement for steady-state natural resource models is

$$rp = -C_x q + f_x p \tag{3}$$

assuming zero amenity benefits from the stock $(D^{*\prime} = 0)$. Equation (3) was discussed in some detail in chapter 7, both in the context of an optimally managed fishery and in the context of a steady-state forest occupying free land. (In the forestry case, extraction cost is taken to be independent of the forest's overall biomass such that $C_x = 0$.)

Since nonrenewables are characterized by $f(X) = 0$, the only possible steady state consistent with exploitation of physically fixed resource stocks is $q = 0$; $X = 0$. This result is the terminal condition for the complete or incomplete exhaustion models described in chapter 2. The only way to "get around" the steady-state exhaustion result in models of nonrenewables is to think of technical change continuously extending the economic resource base over time. This case may be relevant for geochemically abundant resources. If so, exhaustible resource stocks are not really fixed but rather are contingent upon improvements in efficiency over time. As we noted in chapters 2 and 3, it is possible to construct a steady-state equilibrium for the modified Hotelling case in which stock depletion is offset continuously by the appearance of new economic resources due to cost-reducing technical improvements.

Conventional treatments of environmental resources usually stress the social costs caused by flows rather than stocks of pollutants. In the *pure flow* version, the economic efficiency problem is confined to restricting pollution flows to the point at which the marginal social benefit of a flow of pollutants equals the marginal social cost of the flow. The pure flow model assumes that stocks of pollutants do not build up over time.

Chapter 3 also extended the flow pollution model to cases in which pollutants *do* build up: the simplest case occurs when pollutants are persistent so that any flow of pollution becomes a permanent addition to the stock and a permanent reduction in the environmental stock (X). In this case, the marginal cost of pollution includes both the flow damage and the user cost of the added stock. In the stock-flow environmental model with persistent environmental change, equation (2) has to be modified to ignore any endogenous growth of the environmental stock since pollutant stocks do not naturally dissipate. Thus $f_x = 0$. We also assume that the unit cost of using up environmental stocks does not depend on stock size so that $C_x = 0$. Incorporating these assumptions, equation (2) becomes

$$rp = dp/dt + D^{*'}(X) \qquad (4)$$

where $D^{*'}(X)$ is the increase in stock damage caused by an additional unit of the pollutant stock as discussed above. The net price here is the marginal value of additional output made possible by environmental depletion $(\pi - C)$ minus any marginal flow damage caused by the activity (D'). So, holding back on pollution at the margin (increasing the environmental stock) sacrifices immediate net social benefits equal to the net price. The holding cost of this decision is rp. The marginal benefits of holding back consist of the increase in net benefits from delaying the unit of pollution (dp/dt) plus the marginal environmental stock damage that is avoided $(D^{*'})$. Society is choosing how rapidly and how much of its valuable environmental capital is to be used up to generate current net benefits from economic activity that depletes the environment. In the steady state, when $dp/dt = 0$, the net price must equal the present value of stock environmental damage inflicted by an addition to the pollutant stock, i.e., $p = D^{*\prime}(X)/r$.

If we want to make the environment renewable, this can be done by examining cases in which f_x is not equal to zero. Additional units of the pollutant stock tend to dissipate so a *larger* environmental stock X (defined by a lower stock of pollutants) experiences a lower rate of natural recovery. Denoting the recovery rate as $f(X)$, $f_x < 0$ for this case. Restoring the resource stock growth term in equation (4), we have

$$rp = dp/dt + D^{*\prime}(X) + f_x p \qquad (5)$$

Once again, holding an extra unit of the environment stock (one less unit of the pollutant) costs rp. The marginal stock appreciation benefit dp/dt and stock benefit $D^{*\prime}(X)$ are to be interpreted as before. The environmental stock recovery term $f_x < 0$ (multiplied by the net price) is added to the benefit side of (5) indicating that the marginal benefit of holding an extra unit of the environment stock (one less unit of the pollutant) is reduced by the amount of environmental regeneration *sacrificed* by holding a smaller pollutant stock.[3]

Transition Strategies

In most cases, equation (2) must be satisfied in making the transition to an optimal steady-state resource stock equilibrium. In some cases, though, it may not actually be feasible to adjust the resource stock rapidly enough to satisfy equation (2). This possibility was noted in discussing the transition from an existing open-access fishery equilibrium to the optimal steady state in chapter 7. If the net price does not depend on the extraction rate (q), the optimal strategy is to move to the steady state as quickly as is feasible. In the transition from the open-access fish stock to the optimal fish stock, for example, the correct adjustment strategy was to get the rate of accumulation of the stock as high as possible by setting the current extraction rate (q) equal to zero. This was referred to as a "bang-bang" or MRAP-type of stock adjustment. During the transition to the optimal steady state, the holding cost of a marginal unit of capital is less than the benefits of a marginal unit. As soon as the fish stock reaches a level that satisfies equation (3), the rate of extraction jumps from zero to a rate equal to the rate of growth of the stock in the optimal steady state.

This MRAP transition strategy can apply to other resource problems as well. Consider what would happen if the net price is independent of the extraction rate in Hotelling-type models of nonrenewables use. With a constant net price, the marginal benefit from existing stocks of nonrenewables must be less than their holding costs since $dp/dt = 0$. The optimal strategy is to move to the steady state as rapidly as possible. Since the steady state consists of a zero stock of the nonrenewable resource, efficient extraction would be as rapid as is feasible until all (economic) stocks are exhausted. The forestry cases discussed in chapter 6 provide another example of the MRAP strategy. With a constant net price assumed, the extraction rate for an individual stand is set at zero until the appropriate rotation rule is satisfied. At that point, the entire stand is harvested. When the initial state of the forest is characterized by "old-growth" timber (timber beyond the optimal rotation age), the MRAP strategy dictates immediate liquidation of the old growth provided that the stumpage price (p) is not affected by the harvest volume.

When net prices *are* influenced by current extraction rates, the transition to a long-run steady state typically proceeds gradually and equation (2) *is* satisfied along the transition path: the holding cost of the marginal unit of the resource stock equals its marginal benefit at each point in time. Different assumptions can be introduced to make the net price vary inversely with the extraction rate. If the demand curve for the resource product is downward-sloping, then an increase in the extraction rate will reduce the product price π and the net price ($\pi - C$) will also decrease.

Alternatively, we could drop the assumption that the marginal extraction cost C is constant and allow increases in the extraction rate to increase C. A gradual transition to the optimal long-run fish stock or to a normal forest, for example, will be called for when factors of production used in the harvesting process are less than perfectly mobile between resources sectors and the rest of the economy. Building up fish stocks through a sharp reduction in the rate of harvesting fish would lead to unemployment and reduced wages for fishermen and fish-processors in the short run. Thus, an abrupt fall in the harvest rate reduces marginal harvesting cost (C) and leads to a rise in the current net price ($\pi - C$) relative to future (long-run) net prices. Whenever the current net price of a resource rises relative to future net prices, its current extraction rate should be stepped up. Thus the short-run immobility of production factors sends the correct signal to the extraction process: slow down the adjustment process to accommodate limited factor mobility.

An argument for gradual transition to the long-run steady state applies to timber harvesting as well. The presence of significant volumes of old-growth timber and the use of uneconomically long (MSY) rotations suggest that it might be optimal to undertake a burst of harvesting followed by reduced levels of logging in the future. Such an MRAP strategy overlooks factor adjustment problems in forest harvesting. A sudden large change in harvesting, followed by decline, would require the construction of short-lived capital facilities and a temporary influx of labour. The adjustment costs of a "boom and bust" approach of this kind could be quite high. Costs would increase above their long-run level during the harvesting boom and then fall below the long-run level as the harvest declines. These cost movements act to lower the net price (stumpage price) during the boom and raise the net price afterward. This behaviour has the effect of increasing future timber values relative to near-term timber values. Rent-maximizing timber owners will find it rational to slow down the rate of old-growth depletion and lengthen rotations in response to rising stumpage prices. Again, the dynamics of asset equilibrium tends to damp down any tendency to sudden shifts in extraction rates when capital and labour are less than completely mobile across sectors of the economy.

The problem of optimal transition paths forges a link between the short run and the long run in natural resources management. In chapter 1, we noted that the fundamental difference between the short run and the long run lies in complementarity and substitution. If it were possible to move labour and capital into or out of resources sectors quickly, then the economy could move along its production possibility frontier in the short run: changing the output of one commodity would always require an opposite change in the production of at least one other commodity (substitution). When factors cannot move immediately from one sector to another, a fall in output in one sector produces multiplicative declines in the outputs of other sectors (complementarity). Incorporating the effects of rapid factor adjustment in asset equilibrium conditions makes an attempt to recognize that factors are locked into specific sectors in the short run. The purpose of optimal management of society's resource stocks is to maximize discounted real income *including* the incomes earned by imperfectly mobile factors during adjustment periods.

Capital Theory and Taxation

Optimal capital stock decisions provided the basic framework for the analysis of optimal rent capture mechanisms and effective resource taxation in chapter 5. The Resource Rent Tax (*RRT*) was constructed to be *neutral* in its effect on decisions to undertake resource extraction projects in the private sector. Neutrality means that projects that provide before-tax returns that equal or exceed the cost of capital also offer after-tax returns that equal or exceed the after-tax cost of capital. Resource taxation has the effect of *transferring* rents from the private to the public sector without reducing the *total* amount of rent generated by the resource extraction sector. Put differently, a neutral tax system does not attempt to collect taxes on projects that provide before-tax returns equal to the cost of capital: the effective tax rate is zero on such marginal projects. When tax systems are non-neutral, the effective rate of taxation is non-zero on marginal projects. As indicated in the appendix to chapter 5, non-neutral resource taxation also affects the timing of extraction decisions for natural resources.

Recent analysis of effective corporate and resource taxation in Canada, undertaken by Boadway, McKenzie, and Mintz (1989), assumes that resource extraction firms invest in buildings and machinery and equipment up to the point at which the marginal revenue product of these capital assets equals the cost of holding capital, i.e.,

$$MRP = rp_k + \delta p_k \tag{6}$$

Equation (6) can be obtained from equation (1) by assuming that (real) capital goods prices are constant. Equation (6), therefore, defines the capital asset-equilibrium condition for a marginal project. When corporate and resource taxes are introduced to the model, two things happen. First, the after-tax marginal revenue product of capital is reduced to $(1 - T)MRP$, where T is the marginal rate of taxation on net revenue. Second, firms are able to claim a set of present-valued tax deductions which reduces the cost of the capital asset to $(1 - A)p_k$, where A is the present-valued tax deductions. The marginal project must now satisfy the after-tax equilibrium condition

$$(1 - T)MRP = (1 - A)rp_k + (1 - A)\delta p_k \tag{7}$$

which was equation (7) in chapter 5. If $T = A$, then the combined corporate and resource tax system is neutral and the effective tax rate is zero. If $T > A$, then projects that are marginal before taxes earn a lower after-tax return than the after-tax cost of capital and are abandoned when the tax system is imposed. The effective tax rate is positive. When $A > T$, the effective rate is negative: the imposition of the tax system causes private investors to undertake projects that would not have been worth doing without the tax system. Boadway, McKenzie, and Mintz found that the overall impact of corporate and mining taxes on the Canadian minerals sector in the late 1980s added up to a negative effective tax rate.

The variety of asset equilibrium rules, transition strategies, and tax models discussed in this section serve to illustrate the importance of capital theory concepts in optimal natural resources management. Whenever economists develop optimal models of economic activity, they want to move on to the logical next question: can private markets duplicate the results of the efficient models?

■ THE PROPERTY RIGHTS PROBLEM

Well-defined *property rights* turn out to be a precondition for markets to reproduce socially optimal resource management results. Markets cannot operate efficiently unless buyers and sellers have secure title to the returns from marketable commodities. For efficient exchanges to take place, *all* the net social returns from the sale of units of the resource stock, or from holding units of the resource as a capital asset, must be included in the calculations of the individuals or organizations making these decisions.

Titles to Mineral Prospects

Our first encounter with the failure of markets to operate efficiently due to ill-defined property rights was in chapter 2 where it was observed that exploration for mineral deposits often takes the form of a "rule of capture" game under existing institutional arrangements. If society's total stock of exploration prospects is limited, or if current discoveries raise the costs of making subsequent discoveries, exploration prospects should command a positive net price under an efficient resource management regime. The net price reflects the increased cost to other explorers from reducing the stock of mineral prospects. A variety of institutional arrangements are possible here:

> The first is the case in which the user(s) or manager(s) of explorable mineral land have complete property rights and exercise these rights. This may be a case in which private firms have well-defined ownership of explorable mineral land or it may be a case in which the provincial government is the only agent with ownership rights but exercises these rights efficiently by managing the annual supply of land made available for exploration leases. The second is the case of pure common property in which none of the users of the land can exclude or in any way restrict others from using the land.[4]

As we saw in chapter 2, exploration firms can only secure access to mineral deposits in the second case by spending the exploration dollars needed to convert them from mineral prospects to discovered reserves under the exclusive control of the firm. The removal of a valuable mineral prospect from society is worth nothing to the individual firm. Explorable mineral land has an apparent zero net price. As the quotation from Livernois implies, the excessive exploration in case two can be avoided by assigning exploration rights or titles over potential mineral-bearing land to private owners or by limiting the rate at which exploration takes place. Limitation of the rate of exploration could be accomplished by setting "quotas" on the amount of land to be explored (which could be auctioned to exploration companies) or by placing a "depletion tax" on land explored. We should also note that, in some cases, exploration generates external information benefits to explorers on adjacent land. Since the individual firm cannot claim property rights to these benefits, the rate of exploration can sometimes be too low.

Property and the Environment

The notion that ill-defined property rights produce market failure was the central message in the analysis of environmental problems in chapter 3. In this case, the option of private ownership is not available. Environmental quality is a public good in the sense that the benefits of clean air and water are shared by a collective of users. Unless the public asserts its collective property rights to these resources, private producers will ignore the impact of their decisions on the environment by treating "environmental inputs" as free goods. Just as in the case of the provincial owner of mineral-bearing land, the public can assert its control over environmental resource use by limiting the rate at which environmental inputs can be used by private producers or by placing taxes on the rate of environmental depletion.

In a *pure flow* pollution model, the social costs imposed on the public through environmental effects lead to no permanent changes in the environment and can be corrected through a pollution tax set at the level of marginal social cost or by pollution quotas that add up to the optimal flow level of pollution. Making quotas marketable permits polluters to buy and sell quotas to establish a market price for pollution rights. In a mixed *stock-flow* pollution situation in which environmental effects are persistent, the same devices—taxes and quotas—can be used to slow down the rate of environmental depletion and to stabilize environmental quality at a socially optimal level. In this case, taxes and quotas must be set to reflect both flow damages and the user cost of pollution flows on the state of the environment in the future. Individuals polluting the environment must pay for the reduction in the value of the environment to the public.

Persistent pollutants lead to irreversible changes in the environment. If future demands for environmental amenities could be higher than at present or the opportunity costs of providing such amenities could be lower than at present, future environmental values may exceed today's values. But once the environment is irreversibly transformed by current decisions, the possibility of increasing the level of environmental amenities in the future is foreclosed. Irreversibility combined with the possibility that more environmental amenities will be wanted in the future produces an *option* value for resources. If property rights were well-defined, resource owners could save environmental stocks to take advantage of future options and option values would appear as a user cost in current decisions. But the public nature of the environment again requires that option demands be expressed through public decisions.

Fisheries and Timber Resources

Renewable extractive resources such as fisheries and forests provide further examples of the key role of property rights as a precondition for the economic efficiency of markets. Fisheries provide the classic example of inefficient resource exploitation induced by a failure of property rights. Treating fish stocks as a common property resource means that ownership of fish can only be secured by the rule of capture. Fishermen are not required to buy uncaught fish from owners of the stock. The resulting open-access equilibrium, described in chapter 7, leads to an equilibrium stock level that is low enough to dissipate all potential surpluses (rents) that might accrue to the fishery. The mechanism of rent destruction comes about through the impact of reduced stock size on fishing costs. As the stock declines, average harvesting cost increases until net harvesting revenue—the surplus or rent accruing to the resource—is zero. Each individual fisherman is imposing external costs on other fishermen by lowering the size of the fish stock.

As with mineral-bearing lands and environmental resources, depletion taxes or quotas can, in principle, be used to work the fish stock up to an optimal steady-state level. The optimal steady-state stock level, and the path followed to reach that level, simulates the decisions that would be taken by a private present-value maximizing owner of the fishery. Since offshore fish stocks are under federal management, efficient rebuilding of stocks from open-access levels through depletion taxes or individual quotas requires that the public manager behave like a wealth-maximizing private owner. As noted in the previous chapter, many Atlantic fish stocks have been so seriously depleted in the 1980s relative to the number of fishermen dependent on them, that rebuilding is both essential and extremely difficult.

Unlike mineral-bearing lands, environmental resources, and fish stocks, for which ill-defined property rights impede the achievement of optimal management and for which public decisions are essential to efficiency, the ownership and management of timber resources demonstrates an interesting reversal of the property rights problem. The benefits and costs of private timber ownership and management may not diverge from social benefits and costs. The concept of publicly owned timber land in the United States has been open to criticism (Brubaker 1984). Recent changes in timber management arrangements in Canada attempt to take *greater* advantage of incentives to private sector efficiency by spelling out a set of rights and obligations within which private wealth-maximizing decisions can take place:

> ...highly sophisticated forest management agreements...[are]...now found in all the major timber producing provinces. These long-term licenses not only provide their holders with exclusive access to well-defined forest tracts, but also assign to them extensive responsibilities for resource management. The license holders must harvest according to approved long-term plans, build roads and related infrastructure, protect the forest and provide for forest regeneration after harvesting. Within the framework of approved working plans, which form part of the license agreement, the licensees are free to carry on their operations as efficiently as they can without interference from other forest users. For the most part, these incentives lead to operations that are consistent with the public interest in efficient resource use and development.[5]

Private property rights in timber land in Canada could very well be a workable alternative to public ownership and is practised in other countries. Forest products companies managing their own land could be expected to make optimal rotation decisions and to decide to regenerate timber based on comparisons between the expected present value of future timber harvests and the costs of regeneration and other management costs. Since fire or disease could spread from one ownership to others, subsidies for forest protection might be required to encourage individual owners to take account of risks to adjacent owners. Some multiple-use could take place through user fees charged to hunters and recreationalists for the use of private land. Private owners would work out their own harvesting plans and road access in accordance with economic incentives. In some cases, private owners could be expected to lease timber land to forest products companies or enter into harvesting and/or management contracts with firms.

The use of private ownership in timber management would not preclude public management of forests designed to provide nontimber benefits. As discussed in chapter 6, there is something to be said for a separate facilities approach to forest land. Large areas have already been set aside as national and provincial parks or wilderness areas within which timber management is completely secondary to the provision of nontimber values or is proscribed. The current system of forest management in Canada involves confusing and costly tradeoffs between timber and nontimber values on the same forest tract. In many cases, introducing a wide range of wildlife protection and other nontimber objectives as constraints on commercial timber management activities introduces uncertainties, raises timber costs, and offers little assurance that nontimber benefits can actually be realized.

If renewable resources can be regenerated, ill-defined property rights can damage regeneration efforts. In the case of public forests managed for nontimber values, natural regeneration is the standard approach. When timber production is the objective, both natural and artificial regeneration methods are used to re-establish commercial crops. Over large areas of Canadian forest land, costly artificial regeneration provides low rates of return. Establishing private property rights in timber land would not alter this. But in those areas where artificial regeneration offers adequate rates of return, private property rights would offer the right incentives: wealth-maximizing owners would be willing to make the regeneration investments needed to secure future timber harvests since they would receive all the stumpage returns from those harvests. Under the present system, future harvests attract stumpage charges by provincial governments. As a consequence, unless required or subsidized to do so, timber managers have little or no incentive to undertake artificial regeneration spending. Nor are incentives present to alter harvesting methods to save costs on regeneration of the next crop.

On timber land that provides low returns to artificial timber regeneration, two options are available. One option is to allow natural regeneration to take over with the result that future timber crops will be lower or too costly to separate from noncommercial species. The second option is to introduce constraints that require commercial regeneration, subsidize costly regeneration methods, or subsidize the stumpage returns on the future harvests. If artificial regeneration is to take place on this type of land, the costs must be borne by society whatever the nature of property rights.

Incentives to the artificial regeneration of marine stocks also depend on the way property rights impinge on decision makers. For the most part, natural regeneration has been relied upon in the past, since the common property nature of these stocks means that investors cannot usually lay a secure claim to the stocks resulting from investment activities. In some cases, though, private stocking investments may yield reasonable returns, provided the investor can obtain exclusive control over the resulting harvest. Shellfish constitute one example. Another example is the ocean ranching of salmon in which young salmon are released to the sea and subsequently caught as they return to spawn at the point of release. Unlike timber regeneration, the released and growing individuals cannot be distinguished from natural stocks until their return. So commercial and sport fishing take a toll on released individuals and reduce the private return on stocking investments. One way to resolve this problem is to subsidize stocking investments to allow the investor to capture the returns from his investment that accrue to other harvesters.

In all cases, the goal is to achieve *well-defined* property rights. In the absence of externalities, private property rights fulfill this objective. When externalities cannot be eliminated through private property rights, property rights are only well-defined when the external costs and benefits of individual actions are internalized by public policy tools. It is clear from the discussion in this section, that the physical characteristics of natural resources and the institutional nature of property leads to limits on the effectiveness of private ownership. For fisheries and environmental resources, the migratory nature of fish and the public nature of environmental benefits, respectively, means that public policy is required. In order to reflect the costs imposed on others, depletion taxes can be used to force users of fish stocks or the environment to include social costs in their private wealth-maximizing decisions. Alternatively, quotas can be used to limit withdrawals from the stock. These quotas can take the form of pollution permits, for example, or individual landing quotas in fisheries. Under ideal trading conditions, the market value of such quotas or permits equals the marginal social cost of using the resource. Marketable individual landing quotas in fisheries or marketable pollution permits allow firms to utilize social assets (fish or the environment) by paying society to transfer social property to individual permit holders. Incentives to efficient regeneration of publicly owned timber and fish can be interpreted similarly: investors are being rewarded for such investments in accordance with the resulting increases in the value of society's property in these renewable assets.

We also noted that there may be opportunities to extend private property arrangements. Mineral exploration, for example, could proceed more efficiently if the private sector could obtain titles to mineral prospects. Private property in timber land could stimulate wealth-maximizing rotation and regeneration decisions.

■ INFORMATION AND EXPECTATIONS

The decision to use a unit of the resource today has implications for future social benefits and costs. The capital theory models discussed earlier in this chapter assume that all the information needed to accomplish efficient resource management is available or can be made available at modest cost so that it is possible to undertake optimal extraction and regeneration decisions. If markets are to replicate these optimal decisions, public policy must be designed to generate well-defined property rights, in the sense that private and social benefits and costs are brought into equality. But the simulation of well-defined property rights is only a *precondition* for market efficiency. More is required. Markets must be able to accurately transmit information on the future social value of resource stocks so that current decisions can be co-ordinated in the light of future social values.

The Co-ordination Problem

The only theoretically reliable way of transmitting future information to present decision making is through the operation of a complete set of forward markets. Provided the social and private values of resource stocks are equal at all points in time (well-defined property rights), the presence of a full set of forward markets can, in principle, solve the problem of efficient extraction. Taking the example of the simple Hotelling model in chapter 2, resource owners will be willing to enter into forward delivery contracts in a future period only if the rate of return on resource stocks is as high as they could obtain on capital assets elsewhere in the economy. If the rate of return is too low in any future period, they will not supply units in that period and the (net) price for deliveries in that period will rise. If the price is too high in any period, there will be excess supply and the price will fall. Extending forward markets out to exhaustion of resource stocks, provides an end-point or terminal requirement: the resource must be exhausted when the demand for it goes to zero. If quantity demanded goes to zero prior to exhaustion, then the remaining units are worthless and suppliers would shift their planned deliveries to earlier periods. If exhaustion were to occur prior to zero demand for the resource, resource owners could profit by shifting deliveries into later periods. Forward markets are transmitting information and performing a co-ordination function. Forward prices act as signals that permit individual resource owners to infer how other owners are reacting to aggregative information on resource stocks, expected extraction costs, and expected demand conditions.

What would happen if markets were *incomplete* in the sense that some or all of the forward markets were missing? This is the usual case in reality. Suppose that individual suppliers are given information on demand conditions in all future periods. Would this information be enough to reproduce the Hotelling result in the absence of the forward markets? The simple answer to this question is in the negative. *Actual* prices are still dependent on the supply behaviour of an aggregate of individuals. To add further information, suppose each resource owner was to make a provisional announcement, stating how much of his or her resource holdings he or she plans to supply in each period. Based on the announced behaviour of everyone else, the assumed knowledge of the overall demand curve could be used by each individual to accurately predict prices in all periods. These accurately predicted prices could then be used by individuals to modify their announced supply plans in order to maximize the value of their resource stocks. If this *recontracting* process were to be repeated a sufficiently large number of times, it might be possible to reach a stable set of predicted future prices for which all individuals are willing to stand by their announced supply plans. This final (accurately) predicted price set is the Hotelling price set.

To reassure each participant that the Hotelling price set will prevail, it will now be necessary to lock everyone in to their announced supply plans. But to do so requires forward delivery and purchase contracts at the Hotelling price set. So, in effect, we have ended up creating forward markets and establishing the Hotelling price set as the equilibrium set of forward prices. And to do so we have had to provide individuals with information on demand at all points in time and on the conditional supply plans of all resource holders. We have also had to permit *recontracting* (changes in the announced supplies) and to assume a stable outcome. Removing the information assumptions included in the foregoing process leaves resource owners in the dark on future prices. If they do not know demand conditions in future periods and the conditional supplies of other resource holders, resource owners can form no clear view on future prices. Even if they had this information, recontracting would have to be allowed in order to modify the conditional price set until a mutually consistent set of supply plans emerges. And this mutually consistent set of supply plans must still be enforced by forward contracting to ensure that all individuals will abide by the final outcome.

The forward market model will be needed to lead market processes to the optimal result in other models as well. To co-ordinate the amount of pollution that is needed at all points in time to approach an optimal future environmental stock, for example, requires that polluters be able to accurately predict future marginal costs of an increase in the pollution stock. Since the future stock depends on the intervening actions of other polluters, a method must be found to transmit the impact of these aggregate decisions to each individual polluter. An owner of timber land contemplating investing in future timber supplies needs to know the future price of timber. But the future price of timber depends, in part, on the regeneration decisions of other land owners.

Incomplete Information

Co-ordinating individual extraction decisions over time is difficult enough in the absence of forward markets, even when information on resource supplies, technology, and demand conditions is perfect. It is important to realize that existing optimal natural resources management models have been constructed on *very strict* information assumptions. To satisfy the conditions for efficient utilization of mineral resources over time, for example, detailed information is simply assumed to be available on the size of mineral stocks, their present and future costs of extraction, and demand conditions in all future periods. In addition, a suitable discount rate has been selected. If society could form definite expectations, amounting to perfect information, on all these issues, it would not be hard to imagine solving the co-ordination problem using forward markets or planning methods.

In reality, some or all of the information needed to solve optimal extraction models is absent or highly uncertain. This means that the application of optimal exhaustion models may be an imaginary exercise, correct on the assumptions of those models but not relevant to a world of *incomplete information*. If this is true, it is inappropriate to judge the efficiency of actual functioning market-based extraction activity against such an ideal model. Confronted with the same lack of information as the existing market framework, it may not be possible to show that forward markets or planning could improve on the existing situation. If we *really* had all the information required by the ideal models, we could simply compare the prescribed optimal extraction and pricing program against actual market results to identify the extent of market failure and prescribe corrective action. With incomplete information, it is hard to do this.

Forming Expectations

In the absence of complete information and forward markets, resource owners must rely on their *expectations* of future net prices to determine their current supply decisions. On what basis do individuals form their price expectations for resources? One possible approach is to hypothesize *adaptive expectations*. In this model, individuals form their expectations of future real resource prices by taking a weighted average of past prices.

This type of expectations mechanism is a backward-looking one, comparable to the cost-price approach to scarcity discussed in chapter 4. If real resource prices follow a rising trend, the adaptive expectations approach systematically underestimates future prices. Individuals using adaptive expectations would then, presumably, modify their predictions to take account of the past trend and would begin to predict future real resource prices by using a weighted average of recent rates of change in these prices.

Rational expectations models propose that individuals utilize *all* relevent information, not just past price observations, to predict future prices. If new geological or technological information becomes available that reveals new economic stocks of resources or new cost-effective methods of extracting previously uneconomic deposits, the rational expectations model implies that the new information will be factored into price expectations immediately. Unlike the adaptive expectations model, the rational expectations approach is forward-looking and takes account of the physical scarcity measures also discussed in chapter 4.

The forward market model discussed here and in chapter 2 makes the point that forward markets provide a method of discovering how other resource owners or users are planning to change society's aggregate resource stocks. When forming rational price expectations, resource holders must still try to predict the supply behaviour of others. If other holders seem to be anticipating a price increase, for whatever reason, they will be holding resource stocks off the market. This behaviour will lead to the very price increases that they expect and it is rational for any individual to follow the crowd and hold his or her own stocks off the market to take advantage of future price appreciation. Prices can rise simply because everybody thinks they will. Such speculative run-ups or "bubbles" could cause resource prices to depart from the "fundamentals" of the market determined by estimates of marginal extraction and user cost. In the wake of Iraq's invasion of Kuwait in the summer of 1990, for example, crude oil prices increased rapidly, partly due to anticipated shortages and partly due to speculative behaviour. During price "run-ups," consumption/depletion of resources will be reduced and *vice versa* for periods in which prices are depressed by speculation. Over the long run, these departures from price-cost and physical scarcity determinants of resource prices may not be too serious, provided speculative elements do not exert a dominant one-way influence on prices for long periods of time.

■ A PUBLIC POLICY PERSPECTIVE

What role can public policies play in natural resources allocation? It is useful to divide the answer to this question into four parts (Figure 8.1).

First, there are those *general initiatives* that could be applied to natural resources sectors but are not unique to the process of resource

FIGURE 8.1   Public Policy Framework

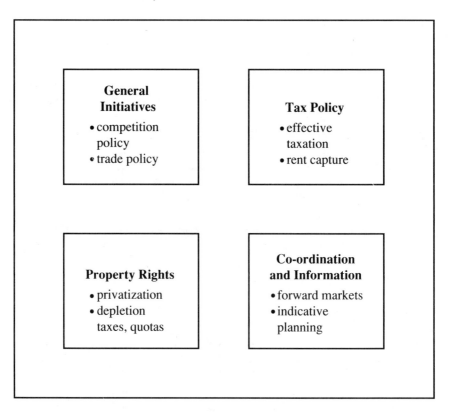

extraction. We have given little attention to this part of public policy. The most relevant examples are competition policy and trade policy. In chapter 2, for example, we noted that the presence of monopolistic influences in the production of resource products generally alters the asset-equilibrium condition for extraction. Competition policy that is designed to simulate marginal-cost pricing in product markets will improve society's allocation of resources. Part of the improvement takes the form of a more efficient allocation of natural resources between present and future uses. In chapters 1 and 4, we also noted that the world prices received for natural resources may be dependent on Canada's exports of resources. This *terms-of-trade effect* has implications for trade policy. The imposition of an export tax that reduces the level of exports could improve the terms of trade for a resource-exporting country like Canada. When world prices are not dependent on Canadian export volumes, attempts to restrict exports lead to domestic losses as we noted in the case of log export restrictions in chapter 1.

Second is the matter of *rent capture and resource taxation*. We have learned a good deal about how to transfer natural resource rents from the private sector where extraction decisions are made to the public sector as resource owner. Like competition and trade policy, the issue of neutral taxation is not confined to resources sectors. Nevertheless, it is an important issue in a country like Canada where the public asserts ownership in a wide range of resource assets. Theories of neutrality and effective taxation have proven very useful in demonstrating how to transfer rents from the private sector to public owners while introducing minimal distortion in private extraction decisions. *Ex-ante* bidding methods, participation, and RRT-style *ex-post* methods of rent transfer clearly dominate alternative types of resource taxation based on product prices or profit measures.

The third area in which public policy can play a role in natural resources sectors is in the definition of *property rights*. As we have noted above, society cannot rely on private extraction and regeneration decisions to solve its natural resources allocation problems unless private decisions fully internalize all social benefits and costs from buying and selling and holding resource stocks. We can be confident that the presence of ill-defined property rights introduces significant market failures in the allocation of many natural resources. With respect to environmental resources and fisheries, for example, the presence of external costs implies that depletion is excessive. Even if we cannot precisely identify the optimal stocks or the optimal depletion rates that would lead to those stocks, we can be certain that some system of taxes or quotas will be needed to internalize the impact of private actions on society. Extension of private property institutions to mineral prospects and timber management might well contribute to economic efficiency of extraction in these sectors. To narrow down the range of appropriate policy action, more information on the magnitudes of external costs must be sought. In some cases, public policy might simply be directed to privatizing natural resources stocks. In other cases, society's stake in efficient natural resources management can only be communicated to individual decision makers through the use of depletion taxes or quotas on the rate of extraction of resource stocks. It is also important to notice that using public policy tools to shift existing resource stocks to optimal levels should take account of transition costs. Optimal regeneration can only be encouraged by subsidizing investment decisions when private ownership is not a feasible alternative.

The fourth area in which public policy can play a constructive role lies in the *co-ordination* of extraction decisions over time and in easing the problem of *incomplete information*. In these areas, we cannot expect too much. Existing optimal management models are built on unrealistic assumptions concerning the amount of aggregate information on the future that is available to society. These assumptions make market-based extraction decisions without forward markets look inadequate. Realistic recognition that information is incomplete suggests that we need more rough and ready ways of assessing the performance of markets in allocating natural resources over time than the benchmarks provided by complete information capital theory models. In the minerals sector, information about aggregate economic stocks is inevitably imperfect. Virtually none of these stocks are owned by private individuals. To establish the magnitude of these stocks and bring them under private control today would require substantial exploration and development investments.

One point to bear in mind is that, with well-specified property rights in place, individual decision makers in resource markets have strong self-interest incentives to make correct predictions about resource values; incentives that are lacking for non-participants. In the case of mineral markets, suppose that past experience and rational expectations concerning future supplies leads market participants to expect that the real cost of extraction will increase in some reasonably predictable way in the future. Suppose, further, that society is willing to accept this assessment. If nothing is done, everyone's best guess is that real resource prices will rise. Provided market participants can secure property rights over existing mineral prospects, there is an incentive for them to hold these prospects off the market to take advantage of expected price appreciation. Co-ordination is imperfect, of course. If everyone holds prospects off the market, current resource prices will rise too much compared to current extraction costs: the current net price will be too high. If everyone believes that others are holding prospects for the future, the current net price will be too low. But the word may get around on the holding behaviour of others and this will induce modifications in individual holding behaviour. Obviously, this is a very rough and ready approach to the depletion problem.

If enough sound information on future real costs is actually available, co-ordination could be improved with forward markets or planning alternatives could be considered. A possible role for public policy in the co-ordination and information process has been described by Solow as follows:

> ...the market for exhaustible resources might be one of the places in the economy where some sort of organized indicative planning could play a constructive role...[with]...the government engaged in a continuous program of information-gathering and dissemination covering trends in technology, reserves, and demand....[S]ome comparison and coordination of the main participants in the market, including the government, could eliminate major errors and resolve much uncertainty. In the case of exhaustible resources, it could have the additional purpose of generating a set of consistent expectations about the distant future.[6]

It might be added that an indicative planning process of this kind may be the best available approach to generating information and co-ordinating the plans of private operators, short of the establishment of forward markets. The approach could be extended to other resources, such as timber and the environment, for which current decisions have long-term implications that depend critically on information about the future.

■ NOTES

1. In all our models to date we have assumed that marginal and average extraction costs are equal so that C is often just referred to as the unit cost. In the discussion of transition strategies later in this chapter, we allow for marginal cost to change as a function of the extraction rate.
2. Equation (1) is sometimes referred to as the Jorgenson equation since it formed the basis for empirical studies of neoclassical capital investment behaviour carried out by Jorgenson and his associates. See D. Jorgenson and C. Siebert, "A Comparison of Alternative Theories of Corporate Investment Behaviour," *American Economic Review* 58 (1968): 681–712; and D. Jorgenson, "Econometric Studies of Investment Behaviour: A Survey," *Journal of Economic Literature* 9 (1971): 1111–47. See also E. Burmeister, *Capital Theory and Dynamics* (Cambridge: Cambridge University Press, 1980), Chap. 2.
3. See also P. Dasgupta, *The Control of Resources* (Oxford: Basil Blackwell, 1982), Chap. 8.
4. J. Livernois, "Marginal Effective Tax Rates for Capital in the Canadian Mining Industry: An Extension," *Canadian Journal of Economics* 22 (1989): 186–87. Copyright: Economic Council of Canada. Reproduced with the permission of the Minister of Supply and Services Canada, 1990.
5. P.H. Pearse, "Property Rights and the Development of Natural Resource Policies in Canada," *Canadian Public Policy* 14 (1988): 311.
6. R. Solow, "The Economics of Resources or the Resources of Economics," *American Economic Review* 64 (1974): 13–14.

■ BIBLIOGRAPHY

Anderson, D.L. "Innovation in Public Rent Capture: The Saskatchewan Uranium Industry." In T. Gunton and J. Richards, eds., *Resource Rents and Public Policy in Western Canada*. Montreal: Institute for Research on Public Policy, 1987.

Anderson, F. "Valuing a Depletable Resource in an Open Economy." *Canadian Journal of Economics* 19 (1986): 730–44.

———— ed. *Selected Readings in Mineral Economics*. New York: Pergamon, 1987.

———— "Optimal Timber Harvesting: Generalizing the Faustmann Rule." Discussion Paper 89–01. Thunder Bay, Ont.: Department of Economics, Lakehead University, 1989.

———— and N.C. Bonsor. "Regional Economic Alienation: Atlantic Canada and the West." In K. Norrie, ed., *Disparities and Interregional Adjustment*. Toronto: University of Toronto Press, 1986.

———— and R.D. Cairns. "The Softwood Lumber Agreement and Resource Politics." *Canadian Public Policy* 14 (1988): 186–96.

Anderson, R. "Resource Conservation and Pricing." *Resources Policy* 3 (1977): 78–86.

Barnett, H.J. "Scarcity and Growth Revisited." In V.K. Smith, ed. *Scarcity and Growth Reconsidered*. Baltimore: Johns Hopkins, 1979.

———— and C. Morse. *Scarcity and Growth: The Economics of Natural Resource Availability*. Baltimore: Johns Hopkins, 1963.

Barney, G.O. (Study Director). *The Global 2000 Report to the President of the United States*. New York: Pergamon, 1980.

Baumol, W. "On the Possibility of Continuing Expansion of Finite Resources." *Kyklos* 39 (1986): 167–79.

———— and J. Benhabib. "Chaos: Significance, Mechanism, and Economic Applications." *Journal of Economic Perspectives* 3 (1989): 77–105.

Benson, C.A. "A Need for Extensive Forest Management." *The Forestry Chronicle*, October 1988, 421–30.

Bernard, J.T., G. E. Bridges, and A.D. Scott. "An Evaluation of Potential Canadian Hydroelectric Rents." Resource Paper 78. Vancouver: Department of Economics, University of British Columbia, 1982.

Bhagwati, J. "Immiserizing Growth: A Geometrical Note." *Review of Economic Studies* 25 (1958): 201–5.

Boadway, R.W., K.J. McKenzie, and J.M. Mintz. *Federal and Provincial Taxation of the Canadian Mining Industry*. Kingston: Queen's University Centre for Resource Studies, 1989.

Boadway, R.W., and J. Treddenick. *The Impact of the Mining Industries on the Canadian Economy*. Kingston: Queen's University Centre for Resource Studies, 1977.

Bonsor, N., N. McCubbin, and J. Sprague. *Stopping Water Pollution at its Source: Kraft Mill Effluents in Ontario*. Toronto: Ontario Ministry of the Environment, 1988.

Borgese, E. "The Law of the Sea." *Scientific American* 248 (1983): 42–49.

Bowes, M., and J.V. Krutilla. *Multiple-use Management: The Economics of Public Forestlands*. Washington: Resources for the Future, 1989.

Boyd, R., and K. Krutilla. "The Welfare Impacts of Trade Restrictions against the Canadian Softwood Lumber Industry: A Spatial Equilibrium Analysis." *Canadian Journal of Economics* 20 (1987): 17–35.

Bradley, P.G., and G.C. Watkins. "Net Value Royalties—Practical Tool or Economist's Illusion?" *Resources Policy* (December 1987): 279–88.

Brobst, D. "Fundamental Concepts for the Analysis of Resource Availability." In V.K. Smith, ed., *Scarcity and Growth Reconsidered*. Baltimore: Johns Hopkins, 1979.

Brooks, D. *Minerals: An Expanding or a Dwindling Resource*. Ottawa: Energy, Mines and Resources Mineral Bulletin 134, 1973.

Brown, E.C. "Business-income Taxation and Investment Incentives." In *Income, Employment, and Public Policy*. New York: Norton, 1948.

Brown, G., and B. Field. "Implications of Alternative Measures of Natural Resource Scarcity." *Journal of Political Economy* 86 (1978): 229–43.

Brubaker, S., ed. *Rethinking the Federal Lands*. Baltimore: Johns Hopkins for Resources for the Future, 1984.

Buongiorno, J., and J.K. Gilless. *Forest Management and Economics*. New York: Macmillan, 1987.

Burmeister, E. *Capital Theory and Dynamics*. Cambridge: Cambridge University Press, 1980.

Cairns, R.D. "Ricardian Rent and Manitoba's Mining Royalty." *Canadian Tax Journal* 25 (1977): 558–67.

——— "Ricardian Rent and the Minerals Industry: The Debate Concludes." *Canadian Tax Journal* 28 (1980): 770–74.

Calish, S., R. Fight, and D. Teeguarden. "How Do Nontimber Values Affect Douglas-Fir Rotations?" *Journal of Forestry* 76 (1978): 217–21.

Cameron, S.D. "Net Losses: The Sorry State of our Atlantic Fishery." *Canadian Geographic* (April–May 1990): 29–37.

Campbell, H., and R. Lindner. "The Effect of the Resource Rent Tax on Mineral Exploration." Resource Paper 90. Vancouver: Department of Economics, University of British Columbia, 1983.

Caragata, P.J. *National Resources and International Bargaining Power: Canada's Mineral Policy Options*. Kingston: Queen's University Centre for Resource Studies, 1984.

Caves, R.E., and R.H. Holton. *The Canadian Economy: Prospect and Retrospect*. Cambridge, Mass.: Harvard University Press, 1959.

Centre for Resource Studies. *Rate of Return Taxation of Minerals*. Kingston: Queen's University, 1977.

Chambers, E., and D. Gordon. "Primary Products and Economic Growth: An Empirical Measurement." *Journal of Political Economy* 74 (1966): 315–32.

Chang, S.J. "Determination of the Optimal Rotation Age: A Theoretical Analysis." *Forest Ecology and Management* 8 (1984): 137–47.

Chappell, D. *From Sawdust to Toxic Blobs: A Consideration of Sanctioning Strategies to Combat Pollution in Canada*. Ottawa: Supply and Services, 1988.

Chiang, A.C. *Fundamental Methods of Mathematical Economics*. New York: McGraw-Hill, 1984.

Clark, C. *Mathematical Bioeconomics*. New York: John Wiley, 1976.

Clawson, M. *Forests for Whom and for What?* Baltimore: Johns Hopkins, 1975.

Conrad, J., and C. Clark. *Natural Resource Economics: Notes and Problems*. New York: Cambridge University Press, 1987.

Copithorne, L. *Natural Resources and Regional Disparities*. Ottawa: Economic Council of Canada, 1979.

Cranstone, D. "The Canadian Mineral Discovery Process since World War II." In J. Tilton, R. Eggert, and H. Landsberg, eds., *World Mineral Exploration: Trends and Economic Issues*. Washington: Resources for the Future, 1988.

Dales, J. *Pollution, Property, and Prices*. Toronto: University of Toronto Press, 1968.

Dasgupta, P. *The Control of Resources*. Oxford: Basil Blackwell, 1982.

Davidson, P. "Natural Resources." In A. Eichner, ed., *A Guide to Post-Keynesian Economics*. White Plains, N.Y.: Sharpe, 1978.

Davis, L., and K.N. Johnson. *Forest Management*. New York: McGraw-Hill, 1987.

Department of Regional Economic Expansion (DREE). *Single-Industry Communities*. Ottawa: DREE, 1977.

Devarajan, S., and A. Fisher. "Hotelling's 'Economics of Exhaustible Resources': Fifty Years Later." *Journal of Economic Literature* 19 (1981): 65–73.

Dixit, A. *Optimization in Economic Theory*. New York: Oxford University Press, 1976.

Dorfman, R. "An Economic Interpretation of Optimal Control Theory." *American Economic Review* 59 (1969): 817–31.

———, P. Samuelson, and R. Solow. *Linear Programming and Economic Analysis*. New York: McGraw-Hill, 1958.

Dupont, D. "Rent Dissipation in Restricted Access Fisheries." *Journal of Environmental Economics and Management* 19 (1990): 26–44.

Easterbrook, W.T., and M.H. Watkins, eds. *Approaches to Canadian Economic History*. Toronto: McClelland & Stewart, 1971.

Economic Council of Canada. *Newfoundland: From Dependency to Self-Reliance*. Ottawa: Supply and Services, 1980.

—— *Financing Confederation Today and Tomorrow*. Ottawa: Supply and Services, 1982.

—— *Western Transition*. Ottawa: Supply and Services, 1984.

Energy, Mines and Resources. *Mineral Policy: A Discussion Paper*. Ottawa, Supply and Services, 1981.

Faustmann, M. "On the Determination of the Value which Forest Land and Immature Stands Possess for Forestry." In M. Gane, ed., Institute Paper 42. Commonwealth Forestry Institute, Oxford: Oxford University Press, 1968.

Fisher, A.C. *Resource and Environmental Economics*. New York: Cambridge University Press, 1981.

—— and F. Peterson. "The Environment in Economics: A Survey." *Journal of Economic Literature* 14 (1976): 1–33.

Forrester, J. *World Dynamics*. Cambridge, Mass.: Wright-Allen, 1971.

Fryer, M.J., and J.V. Greenman. *Optimisation Theory: Applications in OR and Economics*. London: Edward Arnold, 1987.

Gaffney, M., ed. *Extractive Resources and Taxation*. Madison: University of Wisconsin Press, 1967.

Garnaut, R., and A. Clunies Ross. "Uncertainty, Risk Aversion, and the Taxing of Natural Resource Projects." *Economic Journal* 85 (1975): 272–87.

—— "The Neutrality of the Resource Rent Tax." *Economic Record* 55 (1979): 193–201.

Gleick, J. *Chaos: Making a New Science*. New York: Viking Press, 1987.

Gordon, H.S. "The Economic Theory of a Common Property Resource." *Journal of Political Economy* 62 (1954): 124–42.

Gordon, R.B., T.C. Koopmans, W. Nordhaus, and B. Skinner. *Toward a New Iron Age?* Cambridge, Mass.: Harvard University Press, 1987.

Gordon, R.L. (1967) "A Reinterpretation of the Pure Theory of Exhaustion." *Journal of Political Economy* 75 (1967): 274–86.

Graedel, T., and P. Crutzen. "The Changing Atmosphere." *Scientific American* (September 1989): 58–68.

Graham-Tomasi, T., C. Runge, and W. Hyde. "Foresight and Expectations in Models of Natural Resources Markets." *Land Economics* 62 (1986): 234–49.

Gravelle, H., and R. Rees. *Microeconomics*. London: Longman, 1981.

Gray, J. *Stability of Employment within Canadian Resource-based Industries*. Winnipeg: University of Manitoba Centre for Settlement Studies, 1975.

Grubel, H. "Ricardian Rent and the Minerals Industry: A Comment." *Canadian Tax Journal* 27 (1979): 689–92.

——— "Ricardian Rent and the Minerals Industry—The Debate Concludes." *Canadian Tax Journal* 28 (1980): 774–76.

Harris, D.P., and B.J. Skinner. "The Assessment of Long-term Supplies of Minerals." In V.K. Smith and J. Krutilla, eds., *Explorations in Natural Resource Economics*. Baltimore: Johns Hopkins, 1982.

Harris, L. (Chairman). *Independent Review of the State of the Northern Cod Stock*. Final Report. Ottawa: Department of Fisheries and Oceans, 1990.

Hartman, R. "The Harvesting Decision when a Standing Forest Has Value." *Economic Inquiry* 14 (1976): 52–58.

Heaps, T. "An Analysis of the Present Value of Stumpage under a Variety of Economic and Management Conditions." Discussion Paper 284. Ottawa: Economic Council of Canada, 1985.

——— and P. Neher. "The Economics of Forestry when the Rate of Harvest is Constrained." *Journal of Environmental Economics and Mangement* 6 (1979): 297–319.

Herfindahl, O. *Copper Costs and Prices 1870–1957*. Baltimore: Johns Hopkins, 1959.

——— "Depletion and Economic Theory." In M. Gaffney, ed., *Extractive Resources and Taxation*. Madison: University of Wisconsin Press, 1967.

Hirshleifer, J. *Investment, Interest, and Capital*. Englewood Cliffs: Prentice-Hall, 1970.

Hotelling, H. "The Economics of Exhaustible Resources." *Journal of Political Economy* 39 (1931): 137–75.

Howe, C.W. *Natural Resource Economics*. New York: John Wiley, 1979.

Hunter, M.L. *Wildlife, Forests, and Forestry*. Englewood Cliffs, N.J.: Prentice-Hall, 1990.

Jorgenson, D. "Econometric Studies of Investment Behaviour: A Survey." *Journal of Economic Literature* 9 (1971): 1111–1147.

——— and C. Siebert. "A Comparison of Alternative Theories of Corporate Investment Behaviour." *American Economic Review* 58 (1968): 681–712.

Kay, J., and J. Mirrlees. "The Desirability of Natural Resource Depletion." In D.W. Pearce, ed., *The Economics of Natural Resource Depletion*. London: Macmillan, 1975.

Kemp, A. *Petroleum Rent Collection Around the World*. Montreal: Institute for Research on Public Policy, 1987.

Kemp, M., and E. Moore. "Biological Capital Theory: A Question and a Conjecture." *Economics Letters* 4 (1979): 141–44.

Kirby, M. *Navigating Troubled Waters: A New Policy for the Atlantic Fisheries*. Ottawa: Supply and Services, 1982.

Kwon, O.Y. "Neutral Taxation and Provincial Mineral Royalties: The Manitoba Metallic Minerals and Saskatchewan Uranium Royalties." *Canadian Public Policy* 9 (1983): 189–99.

Levhari, D., and N. Liviatan. "Notes on Hotelling's 'Economics of Exhaustible Resources'." *Canadian Journal of Economics* 10 (1977): 177–92.

Lewis, F. "The Canadian Wheat Boom and Per Capita Income: New Estimates." *Journal of Political Economy* 83 (1975): 1249–55.

Livernois, J. "Marginal Effective Tax Rates for Capital in the Canadian Mining Industry: An Extension." *Canadian Journal of Economics* 22 (1989): 184–94.

Mackenzie, B. "Looking for the Improbable Needle in a Haystack: The Economics of Base Metal Exploration in Canada." *CIM Bulletin* 74 (1981): 115–25. Reprinted in F. Anderson, ed., *Selected Readings in Mineral Economics*. New York: Pergamon, 1987.

———— and M. Bilodeau. *Effects of Taxation on Base Metal Mining in Canada*. Kingston: Queen's University Centre for Resource Studies, 1979.

———— and R. Woodall. "Economic Productivity of Base Metal Exploration in Australia and Canada." In J. Tilton, R. Eggert, and H. Landsberg, eds., *World Mineral Exploration: Trends and Economic Issues*. Washington: Resources for the Future, 1988.

Manthy, R. "Scarcity, Renewability, and Forest Policy." *Journal of Forestry* 75 (1977): 201–5.

———— *Natural Resource Commodities: A Century of Statistics*. Baltimore: Johns Hopkins, 1978.

Marglin, S. "The Social Rate of Discount and the Optimal Rate of Investment." *Quarterly Journal of Economics* 77 (1963): 95–111.

Martin, H. and L-S. Jen. "Are Ore Grades Declining? The Canadian Experience, 1939–89." In J. Tilton, R. Eggert, and H. Landsberg, eds., *World Mineral Exploration: Trends and Economic Issues*. Washington: Resources for the Future, 1988.

Martin, H., J. McIntosh, and J. Zwartendyk. "Monitoring Canada's Mine Production." *CIM Bulletin* (July 1979): 43–50. Reprinted in F. Anderson, ed., *Selected Readings in Mineral Economics*. New York: Pergamon, 1987.

Marty, R. "Economic Effectiveness of Silvicultural Investments for Softwood Timber Production." Appendix D in *United States: Report of the President's Advisory Panel on Timber and the Environment*. Washington: U.S. Government Printing Office, 1973.

May, R.M. "Simple Mathematical Models with Very Complicated Dynamics." *Nature* 261 (1976): 459–67.

McCann, L.D., ed. *Heartland and Hinterland*. Toronto: Prentice-Hall, 1987.

Meadows, D.H., D.L. Meadows, J. Randers, and W. Behrens. *The Limits to Growth*. New York: Universe Books, 1972.

Miernyk, W. *The Elements of Input-Output Analysis*. New York: Random House, 1965.

Mitra, T., and H.Y. Wan. "Some Theoretical Results on the Economics of Forestry." *Review of Economic Studies* 52 (1985): 263–82.

Moloney, D., and P. Pearse. "Quantitative Rights as an Instrument for Regulating Commercial Fisheries." *Journal of the Fisheries Research Board of Canada* 36 (1979): 859–66.

Muller, R.A. "A Simulation of the Effect of Pollution Control on the Pulp and Paper Industry." *Canadian Public Policy* 2 (1976): 91–102.

Munro, G. "The Economics of Fishing: An Introduction." In J. Butlin, ed., *The Economics of Environmental and Natural Resources Policy*. Boulder: Westview, 1981.

———— "Fisheries, Extended Jurisdiction and the Economics of Common Property Resources." *Canadian Journal of Economics* 15 (1982): 405–25.

Nautiyal, J. "Forest Tenure Structure in Ontario." *The Forestry Chronicle* 53 (1977): 20–25.

Nemetz, P. "Federal Environmental Regulation in Canada." *Natural Resources Journal* 26 (1986): 551–608.

Nickel, P., I. Gillies, T. Henley, and J. Saunders. *Economic Impacts and Linkages of the Canadian Mining Industry*. Kingston: Queen's University Centre for Resource Studies, 1978.

Nordhaus, W. *The Efficient Use of Energy Resources*. New Haven: Yale University Press, 1979.

Okun, A. *Equality and Efficiency: The Big Tradeoff*. Washington: The Brookings Institution, 1975.

Pearse, P.H. *Timber Appraisal—Second Report of the Task Force on Crown Timber Disposal*. Vancouver: British Columbia Forest Service, 1974.

———— (Commissioner). *Timber Rights and Forest Policy in British Columbia*. 2 vols. Victoria: Royal Commission on Forest Resources, 1976.

———— (Commissioner). *Turning the Tide: A New Policy for Canada's Pacific Fisheries*. Ottawa: Department of Fisheries and Oceans, 1982.

———— "Property Rights and the Development of Natural Resource Policies in Canada." *Canadian Public Policy* 14 (1988): 307–20.

Percy, M.B. *Forest Management and Economic Growth in British Columbia*. Ottawa: Economic Council of Canada, 1986.

———— and C. Yoder. *The Softwood Lumber Dispute and Canada–U.S. Trade in Natural Resources*. Halifax: The Institute for Research on Public Policy, 1988.

Petersen, U., and R. Maxwell. "Historical Mineral Production and Price Trends." *Mining Engineering* (January 1979): 25–34.

Peterson, F., and A.C. Fisher. "The Exploitation of Extractive Resources: A Survey." *Economic Journal* 87 (December 1977).

Pomfret, R. *The Economic Development of Canada*. Toronto: Methuen, 1981.

Ricardo, D. *Principles of Political Economy and Taxation*. London: J.M. Dent, 1933; originally published 1817.

Rovet, E. *The Canadian Business Guide to Environmental Law*. Vancouver: Self-Counsel Press, 1988.

Samuelson, P.A. "Economics of Forestry in an Evolving Society." *Economic Inquiry* 14 (1976): 466–92.

Schaefer, M. "Some Considerations of Population Dynamics and Economics in Relation to the Management of Marine Fisheries." *Journal of the Fisheries Research Board of Canada* 14 (1957): 669–81.

Schneider, S. "The Changing Climate." *Scientific American* (September 1989): 70–79.

Schrecker, T. *Political Economy of Environmental Hazards*. Law Reform Commission of Canada. Ottawa: Supply and Services, 1984.

Schwindt, R. "Public Policy and the Pacific Salmon Fishery's Harvesting Crisis." In T. Gunton and J. Richards, eds., *Resource Rents and Public Policy in Western Canada*. Halifax: Institute for Research on Public Policy, 1987.

Scott, A.D. "Notes on User Cost." *Economic Journal* 63 (1953): 368–84.

———— "The Fishery: The Objectives of Sole Ownership." *Journal of Political Economy* 63 (1955): 116–24.

———— "The Cost of Compulsory Log Trading." In W. McKillop and W. Mead, eds., *Timber Policy Issues in British Columbia*. Vancouver: University of British Columbia Press, 1976.

———— and P. Neher. *The Public Regulation of Commercial Fisheries in Canada*. Ottawa: Economic Council of Canada, 1981.

Sen, A.K. "Isolation, Assurance, and the Social Rate of Discount." *Quarterly Journal of Economics* 81 (1967): 112–24.

Silver, L. *The Pursuit of Further Processing of Canada's Natural Resources*. Montreal: C.D. Howe Research Institute, 1975.

Simon, J. *The Ultimate Resource*. Princeton: Princeton University Press, 1981.

Skinner, B.J. "A Second Iron Age Ahead?" *American Scientist* 64 (May/June 1976).

Slade, M. *Pricing of Metals*. Kingston: Queen's University Centre for Resource Studies, 1988.

Slade, M. E. "Trends in Natural Resource Commodity Prices: An Analysis of the Time Domain." *Journal of Environmental Economics and Management* 9 (1982): 122–37.

Smith, V.K. "Natural Resource Scarcity: A Statistical Analysis." *Review of Economics and Statistics* 61 (1979): 423–27.

Smith, V.L. "Economics of Production from Natural Resources." *American Economic Review* 58 (1968): 409–31.

Solow, R. "The Economics of Resources or the Resources of Economics." *American Economic Review* 64 (1974): 1–14.

Steele, J., and E. Henderson. "Modelling Long-term Fluctuations in Fish Stocks." *Science* 224 (1984): 985–87.

Stewart, I. *Does God Play Dice? The New Mathematics of Chaos*. New York: Penguin, 1989.

Thompson, A. *Environmental Regulation in Canada: An Assessment of the Regulatory Process*. Vancouver: Westwater Research Centre, 1980.

Tilton, J., R. Eggert, and H. Landsberg. *World Mineral Exploration: Trends and Economics Issues*. Washington: Resources for the Future, 1988.

Victor, P. *Economics of Pollution*. London: Macmillan, 1972.

——— and T. Burrell. *Environmental Protection Regulation, Water Pollution, and the Pulp and Paper Industry*. Ottawa: Economic Council of Canada, 1981.

Walker, J.L. "ECHO: Solution Technique for a Nonlinear Economic Harvest Optimization Model." In J. Meadows et al., eds., *Systems Analysis and Forest Resource Management*. Washington: Society of American Foresters, 1976.

Watkins, G.C. "Postscript: Canadian Policy Perspectives." In A. Kemp, *Petroleum Rent Collection Around the World*. Montreal: Institute for Research on Public Policy, 1987.

Webb, K. *Pollution Control in Canada: The Regulatory Approach in the 1980s*. Law Reform Commission of Canada. Ottawa: Supply and Services, 1988.

Webb, M., and M. Zacher. *Canada and International Mineral Markets: Dependence, Instability, and Foreign Policy*. Kingston: Queen's University Centre for Resource Studies, 1988.

Woodbridge, Reed and Associates. *Canada's Forest Industry* (Volume 5: "Fibre Assumptions"). Prepared for the Canadian Forestry Service, Ottawa, 1988.

Zuker, R., and G. Jenkins. *Blue Gold—Hydroelectric Rent in Canada*. Ottawa: Economic Council of Canada, 1984.

Zwartendyk, J. "Mineral Wealth—How Should It Be Expressed?" *Canadian Mining Journal* (April 1973): 44–52.

——— "Mineral Exploration in Canada: The Needs and the Prospects." *Foreign Investment Review* (Spring 1978): 17–18.

■ AUTHOR INDEX

∎ SUBJECT INDEX